Journalism E

Journalism Ethics: Arguments and Cases for the Twenty-first Century explores the major ethical dilemmas facing journalists in the digital age.

Engaging with both the theory and practice of journalism ethics, this text explains the key ethical concepts and dilemmas in journalism and provides an international range of examples and case studies, considering traditional and social media from a global perspective.

Journalism Ethics offers an introductory philosophical underpinning to ethics that traces the history of the freedom of expression from the time of Greek philosophers like Aristotle, through the French and American revolutions, to the modern day.

Throughout the book, Patching and Hirst examine ethically challenging issues such as deception, trial by media, dealing with sources and privacy intrusion. They also explore the continuing ethical fault lines around accuracy, bias, fairness and objectivity, chequebook journalism, the problems of the foreign correspondent, the conflicts between ethics and the law, and the conflicts between journalists and public relations consultants.

Concluding with a step-by-step guide to ethical thinking on the job, this textbook is an invaluable resource for students of journalism, media and communication.

Roger Patching has spent more than half a century in journalism and journalism education. This is the eighth journalism text he has co-authored in the past four decades. In 'semi-retirement', he still teaches part time at Bond University on Queensland's Gold Coast, and his doctorate on privacy invasion is nearing completion. His contribution to journalism education has been recognised with life membership of his professional association, the Journalism Education Association of Australia.

Martin Hirst has been a journalism scholar for more than 20 years. He worked as a broadcast journalist for 20 years, including a stint in the Parliamentary Press Gallery in Canberra, Australia. He is author, co-author or editor of seven books and scores of journal articles. He is a regular commentator on media matters and currently works at Deakin University in Melbourne, Australia.

Journalism Ethics

Arguments and cases for the twenty-first century

Roger Patching and Martin Hirst

Routledge
Taylor & Francis Group

LONDON AND NEW YORK

First published 2014
by Routledge
2 Park Square, Milton Park, Abingdon, Oxon, OX14 4RN

and by Routledge
711 Third Avenue, New York, NY 10017

Routledge is an imprint of the Taylor & Francis Group, an informa business

British Library Cataloguing in Publication Data
A catalogue record for this book is available from the British Library

Library of Congress Cataloging in Publication Data
Patching, Roger, 1944–
Journalism ethics : arguments and cases for the twenty-first century / Roger Patching and Martin Hirst.
    pages cm
Hirst's name appears first on previous editions.
Includes bibliographical references and index.
1. Journalistic ethics. I. Hirst, Martin. II. Title.
PN4756.H545 2013
174'.907–dc23   2013019549

ISBN: 978-0-415-65675-7 (hbk)
ISBN: 978-0-415-65676-4 (pbk)
ISBN: 978-1-315-86745-8 (ebk)

Typeset in Sabon
by Cenveo Publisher Services

Printed and bound in Great Britain by
TJ International Ltd, Padstow, Cornwall

Contents

Table and figures

Table

Figures

Acknowledgements

The first two ethics texts we wrote had their genesis in the mid-1990s while we were teaching at Charles Sturt University in Bathurst, in the central west of New South Wales. We first collaborated on a training manual about law and ethics for the Australian Broadcasting Corporation in 1996–1997. Our collaboration became friendship as we wrote our first book while working in tertiary journalism progammes in southeast Queensland in the early part of the twenty-first century.

The theoretical framework, especially the development of the concept of 'ethical fault lines', owes much to Martin's 2003 doctorate, *Grey Collar Journalism: The Social Relations of News Production*. His recent research has centred on the development of freedom of expression through the ages. We have each also collaborated with colleagues in various ways on other publications. Our common interest also extends to Roger's PhD work on privacy invasion, which is also a rich influence on this book.

The first three chapters explore theoretical and historical references that inform many ethical aspects of journalism, while the remaining chapters look at everyday scenarios taken from media practice. Following our usual practice, Martin drafted the initial theoretical chapters. Roger produced a draft of the preface, the case studies, and the first drafts of the practice-based chapters. The closing chapter was a joint effort.

Positive student reactions, word of mouth and emails from colleagues encouraged us to update and further explore our ethical practice research.

The last Australian text devoted entirely to journalism ethics was written by us in 2007; since then many new cases have emerged, and so have new arguments. Our examples are all new, taken from 'yesterday's headlines'. The cut-off date for developments in ongoing stories, with only minor exceptions, was April, 2013. But ethics is never static. As many of the stories continue to evolve, further ethical dilemmas may present themselves, giving rise to more opportunities for discussion and reflection.

Keeping abreast of the ever-changing ethical landscape of the media, both nationally and internationally, involves both of us in a daily routine of reading a number of newspapers, regular listening and watching of radio and TV respectively, as well as hours spent on the internet searching various media and ethics websites. For us, based in Australia, crikey.com has drawn our attention to many potential ethical dilemmas. The ABC's Radio National's *Media Report* and ABC-TV's *Media Watch* are essential listening and viewing respectively. Overseas, our research has been helped by the team of the Poynter Institute in the United States (www.poynter.org) and by those who report on the media in London for *The Guardian*. Other valuable sources are mentioned in the text.

We appreciate the support and encouragement of our wives, Jenny Patching and Tiffany White, during the production of the book and, in Roger's case, the support of his children. As always, their generous nature has nurtured the creative process for both of us during intermittent bouts of collaborative writing on the Gold Coast and in Melbourne.

We'd also like to acknowledge the help of colleagues at Bond and Deakin Universities, as well as among the wider journalism education community in Australia, New Zealand and globally. Dr Mark Hayes provided some useful words of wisdom after reading the manuscript, for which we are grateful. And, of course, this book would not have been possible without the help of the staff at Routledge, in particular Natalie Foster, Andrew Watts, Sheni Kruger and copyeditor Jonathan Merrett.

All illustrations in this text have been used with the permission of the copyright holders.

Roger Patching and Martin Hirst
Gold Coast and Melbourne, April, 2013.

Abbreviations

ABC	Australian Broadcasting Corporation (Australian public broadcaster)
ACMA	Australian Communications and Media Authority (Australian broadcast regulatory authority)
ACP	Australian Consolidated Press
AFL	Australian Football League ('Aussie rules' football)
AFP	Agence France Presse (French newsagency)
AJA	Australian Journalists' Association (the forerunner to MEAA)
ASIC	Australian Securities and Investments Commission (regulatory authority)
BBC	British Broadcasting Corporation (British public broadcaster)
CBC	Canadian Broadcasting Corporation (Canadian public broadcaster)
CCTV	Closed-circuit television
CEO	Chief Executive Officer (head of a company or organisation)
CIA	Central Intelligence Agency (US spy agency)
CNN	Cable News Network (American 24-hour pay-TV news network)
CPJ	Committee to Protect Journalists
FOI	Freedom of Information
GFC	Global Financial Crisis
ICIJ	International Consortium of Investigative Journalists
IRA	Irish Republican Army
ITV	Independent Television (British commercial television network)
LAPD	Los Angeles Police Department
MEAA	Media Entertainment and Arts Alliance (journalists' union in Australia)
MP	Member of Parliament
MSM	Mainstream media
NBC	National Broadcasting Company (US commercial, free-to-air, television network)
NoW	News of the World (now defunct British Sunday tabloid)
NLRB	National Labor Relations Board (US government regulatory agency)
NPR	National Public Radio (US public radio network)
NUJ	National Union of Journalists (British journalists' union)
ONA	Office of National Assessments (Australian government advisory agency)
PCC	Press Complaints Commission (British print media regulator)
PM	Prime Minister
PR	Public Relations

PTSD	Post-Traumatic Stress Disorder
SBS	Special Broadcasting Service (Australian public multicultural network)
SMH	Sydney Morning Herald
TMZ	American gossip website
UN	United Nations

Preface

Arguments, cases, and fault lines – can journalists be trusted in the wake of the *News of the World* scandal?

> The circumstances of the alleged lawbreaking within News Corp suggest more than a passing resemblance to Richard Nixon presiding over a criminal conspiracy in which he insulated himself from specific knowledge of numerous individual criminal acts while being himself responsible for and authorising general policies that routinely resulted in lawbreaking and unconstitutional conduct.
>
> (Bernstein, 2011)

This is the view of iconic American investigative journalist Carl Bernstein writing for *Newsweek* under the headline 'Murdoch's Watergate?' as the full extent of the criminality and unethical behaviour at the British tabloid *News of the World* began to emerge in July, 2011.

Watergate, which began as a botched break-in at a Democratic Party office in Washington in June, 1972, and ended a couple of years later with the resignation of the American President, was a watershed in American journalism. More than 40 years on, and with the benefit of hindsight, the glamorous portrayal of *The Washington Post* journalists, Carl Bernstein and Bob Woodward, by two of Hollywood's best at the time – Dustin Hoffman and Robert Redford – may have exaggerated their role in the ultimate resignation of President Nixon, but their dogged persistence in chasing the story, often with ethically-suspect behaviour and against intense political pressure, has proved an inspiration for generations of journalists.

Watergate was the journalistic high point of the second half of the twentieth century, and the illegal and unethical behaviour associated with the phone hacking scandal that forced the closure of the *News of the World* is the equivalent in the first part of the twenty-first century. As of February, 2013, arrests associated with the four separate investigations into the scandal stood at more than 100, and included senior players in the British operations of the Western world's most powerful media mogul, Australian-born, but US citizen, Rupert Murdoch. Police officers and other public officials stand accused, alongside journalists, of serious crimes and dereliction of duty in the wide-ranging scandal. News Corporation admitted in early 2013 that the total payout related to the scandal stood at more than $340 million (Neate 2013). The scandal is multi-faceted and will feature in discussion in a number of chapters to follow, but the scope of the criminality and unethical behaviour is breathtaking.

Just as Woodward and Bernstein chased the Watergate story with the support of the *Post*'s editor, Ben Bradlee, their twenty-first-century equivalent, Nick Davies of

The Guardian, followed the *News of the World* story for years with that same dogged determination to uncover the extent of the scandal, supported by his editor, Alan Rusbridger. The breakthrough story about the insidious lengths *News of the World* journalists would go to get exclusive stories was first published on *The Guardian* website in early July, 2011. It revealed that the tabloid had hacked the phone of murdered schoolgirl, Milly Dowler. With worldwide media attention focussed on the unravelling of the *News of the World* through further revelations in the snowballing scandal, Murdoch publicly apologised for the paper's behaviour, closed the paper down, and abandoned plans to take over the British pay-TV operation, BSkyB.

British tabloid journalism has always been a cut-throat business, with the papers guaranteeing bumper circulations with a diet of crime, celebrity and political scandals and topless page three girls. It had long been known that journalists with the 'red top' tabloids (so named for the colour of their mastheads) would cut ethical corners to get the latest scandal first and circulation figures seemed to show that the public was eager to read about the latest celebrity from the arts, sport or politics to fall from grace. Few queried the tactics involved in the scoops. *News of the World* reporters, helped by private investigators, used immoral, unethical and illegal methods to hack into the phone messages of all manner of celebrities, politicians and possibly the voice messages of terrorism victims and fallen soldiers, but it was the hacking of Milly Dowler's phone that nauseated the nation and led to the Leveson inquiry into British press standards. It was not only *The Guardian*'s and, to a lesser extent, *The New York Times*' reporting that brought about the downfall of the *News of the World*, equally it was a handful of British politicians who risked the wrath of the world's biggest media mogul. So while it was reporters from *The Washington Post*, aided by the American judicial system, that brought down President Nixon, it was in part British politicians, prompted by *The Guardian*'s revelations, who brought the jewel in Murdoch's British media empire to its knees.

Then came another scandal that shook the BBC

Before Lord Leveson could recommend changes to the British print media, another scandal erupted at arguably the most trusted media organisation in the world – the British Broadcasting Corporation (BBC). After his death in 2011, the BBC current affairs programme, *Newsnight,* began investigating the network's iconic DJ, TV presenter and charity fundraiser, Jimmy Savile, over allegations of sexual abuse. Editorial management made a monumental blunder in deciding to drop the investigation. Later Scotland Yard investigations would name Savile as a suspect in nearly 200 crimes, including more than 30 allegations of rape (*Jimmy Savile a suspect in 199 crimes, 31 rapes* 2012). By late 2012, 10 people had been arrested in connection with sex crimes stemming from the police investigation. Not only was the BBC challenged over how Savile's sexual abuse could have continued for so long, apparently from 1955 to 2009, literally 'under their noses', but also over the decision not to go ahead with the exposé. In the middle of the Savile scandal, the same *Newsnight* programme ran a story wrongly suggesting that a Conservative Party peer, later identified by social media as the former party treasurer Lord McAlpine, had been involved in paedophilia in the 1980s (Kissane 2012). An internal BBC inquiry into the McAlpine affair found that basic journalistic checks and balances, like correct photo identification of the alleged attacker and a right of reply for the person accused, were lacking (Kissane 2012). The twin scandals shook the respected broadcaster to its core. It was still recovering from those scandals when it was forced to postpone an episode of its flagship TV investigative programme, *Panorama*, amid claims a production team member had offered a potential source a bribe for information. He subsequently resigned (Sweeney and Conlan 2013).

The *NoW* phone hacking and BBC scandals came at the end of more than a decade of change in journalism and the media industry. The Global Financial Crisis (GFC) and the increasing influence of the Internet in not only providing free news content on countless media websites, but also the shift to online of the newspapers' so-called 'rivers of gold' – classified advertising – led to soul-searching at papers the world over. Some stopped their printed editions and moved their content behind Internet pay-walls. Others went from daily to tri-weekly or weekly publications in an effort to remain profitable. In Australia, the challenging media landscape led in mid-2012 to major changes at the two major print groups – Murdoch's News Limited, which dominates print with papers in almost all capital cities and most regional centres and the Fairfax group, publishers of *The Sydney Morning Herald*, *The Age* in Melbourne, and *The Australian Financial Review*. The journalists' union, the Media, Entertainment and Arts Alliance (MEAA) estimated up to 700 journalism jobs would be lost across the two media groups, representing one in seven of the reporting staff (Brook 2012). Figures from the Australian Bureau of Statistics released in late 2012 showed that newspapers had shed about 13 per cent of their journalists in the five years up to the most recent national census in 2011 (*Graphic designer – the most popular cultural occupation* 2012).

The other major ethical game-changer of the latter years of the first decade of the twenty-first century was the release of thousands of government-embarrassing documents through the international whistle-blowing activities of WikiLeaks, founded by the Australian-in-exile, Julian Assange. Add to the mix the impact of social media sites like Facebook and Twitter and you have more and more ethical dilemmas for the twenty-first-century journalist. We'll discuss aspects of the impact of social media in most of the practical chapters and in chapter 12 – a stand-alone chapter devoted to some of the dilemmas social media pose for journalists.

Who's a journalist nowadays and does it matter?

In an age where anyone with a smartphone can record audio, video or text and upload it to YouTube or their Facebook page or Twitter or Instagram feed, and countless bloggers give their opinions on anything and everything on a daily basis, what constitutes a journalist? Technology allows the global publication of pictures, news and information by people who would otherwise not think of themselves as journalists, but who become caught up in events that people want – or need – to know about, like the iconic photo of the 'miracle on the Hudson' plane crash in January, 2009, seen by more than 40,000 on Twitter in the first four hours after being uploaded by Janis Krums using his phone. It's now commonplace and the public expects to see it – news as it is happening, captured by those involved, like the victims of a bushfire, cyclone or torrential rain and flooding.

Is Julian Assange a journalist? Those who decide the Australian equivalent of America's Pulitzer prizes for outstanding journalism, the Walkley Awards, thought so when they awarded WikiLeaks the prize for an 'Outstanding Contribution to Journalism in 2011' (*WikiLeaks takes top journalism award* 2011). Earlier in the year,

Assange had been awarded the international Martha Gellhorn journalism prize because, in the view of the judges, '[WikiLeak's] goal of justice through transparency is in the oldest and finest tradition of journalism' (Deans 2011). We will discuss the impact of WikiLeaks on journalism in the pages that follow.

Are bloggers journalists? Yes, in the eyes of the American First Amendment and those who framed the Australian federal shield law, but not those in some of the states who have produced similar source protection laws. It's another topic we will discuss in chapter 9. Does it matter whether a 'real' journalist publishes the information or you read it on a blog or your friend's Twitter feed or Facebook page? We say it does. Most bloggers (as opposed to working journalists who blog or tweet as part of their daily work) have always maintained that citizen journalists, as they call themselves, operate outside the constraints of reputable journalists – like adhering to legal and ethical obligations. While bloggers crave credibility, while they operate outside the guidelines of professional journalism, they will remain on the periphery of accepted information providers.

Social media and the news

We are in the middle of the 'digital revolution'. In less than a decade, new applications like Facebook and Twitter have created a mini revolution of their own in the way information is circulated. They're called 'social media' because both had their origins in building networks of friends – as a way of keeping in touch in the digital age. The inventors of these applications probably never expected them to replace traditional news services for some or that they would become part of the 24/7 news cycle, or that they would eventually be regarded as essential newsroom tools. Trawling social media sites has become common practice for journalists. A 2012 survey of 600 journalists worldwide found that more than half source and verify news stories using social media from sources known to them. The study showed, however, that the reliance on social media fell between 50 to 80 per cent where the source was unknown or unfamiliar (McAthy 2012). The editor of *The Age* at the time, Paul Ramadge, told author Roger Patching, during a formal interview for his doctorate, that stories, particularly about celebrities, often emanated away from traditional newsrooms, through social media.

> They start there, somebody comments, and then maybe that gets more traction because somebody who is notable comments, and so the momentum builds around it in a way that didn't happen a decade ago.
>
> (Ramadge 2011)

Another aspect of Twitter feeds is the way journalists use the social networking site to alert potential readers/listeners/viewers to breaking news. News presenter for Britain's Channel 4, Jon Snow, says the practice 'leads the information thirsty to water' (Snow 2012). It has led to major media having to develop policies to deal with social media – like whether the parent organisation wants individual journalists to tweet the news first to their followers before filing for their employer's website. There are many facets to the impact of social media on modern-day journalism. A key interest in this book is explaining and interpreting how social media has created new ethical dilemmas and what we call the 'fault lines' that journalists have to navigate.

Why don't we trust journalists?

Journalists have never enjoyed a high reputation for ethics and honesty, and the *News of the World* scandal did nothing to improve it. Over the past decade, we have been keeping an eye on global surveys that measure how much, or how little, faith the public has in the honesty, trustworthiness and ethics of journalists – and the news is not good. In the months that followed the closure of the *NoW*, a series of surveys showed the extent of the loss of public trust in the media. One survey found that more than half the British public said they'd lost trust in UK papers as a result of the scandal (Robinson 2011b). Another found that more than three quarters of the British public wanted stricter regulation of the press and tighter limits on media ownership (Greenslade 2012a). But the extent of the loss of trust was much broader in Australia. Not only newspapers, but the entire commercial media suffered. A survey by Essential Research in late July, 2011, found that fewer people had trust in metropolitan dailies, local newspapers and commercial TV and radio news and current affairs than they had in the previous survey in March, 2010. For instance, trust in daily newspapers had dropped from 62 per cent to 53 per cent and trust in TV news and current affairs had slumped from 64 per cent to 48 per cent. Only the ABC retained the public's trust, with 71 per cent (up 1 per cent) saying they had some or a lot of trust the national broadcaster's TV news and current affairs output (Keane 2011). Nearly a year later, trust in the media was still about the same – 52 per cent for newspapers, 46 per cent for commercial television news and current affairs, and 74 per cent for ABC TV news and current affairs (Keane 2012c). With the exception of the ABC, that means that only about half of Australia's mainstream media consumers trust the commercial media they consume. It's not surprising, then, that another survey a week later found that only 24 per cent of respondents said they read newspapers, compared to 39 per cent who used news websites (Keane 2012b).

The Roy Morgan research group conducts annual surveys rating a total of 30 Australian professions for honesty and ethical behaviour. In 2012, a large majority – 90 per cent – rated nurses as the most ethical and honest profession for the eighteenth year in a row, since they were first included in the survey in 1994 (*Roy Morgan image of professions survey 2012: Nurses still most highly regarded, politicians at 14 year lows* 2012). University lecturers are regularly in the top third of professions, with nearly two thirds of the survey respondents in 2012 believing they are honest and ethical – a great relief for the co-authors of this book. But note in Table 0.1, opposite, the low ratings for Australia's federal members of Parliament and the bottom two – advertising people and used car salesmen. But what of women that sell cars, you might ask?

What the survey shows for would-be journalists is that the public doesn't believe that you are likely to be very honest or ethical. It is a hollow victory for TV journalists, when only one in eight people think they are honest and ethical, that even less think their counterparts in print are honest and ethical.

Table 0.1 shows how a third of the professions listed in the regular Roy Morgan polls have rated over the past five years.

Similar surveys tell the same story overseas. The Gallup survey group conducts similar research in the United States, asking their respondents to rate various professions' honesty and ethical standards in three categories – as either very high or high, average, or very low or low. Their late 2011 survey found that slightly under half

Table 0.1 A selection of results from Roy Morgan 'Trusted Professions' surveys 2008–2012 (*Roy Morgan image of professions survey 2012: Nurses still most highly regarded, politicians at 14 year lows* 2012)

Rating in 2012	Profession	2008	2009	2010	2011	2012
1	Nurses	89%	89%	89%	90%	90%
10	University lecturers	67%	61%	60%	61%	65%
15	Lawyers	35%	30%	32%	38%	30%
16	Public opinion pollsters	29%	23%	27%	34%	28%
20	Talk-back radio announcers	18%	15%	19%	17%	17%
22	TV reporters	16%	14%	16%	14%	14%
24	Newspapers journalists	14%	9%	11%	11%	12%
25	Federal MPs	23%	19%	16%	14%	10%
29	Advertising people	9%	6%	6%	5%	8%
30	Used car salesmen	4%	3%	5%	3%	2%

(46 per cent) rated journalists' ethics as 'average', while almost equal numbers rated their ethics as either very high or high (26 per cent) or very low or low (27 per cent) (Jones 2011). Gallup polls the public's thoughts about 21 professions and, not unexpectedly, nurses top their list, too. Another survey showed that in the five years up to and including 2011, American print journalists' honesty and ethics rating was anchored in the low to mid-20s. They figured in the survey in three of the five years. In the other two years the category of television journalists rated at 23 per cent both times (Gallup 2011).

An international survey of journalists in 46 countries in 2011 found that one in four found ethical rules difficult, and 40 per cent said they had committed an unethical act at work (Szabo and Nunn 2011, p. 6). Research in the Asian, African and the Australian region showed that more than half admitted to having behaved unethically (Szabo and Nunn 2011, p. 7). Asked what to do about the ethical problems facing their profession, three-fifths of the journalists surveyed suggested 'providing more media ethics training for journalists' (Szabo and Nunn 2011, p. 12). As we completed the text, a story emerged showing that newspaper journalists in the US had the worst job of 200 professions surveyed (Hough 2013).

Spinning the news

Another reason why large sections of the population in most English-speaking countries don't trust reporters or news outlets anymore is that they are sick of being misled by public relations, political spin, fake news and hoaxes. A journalism student survey, by the University of Technology, Sydney, in collaboration with the *Crikey* daily e-newspaper, found that more than half the news (55 per cent) in Australian newspapers originated in some form of public relations (*Over half your news is spin* 2010). We revisit that survey in chapter 9, but suffice it to say that with so much PR-generated material in the news these days there is a debate to be had as to whether public relations consultants are the new gatekeepers of news content. We would hope not – we believe there is still a very important gatekeeping role for mainstream media because good, ethical journalism still needs a home.

So what can journalists do about it? They can start to raise their flagging reputations by being accurate, balanced or free of bias, striving to be as fair and objective as possible in everything they write. We feel it is important to make the issue of 'trust' a key ingredient in our discussion of media ethics – an important marker between the 'good', the 'bad', and the 'somewhere in between' when the public scrutinises journalism and journalists more and more nowadays.

Lifting the lid on privacy

Most of us want to be left alone. Nobody likes to have nosy neighbours prying into their business. We'd be a bit worried if a total stranger was monitoring our Facebook status, trawling through our emails or listening to our voice messages. We'd be even more angry if we thought that someone spying on us was a journalist being paid to do it. One of the key lessons from the *News of the World* scandal is that some news organisations, some journalists, and the private detectives they hire, will stoop to anything for a story. To them, invading someone's privacy is just part of the business.

Fortunately, social media and the Internet are giving the public the opportunity to fight back like never before, by not only commenting on the news itself but also on the performance of those producing the news. While a critical Letter to the Editor could be ignored or 'buried' in the paper in the past, mainstream media now openly invite comments on their websites and, by inference, on those who produce the news. We'll discuss this particular case in chapter 10, but Channel Seven was strongly criticised in July, 2012 for their coverage of the death of a teenage girl in a quad-bike accident near Wollongong in New South Wales. The girl's mother, Linda Goldspink-Lord, left a scathing message on the *Seven News* Facebook page, something that would have been unheard of a few years ago. Within hours of the post, more than 30,000 people had indicated their support for the mother's criticism. When the channel removed the statement and accompanying comments, there was an online backlash against the network, with a separate Facebook page called 'Justice for Linda Goldspink-Lord' attracting nearly 3,000 supporters. (*Grieving mum's anger prompts 7 News backlash* 2012).

Journalists have a lot of work to do if they are to raise the reputation of the profession in the eyes of the public. There's an interesting class debate to be had in discussing why you think journalists rate so lowly in those surveys. Is it because the public only remembers the commercial current affairs and gossip magazines invading people's privacy, or perhaps because the media is invariably the bearer of bad news? Or is it because they appear to be always criticising someone we like?

Who's watching the watchers?

The less-than-savoury actions of the media that we've already outlined, plus the changes brought on by social media and the newly-minted 'journalists' like Julian Assange, has led to a backlash in some countries, notably in Britain and Australia, and to a lesser extent in New Zealand and the United States. Governments have reacted by mounting a number of inquiries, most notably the Leveson inquiry in Britain, and the Finkelstein and Convergence inquiries, and the ill-fated proposal for an invasion of privacy tort in Australia.

The former Australian High Court judge, and the country's most prominent advocate for strengthened privacy laws, Michael Kirby, said in late 2011 that if the Australian government did not introduce a law against serious invasions of privacy in the wake of the British phone hacking scandal then it would never happen (Le Grand 2011). He first proposed a privacy tort in 1979. Given that the Australian government announced early in 2013 that it was sending the proposal back to the Australian Law Reform Commission for 'further consideration', that probably qualifies as a 'never'.

Justice Kirby's view brings us back to where we started our initial discussion of media ethics. We have flagged a series of issues. We hope this book will help answer them. The central question that underpins all the others that we ask and hopefully answer is: 'What can we do about it?' We can only answer that question with another one: 'What will you do about it'?

How to use this book

We chose the title of this book carefully. As noted above, the first 'decade-and-a-bit' of the century has provided massive challenges to mainstream media worldwide, like how to survive the Internet, social media, the global economic crisis and the continuing ramifications of the phone-hacking scandal. We deliberately chose the order – arguments and then cases – because it reflects the way in which we believe working journalists, editors, and students of journalism can best develop their own thinking about ethical issues and fault lines. The process of becoming a better reporter is also a process of lifelong learning. Our ideas, attitudes and knowledge are constantly developing in a cycle that educational theorists call 'action learning'. Put simply, this is the process of adapting and changing our behaviour in response to our experiences of, and in, the world around us. Action learning involves a circular, or spiral, process of thinking about how to do something, doing the task, reflecting on our actions, and then another round of doing and so on. In this way learning – the gaining of new knowledge and insight – relies on a combination of both theory and practice, and the application of one to the other.

Each chapter is structured in such a way that it mirrors this logic. First, you are invited to read, consider and debate the contexts and arguments put in each chapter. Second, to reinforce the arguments in the 'practical' Parts II–IV, we invite you to put yourself into the situation with some provocative questions about the principles, arguments and context of each case. The questions at the end of each case study run the range of differing opinions on the various issues and, as such, don't necessarily reflect the opinions of the authors.

You might have noticed the term 'fault line' in the chapter heading and in an early paragraph of this chapter. That's how we describe the everyday activities in newsrooms the world over. Think of fault lines as being like fissures in the ground caused by tremors – some are quite mild, leaving cracks that are barely noticeable; others can be quite strong, with almost earthquake-like intensity. The latter can cause massive structural damage, like the on-going fallout from the British phone hacking scandal. Fault lines in journalism manifest themselves every day in a million small decisions reporters and editors make about what to write about, how to write it, and whether it goes on the front page or is left out.

The purpose of the book is to position the arguments about fault lines and the philosophical traditions in which ethics are usually discussed within an overall theoretical framework, a framework that we think will help you both as a student and as a working journalist. It is a framework that provides you with the analytical skills and sound arguments for making ethical decisions.

Within these pages you will find a critique of some competing and complementary ethical philosophies and the case for a holistic approach, which we have broadly defined as the dialectic of ethics, following the work of American journalism scholar, John C. Merrill (1989), on the workings of the dialectic in journalism. Each general and specific argument is assessed using the dialectical method and then measured through its application to specific cases from around the globe.

There is one certainty about journalism ethics – there's always plenty to talk about.

Part I

The theoretical framework for arguments and cases

Overview and objectives

The following three chapters set out the theoretical framework for the practical discussions and cases that follow. The purpose of this part is to introduce a theoretical and historical context to our study of arguments and cases in journalism ethics.

The first chapter examines the philosophical principles and traditions on which journalism ethics has been built. Here we explore various ways in which ethics have been explained and explored over the past 2000 years. We make the point that ethics and philosophy have a close, and sometimes problematic, relationship with journalism. In our view, journalists are important public intellectuals who contribute to debate and inform our ideas of both history and philosophy.

The second chapter explores the historical development of ideas that inform our understanding of press freedoms. We show how the economic and political history of the last 300 years has shaped what we know today as 'freedom of the press'. This chapter outlines how revolutionary change – the emergence of capitalism from feudalism – helped define, and was in turn defined by, the development of a commercial press and the emergence of journalism in the seventeenth century.

The final chapter in this part brings our historical review up-to-date by briefly describing the period of 'industrial journalism' that emerged in the nineteenth century alongside the Industrial Revolution. We then explain how the ideology of journalists today – a belief in the market system and the 'fourth estate' role of the news media – is built on contradictions and fault lines that create the ethical dilemmas discussed in Parts II, III and IV of the book.

After reading the three chapters of this part you will have an understanding of the importance of philosophy, history and theory in any discussion of arguments and cases in journalism ethics, including:

- the philosophical foundations of several traditions that inform journalism ethics today
- the history of freedom of expression, free speech and press freedom and what they mean today
- the concept of ideology and its importance to the debate about journalists' ethics
- the definitions of common terms: ethics, ideology, public interest, accuracy, balance, bias, fairness and objectivity
- the place of these concepts in a discussion of journalism ethics

- the importance of historical and contemporary debates among journalists, their supporters, and their many critics
- the role of journalists and editors as public intellectuals – with a role in the production and circulation of ideas.

1 Ethics and philosophy

Journalists: philosophers of the everyday

> Philosophy gave me an insight into my madness. The madness of being a hack ... For the last fifteen years I'd been thinking in an irrational way.
>
> Graham Johnson, *Hack*

Former *News of the World* reporter Graham Johnson (2012, p. 293), says a chance encounter with philosophy saved his life. Johnson spent years as a tabloid journalist willing to do anything for a story; surviving by suppressing his own moral compass. Johnson's tale of 'sex, drugs and scandal from inside the tabloid jungle' reminds us that ethical dilemmas do not just happen in single remarkable moments. As Johnson's confessions demonstrate, some ethical fault lines can take years, or even decades to develop. We now know that the phone-tapping and bribery that came to characterise the *NoW* newsroom had been encouraged and sanctioned by a succession of editors and senior staff over many years, including those in charge when Graham Johnson was a loyal tabloid hack. Johnson's recovery is a timely reminder that journalists would be better if they discovered philosophy at the beginning of their career, not at the end.

It is not just in moments of quiet desperation, or Johnson's existential angst, that journalists come into contact with philosophy. Journalists are actually everyday philosophers themselves. Journalism is a key social force for the popularisation and dissemination of ideas and, broadly speaking, journalists can be described as the everyday intellectuals who provide the public with a means of understanding the world around them. So there is a strong link between philosophy and journalism, even if the deeply ingrained pragmatism of most journalists leads them to deny it. As J. Herbert Altschull notes, in a history of the ideas behind American journalism, most reporters 'are reluctant to confess to holding a philosophy'. Altschull sums it up very well: journalists and editors do have a philosophy – even if it is only a belief in the shop-worn ideal of objectivity. Newsworkers arrive at their philosophical understanding of the world, 'through the assimilation, usually unnoticed, of intellectual concepts that form the basis of Western civilization' (Altschull 1990, p. 2). We will explore some of these foundation concepts in this and subsequent chapters as no journalist or editor can today ignore their profound and ongoing influence.

It is commonly accepted that journalists and the news media play a gate-keeping role; perhaps not telling us what to think, but certainly providing strong indicators of what to think about and how to go about thinking about these things. So, it is obvious that journalists themselves must think about things, in fact they are engaged in a form of mental labour (Hirst 2012a; Poulantzas 1978; Sparks 2006) that marks out their work as being intellectual in some sense. The thinking work of journalists is then presented as a series of factual accounts and opinion-inflected analyses of the world around us and, because the power of journalism is legitimised by its supposed public interest and professional motivations, it becomes a guide to social action. While not perhaps on the same publicly-recognised level of intellectuals such as scientists, theologians, eminent scholars and literary figures, journalists deserve to be considered among the ranks of public intellectuals and, in many accounts that describe the history of public life, they are accorded that position. Journalists provide a 'bridge' between science, technology and specialist knowledge and the news consuming public (Simmons 2007, p. 10). There was also a time – though we would not call it a 'Golden Age' – when journalists and editors were much closer to contemporary philosophers, particularly during the period of the American and French revolutions of the eighteenth century (Burns 2006; Daniel 2009; Stephens 2007). Today, the division of mental labour is much greater than it was even 20 years ago and the gap between journalism and philosophy seems much wider than it actually is. Nevertheless, it is possible to point to many journalists who have also become significant public intellectuals (thinkers and philosophers of the everyday) in their own right. The 'father of electricity', Benjamin Franklin is one; not only was he an inventor and a dabbler in science, he was a newspaper editor and writer, a diplomat and a participant in one of the most significant political revolutions of the modern age – the American war of independence against British colonialism. We could also add more modern figures like George Orwell to this list; his vast body of work collected in over 40 volumes encompasses fiction (*Keep the Aspidistra Flying, Burmese Days*), science fiction/futurism (*Nineteen Eighty-four, Animal Farm*), numerous essays on imperialism (*Shooting an Elephant, A Hanging*), pamphlets on socialism, nationalism and war (*Homage to Catalonia, The Lion and the Unicorn, Down and Out in Paris and London,* and *The Road to Wigan Pier*) and hundreds of articles on literary criticism (*Politics and the English Language*). Orwell's work not only gives us an insight into the period in which he was an active journalist and author (roughly 1930 to 1950), it continues to provide insights and reflections that are relevant today.

George Orwell was one journalist who was not afraid to admit he had a philosophy of life, or world-view, which informed his writing. The twentieth century has given us a range of journalist-intellectuals who sit right across the political spectrum. Some are heroes, some are villains and in the end it perhaps depends on your own political, cultural and philosophical outlook how you would describe them. A brief list of some of our favourites would include Ernest Hemingway and Martha Gellhorn; John Reed, Louisa Bryant, Hunter S. Thompson; PJ O'Rourke, Ida Tarbell, Christopher Hitchens, Robert Fiske, Michael Moore, Susan Faludi, Naomi Klein and John Pilger. Whomever you might regard as a leading light on this list or your own version, the key point is that for more than 400 years, since the beginning of the Enlightenment in the sixteenth century, there has been a strong link between journalism, newsgathering, news-writing, opinion-forming, philosophy and the growth of democratic public discourse. A discussion of ethics must canvass all of these areas.

An emotional attitude

> I write it because there is some lie that I want to expose, some fact to which I want to draw attention ... But I could not do the work of writing a book, or even a long magazine article, if it were not also an aesthetic experience.
>
> (Orwell 1946)

Exposing official lies is an honourable and ethical ambition that continues to motivate the best journalists of the past and the present. In his 1946 essay, *Why I Write*, George Orwell says that most journalists and writers will develop a world view, an outlook on life from which they 'will never completely escape'. Orwell calls this the 'emotional attitude' that is fabricated from all the social relationships that a person is involved in, including their working life. The term 'emotional attitude' is perhaps synonymous with what others have called the 'world view', or the working philosophy of journalists. It is an attitude that affects ethical thinking and decision-making (Cuillier 2009). We like to use the term 'emotional attitude' because it evokes the important idea that the way we think and what we think are very clearly linked to our human emotions. This is doubly important in a discussion about ethics, which involves important emotions like empathy, disgust, love, respect, hate, and fear.

The fault lines in emotional attitudes of journalism today centre on questions of ethics: the 'right' way to gather news; the values of 'accuracy' and 'objectivity'; notions of 'bias' versus public service; the impact of 'infotainment' on news values; the pressures generated by broken business models and the rising tide of 'user-generated news-like content' (Hirst 2011). These are the fault lines, or what John Merrill (1989) calls the 'antinomes': the contradictory positions and ideas within journalism.

The emotional attitudes that reporters and editors hold, and which colour their view of news, are created in a dialectic: the interplay of opposing ideas (Merrill 1989) and opposing social forces (Hirst 2001). Thus we can talk about an 'emotional dialectic' (Hirst 2003): the fluid, contested, and challenging continuum of ideas, attitudes, and ideologies that reporters and editors hold and work within. The emotional dialectic is the process that determines a person's view of the world, builds their philosophical outlook and forms their consciousness. In news media, the 'interplay' of opposing forces – the emotional dialectic – carries over into the news agenda and into decisions about how and why a story should be reported. We call this the 'dialectic of the front page'.

It stands to reason that reporters and editors, like every other citizen, have a range of opinions about many issues. In the case of journalists, the important additional point is that these attitudes have a direct bearing on the work they do. In order to fully understand and appreciate the emotional dialectic of journalism and its relationship to media ethics, we must understand the philosophical roots of the ideas and concepts that inform both the theory and the practice of news reporting. We must also understand how the news product is produced and the conditions of its production. Finally, we need to understand the social context in which the news is both produced and consumed, and the significance of embedded (ideological) meanings.

Philosophy and the news industry

> It's essential for young journalists to understand how our peculiar institution developed, and that it is not a natural kind – it can be changed and reformed.
>
> (Romano 2009)

Carlin Romano makes a compelling case for why a philosophy of journalism is a good idea: young reporters need training in philosophical thinking to hone their 'intellectual instincts and reflexes' in the search for truth. It may not be quite so obvious as the link between philosophy and ethics, but there is a strong connection between philosophy and the news industry too. In part the link is very basic – without the circulation of ideas through news and journalism there is very little material for philosophers to think about. Nor would we know of the work of philosophers without the popular media – journalism, magazines, books, etc. But at a deeper level there is a common historical element that becomes clear when the history of philosophical thinking and the history of news and journalism are placed side-by-side. The thesis that we will explore in this and the next chapter is that the development of modern journalism ethics – as exemplified by ethical codes and practices – arises out of the historical needs of the news industry from the fifteenth century onwards and its intersection with post-Enlightenment philosophies of freedom of speech and freedom of the press. This does not seem such a far-fetched proposition if we simply remember that among the first uses of the Gutenberg printing press, invented in the 1450s, was the reproduction, on a mass scale for public consumption, of one of the most enduring philosophical tracts in human history: the Protestant Bible. Gutenberg's edition of the Bible was influential and sparked a challenge to the political dominance of the Catholic Church in European life. Gutenberg's Bible, published in vernacular language, not high Latin, created a religious schism in Europe that eventually helped break the hold of the Pope and his archbishops, led to the establishment of the 'New World' as a haven for religious dissidents and paved the way for breakthroughs in science that created the modern world. The scepticism and pragmatism of contemporary journalism is predicated on the scientific and social revolutions ignited by the sparks that flew from Gutenberg's printing press. For nearly 400 years, the fires of freedom were fed by generations of writers, publishers and editors, many of them the ancestral predecessors of modern journalists. It was their passion, determination and refusal to accept the censorship of clerics and kings that laid the foundation for modern news media ethics.

What is philosophy?

Our study of ethical debates only makes sense with reference to first principles and a brief discussion of philosophy. There is a very clear and long-established link between philosophy and ethics; they are not exactly synonyms, but they are closely related. A sample of easily-accessible definitions of philosophy and ethics demonstrate the links between them

philosophy [fi-los-uh-fee] (noun):

- the rational investigation of the truths and principles of being, knowledge, or conduct
- the critical study of the basic principles and concepts of a particular branch of knowledge, especially with a view to improving or reconstituting them
- a system of principles for guidance in practical affairs, or a system of values by which one lives
- a set of ideas or beliefs relating to a particular field or activity; an underlying theory.

ethics [e-thiks] (noun):

- the discipline dealing with what is good and bad and with moral duty and obligation
- the principles of conduct governing an individual or a group; for example *professional* ethics.

In fact, ethics is often considered to be a branch of philosophy as Dictionary.com defines it:

> **Ethics**: that branch of philosophy dealing with values relating to human conduct, with respect to the rightness and wrongness of certain actions and to the goodness and badness of the motives and ends of such actions.

The more upmarket *Oxford Dictionary* agrees: ethics is 'the branch of knowledge that deals with moral principles'. We need not go on – ethics and philosophy are generally symbiotic. Some of the most important issues in philosophy over many centuries have been to do with communication rights and freedoms. There have also been arguments about who could communicate and with whom; about what could be communicated and who controlled the communication. The philosophical discussion about news revolves around freedom of speech and censorship; the dialectical relationship between them is at the heart of journalism ethics. It is the opposition between these two powerful ideas that forms one of the many contradictions in the history of both philosophical thinking and thinking about news and journalism.

You might well be asking: 'What has this got to do with journalism ethics today?' The first answer is that the centuries-long fight against censorship of the news by Church and State, from the fifteenth century on, forms an important theme and thread in the development of modern journalism ethics. From the fifteenth century, publishers fought to establish a 'fourth estate' in relation to the 'divine' powers bestowed on and enjoyed by monarchs and clerics and judges. This was one of the positive outcomes of the American and French revolutions in the eighteenth century. Also, historical accounts are important to our understanding because yesterday always weighs heavily on today. Some of the earliest forms of news gathering and dissemination – what we now call journalism – were carried out by people we would now call 'philosophers'; chief among them figures such as the early Greeks, Socrates, Aristotle and Plato. These figures are important, too, in the development of ethical practices and ways of thinking about ethics. A whole branch of philosophical thinking is devoted to a discussion of ethics: the good and bad; the moral and immoral; the sanctioned and the permissible. Having some understanding of, or at least a passing acquaintance with, some key ideas in the philosophy of ethics is an important foundation for journalists and journalism students.

Theories and origins of ethics

There are many variations in theories and systems of ethical thought, discussion, and, ultimately, decision-making. We have chosen to include a brief overview in this chapter before outlining our own philosophical framework of the dialectic – the idea of tensions, contradiction and resolution of conflict within the world of ideas and social action. In early, pre-scientific, attempts to understand the physical world, religion and mythology appeared to provide many answers and the concept of a supreme being was at the core of most ethical systems. God's laws were seen as being synonymous with natural law. However, as the power of science has grown, these notions have also shifted and we now look to the material conditions of our lives for many explanations that would previously only have been known as mystical phenomena. This is an important development in philosophy because it begins to assume that human beings are capable of materialised thought and action *independent* of a higher authority. Karl Marx was an early writer in this tradition. In particular, Marx argued, it is a human being's ability to labour as an individual, and also to work collectively in refashioning nature, that sets our societies apart from those of other animals on the planet. This might, at this point, seem a little obscure for a text about journalism ethics, but it is at the very core of our arguments and cases. As we demonstrate in the following chapters, it is the ways in which reporters and editors go about their daily tasks in the newsroom – the social organisation of the news production process – that finally impacts upon and helps determine many ethical and unethical attitudes in the newsroom.

When considering systems or philosophies of ethics, a broad distinction can be made between those that simply describe situations, and those that codify a list of rules, recommendations, or proposals. The 'descriptive' methods are those that simply lay out the facts for our consideration. They describe a situation and invite us to make up our own minds, or to imitate the good behaviour as it is described. On the other hand, systems of ethics that are 'normative' are generally ones that define 'good' and 'bad' behaviour and demand that we stay within the rules and boundaries (norms) of good behaviour. Normative systems are also sometimes described as 'evaluative', or 'prescriptive' (Bullock and Trombley 2000, pp. 594–5).

The earliest written records of ethical debate are about 5000 years old – developed in Mesopotamia, Egypt, and the Hebrew world. It is therefore no surprise that ethical traditions are often historically associated with religious movements, churches, and philosophies. Hindu, Buddhist, Taoist, Jewish, Christian, and Islamic thinkers have all proposed life codes that suggest ethical ways of existing in harmony with other human beings and with nature, often in a relationship with a spiritual world. Each poses and answers in its own way questions such as:

- How can I know what is right?
- What is the ultimate criterion for right action?
- Why should I do what is right?
- What sanctions and/or punishments should apply for transgressions of the moral code?

All of these questions are also applicable in a study of journalism ethics, at both a philosophical and a practical level. For example, most codes of ethics contain some type of enforcement clause that includes penalties for non-compliance. It is fairly obvious, then, that codes of ethics in the media might usually be normative: they set out in reasonably precise terms the 'rights' and 'wrongs' of ethical behaviour. One final point about normative systems – they tend to be socially determined. That is, the standards and values prescribed in the code tend to be those of a particular group, or are based on standards of behaviour that are broadly acceptable to 'mainstream' society (whatever that is defined as). In journalism and the news media, most codes of ethics, charters of editorial independence, and other written instruments for classifying ethics are said to be normative. They are systems that recommend, and sometimes enforce, the standards that are deemed valid by the drafters of the code. Such codes are also historically situated – that is, they reflect the social norms of the time in which they were drafted and promulgated. This is why, from time to time, even the most effective and efficient code will need to be updated (Hirst 1997).

Deontological versus teleological systems of ethics

The first distinction to be made is between deontological and teleological systems of ethical thought and decision-making. Deontology is primarily concerned with obligations and duties that are imposed upon individuals. Teleology is primarily concerned with the consequences of our actions. Some codes of ethics contain both deontological and teleological elements. Immanuel Kant's *categorical imperative* is the best-known form of deontological ethics; we should examine the reasons for our actions, not necessarily the outcome that they achieve. In Kant's schema, *imperative* implies a command, a 'must-do', and *categorical* means that it is unconditional, the imperative applies at all times and under any circumstances (Johnson, R. 2012). The Ten Commandments issued by God to Moses are a good example of the categorical imperative. People were expected to obey God's laws. In terms of the categorical imperative, what constitutes right action is always right.

The 'actions' versus 'consequences' contradiction between deontology and teleology then leads us to consider the distinction between 'intention' and 'foresight':

- Do we intend to always act in an ethical manner, in accordance with the duties and obligations (responsibilities) of being a journalist? A deontological approach is one that makes us always consider our actions ahead of any consequences. We should do what is *right*, not necessarily that which creates *good* consequences (Alexander and Moore 2012).
- What do we intend our actions to achieve? This is a teleological approach in which we look at possible consequences, both positive and negative.
- Can we foresee any unethical consequences? In considering teleological questions, can we look ahead and predict both good and bad results of our actions?
- Can we predict outcomes before they happen? If we always behave ethically following the principles of deontology, can we apply a predictive teleology to double our chances of being ethically good?

Deontology

Journalists have an obligation (duty) to tell the truth because, under all circumstances, telling the truth is the right thing to do. This is a deontological concept, which postulates that our actions are based on duties or obligations to others. Deontology is derived from the Greek word *deon* meaning duty and regards moral and good actions as 'self-evident and not necessarily derived from any higher, or more fundamental truths' (Bullock and Trombley 2000, p. 213).

A key aspect of deontological systems is their implication that we ought to live by moral rules, and that these rules should not be broken – even if better things may come from breaking them. In other words, unlike teleological (or 'goal-oriented') ethics, it is not the consequences of our actions but their inherent moral value that should determine what we do. Hence, we need to know how rules are to be framed, and what actions constitute a breach of these rules. Kantian ethics is then, quite clearly, a form of deontological ethics.

The formulation adopted by Kant in his manuscript, *Groundwork on the Metaphysics of Morals* (1996; originally published 1785), is that all our actions should be 'willed without contradiction as a universal law' (Bullock and Trombley 2000, p. 108). In other words, we should do what is right, because it is right. Kant's system is prescriptive and therefore in the normative tradition; the 'categorical imperative' must have 'universal application' (Sanders 2003, p. 18). The Kantian imperative implies that we should never treat people as a 'means to an end', but as an 'end in themselves'. In other words, we should never take advantage of other people. This is crucial for journalistic ethics because it implies that reporters must not take advantage of people, or put them at risk just to get a story published or broadcast. Karen Sanders' (2003, p. 19) critique of Kantian ethics is that it leaves 'the moral significance of the emotions insufficiently explained'.

Teleology and the utility principle

Teleology is another strand of ethical decision-making where a decision is reached after considering the consequences of the action. The basic teleological proposition is that the purpose of an action is more important than the action itself and, perhaps, more important than the impetus that gives rise to the action. It directs us to first know, and then understand, all the possible consequences of our actions. This is obviously important in journalism, particularly in situations where the consequences of publishing, or broadcasting, a story can be life-threatening.

The idea of utilitarian ethics is the classic teleological model. The well-known English philosopher of the nineteenth century, John Stuart Mill, is credited with modifying, or at least articulating, the utility principle, which was first proposed by Jeremy Bentham. We know of J. S. Mill through the aphorism: 'the greatest good for the greatest number of people'. According to the theory of utility, the rightness of an action is in direct proportion to its ability to bestow happiness, 'pleasure and the absence of pain' (Internet Encyclopedia of Philosophy).

Mill's utility principle is altruistic – that is, it does not rely on us being motivated by an egoistic impulse to act in our own best interest. Instead, as individuals, we are encouraged to act in pursuit of certain collective, or social, benefits. But this begs a further question: What things are good in themselves? It is obvious that we cannot answer this question in a vacuum, hence we must begin putting our ethical considerations into a socially constructed framework. What feels right and proper to one person may cause excruciating agony to another person with different sensibilities and thresholds. Many scholars of journalism ethics regard Mills' utilitarianism as perhaps the most important ethical principle because it is embedded in the democratic traditions of the eighteenth and nineteenth centuries. They argue that utilitarianism is the foundation of public service journalism and professionalism (Friend and Singer 2007, p. xxi). We would not dispute the importance of utilitarianism, but might add only that ethical questions cannot be separated from questions of social structure, and therefore cannot be easily separated from questions of social control or from institutions of power. It is not possible to abstract Mills' utilitarian principles from the social milieu in which they were forged. We will come back to these questions in subsequent chapters.

Rawls' 'veil of ignorance'

The American political philosopher John Rawls outlined a theory of justice and fairness that is often referred to as the 'veil of ignorance' when discussed in relation to journalism ethics. The veil of ignorance is a form of Kantian imperative that also relates to social contract theories of ethics (see below). The veil of ignorance is what philosophers call an 'original position' – that is a position taken without (as far as possible) any prejudice or pre-conceived ideas about processes or outcomes (Travis 2010). Rawls' theory has both deontological and teleological elements; it asks us to consider both right actions and consequences. In everyday terms, we can describe the veil of ignorance as an invitation to 'walk a mile' in someone else's shoes. It is a call for us to consider how our actions (or the actions of others) might affect people who come into contact with the consequences of the action. In terms of journalism, this means considering the consequences of reporting, prior to commencing the action (Skorpen 1989). Rawls' veil of ignorance is really no more than a thought experiment; it is virtually impossible for any of us to forgo all prior knowledge of our social conditions. The veil of ignorance also assumes a power vacuum in which there is no advantage or disadvantage attached to ethnicity, class, gender, sexual orientation or other markers of social differentiation (Internet Encyclopedia of Philosophy). Rawls' critics argue that the veil of ignorance is only useful as a hypothetical thinking exercise, with little practical application. However, there is one practical question that makes Rawls' theory relevant in journalism: 'How would you feel if this story was about you?'

This is not a blanket rule. Obviously, uncovering wrongdoing in public life is going to make the subject of the story feel terrible – mainly because they have been caught – but it should not be a reason for abandoning the report. On the other hand, 'How would you feel if this story was about you?' can be applied effectively to routine stories with little or no real public interest – for example, reporting that merely embarrasses ordinary people for the titillation of the audience. How would you feel?

A further criticism that can be levelled at Rawls is that his theory of justice and fairness is historically situated in twentieth-century liberal-democratic capitalism. It therefore normalises existing inequalities by assuming (behind the veil of ignorance) that there is actual equality before the law and in the laws of economics (Freeman 2012; Roberts 2012). However, we cannot separate hypothetical individuals out from unequal social relations and power structures and in this sense Rawls' theory is weak (Cheshire 1997; Plaisance 2002). Inequalities based on ethnicity, gender and sexual orientation are endemic and integral to capitalist society, as are power differentials based on income and class status. Despite these caveats, Renita Coleman (2011) argues Rawls' work is useful in examining situations where vulnerable subjects – such as children – are used in a news context. Rawls' veil of ignorance provides an individual journalist with a shorthand way of asking an important question about the consequences of their actions, but it is not the most effective theoretical account of journalistic ethics. Perhaps it finds its greatest use in the consideration of when is it OK to invade privacy for a story (Kieran et al. 2000); this is when the 'How would you feel?' question is most relevant.

The tradition of the social contract

One of the primary directives for journalists is to honour their contract with readers, viewers, and listeners – to give them the truth, the facts, and the context for the stories they report. This contractual obligation is a cornerstone of the expected role of journalists in a liberal democracy. As Stephen Ward (2010, p. 50) suggests, at the heart of this compact is the presumption that journalists are given freedom to report without restraint in return for being responsible. The social contract implies that, at the level of ethical behaviour, morality is an implicit agreement we make with other human beings. In general terms, a social contract implies an unwritten agreement that we will all behave responsibly towards each other (Bullock and Trombley 2000, p. 799). We do this voluntarily, in good faith, and in order to collectively gain a share of any benefits derived from human endeavours towards establishing and sustaining a healthy society. In ethical systems constructed on the basis of a social contract, we begin to get the first sense of a materialist ethic separated from the spiritual elements of the ancients and an infallible, or unquestioning, belief in the divine omnipotence of a god. The idea of the social contract goes back to the eighteenth century and references to it can be found in the work of Kant, Rousseau, Hobbes, Locke and others. While there are differences in emphasis among the various philosophers who are today credited with influencing our understanding of the social contract, a fundamental similarity remains: the contract is the basis on which civil society is built and it implies a certain level of consent on behalf of subjects in relation to sovereign (political) power exercised by government (Cudd 2012). The social contract is also a foundation for the ethical concept of the public interest. The contract between journalists and audiences is predicated on rights and duties (on both sides) and on a mutual obligation to uphold freedom of the press (Sjovaag 2010).

Virtue theory

A virtue is described in the *Australian Concise Oxford Dictionary* (Moore B. 1997, p. 1532) as 'moral excellence; uprightness, goodness'. The dictionary also tells us that virtue is a 'good quality'. As Stanley Cunningham (1999, p. 7) noted in his interpretation of Aristotelian ethics in journalism, virtue is to be understood in terms of 'excellence and rightness' and as an act of 'moral agency and responsibility' to do the right thing under all circumstances.

Aristotle's ethical guide, the 'Golden Mean', is a good example of virtue theory – or virtue ethics – where moral virtue is the *mean* (or middle ground) between two extremes. The Golden Mean is the view that moral virtue lies between the extremes of doing or feeling too much, or too little. Thus virtue lies in a balance that can be found in the exercise of good judgment – the 'right amount' of anger, for example. Therefore, it should not necessarily be seen as some measurable mid-point, equidistant from the two extremes. The Golden Mean is the most virtuous path and the extremes are defined in relation to it, not the other way around (Cunningham, S. B. 1999, p. 8).

Instead of asking, 'What ought I do?' virtue theory asks, 'What kind of person should I be?' Virtue theory puts the ethical spotlight on characteristics that compose a 'good' individual, rather than the social consequences of our actions. In this tradition it is argued that a virtuous character will always act ethically.

Aristotle referred to virtues as 'dispositions' and believed they could be developed over time through education and repetition – assuming, of course, that we are prepared to be rational and intelligent in our choice-making (Sanders 2003, p. 15). In Aristotle's case, the Golden Mean is that space of comfort between excess and deficiency. For example, *courage* is the mean between *cowardice* and *temerity*. This process emphasises character over action, believing that actions are the result of innate attributes. Importantly, the mean is not found using simple mathematical formulae; the mean is determined by reference to circumstances and necessity.

Andrew Belsey and Ruth Chadwick (1992) suggest that while not necessarily always temperate in their behaviour, particularly where the consumption of alcohol is concerned, a good journalist should display the positive virtues of 'fairness, truthfulness, trustworthiness and non-malevolence'. They then go on to ask whether this is in fact a good foundation for ethical behaviour because virtue might also be defined as respecting the rights of others or promoting the general good, both of which might conflict with what journalists actually do (1992, pp. 11–12).

John O'Neill (1992, pp. 19–20) suggests that the virtues of truth-telling, honesty, and integrity might be appropriate for media professionals. At the same time, O'Neill recognises that the oft-cited journalistic virtue of 'objectivity' 'is often rejected by some of the best journalists of our day' (1992, p. 20). Indeed, we'll be returning to the problematic issue of objectivity in subsequent chapters.

Finally, it is important to note a caveat on the idea of virtue ethics and Aristotle's Golden Mean, which is not a fixed capacity and can vary according to circumstances. Sanders (2003, p. 16) uses the example of a war correspondent who takes risks to get a story from the front lines. Depending on the circumstances – the precautions taken and the news value of the story – one could imagine the reporter being either brave or stupid.

Pragmatism

Pragmatism is a relatively recent philosophical tradition most closely associated with American thinkers from the late nineteenth to early twentieth centuries – William James, John Dewey and, to some degree the journalist and public relations theorist Walter Lippmann. Some scholars regard pragmatism as journalism's most significant philosophical approach because of its strong association with the 'search for "facts"' (Altschull 1990, pp. 235–6). Despite coming onto the scene relatively recently, pragmatism shares the concerns of philosophy generally – the attempt to reconcile empiricism with belief and to resolve metaphysical disputes: 'How we can reconcile the claims of science, on the one hand, with those of religion and morality on the other' (Hookway 2010). The facticity of pragmatism lies at the heart of its appeal to journalists and to journalism scholars like Altschull because it appears to justify an approach that is neutral or objective. If the 'facts' speak for themselves then there is no reason for reporters to embellish or interpret. This appears to work well in the abstract, but, as we've already suggested, in practice it is a little more complicated because the world-view of the journalist – their day-to-day philosophy or ideology – will always colour the selection and prioritising of any given set of supposedly neutral 'facts'.

Determinism versus free will

Determinism generally means a belief in an overriding causal law – that every event has a cause and effect. For ethicists and political thinkers like J. S. Mill, the law of determination is the 'most general and comprehensive of all the laws of nature' (Bullock and Trombley 2000, p. 217). In life, as in philosophy, there is tension between what is pre-determined (nature) and what is an act of free will (the human intelligence). It is an ethical dilemma that we cannot ignore. The argument about determinism in ethics says there is a causal explanation for everything that happens in the universe, hence we have no freedom of choice, and therefore we are not morally responsible for our actions. In other words, we cannot do other than what we do, because it is pre-determined for us, through nature.

On the other hand, the free will argument is that moral decision-making is based on an assumption that individuals are responsible, and should therefore be held accountable, for what they freely choose to do. The concept of free will is very important in bourgeois ideologies and therefore, one could argue, central to any discussion of media ethics in a normative, capitalist society. If we are free to choose our actions, we must accept responsibility for their inherent moral value and the consequences that flow from what we choose to do. As Bullock and Trombley note, 'determinism and free will seem, on the face of it, to be incompatible' (2000, p. 337). In our view the apparent contradiction between freedom and responsibility in journalistic practice, as characterised in the determinism versus free will debate, is crucial to an understanding of the fault lines in contemporary journalism theory and practice. Is freedom of the press today an actual right, or is it a privilege? And who does it belong to – the media owners, media workers or the public? John Merrill (1989, p. 33) argues that the pendulum of freedom is swinging away from the press, particularly as public access to the media becomes more common and news moves from a 'lecture' format to a 'conversation' that involves the audience on an equal footing with the reporter. As we will discuss in subsequent chapters, this is an important issue as web-based journalism and user-generated news-like content become more popular (Hirst 2011; Hirst and Harrison 2007). Also, Merrill (1989, p. 53) points out that responsibility in journalism is not without its own problems – to whom is a reporter responsible and how should conflicting responsibilities be prioritised, or reconciled?

Universal versus relative ethics

> It might be said that journalists are, really, absolute believers in relativism – or relativistic believers in absolutism. They are both egoists and altruists ... – creatures of the clash between inflexibility and flexibility and between all the other contraries that impinge on their lives.
>
> (Merrill 1989, p. 10)

As the American ethicist John Merrill pointed out, relativism and absolutism are, of course, contradictory and it is therefore difficult for one person to be philosophically a universalist and a relativist at the same time – at least not without causing him/herself a headache. According to the relativists, there are no absolutes, no universal truths, and all forms of morality are particular to specific social formations and cultures that are historically determined: 'moral truth or justification is relative to a culture or society' (Gowans 2012). For example, just because a statement holds true for you, here and now, does not mean it will be true for other people under different circumstances. Relativism is usually associated with cultural differences that exist over distances, and between various nations or societies (Bullock and Trombley 2000, p. 742). This leads relativists to advance the argument that we should not pass judgment on, nor should we attempt to change, the moral, social, and ethical values freely expressed in other cultures. By the same token, they should not interfere in our world either. We can see how difficult it is to apply this concept to the world around us when we look at the way Islam is reported in the media and in contemporary debates about what might constitute the 'absolute' values of 'Western civilization' and how this might clash with fundamental tenets of the Muslim faith. As journalism scholars have noted, there is a tone of 'cultural incompatibility' in some reporting of Islamic affairs, the so-called 'war on terror' and in coverage of the Middle East, or other parts of the Muslim world (Irfan 2010; Vultee 2009).

The simple argument in terms of journalism ethics is that one journalist or newsroom editor might choose to do things one way, but if another individual or newsroom chooses a different way, it doesn't matter. In a relativist world there are no universals such as fundamental human rights. Of course, ethics are relative to a large degree and no two newsrooms will be exactly alike; there could be regional, national, language and other differences that separate out several journalism cultures (Hanitzsch 2007).

What might unify journalism and provide some universality is the pursuit of truth and a dedication to the public interest. Perhaps this is true of Western-style journalism, but attempts to universalise ethics beyond that are problematic because of national and regional differences (Brislin 2004).

Rights-based ethics systems

> I shall advance the thesis that if there are any moral rights at all, it follows that there is at least one natural right, the equal right of all men to be free.
>
> (Hart 1955, p. 175)

Natural rights are those rights that human beings have and enjoy as a condition of their existence; that is, they are not dependent on the existence of a particular type of society and they are universal in that they extend across all social formations equally. Natural rights are those that are said to exist in nature, or in earlier times those bestowed by God (when God and nature were philosophically seen as essentially one and the same thing). They are rights 'inherent in the human personality' (Tierney 2001, p. 20). Natural rights are often defined in relation to moral rights – those rights that exist socially and that are 'created or conferred by men's voluntary action' (Hart 1955, p. 175). 'Rights' often form the basis for ethical considerations in the context of news and journalism – the 'public right to know', for example, that is often cited by reporters to justify some potentially dubious practices, including breaches of the right to privacy of individuals in the news spotlight.

Scholars have determined a classification system for rights and the various elements from which they are composed. The four basic elements of any right are 'the privilege, the claim, the power, and the immunity'. A privilege is a right that exists without any negative obligation. You have a right (privilege) to do something if there is no mandated prohibition against doing the action (Wenar 2011). For example, you have a right to wear red shoes. A person has a right (claim) to something if a third party has an obligation to provide it. The right to a fair trial is a claim because the State has an obligation to ensure that the accused person does receive a fair trial. If a trial is deemed to be unfair, then the accused has a right to seek redress. A power is the right to determine the fate of another person. A ship's captain can order a crew member to carry out functions to keep the vessel in good order (Wenar 2011). Immunity is a right not to be subject to the power of another's right. For example, in some legal cases, witnesses have a right (immunity) not to incriminate themselves in the evidence they give. Rights are also sometimes given designations of either positive or negative, which can be simply interpreted as the freedom to (positive) or freedom from (negative). Finally, it is important to recognise that within any society there are social limits imposed on the exercise of rights. You may have a right to throw pebbles from the beach into the sea, but if there are people in front of you swimming or paddling on the shoreline, you do not have a right to throw stones if swimmers or paddlers could be injured by your actions. Thus in any historical and social context, the complexity of rights, obligations and mutual considerations increases as the society becomes more complex.

To codify the application of rights many are now included in legal provisions and statutes, particularly in relation to political, civil and property rights. For example, a driver's licence gives its holder a right to drive a car, but only in the context of road rules which are designed to maintain the rights of other drivers, cyclists and pedestrians. Moral and legal rights can sometimes overlap and certainly J. S. Mill thought that some moral rights should be enforceable by law when considering the principles of utilitarianism (Campbell 2011). Civil rights are a form of legally enforceable privilege and they are generally designed to protect the rights of citizens within and against the power of the State; their origin, too, is in the political philosophy of Aristotle (Altman 2012).

In the middle of the twentieth century, a number of natural, political and civil rights were codified into a statement authored and endorsed by the newly-formed United Nations and this is a good example of a 'complex, layered structure of rights' (Wenar 2011) that gives expression to both positive and negative types of freedom, as we've just discussed. Human rights are freedoms that set out how citizens should be treated by their governments and in the context of global travel or migration. Human rights prohibit discrimination (a negative freedom) and impose duties on governments regarding the treatment of their citizens (a positive freedom) (Nickel 2013). The Universal Declaration of Human Rights covers a lot of territory – everything from the right to life and education to the right not to be tortured. The key right for our purposes is the famous Article 19.

Article 19

> Everyone has the right to freedom of opinion and expression; this right includes freedom to hold opinions without interference and to seek, receive and impart information and ideas through any media and regardless of frontiers.
>
> The Universal Declaration of Human Rights

The right to freedom of expression is enshrined in the United Nations' Universal Declaration of Human Rights and it is held to be universal. This declaration was made in 1948 – as the world was recovering from the Second World War and the scourge of Fascism in Europe. It was meant to enshrine these values in a global body that would ensure no such conflict could occur in the future.

The declaration is universal in that the rights expressed exist for, and are (theoretically) available to, every person on the planet.

The Declaration is an admirable document; it is full of good intentions, but at times it seems as if the document is not worth the very expensive paper it is printed on. The UN's declaration is not a treaty, it is not legally binding and it is most often honoured in the breach. The right to adequate food and shelter does not stop famine or illegal land-clearing and forced population movements. No right on this charter has prevented war crimes or State torture. The declaration of a theoretical universal right is immediately compromised in practice by the very existence of alienation and exploitation, as a condition of life under capitalism, for the majority of the world's current and future population.

In the realisation and application of human rights, contradictions appear and this is particularly the case when we are talking about rights in relation to journalism, journalists and the news. We will confront this issue in nearly every chapter of this book, but for now a few simple illustrations will suffice.

Think about a recent, high-profile court case that you are familiar with. Are there any instances you can remember in which the rights of the accused person – the right to a presumption of innocence and the right to a fair trial – were threatened by media coverage of the case?

The public right to know is often cited by journalists as a reason for aggressive, 'in your face' reporting. The news media's role is to inform the public; in particular, to inform the public about things that governments might want kept secret for reasons of national, military or economic security. Yet governments will also claim to be acting in the public, or the national, interest when they refuse to disclose information. How can we know who is right under such circumstances? The right-to-know and the right to privacy are also often in competition, despite both being either directly or implicitly covered in the Universal Declaration.

The systems of ethics that base themselves on the exercise of certain rights can only function according to the rule that we should always respect the rights of other individuals. However, we need to ask and answer the following question before proceeding to a discussion of application: Can ethics and morals be based on rights, or are rights derived from more fundamental moral principles? In a very concrete sense, what is the 'right to life'? Or, perhaps more applicably, we should ask: What is the right to freedom of expression? Is it a right that everyone has regardless of its conflict with other 'rights', such as a 'right to peace and quiet'? In other words, are rights universal or relative?

Universal prescriptions about the value, sanctity, and application of human rights have some weight in many systems of national and international law. They are becoming increasingly important, and incorporated into descriptions of ethical behaviour. For example, federal and state anti-vilification laws exist on the basis of Australia's signature on the International Covenant on Civil and Political Rights. On the other hand, the Australian constitution, unlike the American, does not include a 'right' to freedom of expression. However, the Australian High Court has ruled that the constitution contains an 'implied' right to freedom of political speech (for a good discussion of these issues in a legal context, see Pearson and Polden 2011, pp. 33–8 and 229–32). One line of argument suggests there might be contradictions and pitfalls associated with a rights-based approach to media ethics. For example, if people have a right not to be deceived, then deception in investigative journalism, even for results which would be for the general benefit of the public, would not be permitted at all (Belsey and Chadwick 1992, p. 11). In our modern societies these issues are at the core of debates about ethics.

The interplay of rights, free will, virtue, determinism and freedom of expression creates particular tensions and paradoxes within the field of journalism and in its relations to other social structures, relations and institutions. Like John Merrill, we understand these contradictions as an expression of the dialectic in journalism. The dialectic is a tool of logic – a method of thinking – and the mode in which history moves forward in a series of clashes and resolutions in ideas and in practice.

Contradiction, paradox, and fault lines: What is the dialectic?

> Paradoxes abound in journalism. But conflicts and disagreements in journalism are healthy, not unhealthy. Contraries abound and clash, and that is good.
>
> John C. Merrill, *The Dialectic in Journalism* (1989, pp. 4–5)

American scholar John C. Merrill was one of the first theoreticians to introduce the dialectic into the study of journalism in *The Dialectic in Journalism* (1989). Here, Merrill writes of the 'triadic movement that pushes thought forward and to higher levels through the recognition of flux and the merger of conflicting concepts'. According to Merrill, journalism is filled with such concepts needing reconciliation, two of the chief among them being 'freedom' and 'responsibility'; others might be 'disclosure' versus 'privacy', or 'objectivity' and 'subjectivity'. Merrill argues that in a debate about journalistic ethics, the notion of freedom is in contradiction to, and clashes with, the idea of responsibility, and the synthesis is a new ideology: *social responsibility* in journalism. This interpretation of the new synthesis is, of course, itself open to debate, challenge, and eventual mutation into something else.

The contradictory elements of any dialectic in journalism will necessarily revolve around social issues, each impacting on news media ethics. Merrill emphasises changes in ideas driving a change in practice, and the philosophical heart of his dialectic in journalism is Aristotle's idea of the Golden Mean: that between two extremes there lies a more reasonable and acceptable middle path, one that avoids both carelessness and being overly cautious. The application of the Golden Mean to debates around ethics implies that the resolution of the conflict lies in a synthesis that is somewhere in the middle, between the two extremes. We can see this in how Merrill attempts to solve the contradiction between the individual freedoms that news workers enjoy and the need for some form of social control over the news media. In Merrill's synthesis, it is responsible journalism that takes a middle way, through a process of gentle reform, rather than massive upheaval or revolution.

Like many of the philosophical ideas underpinning a study of journalism ethics, the concept of the dialectic is a very old one. Raymond Williams (1989) traced it back to the Greek philosopher, Plato (427–347 BC), and noted that it has been used in modern philosophical discourse since the fifteenth century. Harsh Narain (1973, pp. 1–25) disputes Williams's attribution to Plato, though he agrees the dialectic is almost as old as philosophy itself. It seems it may have been Heraclitus (around 500 BC) who first outlined two concepts central to the dialectic. The first is 'flux' and Heraclitus is thought to have explained this with the famous aphorism that we never step into the same river twice. The second is the 'unity of opposites' and Heraclitus used another water analogy to explain this: 'Sea is the purest and most polluted water: for fish drinkable and healthy, for men undrinkable and harmful' (cited in Graham 2011). A third concept is important to a full understanding of how the dialectic works in practice and that is the process of combined and uneven development, which brings the dialectic firmly into an historical context. Combined and uneven development links the development of a society's economic capacity (its abilities to produce the conditions of its own survival and growth) to the ways in which different levels of capacity combine to produce concrete social structures and varied patterns of intellectual, social and cultural life. Despite its application in historical and social studies, the concept of combined and uneven development itself comes from observations of nature:

> All the constituent elements of a thing, all the aspects of an event, all the factors in a process of development are not realised at the same rate or to an equal degree. Moreover, under differing material conditions, even the same thing exhibits different rates and grades of growth. Every rural farmer and urban gardener knows that.
>
> (Novack 1968)

Certainly, the major philosophers of the ancient Greeks drew on the dialectic for their explanations of both the natural and the social world and its intricate patterns of flux, certainty, and uncertainty. It was in the hands of German philosophers Immanuel Kant and Georg Hegel that the concept of the dialectic came to refer to the principles of contradiction, and constant tension between competing ideas or social forces. What Kant, Hegel, and later Karl Marx, believed possible using the concept of the dialectic was to 'make sense of the connection between the material world and consciousness, in both its theoretical and practical forms' (Hunt 1993, p. 6). The process of combined and uneven development is central to our discussion of how freedom of the press developed as a philosophical and ideological construct during the revolutions that occurred across Europe from the sixteenth to eighteenth centuries and in the United States from the middle of the seventeenth century. The dynamics of these revolutions demonstrate clearly the effects of uneven development of the economic base of societies and the ideas that flow from different material circumstances (Le Blanc 2006).

The word 'dialectic' originally stood for logic and systematic thinking; later it came also to mean the process of contradiction and resolution between conflicting sets of ideas. In modern European philosophy, the roots of the dialectic as a method of reasoning can be traced to the philosopher Immanuel Kant, and later to Georg Hegel, who hypothesised that the inherent contradictions between an idea and its opposite would be resolved at a higher level of meaning. Hegel further refined the concept to refer to the principles of contradiction, and constant tension between competing ideas or social forces. According to the philosophy of dialectics, everything tends to clash and merge with its opposite (the 'unity of opposites'). Development and change is everywhere in nature, and in society. Dialectically, the development of nature and human discourse proceeds by the process of an idea (thesis) conflicting with its opposite (antithesis) to produce a new idea that combines elements of the previous ideas (synthesis), which in turn produces a new thesis, and the process begins again. If we look briefly at the writing of the American media scholar, Vincent Mosco, we can gain a sense of his modern interpretation of the dialectic. He calls this a process of 'mutual constitution': the interaction of social, economic, cultural, and political forces 'which transform them into different dimensions of the same historical process – the disintegration and reintegration of the modern world' (Mosco 1996, p. 5). There is no reason, particularly in terms of the applicability of philosophical concepts, that we should exclude journalism from this process. The practice, and the theory, of journalism are subject to the same buffeting social forces that shape our lives on a daily basis. As John Merrill (1989, p. 8) puts it: 'Flux is king in journalism. Dynamic thinking and dialogue is essential to journalistic progress.'

The ethico-legal paradox

This is a book about journalism ethics, it is not a text about media law, but we cannot ignore the dialectical relationship between law and ethics. Instead, we have to articulate the complexity of the fluid relationship between them. We do this using the concept of an 'ethico-legal paradox', which is how we have chosen to describe the flux and dialectical unevenness that often exists between the law and ethics. Simply defined, the ethico-legal paradox is the confusion or contradiction that arises when the legal and moral/ethical obligations of a journalist conflict with each other. Several of the ethical fault lines discussed in this book are the result of this paradox. An action may be legally wrong (or at least questionable), but from the standpoint of ethical actions the same action could be justified – perhaps, for example, on public interest grounds.

We have always argued that, unlike the very black and white nature of law (something is either legal or illegal), ethics and ethical philosophies deal with the grey areas. Of course, not all ethical issues are shrouded in doubt; some ethical principles do come with imperatives or absolutes. The first principle of the medical code, 'first do no harm', is one such imperative and in journalism telling the truth is an absolute that should never be compromised. But what about breaking the law – for example, trespassing on private property – in order to secure a story? Or how about lying to authorities or to a source in order to hide your true intentions on a story you are chasing? Instead of trying to answer these questions here, we will leave that discussion for later chapters; our purpose now is only to pose the ethico-legal paradox as an issue that sits at the heart of arguments about both the theory and the practice of journalism. The ethico-legal paradox is an example of the dialectic as it operates within the journalistic field.

The dialectic: Idealism versus materialism

Dialectical thinking is a way of coming to terms with the competing ideological tides of thought that surround journalism today; as Fredric Jameson puts it, dialectical thinking is a method for 'lifting ourselves above' these competing ideologies to get 'a little distance' in order to critique them (Jameson 2009, p. 281). But in order to rise above – hence to see clearly – the contradictions, we have to understand the materiality of ideas and begin to understand the 'paradoxes of capitalism itself' (Jameson 2009, p. 55).

In Merrill's account, the dialectic is a clash between two ideals that creates the social pressures leading to changes in journalism. We argue that this is an idealist philosophy based on Kant's and Hegel's conceptions of the dialectic. Idealism is the theory that the only things that can really exist are mental constructs or ideas (Narain 1973, p. 26). Hegel's eighteenth-century idealism, articulated in his books *Phenomenology of Mind* and *Philosophy of Nature*, centred on the notion that there has only ever been one, all-encompassing mind, or spirit, and that our individual thoughts are dependent fragments (Bullock and Trombley 2000, p. 412). Narain (1973, p. 29) quotes from *Philosophy of Nature*: 'God has two revelations, as nature and as spirit, and both manifestations are temples which He fills and in which He is present.'

The antithesis of idealism is the philosophical tradition of materialism, or dialectical materialism, developed by two more German philosophers who both studied the work of Hegel. Karl Marx and Friedrich Engels extended the scope of dialectics to the natural world, and to the formation and transformation of human society (Callinicos 1987, 1995). According to a materialist dialectic, gradual quantitative changes will generally lead to a qualitative (revolutionary) change. Further, any synthesis is inherently unstable, leading to new contradictions and further dialectic development.

Marx and Engels argued that historically and empirically measurable changes, such as between modes of production – from slavery to feudalism, and from feudalism to capitalism – were the result of cumulative changes brought about by the clash of economic, social, and political forces. In their view, this clash was based on the existence of antagonistic social classes and real social forces, not just a clash of ideas and ideals (Callinicos 1995, p. 101). This clash of social forces does not occur all at once, or at a steady rate across all nations or social formations.

We will employ this argument in the following chapter to outline how the struggle for a free press was part of the slow but necessary transition from feudalism to capitalism and how, in the context of combined and uneven development, this led to the gradual evolution from the partisan press of the eighteenth century to the form of industrial journalism that dominated the twentieth century. From a materialist perspective, the important clashes in the world are the 'fettering of the productive forces by the relations of production', and 'the class struggle between exploiters and exploited' (Callinicos 1995, p. 102). We can apply this analysis to journalism to demonstrate that the major contradiction, the fault line, in the news media today is based on the relations of production in the newsroom – that is, how the news commodity is produced (see chapter 3). Briefly, what drives the development of a dialectic in journalism is not only a clash between ideals (freedom and responsibility), but also a clash of material forces. The contradiction in the news media is the gulf between the need for the news commodity to sell and produce a profit for the owning class, and the supposedly democratic function of the news media to provide information to the public without fear or favour. This very material contradiction is contained in what we call the 'duality of the news commodity' (Hirst 2003; Hirst and Patching 2007); it is both information (use value) and a manufactured product with an exchange value against other goods and services. Journalists hold this contradiction in their heads: on the one hand a belief in the public interest and ideals of the fourth estate; on the other a belief in the freedom of the marketplace. It is the expression of this dialectic in their work that makes journalists the philosophers of the everyday.

Thus, the final question in this opening chapter is to ask: How do reporters develop their philosophical views, their emotional attitudes to the world around them? There is no doubt that they are *expressed* in the form of ideas and consciousness, but they are formed in the everyday social interactions that occur between human beings. Our social interactions are determined by many things – gender, ethnicity, where we were born or grew up, where we went to school, our family's access to wealth and power – and these relationships are based in the material world. As we discussed above, it was Marx and Engels who developed this materialist approach to the workings of the dialectic. The Marxist method – sometimes called historical materialism, or materialist dialectics – dictates that ideas that arise must be carefully examined in the context of the historical and material conditions that gave birth to them; in particular, the process of combined and uneven development between economic and other social or political forces. Or, put another way, we must examine the historical period in which human beings give expression to certain ideas and not others. For example: Why did ideas about freedom of the press develop and mature when they did between the sixteenth and nineteenth centuries? What were the material conditions that led to arguments about the need for, and desirability of, press freedom? It is to these questions that we will turn in Chapter 2.

2   An age of revolutions
Journalism, ethics and freedom of the press

The trial of Socrates: freedom of expression in the ancient world

> The Athens of Socrates's time has gone down in history as the very place where democracy and freedom of speech were born. Yet that city put Socrates, its most famous philosopher, to death. Presumably this was because its citizens did not like what he was teaching. Yet he had been teaching there all his life, unmolested. Why did they wait until he was 70, and had only a few years to live, before executing him?
>
> (Stone 1979)

Four hundred years before the birth of Christ, the Greek philosopher Socrates fell foul of the religious authorities and was tried for heresy in Athens. Many philosophers of the eighteenth and nineteenth centuries relied on philosophical insights of the ancient Greeks for their own ethical arguments, particularly about freedom of expression. John Stuart Mill, in his famous pamphlet *On Liberty*, published in 1859, wrote that 'Socrates was put to death, but the Socratic philosophy rose like the sun in heaven, and spread its illumination over the whole intellectual firmament' (Mill 1859). However, it seems Socrates was not the saint that many might think him to be. According to scholars of Ancient Greece, Socrates himself was not a believer in the right of all Athenians to speak in the agora (public forum). He was, by some accounts, quite aristocratic and elitist in his own views. According to reconstructed documents, the charges against Socrates were damning: 'Socrates is guilty of refusing to recognize the gods recognized by the State, and of introducing new divinities. He is also guilty of corrupting the youth. The penalty demanded is death' (cited in Linder 2002).

The democratic republic of Greece was founded on a contradiction between the free and the unfree. The economy was heavily reliant on slavery and slaves were not free. Even as Greek society developed, real freedom of speech was limited to the aristocratic classes. There was formal equality for this caste, but in practice there were social and economic inequalities: 'Slaves, foreigners, and women did not have the liberty to speak freely' (Berg 2012, p. 9).

Athenian free speech was also limited by legal restraints, particularly for what we would call libel today, and also by a form of qualified privilege for government officials. The later Roman empire, under Augustus, also used laws against treason and *lex maiestatis* (writings against the Emperor) to squash dissent and freedom of speech. Under Augustus' successor, Tiberius, writers were expelled from Rome for treason and their manuscripts destroyed (Berg 2012, p. 20).

There is no doubt that the first debates and arguments about freedom of expression took place during the ancient Greek and Roman republics. However, the two societies differed in their understanding of freedoms and their approach to freedom of speech.

The Athenians believed freedom of expression was a cornerstone of democracy, but the Romans believed it was 'a foundation principle of their liberty'. Berg adds that these competing conceptions of freedom of speech and expression 'have echoed through history and still define the contemporary debate' (2012, p. 5). However, we have to be careful in making an assessment of these freedoms as exercised nearly 2000 years ago. Both Greek and Roman societies were founded on slavery: How does that square with ideas of democracy and personal freedom?

The present on the shoulders of the past

The purpose of this chapter is two-fold. Firstly to look historically at how the social practices of journalism today were developed over a period of several centuries and how this development is intimately bound with emerging arguments about freedom of expression, freedom of speech and freedom of the press. The second aim is to show how the period of bourgeois revolutions from the seventeenth to the nineteenth centuries laid the political foundations for capitalism to become the dominant economic system under the social control of the bourgeoisie – a new ruling class. This overview is necessary because, although we might speak generically about journalism through the ages, the social conditions and content of journalistic practice (and outputs) vary significantly from period to period. The journalism that delivered news of Greek military expeditions back to Athens, or provided intelligence to Rome about the far-flung parts of its empire, was not the same thing as the journalism of newsbooks during the Middle Ages. The newspapers that followed the newsbooks were different again. As well as containing news briefs, often days or weeks out-of-date, their main purpose was propaganda. In the sixteenth and seventeenth centuries, publishing and journalism were often used in the service of doctrinal battles within the broad Christian Church. Ideas of religious freedom – particularly Reformist and Protestant movements against Catholic hegemony – were widely circulated for the first time after the invention of the printing press in 1450 and newsbooks were important throughout Europe for the role they played in spreading religious freedoms (Berg 2012). The news delivered by the publishers, editors and journalists in eighteenth-century America was mostly framed in terms of support or opposition to the cause of independence (Burns 2006). The explosion of the free press in France during the revolutionary years gave birth to hundreds of newspapers, but their function was to support one or another of the political factions, not to deliver a simple diet of facts and information to their readers (Stephens 2007). It perhaps goes without saying that none of these types of journalism bear much resemblance to the industrial models of news production that were born in the nineteenth century and continue to dominate journalism today. The theme of freedom of the press parallels the story of journalism through the ages and it was the struggle to define, fight for and defend this freedom that helped forge the ethics of journalism today.

The Acta Diurna: *freedom of expression in ancient Rome*

The first flows of news were of course by word of mouth. Information, gossip and interesting snippets were passed between families, clans and villages as people moved around. However, as societies became larger and more complex, spread over greater distances, governing elites needed to be sure that information was accurately gathered and relayed. As Mitchell Stephens (2007, p. 52) notes it was just as easy for a runner to carry a message hand-written on papyrus (an early form of paper) as it was for him to commit the information to memory. It was also likely to be more accurate when it reached its destination. In the Roman empire, news was circulated in letters between leading figures of the day. In ancient Rome we see the first examples of 'professional' newswriters, scribes who would compile and copy news for circulation among the empire's rulers (Stephens 2007, p. 55). Even 2000 years ago the key questions for the news of the day were speed and accuracy.

The first *acta* were probably written about 130 BC as records of important legal cases and were later expanded to include other public notices. They were displayed in public squares for several days before being archived (Atwood 2011). Early official records were also important to the circulation of news-like information. The Roman Senate – the empire's highest decision-making body – kept written records of its activities, known as *acta senatus* and also of significant events in the daily lives of its citizens, known as *acta diurna*. The emperor Augustus banned daily publication of the *acta* for a time, but they were still deposited in Roman libraries and could be consulted with permission (Smith 1875). The *acta senatus* was akin to the minutes that a secretary might make of a meeting; they would name the important speakers and give a summary of their arguments and any decisions made by the Senate (Martin, R. 1981, p. 201). The modern equivalent would be Hansard (a record of proceedings in Parliament or the daily records of the US Congress). The *acta diurna* appear to have had a different purpose and quality; no copies survive, but from contemporary accounts it seems the *diurna* were a combination of news about the city or market and a register of notable births, deaths and marriages (Stephens 2007, p. 56).

News in the Middle Ages

In the so-called Middle Ages, also known as the 'medieval' period, generally believed to begin with the Vandals' sacking of Rome in about 456 AD, spoken word news tended to dominate. The Middle Ages lasted for around one thousand years and the printing press may have had something to do with its ending in the fifteenth century. Printing was not developed in Europe until the end of the Middle Ages, though in China and Korea there were experiments with moveable type made from bronze (Stephens 2007, p. xii). During the medieval period, particularly the years of the 'Dark Ages' (500–1000 AD), general literacy declined and political power became concentrated in the hands of the clergy and nobility. However, these early 'Middle Age' years were also a time of intellectual endeavour – even if reserved only for the rich and powerful. The first universities, the beginnings of modern jurisprudence and scientific enquiry developed in this period (Frater 2008; Swan, R. 2012). The Middle Ages ended with the Renaissance and Enlightenment. One of the key developments of the later Middle Ages was the drafting of Magna Carta (Great Charter) in England. This document went through several versions before finally being adopted as part of the British (unwritten) constitution in 1225.

Magna Carta: the first written rules of freedom

Magna Carta was a document drawn up to signify a truce in ongoing disputes between the King (John) and his feudal barons over abuses of royal power and what the barons thought were extortionate demands upon their wealth. The charter was first drawn up in 1215 but went through several drafts over the next 80 years leading to a final version written in 1297. All but three of the clauses in Magna Carta have since fallen into disuse or been repealed. The key clause that is still operational in the laws of the United Kingdom today is that relating to *habeas corpus* – the right to a fair trial and not be subject to arbitrary arrest or denial of liberty (British Library n.d.). Magna Carta also signalled something else important – a gradual but irreversible transfer of political and economic power from the countryside to the towns and cities: 'the city of London shall have all it ancient liberties and free customs, as well by land as by water; furthermore, we decree and grant that all other cities, boroughs, towns, and ports shall have all their liberties and free customs'. A second clause also points in this direction as it secures free passage for 'merchants' and their rights 'for buying and selling by the ancient and right customs, quit from all evil tolls' (Magna Carta (Great Charter) *c.* 1215). Magna Carta is still considered an influential document and traces of its sentiment and clauses can be found in the United States Declaration of Independence and the Universal Declaration of Human Rights endorsed by the United Nations in 1948.

Writing, printing and the birth of journalism

> When combined with papyrus, the alphabet spelled the end of the stationary temple bureaucracies and the priestly monopolies of knowledge and power.
>
> (McLuhan 1967, p. 90)

There is a long oral tradition in journalism and news-telling, but it is the invention of printing and the growth of mass literacy that began to break down religious and royal monopolies over knowledge and power. At the same time, the rise in literacy and the growth in the circulation of news via technological means created a greater divide between those empowered to 'tell' the news and those whose role had become the passive reception of news and information. It is in this context that ethics and philosophy are joined together. Philosophy develops when knowledge can be stored, studied, copied, edited, questioned and extended through the acquisition of new knowledge and the testing of new theories. Ethics is a branch of philosophy that impacts implicitly on the process of news-telling. Obviously, audiences have a right to expect to be told the truth (no matter how unpalatable) and therefore, they have an expectation that those now tasked with gathering and telling the news will do so honestly – without 'fear or favour'.

Since the embedding of written versions of the news (and now electronic versions based on textual systems) there have been two issues in the news business that cause consternation among publishers, consumers and government regulators: accuracy and credibility on the one hand and censorship on the other. As we shall see in this chapter, the separation of priestly and kingly authority from the news-telling process has been a double-edged sword: on one side it might be argued that there has been a democratisation of the news process; on the other, it can be equally postulated that modern forms of censorship and control are just as effective as the control exercised by the royal court or the priests in their temples and cathedrals. Either way, we need to address these issues historically and from the perspective of philosophical and theoretical thinking in order to arrive at an approximation of the truth. As the news historian Mitchell Stephens (2007, p. 48) writes: 'Under the influence of literacy, news may have taken the first hesitant step on the long, perhaps endless, road toward objectivity'. All we would add is that the 'road toward objectivity' is winding, full of potholes and, ultimately, may lead only to a cul-de-sac. What we can agree on with Stephens is that literacy and the spread of published news opened up new philosophical debates about journalism that led, in the early years of the twentieth century, to the codification of ethics in news reporting for the first time. However, it is a debate that has its roots firmly in the past.

The importance of Johannes Gutenberg's mechanical press

> The printing press did not merely accelerate existing trends, but was itself a coherent and independent revolution.
>
> (Berg 2012, p. 44)

Johannes Gutenberg's printing press comes into first use in 1450 and in 10 short years there was an established printing industry across Europe. In 1455 Gutenberg published his first book, The Bible, and began selling it to the general public. This was the first time that an unauthorised version of the Bible was widely available and it inevitably led to a decline in the power of the official Roman Catholic theologians. The invention of moveable metal type and the reduced costs of reproduction by printing are generally credited with striking an almost fatal blow to the Catholic hierarchy and the royal courts of Europe: 'when ordinary people may read and write, what control can their rulers retain over their thoughts – or indeed their actions?' (Altschull 1990, p. 34)

The printing press also became the catalyst that generated one of the original and most enduring fault lines in journalism and the provision of news-like information: the dialectic dance of mutual need and distrust between the news providers and the power of the State apparatus (whether in a monarchy, a liberal democracy or a republic). Printers needed the State to sanction their work and the State needed printers to manage public discourse and to suppress dangerous ideas. It is from this basic need that all forms of press licensing descend.

The first form of privilege (as the licence to print was then known) was given to owners of Dutch printing presses in about 1467. Effectively these privileges were a form of licence to print official documents and also general books. Licencing of the press became a major source of conflict in the Renaissance and Enlightenment period as emerging new social classes came into conflict with hereditary and ecclesiastical power. Feudal rulers were not above manipulating the new technology of the printing press and many of the first newsbooks were favourable to royalty; they were written with the express purpose of neutralising opposition or rallying support. Licensing presses also helped, as no press could legally operate without a royal warrant. From the middle of the fifteenth century, and for the next 200 years, religious disputes – mainly between the Catholic Church and dissenting Protestants – were the reason for most acts of censorship. According to Stephens (2007, p.81), it was religion 'that caused many a printer to risk a fine, a jail sentence, a flogging or even death'.

A church edict issued by Pope Julius the second during what became known as the Fifth Lateran Council of 1512–17 established a formal process of pre-publication censorship 'across the Catholic world' (Berg 2012, p. 45). The context for this was a schism within the Church – between Rome and Catholics in France. The cardinals and other noteworthy church officials demanded that heretical and schismatic texts that contravened the teachings of the church should be banned because they contained 'errors opposed to the faith as well as pernicious views contrary to the Christian religion and to the reputation of prominent persons of rank' (Papal Encyclicals 1515). Of course the persons 'of rank' referred to here were the leaders of the church, including Pope Julius and his successor, Leo X. Unauthorised texts were to be burned and printers who published and distributed such works were to be excommunicated from the church. According to Chris Berg, it was the print medium itself – because it allowed rapid and widespread distribution of materials – not the message of Protestantism which was the origin of restrictions on freedom of the press (Berg 2012, p. 46).

The Catholic Church was not the only body to censor printing in the sixteenth century. In England Henry VIII held a royal monopoly on printing; the works of the German Protestant Martin Luther were banned in his homeland and in 1563 Charles IX introduced the licensing of books in France (Berg 2012, p. 47). In 1538, licensing of printed works was introduced in England and the Stationers' Company was formed with a royal warrant to police and enforce the system (Stephens 2007, p. xiii).

In the sixteenth century, people began to realise the social and political importance of news and the advantages that accrued from being the first to receive it. For the first time, the wealthy and powerful began to see control over the flow of news as a way of increasing their wealth and securing their power (Harris 1996). The first recorded financial newsletter was produced by the European financiers, the House of Fugger, in 1568. The hand-written letters were only available to subscribers (Stephens 2007, p. xiv). This was the forerunner of Reuters and other news services of the late nineteenth century. Until the fifteenth century, news circulated among the kings and clerics of Europe through such hand-written newsletters, but as the century progressed more printed sources of news began to appear. The audience for this news was not only 'princes, statesmen and nobles,' but also 'Europe's growing contingent of news-hungry traders and financiers' (Stephens 2007, p. 64). Despite the growing number of written and printed news sources, at least some of the information was found to be unreliable. In at least two, well-documented cases the death of a king was announced and mourned while the monarch was very much alive. News was also notoriously slow to circulate, sometimes taking weeks, months or even years to reach distant places.

The importance of the Dutch Republic

The Dutch Republic was founded in 1572 and within the decade the port city of Antwerp became one of the first towns in Europe to adopt statutes enshrining religious tolerance. However, there is another factor at work here that we need in order to fully understand the changes taking place towards the end of the sixteenth century: the emerging class of merchants and traders in Antwerp and the other port towns of the Republic needed to be able to trade with other nations within Europe and further afield. Religious intolerance got in the way of this trade and interfered with the ability of the merchant class to profit from expanding global commerce. Tolerance of religious difference was also linked to freedom of expression in the republic. It may be a coincidence that one of the Republic's influential philosophers of religious pluralism and freedom of speech was the engraver, printer and theologian Dirck Vockertszoon Coornhert. Coornhert was a key figure in the Dutch Republic, holding official positions in the administration and influential in debates about theology and religious schisms of the day (Berg 2012, pp. 56–7; van der Zijpp 1953). Despite no formal provision for freedom of expression in Dutch law, it seems that printers and writers such as Coornhert were able to work without fear of interference and that freedom of speech became the norm for the 'educated and political classes' (Berg 2012, p. 57). We can see from this that the pursuit of individual freedoms – of religion and expression – in the sixteenth century began to inform the consciousness of the emerging burghers (*bourgeoisie* in French) who came to dominate the economic life of the Dutch Republic. The printers of the Republic were able to turn a tidy profit from the publication of works banned in other European nations. Within a century of its introduction, the commercial printing press had begun to undermine the old ruling order by transferring some of the power over knowledge and ideas (if not at this time, all of it) from 'scribes in the monasteries to printers in the cities' (Stephens 2007, p. 113). The Dutch press had influence beyond the Republic because of the key shipping routes that passed by its coast and provided trade routes in and out of Europe; but not all European monarchs were as keen on religious toleration and freedom of ideas as their Dutch counterparts.

In England, during the reign of Elizabeth I, the feared and secretive Star Chamber regularly dealt severely with enemies of the crown. The decree establishing the Court of the Star Chamber in 1586 made unlawful any writing unacceptable to the established order (the Crown and the Church). The Star Chamber was established by Elizabeth's father Henry VIII and during the time of its powers – 1586 to 1637 – it came to stand for the most oppressive form of censorship based on secrecy and torture. The Star Chamber had its own police force that could confiscate and destroy printing presses (Altschull 1990, p. 35). However, the extent of the Star Chamber and censorship in many parts of Europe could not dampen the growing public enthusiasm for the printed word.

Seventeenth-century Europe – an explosion of printing and news

> Despite the added reliability imparted by the printing press, journalists in the early seventeenth century clearly had something of a credibility problem … 'Truth,' as one seventeenth-century journalist noted, 'is the daughter of time.'
>
> (Stephens 2007)

In the early seventeenth century, a 'strange and monstrous Serpent (or Dragon)' was living in the Sussex countryside it was reported in the *Harleian Miscellany*. A detailed description of the creature is given; it is reputed to be 'nine feete, or rather more, in length, and shaped almost in the forme of an axeltree of a cart; a quantitie of thickness in the middest, and somewhat smaller at both endes' (cited in Staveley n.d.). Of course this sensational news would help to sell copies of the Miscellany and many readers would no doubt, at the time, consider the existence of serpents and dragons as a natural phenomenon. Perhaps, in 400 years time, when the history of the twenty-first century is being pored over and picked apart by ethicists, people will chuckle over some of the stories carried over the years in the American supermarket magazine *The National Inquirer*, which regularly brings back to life Hitler and Elvis Presley, not to mention it being the only news outlet that regularly features eyewitness and first-hand accounts of the vastly under-reported phenomenon of alien abductions. *The Inquirer* has been around for 90 years and has published some famous scoops – most related to celebrity and political scandal – but as one reporter who was caught fabricating stories for the magazine noted when he was found out and suspended from his job with the *Salt Lake City Desert News*: 'When I dealt with the *Enquirer*, I never dreamed that I was accepting money for "information"' (Dillon Kinkead 2003).

The first newspaper printed in England was the *Corante* of 1621; it was dominated by news from Europe, most of it about commercial or political developments on the continent. The publication of news about events in Britain itself does not appear for another 20 years and only then because the authority of the king, Charles I, was weakening and the country descending into civil war. In 1643, the British Parliament passed a law to regulate printing throughout the Commonwealth, commonly known as the Licensing Order of 1643. This order is what effectively gave the Stationers' Company a monopoly over printing and publishing in Great Britain. It was also around this time

(1644) that *Areopagitica*, John Milton's famous pamphlet arguing for freedom of the press, was published. The English civil war led to the execution of Charles I in 1649 and, of course, this was widely reported in newspapers that began to enjoy their own new-found freedom. Milton's *Areopagitica* was written as a riposte to the licensing order and was influential among the bourgeois revolutionaries.

John Milton – Areopagitica

The British philosopher John Milton wrote what is commonly held to be one of the first arguments against censorship in his essay *Areopagitica* in 1644. Along with *Leviathan*, Thomas Hobbes' pamphlet about the rising power of the State, Milton's *Areopagitica* is considered a foundation document of the Enlightenment (Altschull 1990, p. 35). Milton wrote *Areopagitica* to argue that freedom of the press was a long-standing liberty that had its roots in ancient Athenian democracy. For good measure, he also sought to link seventeenth century censorship to the Inquisition and other Catholic crimes against reforming Protestantism. Milton believed that truth would trump falsehood if the press was free from any government interference or licensing (Berg 2012, p. 66). One oft-quoted passage argues for freedom of conscience as a key aspect of individual freedom: 'Give me the liberty to know, to utter, and to argue freely according to conscience, above all liberties' (Milton 1644). However, critics argue that Milton's defence of free speech was actually less than fulsome. For example, it did not extend to heretics or to Catholics and he also favoured severe punishments for those who produced blasphemous or seditious work. For Milton, it was the case that some forms of speech should be curtailed by authorities and institutions, particularly if it could be proven 'subversive of its core rationale' (Fish 1994, p. 104).

Milton's *Areopagitica* was written at a time when England was in turmoil and a civil war was raging. The Protestant rebel Oliver Cromwell recruited an army to serve the English Parliament (the Long Parliament) in its war against the Catholic monarch and his supporters. Three serious periods of conflict make up the English civil war, which lasted from 1642 to 1651. Milton himself was a well-educated commoner, versed in the Greek and Roman classics and the class nature of his appeals in *Areopagitica* can be seen in this biographic history. The rising class of merchants, traders and self-employed artisans – Milton's father was a legal scribe himself involved in the book trade – was chafing at the continued rule of the Tudor (Henry and Elizabeth) and Stuart (Charles I and Charles II) families and their aristocratic courtiers. It was in the ranks of these nascent bourgeois (known as the burgess in England) that Puritanism (anti-Catholic religious ideals) took hold and revolutionary sentiment was fomented (Altschull 1990, p. 38). What is important to recognise here is that this resentment against royalty and the oppressive Anglican church had both political and economic causes (Davidson 2012). However, Milton himself is not above criticism – for 21 years he served Cromwell's Council of State in a censorious role used effectively against the rights of Catholics (Altschull 1990, p. 41).

It is not a coincidence that Milton produced *Areopagitica* at this time – by the middle of the 1600s the rising merchant class was clamouring for news, particularly if it concerned events that might impact on the profitability of their business enterprises. Milton's sentiments held direct appeal for this emerging social caste and the increasingly common corantos (newsbooks) published in Amsterdam quenched their thirst for up-to-date (as much as was possible in the age of sail) news from around the world. Nine years after Milton's *Areopagitica,* his contemporary Thomas Hobbes published *Leviathan*, which is a defence of the power of the State by means of a social contract. Under the terms of this covenant, citizens must give up certain rights and freedoms in return for protections offered by the State. In this context, freedom of expression is a moot point because only those expressions acceptable to the sovereign power – which Hobbes described as a mortal God – would be allowed (Altschull 1990, p. 46). Sovereign power could be the monarch, or an assembly of men elected, as to a Parliament or Congress, but whichever case, by agreeing to the convenant, all subjects are bound in loyalty. It is also the role of the State – Hobbes called it a 'Commonwealth' – to determine what speech or writing is allowed: 'it is annexed to the sovereignty to be judge of what opinions and doctrines are averse, and what conducing to peace' (Hobbes 1651).

A brief period of relative press freedom existed in England after King Charles I was executed in 1649. There was an explosion of new London weeklies following the death of Charles and they keenly reported on events in the English Parliament. According to Stephens (2007, p. 148), 'the free practice of newspaper journalism was straining fitfully to reinvent itself in England, in a hurry.' It was in the second half of the seventeenth century that the newspaper as we know it today – containing a wide selection of items of general interest – came fully into existence. It was, says Mitchell Stephens (2007, p. 158) a 'symbiotic relationship between news and business' that led to the creation of the modern newspaper and to the commercial class becoming the 'most loyal and valuable' of customers for news and a target for the 'gentle grab and fleece trick' of newspaper advertising.

However, as European trade with the Far East and the Americas became more important, the nature of news and news publications also began to change. Stephens notes that to be properly called a 'newspaper' that we would recognise today, four conditions need to be met:

- the publication must be available 'to a significant portion of the public'
- the publication must be regular and frequent; for a newspaper this means 'at least weekly'
- a newspaper must include a variety of articles, not just one long story
- it must display a 'consistent and recognizable title or format' (Stephens 2007, p. 131).

It was during this time that many techniques we now take for granted in newspapers first came to notice: stacked headlines on the front page; the use of children to hawk the papers on the streets of major cities and towns; and, for the first time, 'spirited coverage of national news' (Stephens 2007, p. 149).

The existence of the opposing views of Milton and Hobbes is a clear indication of how history works through paradox and contradiction. Ideas and social forces clash in a struggle for supremacy. In the seventeenth century the central contradiction was the delicate balance required to hold civil society together – between individual and collective will. It is also clearly evident in the writing of John Locke, an English philosopher whose influence overlapped that of Milton and Hobbes. Locke is also an important thinker in the explication of bourgeois rights. Throughout his work, Locke emphatically argued for the sanctity of private property, the cornerstone of bourgeois economic and political demands (Altschull 1990, p. 54). For Locke, the right to possess property was a defence against oppressive State interference in one's life and pursuit of liberty. Taken together, Milton, Hobbes and Locke form a formidable triumvirate of seventeenth-century philosophers whose work contributed to the eventual overthrow of absolutism and the period of history known as the Enlightenment.

The Age of Enlightenment

The Age of Enlightenment, from the middle of the seventeenth until the end of the eighteenth century, is the period of history that signals the end of the Middle Ages. The Enlightenment was built on the basis of significant revolutions in science, politics, arts and philosophy (Bristow 2011). Reason and science replaced religion as the grand theory that explained human existence. History was seen as a progression of stages linked to economic development or 'modes of subsistence' and human beings were conceived as possessing natural and inalienable rights. The Enlightenment also saw the emergence of a new social class that would eventually, over a period of 200 years, challenge kings and priests in a battle for the hearts and minds of citizens. This series of revolutions, which culminated in the American war of independence 1775–1780 and the French revolution of 1789, began with the parliamentary uprisings against English monarchs in the second half of the seventeenth century, roughly 1645–1690. Importantly, this political revolution also signalled a globally-significant and irreversible change in the power of economic control which was beginning to shift from feudal landowners to the rising class of merchants and manufacturers based in the cities. The social basis of the bourgeoisie was new relations of production, those based on ownership (or non-ownership) of capital – in Marxist terms 'the means of production' (Davidson 2012; Hallas 1988).

Many of the principles of press freedom that we either celebrate or bemoan today owe their existence to the sometimes fierce struggles for press freedom that occurred during the Enlightenment, and in particular during the revolutions of the seventeenth and eighteenth centuries. Throughout this time, there was constant pressure from governments in England, the New World and across Europe to curtail press freedom through the imposition of taxes (stamp duties) on paper and on advertising.

Under the influence of the Enlightenment's philosophers, the emerging bourgeois class mounted pressure against stamp taxes and the licensing laws. As these restrictions began to lapse, newspapers began to flourish again. However, it is important to remember that at this time literacy was limited to the wealthier classes and those artisans, tradesmen and merchants who had a need to know their letters and numbers. According to some estimates, literacy levels were as low as 40 per cent (Stephens 2007, p. xvii).

In 1694, English philosopher John Locke wrote a pamphlet sent to the House of Commons in which he outlined several reasons why censorship of the press should be ended. His key argument was essentially economic in nature and a defence of private property rights – such as those that artisan printers held in their presses. The government had no right to take away a man's property, nor the right to tell him how he should use it, as long as no law was broken by its use. However, like many of his contemporaries, Locke was not an anarchist. He believed that the State had the power to suppress opinions that might harm civil society (Altschull 1990, p. 58). The qualifications employed by Locke are consistent with those of Milton and others who were not in favour of all cases of revolution, only those that served the interests of the property-owning class of free men in their struggle against absolutism.

Journalism and the bourgeois revolutions

Mitchell Stephens (2007, p. 164) poses the question: 'Why were newspapers, with investments and reputations to protect, leading revolutions?' The answer is that the class whose interests were represented in the newssheets of the late seventeenth and early eighteenth century was fighting for political and economic control over the whole of society. The political aim of the bourgeoisie was to create the social conditions that would lead to its dominance over the economic system of capitalism that we know today (Davidson 2012).

From the sixteenth century through to the Industrial Revolution, economic, social and political power gradually, but decisively, shifted away from the feudal kings and barons (and from the Church hierarchy) to the entrepreneurs, traders and artisans of the cities and towns. Manufacturing and commerce had begun to replace agriculture as the economic engine of growth and where the money goes, so too goes the political power. However, the old order of kings, popes and bishops was not going to simply fall over, or die out. It had to be resisted and overcome and newspapers filled an important niche in the armoury of weapons that the bourgeoisie could bring to bear against its class enemies. We can see this clearly as the eighteenth century matured – by the time the American revolution and war against Britain began in 1776, newspapers had become indispensable to the organising and propaganda efforts of this new mercantile class. However, these revolutionary newspapers did not just appear overnight. Their evolution into politically-charged organs of rebellion took nearly 100 years to develop (Stephens 2007, p. 164). Along the way there were victories and setbacks; the newspapers developed in a process familiar to historians – that of combined and uneven development. Throughout the eighteenth century, there were numerous battles between editors and the authorities over issues of sedition, libel and onerous taxes on newspapers. Many editors, including now famous pioneers like Daniel Defoe, spent time in jail or exile as they led the struggle against autocracy and for a new franchise in favour of their class, the bourgeoisie.

The emerging print media, and the editors who made it possible, were key players in the struggle of the bourgeois revolutionaries, but – as is usual in situations of extended political crisis – the political changes did not all happen at once or without setbacks. The historical process of combined and uneven development is characterised by the saying 'two steps forward, one step back'.

The ignoble birth of the first reporters

In the early 1700s, newssheets in colonial America relied heavily on local classified advertising, often covering their entire front page with ads, including for the sale of slaves or the capture and return of runaways. Another source of funding which contained implications for the way the American press developed in the 1700s was subsidies provided by political patrons. There are countless stories of proprietor-publishers seeking loan funds from wealthy friends, often in return for using their paper as a mouthpiece for particular viewpoints on issues of the day. This practice continued well into the the nineteenth century; important American newspapers were still requiring subsidies as late as the 1840s (Baldasty 1992).

In 1704, Daniel Defoe published his first edition of the *Review* in London to comment on politics. The paper was to last until 1713 and during the period of its existence Defoe was imprisoned for his attacks on the Anglican establishment. Defoe was a protagonist in the free speech battles of his time. In 1704, he published a tract called *Essay on the Regulation of the Press*: 'To put a general stop to publick Printing would be a check to Learning, a Prohibition of Knowledge, and make Instruction Contraband' (Defoe 1704).

In 1712, a stamping tax was imposed on newspapers in England, 'clearly designed to keep news out of the hands of the lower classes' (Stephens 2007, p. xvi) by making them too expensive. Within a little over 50 years this would have profound implications for Britain's control over the American colonies. The economic pain of poor profits – which some blamed on the stamping of newspapers – led many American editors into revolutionary politics. In this brief summary we can only mention a few. Among them was Benjamin Franklin who became a newspaper editor in 1729 when his brother James was jailed for allegedly using his paper to 'mock religion and bring it into disrespect', but really for printing pro-independence and anti-British sentiments. At the same time as the American colonists were building their arguments for the overthrow of British rule, the French bourgeoisie was also fomenting revolution.

The philosophes: *ideas to a French revolution*

Voltaire was one of several French philosophers (*philosophes* in French) who are important to the development of free speech and free press arguments in the eighteenth century. While each of them – and their English or American counterparts – deserves recognition for their intellectual endeavours, it is important to bear in mind the dialectic approach: for every argument the *philosophes* advanced about freedom of speech, there were important caveats, disclaimers and exceptions. Often these contradictions were embodied in the utterances or writings of those regarded today as the heroes of liberalism.

Voltaire was very influential over the course of his lifetime and, uncommonly for his day, he lived to be 83. Today, he is regarded as one of the leading intellects of the Enlightenment and his contributions to the study of modern history are regarded as the foundation of methods of historical inquiry (Force 2009). Voltaire was a believer in scientific method and argued that there was a strong link between morality, ethics and reason. Freedom of thought and of action was a result of the ability to reason – that is, to think clearly and logically from first principles. But, like his contemporaries, Voltaire also believed that religion was necessary in order to control those elements of the lower social order which he believed were not capable of reason. Thus, there is a series of contradictions in Voltaire's world view: 'Voltaire echoed these ideas in his political musings, where he remained throughout his life a liberal, reform-minded monarchist and a skeptic with respect to republican and democratic ideas.' (Shank 2010).

Voltaire, whose real name was François-Marie Arouet, came from a wealthy background, but not of the nobility. He spent some months in the Bastille for writing seditious and satirical poetry against the French monarchy and three years in exile after a nobleman he insulted had him beaten and imprisoned again. No doubt these experiences shaped his views.

In 1748, the French philosopher Montesquieu wrote an influential text called *The spirit of laws*, which is said to have had a strong impact on the American revolutionaries of 1776. A central idea in Montesquieu's writing was the separation of powers between different branches of government to provide a system of checks and balances. Despite being a champion of more democratic forms of state, Montesquieu was himself a member of the nobility and, according to Altschull (1990, pp. 73–4), he would not have extended free speech to 'the yeoman farmer or the carpenter'. This was perhaps a natural pattern of thought in the eighteenth century and among the French *philosophes* more generally. As Altschull tellingly reminds us: 'When they urged freedom of expression, they were speaking of such freedom for representatives of their own class' (1990, p. 71).

The social contract of Jean Jacques Rousseau

A decade before the American revolution, and 27 years before the French revolution, the Swiss-French philosopher Jean Jacques Rousseau published his most famous work *The Social Contract* (Du Contrat Social) in which he attempted to reconcile the contradiction between freedom and authority by defending the proposition that the general will of the population finds expression in the monarch. This dialectic is expressed in the famous paradox from the opening lines of *The Social Contract*: 'Man is born free, but is everywhere in chains'. Rousseau attempted to legitimise the chains by asserting that they are automatically and readily agreed to by free men when they choose to combine into a society. Such citizens, Rousseau suggested, achieve 'moral freedom' by agreeing to be subjects of a monarch or other form of government. For Rousseau, abdicating from unfettered natural rights leads to a form of stable society in which people enjoy civil rights that are formally equal under the law (Bertram 2012). According to Berg (2012, p. 117), the contradictions in Rousseau's arguments are open to an interpretation that legitimises 'nearly unlimited opportunities for government to censor and repress seditious, heretical, or obscene views'. We get a slightly different view of Rousseau from the journalism scholar J. Herbert Altschull. He argues that Rousseau's politics were more favourable to commoners than to the bourgeois and that his belief in the formal legal equality of citizens was a way of socially overcoming the physical inequalities that existed between men in their natural state (Altschull 1990, p. 87). One school of thought among journalism scholars suggests that Rousseau's social contract is the foundation for journalism ethics, the freedom of the modern press in its role as the Fourth Estate and the guarantor of liberal democratic market society (Sjovaag 2010).

Journalism and the American revolution

The American war of independence was largely fought in colonial newspapers long before the first shots were fired at Lexington Green, Massachusetts on 19 April 1775. Newspaper editors were among the most vocal critics of the British for nearly 40 years before the war began. They were not well-liked by the colonial administration, but garnered wide public support among the new Americans. Their stories are well told in the many books about the history of American journalism. Two are worth mentioning as examples of the radical editors who led the American revolution:

Benjamin Franklin

> Without freedom of thought there can be no such thing as wisdom and no such thing as public liberty without freedom of speech.
>
> Benjamin Franklin, 1722

Benjamin Franklin is best known for the story about him flying a kite during a storm and subsequently inventing the lightning rod. It's a true story and the incident occurred when Franklin was in middle age and already successful in many fields. He was a true Renaissance man who, in the spirit of his times, could turn his hand to anything.

In the 1720s, Franklin began work as a printer's apprentice with his elder brother James on the *New England Courant*. In 1729 Franklin took over editing the *Courant* and it became one of the best colonial newspapers (Stephens 2007, p. xvi).

Benjamin Franklin became an important figure in the public life of the United States after the war of independence and he learned his politics at an early age. Franklin is also an important figure in the discussion of journalism ethics because he once argued for an interesting definition of truth in which the facts were less important since they only represented 'truth as niggling minds defined it'. For Franklin there was truth, in the larger sense, 'as the cosmos recognized it' (Burns 2006, p. 89).

According to the American news historian Eric Burns (2006, p. 91), Benjamin Franklin was 'as ethical a journalist as America produced in the eighteenth century' and only occasionally deceived the readers of newspapers he edited 'because he thought it a better way to tell a story'. Benjamin's brother, James Franklin, was not the only editor to feel the wrath of the British authorities in colonial America.

John Peter Zenger

In 1735, the publisher of the *New York Weekly Journal*, John Peter Zenger, was acquitted of seditious libel in what is still widely regarded as one of the first victories for press freedom in the American colonies. Zenger had used the pages of his paper to attack the governor of New York (still then a British colony) William Cosby. Zenger's lawyer, Andrew Hamilton, was able to persuade the jury in the Zenger trial that his client had been truthful in his libellous descriptions of Cosby and his victory was celebrated as a blow for freedom of the press (Stephens 2007, p. 165). As J. Herbert Altschull (1990, p. 110) notes, the Zenger case was the first in which truth was accepted as a defence to libel (this is now common practice in most English-speaking jurisdictions). It is also a foundation stone of modern journalistic belief systems, which Altschull describes as 'the press as a restraint on tyranny and the abuse of power'; but at the time, despite the celebrations of Zenger's supporters, it was an isolated victory and over the next 50 years many more American editors were accused and convicted for truthfully libelling their social superiors.

In the decades before the war of independence, the colonists' grievances against the British were both political and economic – summed up in the slogan 'No taxation without representation' and the infamous Boston Tea Party. The protest was planned at the house of a *Boston Gazette* editor. The *Gazette* may have been one of the most revolutionary newspapers in the American colonies, but it was not the only one. In his book, Eric Burns (2006) mentions several prominent newspaper owners and editors who were vigorous proponents of American independence. They were inspired by agitators and philosophers like the famous, bourgeois radical, Thomas Paine. Paine's first pamphlet *Common Sense*, in 1776, helped to coalesce support for the revolutionary war. Later that same year the Second Continental Congress adopted the Declaration of Independence, with its famous passage:

> We hold these truths to be self-evident, that all men are created equal, that they are endowed by their Creator with certain unalienable Rights, that among these are Life, Liberty and the pursuit of Happiness.

Within a decade of the successful rout of British forces from the continental United States, the American constitution was adopted at a convention in Philadelphia in 1787 and came into effect on 4 March 1789. A few years later, in 1791, Congress adopted the Bill of Rights. The Bill of Rights grouped together the first 10 amendments to the Constitution of the United States. Several states had refused to ratify it unless it contained a bill of rights that set out constitutional limits to what the Federal government could do in relation to the rights of American citizens (The Bill of Rights: A brief history 2002).

The first amendment is perhaps the most famous and it enshrined rights to freedom of expression and religion in the constitution in an oft-quoted passage:

> Congress shall make no law respecting an establishment of religion, or prohibiting the free exercise thereof; or abridging the freedom of speech, or of the press; or the right of the people peaceably to assemble, and to petition the Government for a redress of grievances.

The signing into law of the constitution, and the amendments of 1791, was a political victory for the American bourgeois class in its nearly century-long battle against the old order of Europe, represented by the British crown.

There was never a counter-revolution to reverse the gains won during the fight for American independence, but by late in the eighteenth century there was a backlash against what was seen as too-revolutionary sentiment in some quarters, including sections of the press. The newly-consolidated American government wanted stability, and enthusiastic support for the French revolution was seen as potentially destabilising at home, too. By the mid-1790s, the excesses of the French revolution began to upset some of the more conservative American leaders.

In 1798, President John Adams signed into law the Alien and Sedition Acts in response to a backlash against alleged foreign agitators (mainly Irish and French nationals) who it was feared would undermine the gains of the American republic since the War of Independence. The Sedition Act outlawed the writing or publishing of material prejudicial to the aims of the American government. Throughout this period there is tension and, sometimes, open conflict between the two wings of American bourgeoisie, the Federalists and the Republicans which is reflected in their various partisan newspapers (Burns 2006; Daniel 2009). At the heart of their dispute is an emerging difference of opinion about the successes and excesses of the French revolution.

Journalism and the French revolution

It is perhaps no coincidence that, within a generation, the French, too, were in revolt while the American War of Independence raged in the 'New World'. In 1777, the first French daily newspaper, the *Journal de Paris*, was published. The first American daily was not published until 1783, the same year that parliamentary reporters in England took another step towards professionalism by adopting shorthand to take notes and report speeches (Stephens 2007, p. xvii).

By 1789, a key year in the French revolution, mercantilism (trade between nations) was already an important form of economic life that had been embraced both by the bourgeois *citoyens* (city-dwellers, citizens) and by the absolutist French state. These two camps – the nobility and the bourgeoisie – agreed that commerce was becoming increasingly important; where they disagreed was in the amount of political freedom that the state was prepared to concede and that the citizens were demanding. Thus, there was (as always) a dialectic in play, holding in tension the economic and political contradictions of the day. This paradox is manifest in the application of the formal censorship régime then in place. It was a 'two-tiered' system that tolerated dissent as long as it did not go too far. It is also evident in the attitudes to freedom of speech held by some of the leading French intellectuals of the day. Freedom of expression was permissible only while it did not upset the 'general order' of things and did not excite the lower orders (peasants and proletarians) with democratic aspirations beyond their station (Berg 2012, p. 114). Such contradictions are inherently unstable and a split between the old régime and the emerging new order was inevitable and took place when the Estates General was convened in May 1789. The faction of citizens – the merchants and business class – broke away from the nobility and the clergy to form the Constituent Assembly (Rudé 1964). It was in this context that the discussion of freedom of speech and its limits took place. Freedom of speech, or expression, or of the press was not to be absolute (Berg 2012, p. 115).

The storming of the Bastille took place on 14 July 1789, and a few months later the Declaration of the Rights of Man and the Citizen was promulgated by the Constituent Assembly – it includes the freedom to communicate 'thoughts and opinions' as the 'most precious' of rights (Stephens 2007, p. xvii). At this time, the official French press – licensed and censored by Louis XVI – did not report the storming of the Bastille and it was such 'gaping omissions' that drew readers to the unsanctioned press (Stephens 2007, p. 174). In 1788, only four newspapers were published in Paris (most sanctioned by the king); by 1790 this number had exploded to over 300. Some expressed loyalty to the people, some to the king and some to the various factions of the Constituent Assembly (Stephens 2007, pp. 176–7).

The French Declaration was inspired by the American Declaration of Independence (1776) and in August 1789 the American revolutionary leader Thomas Jefferson was in France on a diplomatic mission. French and American democrats and revolutionaries were in general agreement at the time and in constant contact; Benjamin Frankin and Thomas Paine visited France and French radicals often made the trip to New York or Boston to see the American revolution in progress.

It was the ideals of the Enlightenment and a belief in the natural rights that men enjoyed as a gift from God that guided the eighteenth-century revolutionaries. The leading figures of the American and French revolutions were in broad agreement about the necessity of overthrowing absolutism and instituting a more democratic and representative form of government. From 1770 to 1800, developments on both sides of the Atlantic were moving inexorably in the direction of a successful and completed bourgeois revolution.

Property rights – including the right to edit their papers as they saw fit – were as important to the bourgeois revolutionaries of Europe and America as their political rights. Translations from French to English vary slightly in wording, but in the Declaration a right to property is elevated to the status of a natural right. However there is no property right in nature because there is no property invested in human beings when they exist in their natural state. Unlike freedom of expression, the right to property is not natural, it is a social relationship. The Declaration also set out legal limits to the expression of rights and this, too, is a social construction. As we have seen, Voltaire was among the philosophers of the Enlightenment who did not think freedoms could be safely extended to the lower classes. Things or actions are deemed lawful or illegal on the basis of decisions taken within a particular social context, which is, to a large part, dependent on relationships of inequality – between the powerful and the subjugated. Like Magna Carta of the thirteenth century, the Declaration of the Rights of Man and the Citizen was a product of historical circumstance and the rights that it holds 'sacred and inviolable' are socially constructed to reflect the conditions of the French revolutionaries – to secure their rights as a class. In the later years of the eighteenth century this meant that such declarations could only represent the interests of one group – the revolutionary bourgeoisie. It was not long, therefore, before the newly-triumphant, revolutionary bourgeois of France were implementing their own forms of censorship and calling seditious any writing or opinion that challenged the authority of their class: 'By 1793, even calling for the dissolution of the revolutionary government was punishable by death' (Berg 2012, p. 118).

The (unequal) Rights of Man and Woman

A year after the Bill of Rights became law in the United States, Thomas Paine's *The Rights of Man* was published. In the same year, the London Corresponding Society was formed to campaign for electoral reform and for 'Tradesmen, Shopkeepers and Mechanics' to have the right to vote and to parliamentary representation. The Society was open to anyone who believed in the reform of parliament in a democratic direction. The founding treasurer was a shoemaker called Thomas Hardy. Two years later, he was arrested on a charge of high treason. The case against Hardy was dismissed and for a time it seemed that the Society might prosper. However, by 1800 the Society had been outlawed and *The Rights of Man* had been banned (Thompson 1963, p. 19).

When writing about and discussing the politics of freedom and freedom of the press in the eighteenth century, it is common to use the term 'man' to mean both men and women. Of course it was common, up until very recently, for this convention to be employed without thinking. However, to set the record straight and to get a full understanding of just how revolutionary the eighteenth and nineteenth centuries were, we cannot ignore one of the earliest 'feminists', Mary Wollstonecraft. In 1792, Wollstonecraft published an important tract on the human, civil and political rights of women, *A Vindication of the Rights of Women*. Unlike many of her male contemporaries, who were from genteel backgrounds and engaged in speculative philosophical writing, Mary Wollstonecraft was from a decidedly working-class background and was employed as a governess, lady's companion and teacher at various times. Her life was, at times, very unhappy, but a year before she died Mary gave birth to a daughter, also known as Mary and author of an early Gothic novel that you might have heard of – *Frankenstein*. Wollstonecraft's contributions to the debates of her day – about the nature of democratic society, the links between natural rights and the civil rights of women, the role of the family and the outcomes of the French Revolution – were equal to those of her male contemporaries and display a firm command of the arguments (Tomaselli 2012).

Throughout the period of its revolutionary struggle (from the late 1700s to the middle years of the nineteenth century) the French bourgeois were all too aware of the important role freedom of speech and expression had played in fomenting their revolution against the old order. One of their most eloquent theorists, a generation behind Rousseau, was another Swiss-French revolutionary, Benjamin Constant.

Constant's view was that the gains of the bourgeoisie's own revolution had to be consolidated and this required that 'power and property must be in accord'. He continued this train of thought in his book *De l'esprit de conquête et de l'usurpation* (*The Spirit of Conquest and Usurpation*):

> If you divide them [power and property] there will be a struggle, and at the end of the struggle either property will be invaded or the government will be overturned.
>
> (Constant 2002, p. 93)

This was indeed the lesson that the French bourgeois had learned from their own revolution when the economic power of private property was separated from the political power of the old order. It was the old order that was destroyed. Constant recognised the growing importance of industry and according to some scholarly accounts he had one foot in the idealism of the Enlightenment and another in the Industrial Revolution of the nineteenth century (Gossman 2004). For Constant it is the culture of commerce that will be the engine of history following the French revolution (Gossman 2004, p. 15). Constant presents an argument about how the newly triumphant bourgeois state might deal with freedom of speech. This is why it does not have the same angry and revolutionary tone of some earlier tracts on the topic of freedom of the press. A key point that Constant makes in these passages is that the government can tolerate dissenting voices as long as this is not turned into action against the state. The logic of this reasoning then suggests that the best way to prevent seditious voices or seditious writing from turning itself into action, is to leave it alone; to tolerate but neither encourage, nor repress it. By the late eighteenth century, the bourgeois political revolution was almost complete and the new ruling class had taken over the state apparatus. Under the circumstances, an absolute belief in freedom of speech was replaced with a more selective application of its principles. The news media and the intellectual work of journalists and editors was no longer required to drive revolution and change, instead their purpose was to consolidate and support the new ruling class. This required some changes in the ideological positioning of journalism. In the nineteenth century, and then into the twentieth. Journalism became less about fiery rhetoric and more about commercial realities. Instead of firebrand editors, the news media came to be dominated by wealthy members of the new ruling elite. Their purpose was not to preach revolution, but to reap profits from the sale of commodities and manufacturing.

The age of media barons

> Before the century closes schools of journalism will be generally accepted as a feature of specialized higher education, like schools of law or of medicine.
>
> (Pulitzer, 1904, p. 642)

An Hungarian-born migrant to the United States, Joseph Pulitzer, became an accidental newspaper reporter after an encounter with two German-speaking chess players in the St Louis Library in 1872. The players, impressed with Pulitzer's intelligence, offered the young man a job on their German-language newspaper. By the age of 25, Pulitzer had taken over the paper and was ready to make his leap into the mainstream of American journalism. In 1878, Pulitzer bought two St Louis newspapers and combined them into the *St Louis Post-Dispatch* (Stephens 2007, p. xxii). Five years later Pulitzer made his move on New York and bought the struggling *World* newspaper. Pulitzer was able to put both the *Post-Dispatch* and the *World* onto a stronger financial footing and consolidate his place in history as one of the original media barons.

The occasion of establishing the first 'college of journalism' in the first years of the twentieth century confirms the arrival of the age of industrial journalism. Putting journalism training onto a professional footing, alongside medicine or law, was symbolic of the changes that would soon occur in the field of journalism and news production. The key objective of this new type of journalism was not so much persuasion to a revolutionary cause as it was in the seventeenth and eighteenth centuries; instead it was the production of a profit for investors based on the efficient and cost-effective delivery of a brand new commodity – the daily news. Pulitzer knew that this future demanded a new type of journalist – one not so much motivated by political passions – who could turn his or her hand to the gathering and marshalling of facts, to the process of bright and attractive writing and who knew the value of a dollar. Pulitzer may be the first media baron, but other wealthy business figures would soon follow in his footsteps.

In 1887, William Randolph Hearst took over the *San Francisco Examiner* from his father and, within a few years, he had turned around the ailing newspaper by following Pulitzer's lead. Under Hearst junior the *Examiner* became a crusading paper that was also very good at self-promotion (Stephens 2007, p. xxii).

Industrial journalism soon became the new standard on both sides of the Atlantic. In 1894, an unassuming young Irishman, Alfred Harmsworth, entered the British journalism scene when he bought the nearly bankrupt *Evening News* for the modest sum of £25,000. Harmsworth and his brother Harold were already involved in magazine publication at this time and profits from their successful magazine *Answers from Correspondents* enabled Alfred to buy his way into newspaper history (Simkin 1997). Within a short time, by 1898, Harmsworth had turned the *Evening News* into a successful masthead that boasted daily sales of over 800,000, turning an annual profit of £50,000 and a very good return on the original investment. A chance meeting with Joseph Pulitzer in 1901 – they were passengers on the same luxury trans-Atlantic steamship – led Harmsworth to accept a challenge to redesign Pulitzer's *World* newspaper. His work resulted in a 'small, breezy, well-illustrated paper'. This format broke the mould of broadsheet layouts and became the precursor to the successful tabloid format (Stephens 2007, p. xxiii).

The emergence of Hearst and Pulitzer in the last decades of the nineteenth century was a clear signal that the American newspaper industry had changed forever. Between 1870 and 1900, the number of established American newspapers jumped from about 500 to nearly 2000. Newspapers were no longer written, edited and published by lone proprietors, or small family operators, for the benefit of their immediate community. By the turn of the century, newspapers had become prosperous businesses. By 1910, it is estimated that around 2600 daily newspapers were in circulation in the United States and on the eve of World War One an estimated 323 socialist newspapers were in existence across the country (Stephens 2007, p. xxiii).

The economic power of the emerging newspaper barons in the United States and in England began to assert itself at the end of the nineteenth century. There are many examples of the rich and powerful newspaper owners of the day involving themselves in politics. William Randolph Hearst formed his own political party to endorse his bid to be mayor of New York, and even suggested himself for the Presidency in 1904. In England, not only did both of the Harmsworth brothers – owners of several newspapers and magazines – become peers in the House of Lords but a Canadian newspaper figure, Max Aitkin, became Lord Beaverbrook and also took a seat in the House of Commons. This trend continues today and modern media moguls, like Rupert Murdoch, continue to seek advantage and influence through their relationships with political leaders and the wealthy 'one percent'. Murdoch has powerful friends on both sides of the Atlantic, in Australia and in southeast Asia. Despite the travails of *News of the World*, Rupert Murdoch continues to enjoy close and powerful friendships with business figures and politicians all over the world (McKnight 2012; Watson and Hickman 2012; Wolff 2008).

One of the enduring metaphors surrounding journalism and the news industry today is that it represents the 'fourth estate' and that it has a 'watchdog' role over the actions of governments and political institutions. It is often invoked alongside theories about the 'marketplace of ideas' to explain the role of journalism today (Horne 1994). Such ideas are the foundation of the liberal democratic paradigm many journalism scholars use to explain the function of journalism and news – particularly in English-speaking nations with a traditional of parliamentary democracy and built on a political economy of private enterprise (see Sjovaag 2010 for more on this). In chapter 3 we will provide a critique of this view and explain our position – that critical reflection on the assumptions underpinning the liberal-democratic paradigm is necessary for the survival of good journalism in the twenty-first century.

Another important contributor to this debate was the German critical theorist, Jürgen Habermas. His discussion of the rise of a 'public' or 'civic sphere' (Habermas 1989, 1992; Bernstein 2012), arising in European and especially British coffee houses in the seventeenth century, is important to our understanding of news and journalism. The coffee houses of Paris, London, Berne and Berlin were where businessmen gathered to gain information and discuss issues of the day. While the historical accuracy of Habermas' discussion has been debated, the concept of 'the public sphere', a social space located between the institutions of the state and the marketplace, where citizens were, at least theoretically, free to discuss matters of significance and importance, had gained enormous influence. To be sure, only people – almost exclusively men – of property engaged in commerce participated in this 'free and open discourse' about important matters, hence the description of 'the bourgeois public sphere' in Habermas' work, and contributions to or critiques of it.

What is often overlooked in Habermas' work is his equally influential theory of communicative action (Habermas 1984, 1987, 1990), which posits the 'emancipatory quality' of human discourses oriented towards greater enlightenment and rationality. We should remember his warnings about how the public sphere continues to be colonized by the instrumental rationality of tightly focused business or state interests. Journalism so colonized becomes simply another business oriented to make money, or as a mouthpiece for a particular regime or government's propaganda. A colonized public sphere views citizens only as consumers and/or supporters of the interests of particular regimes or governments. Nevertheless, the notion – even hope or belief – that all journalism can and indeed should constitute a genuine public or civil sphere where free and open discussions about important matters can occur remains extremely important and influential in many activist and scholarly domains.

Journalism, the public sphere and freedom of speech are historically and philosophically entwined (Steel 2012), but they are not the same thing. Today there are codified rules and social norms that govern the practice of journalism and, despite their history being obscured, these rules and norms are firmly based on the ideas of the Enlightenment and the bourgeois revolutions of the eighteenth and nineteenth centuries.

3   Journalism ethics today

The links between philosophy, ideology and journalism ethics

So far we have covered some important historical perspectives on the development of journalism ethics; now it is time to turn our attention to some of the key philosophical principles and arguments in the field today. In this chapter we examine the core ideas that frame journalism ethics and critique two major ideological frameworks that are used in discussions of journalism and the news industry. The first is the 'free-market' model which overlays a neo-classical economics discourse over the exchange and flow of information; the second is the political equivalent, the 'fourth estate' model of journalism's public interest role. These taken-for-granted ideas help to structure the social field of journalism. They are what Pierre Bourdieu (1998, p. 1) calls the 'hidden constraints' on journalism practice today.

The first task is to define the contemporary relationship between philosophy, ideology and world-view. We do not see a huge difference in meaning between these words and certainly our use of Orwell's phrase 'emotional attitude' indicates the close relationship between the three terms. If anything, philosophy is a more formal word that has implications of something grand and on a huge scale. Certainly this is the case when talking about 'capital P' Philosophy. At one end, philosophy is the study of many of life's big questions – the point of existence and so on. But today, we also have the word science, which covers much of the same ground and, as our historical survey showed, science began to encroach on the realm of philosophy during the Middle Ages. Ideology is a much more modern word, but its meaning is close to philosophy at one level: 'the science of ideas; the study of their origin and nature'. It is also, according to the same dictionary, 'a system of ideas and ideals, especially one which forms the basis of economic or political theory and policy' (Oxford Dictionary). It is in this sense that we talk of a 'professional ideology' of journalism today. A world-view is something close to both philosophy and ideology; it is the ideas (or, if you like, emotional attitudes) that we carry around in our heads and use to operationalize our belief system into everyday actions. One dictionary defines world-view in such a way that distinguishing it from either philosophy or ideology is difficult: 'a comprehensive view of the world and human life' (The Free Dictionary).

We can make sense of the similarities and differences between the concepts of philosophy, ideology and world-view in the following way. A philosophy is a system of beliefs that is defined primarily by a set of clearly-defined principles; it is a coherent body of thought based on key central ideas (for example, Stoicism, Confucianism and Marxism are terms commonly used to define systems of philosophical thinking). An ideology is a set of beliefs common to a particular social group (for example, a class or caste) or social system, but not necessarily based on a set of clearly-defined philosophical principles; we can talk about the ideology of socialism, or capitalism, or perhaps even an ideology of ideas like sexism or racism. An ideology often contains within it associated social practices that embody its ideas. A world-view is a more individual form of ideology and it is the outlook that we might have on life that distinguishes us from our peers or those whom we see as being different from ourselves. A world-view can often be a mix of philosophical principles and ideological ideas or practices. For example, if you adhere to a Christian philosophy, it may lead you to have a shared ideology with fellow believers, while allowing for differences in world-view around particular issues, such as abortion, gay rights, etc. Journalists, therefore, may adopt a variety of world-views in relation to particular issues, but we would argue that most would hold to a shared ideology based on an understanding of what it means to be 'professional' and to behave ethically. In turn, we could suggest, this professional ideology is based on values of normative philosophy (pragmatism, for example) with deep roots in the principles and traditions of Western thought since the Enlightenment (Hartley 1996; R. Johnson 2012; Kant 1996; Lucy and Mickler 2006; MEAA 1997; Pilger 1998; Schultz 1998; Simkin 1997; Stockwell 1999).

This world-view is normalised and operationalized in journalism through both the marketplace of ideas (Horne 1994) and the fourth estate discourse. True to its bourgeois origins, industrial journalism makes news that does not upset the ruling class and a narrative that does not challenge the core structures or ideas of capitalism itself (Bourdieu 1998, pp. 44–5). Public broadcasting organisations are not immune from these pressures; in fact, their close links to the apparatus of government make the problems all the more acute.

The fault lines in journalistic ideologies

The core values of the BBC – one of the most respected public institutions in the world, at least until recently – are in line with the normative ideological ideals of Western liberalism: 'individual reason, personal liberty and autonomy, the existence and necessity of civil society, with an informed citizenry, civic responsibility, parliamentary representation, ethnic, cultural and religious pluralism, and public debate'; but it seems there is an ethical paradox at the heart of this renowned international news organization (Frost et al. 2011). According to Chris Frost and his colleagues, the very existence of the ethics of 'due impartiality' at the core of the organisation's professional ideology is in direct contradiction to another of the broadcaster's social responsibilities: to uphold the ideological values that are 'deemed fundamental to British society'. In particular, the researchers argue, the BBC's journalists face an ethical dilemma that is rooted in the clash of these conflicting ideologies whenever they are covering 'complex, contentious areas, where issues of domestic and foreign policy, law, civil rights and cultural traditions collide' (Frost et al. 2011, p. 222). The problem for the BBC is institutional, according to Frost and his co-researchers: 'its access to British elites, its perception of itself as a bulwark of the national interest, and its support of consensus on fundamental civic values require it to be a voice of the established political and social order' (p. 224).

The problem is not just confined to the BBC, though no doubt the broadcaster feels it acutely. What Frost and his colleagues are pointing to is a general problem associated with professional journalism across the Western hemisphere and particularly in English-speaking nations. There is a fundamental conflict between the idea of neutrality (balance, objectivity and fairness) and a journalist's own identification with the social values inherent in the capitalist market system. Any journalist or news organization that is required to be 'a voice of the established political and social order', whether by legislation or expectation, is already compromising the ethical principles associated with neutrality.

Unfortunately, most journalists and editors (with a few exceptions) are oblivious to this contradiction and never question it. Most journalists rarely challenge their deeply held assumptions about the nature of democracy and the market, or the social values associated with them. The pragmatism of their shared ideology produces a contradictory class consciousness in journalists and an unfortunate perceptual blindness to the contradictions of global capitalism (Hirst 2012a). The problem is, then, one of an in-built bias that is hardly ever acknowledged: 'it forms the ideological frame through which political news content will be perceived and represented' (Frost et al. 2011, p. 224). In the case of the BBC, Frost and his colleagues also note that there is an element of political economy in the equation; they suggest that the operating climate – 'increasing competition between providers of news, the advent of user-generated content, the demands of the 24-hour news cycle and the high cost of primary newsgathering' – is a factor in driving and widening the ideological fault lines apparent within the BBC's news culture (p. 225).

In order to fully explore arguments and cases in media ethics, we need to explain this paradoxical relationship between journalism and ideology. We also need to understand how conflicting ideologies compete for attention and influence in the ongoing debate about media ethics (Richards 2002). Ideological positions and arguments don't impact on journalism ethics in an abstract way, they manifest themselves in very real fault lines – not only between the news media and the public it serves, but also in arguments between reporters about personal conviction, political beliefs, and loyalties. Understanding this conflict, or dialectic, and debate at the heart of journalism is helped by an understanding of the role and power of the assumptions and ideas embedded in journalists' heads.

A common ideological belief is that journalists are part of some supposed 'elite' of opinion-formers, wise figures, and pundits who are basically courtesans in an 'electronic whorehouse' (Sheehan 2003). In *The Electronic Whorehouse*, Paul Sheehan (2003) argues that the media is dominated by a 'left and liberal media establishment'. In a review of Sheehan's book, another senior journalist and editor, Max Suich, contends this argument is at best 'unpersuasive'. Suich (2003, p. 15) goes on to suggest that the 'noise of all these opinions, including Sheehan's, may be the reason … there is growing disillusion … with the quality press'. In supporting the public role of journalists in creating and shaping public opinion, Mark Davis (2002) argues that any society needs people with ideas, 'especially those humanitarian elites that conservative commentators love to disparage'. Davis is making the argument that journalists are among the group of general public intellectuals that encourage, challenge, and lead debates. We agree – the very fact that reporters and columnists engage, often loudly, in public debate and the circulation of opinion means they deserve to be taken seriously as public intellectuals. That there is such a wide gulf between 'right' and 'left' is then no real surprise. These political tensions inform many debates in journalism ethics. Whichever way you slice it, there are great fault lines within and around journalistic ideologies and in the way that journalists judge the validity of their own ideological positions against others. We are constantly amused when senior columnists and editorial writers attack their fellow columnists – usually in rival media outlets – for their elitist and biased views. The irony of such claims, coming from similarly elitist positions, seems lost on the protagonists. Rupert Murdoch's *The Australian* is one newspaper that delights in repeatedly attacking the nameless 'intellectual elites' and 'so-called progressive intellectuals who manipulate the language' to fulfil 'the intelligentsia's utopian dream' (Newman 2013, p. 10). *The Australian* is the most elitist of Australia's quality newspapers; it has a tiny national circulation of around 125,000 in a country of nearly 21 million and all of its columnists are handsomely paid for their intellectual opinions. Bourdieu remarks sarcastically (1998, p. 47) that members of the journalistic elite feel able to 'impose' their 'vision of the world' and their 'view of things' on a less intelligent public mind. The corollary is that senior journalists and columnists can also be sneeringly anti-intellectual in their attempt to appeal to a mass audience (Bourdieu 1998, p. 58).

There is no straight right–left split between reporters and commentators, but political fault lines can impact on journalistic ethics. Dennis Glover (2004, p. 29), argues that while 'truth has become contested and politics more ruthless', at the same time 'the whole notion of objectivity has itself been undermined and too few journalists do anything to call our politicians to account'.

There is no doubt that since 11 September 2001 the media has been dragged into an ideological battle. It is a conflict in which, according to Glover (2004, pp. 72–3), the conservative opinions of 'right-wing commentators' have 'finally become the new orthodoxy', which pretends to be brave by questioning 'politically correct' supporters of more liberal or left-wing ideas. Mark Davis (2002) describes this form of abuse by conservative commentators as 'clever', because 'it helps mask the fact that those who attack elites are themselves part of an elite'. He goes on to ask how many 'ordinary' people have radio shows or newspaper columns that they are free to use against their ideological opponents.

In their pioneering work on what ideologies are, and how they come into being, Karl Marx and Friedrich Engels defined one aspect of ideology as the ruling ideas of the class that controls the economy and production. In his pamphlet, *Theses on Feuerbach*, Engels wrote that ideology is 'nothing more than the ideal expression of the dominant material relationships, the dominant material relationships grasped as ideas' (Engels, cited in Williams 1989, p. 115). One would therefore expect, in a capitalist society, that the wealthy class that owns most of the economic resources, including the news media, would exercise its advantages in both the economy and politics in ways that can undermine political equality (McChesney 2000a, 2007, 2008). McChesney's argument is that news media deal extensively with issues of political education and debate, but that capitalist media systems do not 'exist to serve democracy'. He suggests their aim is not information, but to 'generate maximum profit to the small number of very large [media] firms and billionaire investors' (2000a, p. 2). Dennis Glover makes a similar point: by drawing attention to an alleged 'left-wing' conspiracy among the news 'elite', the conservative ideologues attempt to 'distract' citizens from 'far more important issues that involve their real interests, such as ... the steady transfer of wealth to the [already] rich' (2004, p. 72). This has certainly been the case in Australia since the Finkelstein inquiry of 2012. Newspapers in Rupert Murdoch's News Limited stable have taken it upon themselves to champion a heavily libertarian view of freedom of the press in what they describe as a 'war' over rights and freedoms in which government attempts to address public perceptions of bias in the media have been met with outright hostility. The media inquiry's recommendations have been misrepresented in the Murdoch papers amid a relentless chorus of editorials, opinion pieces and slanted news reports designed to give the impression that freedoms of expression, speech and the press are under attack from left-wing academics and bureaucrats intent on bringing a critical media to heel. The

Leveson inquiry in Britain was also met with distrust from editors and political figures who argued that it represented an attack on press freedom. We are not advocates of greater government intervention into, or control of, the news media; however, some of the opposition to Leveson and Finkelstein from editors appears to be self-serving.

Core ideas in the ideology of journalism

The ideology of journalism in a western, free-market, liberal democracy (like the UK, the USA, Australia, South Africa, most of Europe, and parts of Southeast Asia) is a complex and tangled set of ideas and ideals, many of which appear to be in contradiction with each other. In this part, we outline what each of these competing concepts are, how they relate to each other, and how they are being revised on an almost daily basis. It is interesting, in passing, to note the emphasis that various authors in journalism ethics place on each of these concepts. Belsey and Chadwick (1992) make no mention of accuracy, fairness, responsibility, or accountability in their index, but they do mention bias and objectivity. Hurst and White (1994) include accuracy, balance, bias, fairness, responsibility, and objectivity in their index. Patterson and Wilkins (1994) mention accuracy, but not accountability, though they do include bias, balance, fairness, and objectivity. *Journalism ethics at work* (Tanner 2005) mentions accuracy (but not accountability), bias (but not balance), fairness, objectivity, public interest and responsibility. On the other hand, Johan Retief (2002) devotes a chapter each to accuracy, fairness and objectivity; public interest is dealt with in two pages. Tony Harcup (2007) has a chapter on the public interest, while accuracy, bias and fairness appear in the index, but balance and objectivity are not mentioned. This is not an exhaustive list, but it is illustrative of the various approaches and emphases that scholars of journalism ethics take to or place on various principles and concepts. The concepts are treated here in alphabetical order, but the relationship of each to the others is constantly reinforced.

Accountability

In this part we have chosen to use the term accountability, but it is synonymous with 'responsibility to' or 'duty to', and in a general sense involves being accountable to the news-consuming public. Inside the concept of accountability we also find the term 'trust'. The public has to be able to trust journalists and the news media to tell the truth. However, there also needs to be a level of accountability and trust within the media organisation, particularly to the business side of the organisation, and an important responsibility towards the sources of news information. Hurst and White (1994, p. 6) also mention a moral accountability to self and society, and the contradictions inherent in conflicting loyalties.

Accountability is a vexed issue in journalism ethics precisely because of these conflicting loyalties. Should a reporter's loyalty to their employer override accountability to the public trust? Equally, should the public interest come before self-interest? This dilemma can be potentially catastrophic for a reporter caught between the wishes of their employer and the needs of the public. It becomes even more complicated in a situation where a reporter might consider it permissible to lie in order to get to a greater truth. This is the fault line between what Jackson (1992, p. 99) calls the 'perfect' and 'imperfect' duties of the investigative journalist: 'The argument that those to whom the journalists would lie are themselves liars is doubtfully relevant and, in any case, not conclusive.' In this situation, accountability to the source – the person being lied to – is thrown out the window, and the principle of the 'greater good' is invoked to justify dishonesty. Is this really a case of a more important duty, that of being accountable to the public? Under such circumstances, it becomes difficult to discern which duty is more compelling for the reporter, and which should take precedence. In our view the threshold has to be a very high level of public interest.

Like many issues in journalism ethics, it would seem that accountability is in the eye of the beholder, and that it might be a physical as well as an intellectual impossibility for the news media to be accountable to every competing interest all the time. Is there also a case for being accountable to your colleagues in the newsroom to produce the best material you can and not to bring the profession into disrepute? Johan Retief (2002, p. 2) seeks a solution in the concept of accountability in the capitalist market but this is not necessarily the best arbiter of responsibility. Nor is it necessarily the most effective guardian of accountability, given the overriding imperative of market forces to garner profit from the activities of reporters. The committee of eminent Australians who reviewed the AJA Code of Ethics in the 1990s was aware of this contradiction, though perhaps not able to resolve it in terms of reconciling public interest in journalism with the private needs of media owners. However, the committee recommended, and the journalists' union adopted, a Preamble to the revised Code that attempted to deal with the issue of accountability by connecting 'power with accountability, accountability with trust, and trust with the fulfilment of the public service role of journalism' (MEAA 1997, p. 20). In our view the success or failure of the MEAA's revised Code to finally address this issue is still open to question.

Accuracy

It would be a mistake to think that accuracy is something that we can take for granted in the news media. Reporters frequently get things wrong – most annoyingly this often means getting names wrong. In one celebrated case, a senior partner in a Sydney law firm sued the *Sun-Herald* newspaper for describing him as a man who engaged in homosexual bondage games. Oops, it turned out it was the wrong man and the case was sent to trial before a civil jury where Justice Levine agreed that wrongly describing a person as gay, and into sado-masochism, could be defamatory (Milligan 2003). Accuracy is also an issue of trust when it comes to dealing with media releases, leaks and whistle-blowers. Sadly, a survey of journalists and editors at 50 Dutch daily newspapers found that while the journalists acknowledged that leaked information was often 'unbalanced, incomplete and lacking in detail', in only a third of cases did they check its accuracy. While they rarely checked the accuracy of leaked stories, not one believed using the information leaked to them posed a moral or ethical problem (Duke 2005).

While it may seem that accuracy is a constant (and a given) in news, and something that reporters should take great pride in, there are times when the pressure of competition, or just laziness, takes the edge off accurate gathering and writing of the facts (Hurst and White 1994). Accuracy is also an issue when reporters and editors wish to claim that their reporting of a controversial or potentially defamatory issue should be privileged. For example, to claim privilege as a defence in a defamation or contempt action, the account given in a news story must be substantially accurate.

The news media cannot afford to make mistakes of fact or accuracy. There have been many cases of the media getting it wrong when racing to be first with what appears to be an important piece of news, including what Hurst and White call 'converting suggestion into fact' (1994, p. 100). This is a big problem when relying on a media release or statements from sources with a particular line to push. A good example of this occurred in early 2013 when a fake news release caused a mining company to lose value on the stock exchange. Journalists raced to publish without a full check on the authenticity of the source. A similar situation can occur when a reporter at a news event is forced to rely on eyewitness accounts from people at the scene. Eyewitness accounts can provide dramatic quotes and imagery for a news story, but they must be treated cautiously as they can often be unreliable and inaccurate. Journalists themselves have reported that the temptation to take eyewitness accounts as 'gospel' is primarily a response to the pressures of tight deadlines and limited research, or fact-checking resources (Schultz 1994, p. 41).

In a general sense, it is not difficult to be accurate. The simple checking of names, places, dates, and so on (the reporter's 5W and H questions – who, what, where, when, why, and how) is the first line of defence in the newsroom. The attribution of material to named sources would also help, but on its own it does not lessen the responsibility on the reporter and editor to get things right. However, it is a different story when accuracy is deliberately thrown out of the window for the sake of a good headline. When Kelvin McKenzie was editing Rupert Murdoch's *Sun* newspaper in London in the 1980s, he was regularly accused of making up material for front-page stories. Sometimes the stories were relatively harmless, like the famous 'Freddie Starr ate my Hamster' story on 13 March 1986. Starr was a comedian who had pretended to eat a hamster as part of his act. The fact that no hamster was consumed did not stop McKenzie on this occasion. There were more serious consequences when *The Sun* accused fans of urinating on rescue workers when a stand at the Hillsborough soccer ground in Sheffield collapsed during an FA Cup semi-final between Liverpool and Nottingham Forest on 15 April 1989 (Hargreaves 2003, p. 114). Ninety-six people lost their lives at Hillsborough that day and *The Sun* was one of many newspapers found to have carried exaggerated and false reports of bad behaviour by Liverpool fans; some of the misinformation also came from police and officials at the ground (Hillsborough Independent Panel 2012). There is no excuse for such blatant making up of 'facts' or angles, purely for the sake of selling more newspapers, or attracting more viewers. The Hillsborough case also provides a lesson for reporters: always question the motivation of sources. In this instance, the police had their own reasons for lying about the causes of the tragedy – to cover up their own incompetence on the day and in subsequent inquiries.

Balance and bias

If journalism is merely about the reporting of facts, then striving for complete accuracy would be enough. However, journalism is more than the reporting of facts – it is also about interpretation – thus there is the potential for bias. Andrew Edgar (1992) argues that any act of interpretation within journalism involves the 'selection and ordering' of the facts. This selection is part of an incomplete process, and necessarily 'biased by the horizon in which interpretation occurs' (Edgar 1992, p. 114). The concept of 'horizon' is very close to what we call the world-view, the ideology, or the emotional attitude of the news worker. It is a dialectic arrangement of competing social forces and ideas that combine to make up 'the stock of knowledge and competencies, typically taken for granted by the journalist' (Edgar 1992, p. 117). These are the ideas and beliefs – the social values – against which the news value of an item is assessed. Thus, the question of bias and balance is primarily one of journalistic ideology, and we can therefore talk about balance as being the fair presentation of both sides of an argument, or conflict, and bias as a definite propensity to favour one side over another. Bias is such a difficult concept to deal with in journalism, and equally difficult to pin down, primarily because the assumptions on which a reporter's views are based can be largely subconscious. There may also not be a perception of bias if the slant on the story appears to be one simply 'dictated by the perceptions of prevailing values in the community', or by 'the acculturation that occurs in all newsrooms' (Hurst and White 1994, p. 29).

Balance is also, at times, a question of editorial independence – independence from pressures both within and outside the newsroom, in particular pressures to include, or omit, information in a story. Such distortions can rob the readers or viewers of the opportunity to decide for themselves about the validity of a report. One important bias that reporters and audiences are aware of (most of the time) is the tendency for news outlets to represent the views of their owners in editorials and political coverage. This is a situation in which reporters must juggle their competing loyalties. Johan Retief (2002, p. 40) points out that the context in which a news item appears is important, as well as the presentation of competing points of view. In terms of ideological bias, we also have to account for the social, historic, political, and economic contexts in which the news communication occurs. Certainly we must be conscious of the political position of the journalist, and the publication/broadcaster for which they work, but we must also consider the very conventions of news reporting. This means understanding, and critiquing, the ways in which the media applies a narrative structure to ambiguous events in order to create a coherent and causal sense of them. We might call this the 'bias of convenience'; it is the reporter's path of least resistance. This form of bias may often be unconscious, but it is the skewing of a story or selection of information based on common sense, rather than a critical investigation of fact and circumstance. It is a particular trap in the age of the 24-hour news cycle that relies more on recycling and embellishing what is already known, rather than uncovering new material (Hirst 2012b). A second form of unconscious bias is reporting in the 'perpetual present'. This bias occurs when the past and previously available information is ignored in favour of reporting only the 'new'. As Bernard Keane notes, it is often deployed in reporting politics where messy and tedious explanations of past events and actions are ignored in favour of 'pack' reporting, 'in which what happened two days ago, let alone two years ago, is forgotten' (Keane 2010).

It's also important to be aware of other unconscious forms of bias that exist in news and journalism. Some, like gender bias, are deeply ingrained in our culture; others like the Google bias when searching online are relatively new and under-explored. Sexism is all around us; numerous scholarly studies over decades have shown that women are under-represented in the news, in newsrooms and in boardrooms. Women are placed in domestic roles, or identified by being 'wives' or 'mothers' or 'the girlfriend of'; they are more likely to be identified by the clothes they're wearing or objectified according to secondary sexual characteristics (breast size, for example). Unless you are conscious of this and actively fight against it, chances are you will be merely repeating old mistakes or adding to the layers of sexist myths. In some countries there are now more women than men in journalism; though the gap is shrinking on the newsroom floor, at senior levels the news is not so good (Hanusch 2013b). Gender may also have an important influence on the professional roles and identities of journalists (de Bruin 2000; Hanitzsch and Hanusch 2012), as well as on story selection and choice of angles – all of which contribute to a gender bias.

Fairness in reporting

Fairness is linked to balance and increasingly it is being seen as the 'holy grail' for reporters, replacing the difficult and, as some would argue, out-dated concept of objectivity. By the same token, others point out that bias is in the perception of the audience. While acknowledging the fact, the conservative Australian commentator Ron Brunton is alarmed that such a statement implies there are no 'objective standards' by which claims of bias can be judged. He laments that bias in news is an issue usually raised by 'people who are hopelessly biased themselves' (Brunton 2002). Fairness is linked to objectivity in the same way as bias and impartiality, but also to the concept of using fair means to obtain information for a news story (Retief 2002, p. 40). For example, it would be unfair to take advantage of a grieving mother to obtain information about a child who died under tragic circumstances.

Like the other concepts discussed in this chapter, fairness itself relies on trust, truth, honesty, and a clear representation of the facts in a story. The duty of a reporter is fair disclosure to the audience. It is an essential duty because if the news-consuming audience cannot rely on the reporter to be fair and accurate, how can they judge the truth of what is being reported? This issue of trust is at the heart of the relationship between journalist and citizens, and 'if that trust is misplaced then media credibility suffers' (Hurst and White 1994, p. 40). But fairness in reporting must go beyond accuracy and into the area of competing opinion. This is not just about the competing opinions of editorial writers and columnists, which are often in a narrow band of mildly conservative and conformist views circulating around a core consensus of ideas (Hallin 1989; 1994); crucially, it is also about access, and who gets to have a point of view. In a period in which there has been an almost unprecedented growth in the concentration of media ownership, and a simultaneous shrinking of media outlets, it is becoming harder each day for diverse voices to get a fair hearing in the mainstream media. The rise of blogs and citizen journalism is, in part, a response to this lack of diversity (Hirst 2011). It was in this context that the MEAA Ethics Review Committee commented that the 'public service role of journalism is in danger of being eclipsed by the commercial pressures of media businesses' (MEAA 1997, p. 7).

The curse of objectivity

> Some people will say that words like scum and rotten are wrong for Objective Journalism –
> which is true, but they miss the point. It was the built-in blind spots of the Objective rules
> and dogma that allowed Nixon to slither into the White House in the first place ... You had
> to get Subjective to see Nixon clearly, and the shock of recognition was often painful.
>
> (Thompson 1994)

For someone as outrageous and cynical as the late, great American gonzo journalist Hunter S. Thompson, there can be no question that objectivity is a curse for journalists. In an obituary published when disgraced former American president Richard Nixon died, Thompson (1994) argued that by attempting to be objective, or at least by paying lip service to the ideology of objective reporting, in fact most news workers fall back on conscious and unconscious prejudices. Hunter S. Thompson is not alone in dismissing the idea of objectivity. In the period of the 'partisan' press in nineteenth-century America, objectivity was dismissed and advocacy of political parties was expected of editors (Avery 1995).

A well-respected Australian editor of the 1950s and 1960s, Sydney Deamer, is reputed to have once counselled a young reporter, Don Whittington, to forget about objectivity, and to instead 'strive to be fair'. It was a sage piece of advice that Whittington took to heart, later using the phrase as the title for his memoir about life in the Canberra Press Gallery (Whittington 1977). Accuracy, fairness, balance, and accountability might well be news virtues, but objectivity may not deserve a place in this list. However, objectivity is important because it has been a normative value in journalism for nearly 100 years and the idea still exerts a strong influence on thinking about journalism (Maras 2013).

The ideology of objectivity conceals a key fault line in contemporary journalism, and there are no easy answers. Objectivity is in the 'positivist' tradition of philosophy that takes a 'common sense' approach to knowledge: we can only know that which we can verify with our senses, but to do so we must put aside our judgement or preferences (Wien 2005). It is on this basis that all young reporters are told – often in no uncertain terms – to leave their opinions at the door and to stick to the facts. This is a difficult balancing act; we all bring our own opinions and prejudices to the table and journalists are no different. Objectivity is problematic, to say the least. Objectivity has the tendency to make us complacent and passive receivers of the news rather than 'analyzers and explainers' (Cunningham 2003, p. 26). Cunningham argues that objectivity makes reporters and editors reluctant to confront too directly those in power: 'objectivity makes us wary of seeming to argue with the president – or the governor, or the CEO – and risk losing our access' (2003, p. 26).

The dialectic contradiction inherent in the conceptualisation and implementation of objectivity is one of the central and recurring dilemmas that confront journalists in all media organisations. For just over a century, the conflict over objectivity has been one of the most volatile fault lines in the ideology of reporters, and in their, often acrimonious, relationship with the public (Kaplan 2006). One historian of journalism has argued that objectivity became a normative value in American journalism in the first decades of the twentieth century, but not as an ideal worth striving for. Instead, it was a deliberate and cynical move to protect the commercial interests of American newspaper owners and 'used to camouflage or even further the press' material interests: increased profit, advertising, and circulation as well as protection from legal sanctions' (Porwancher 2011, p. 186). The ideal of objectivity did not gain easy acceptance and, according to one account, it was not until the 1960s that American newspapers began to take it seriously, perhaps, as Feighery (2009) suggests, because of pressure from the public and government.

British media philosopher John O'Neill ties quality and ethical reporting to the virtues of a good journalist, which he says are honesty, perceptiveness, truthfulness, integrity, and the contested virtue of 'objectivity'. However, he does have an interesting and slightly different interpretation of 'objectivity'. O'Neill defines objective journalism as a style of reporting that 'best allows the audience to appreciate the complexities of a situation [and] may be better served by non-objective presentation of events' (O'Neill 1992, p. 20). We take this to mean that there are circumstances where merely laying out the facts does not give the audience a true picture and that one interpretation is actually more accurate and better serves the public interest, rather than leaving ambiguity in place.

That's a look at objectivity in the macro sense, but there's also objectivity in the micro sense, as practised by individual journalists within individual stories. It is in this context that dictionary definitions of 'objective' come into play: 'external to the mind; actually existing; real' (Moore B. 1997, p. 922). You can see that already this might tend to contradict or clash with Orwell's 'emotional attitude'; it is hard for an individual to completely lose their personality and not bring any of their own feelings to a story. We have to ask the question: Can any story be reported objectively by the individual journalist?

While there are many who would argue that there are reasons why no story can be truly objective, that is no reason not to try to be as objective as possible in every story you produce. As a working journalist you will make decisions about who will give a comment, what you will use from what sources say, and who you won't contact and thereby ignore (usually using the excuse of deadline pressure), etc. If these decisions are made fairly, and with the best interests of the audience and the story in mind, you will be on the right track. Our advice is that you always check your own emotional attitudes and have some self-awareness about your own prejudices, biases, and beliefs.

Despite our differences, we agree that true objectivity is probably impossible to achieve on a regular basis given the pressures on modern-day journalists, but your own personal ethics should dictate that you take as much time on a story as you can in order to cover it as objectively as you can. It is clear from our analysis in this chapter, and within a framework of dialectics, that ideological positions and emotional attitudes of news workers are necessarily contradictory and impossible to avoid. So, too, is the existence of bias in the news audience!

The public interest

The public interest, simply defined, is the maintenance of the general social welfare of the population. There is general agreement that the public interest is operationalized as an alignment of social policy with 'a common concern among citizens in the management and affairs of local, state, and national government' (Lehman 2008).

The concept of a public interest is an aspect of the social contract philosophy articulated in the eighteenth century by the great bourgeois thinkers of the day. The principle also relies on an argument about the 'greater good', 'in essence asking that we put aside individual differences for the benefit of the best outcome' (Sjovaag 2010, p. 879). Journalists and editors make a strong claim to be representative of the public interest and acting for the greater good in almost everything they do; it is particularly effective in the pursuit of corruption or malpractice by government and business leaders. But how do journalists and editors know what is in the public's interest? It is not that easy to pin down the public interest in practice. The fourth estate role of the press requires it to be critical (but not too critical). This tension is well expressed in relation to government-funded broadcasters like the BBC, ABC and SBS and publicly funded outlets like PBS in the US that also take advertising, but it is evident in all major news media outlets. The ideology of professionalism requires the public interest to be defined through the eyes of the State. In this regard, the news media's critical role is constrained by the ideological need for it to be esteemed as 'a bulwark of the national interest' and 'a voice of the established political and social order' (Frost et al. 2011, p. 224). This is the default position of most news media and most journalists; it is clearly in operation during times of conflict when support for the military and for the war aims is seen as the right thing to do. As we shall see in chapter 6, when talking about war and terrorism, the convention of only offering polite and mild criticism has been in almost continuous operation in relation to Iraq and Afghanistan since 2001. Daniel Hallin (1989) has provided one of the most robust critiques of media complicity in substituting state and national interest for a broader definition of the public. He called it the sphere of consensus and limited controversy. There are core ideological beliefs that lie beyond challenge and then an agreed radius of allowable criticism that should never extend to an attack on the consensus ideals. Hallin's idea is resurfacing today, but in some discussions it is referred to as the 'Overton Window' after the political scientist James Overton who first described it.

Definitions of the Overton Window are remarkably similar to Hallin's spheres of consensus and limited controversy:

> for any political issue, there's a range of socially acceptable positions that's narrower than the range of possible positions. Positions within the Overton window are seen as mainstream and uncontroversial, while those outside it are viewed as shocking, upsetting, and dangerously radical.
>
> (Lee, A 2011)

Daniel Hallin defines consensus and limited controversy in very similar terms:

> Within this [consensus] region journalists do not feel compelled to offer competing views [and] play an essentially conservative, legitimizing role ... Beyond [consensus] lies what can be called the sphere of legitimate controversy ... where objective journalism reigns supreme ... Beyond [legitimate controversy] lie those political actors and views which journalists and the political mainstream of the society reject as unworthy of being heard.
>
> (Hallin 1994, pp. 53–4)

The public interest is problematic and not just because it is linked to the much narrower State interest of the ruling elites; it is problematic because defining exactly what 'the public' is has never been easy. In fact, it is the media that helps to define the public in ways that suit its own needs, not necessarily those of the public interest. The 'public' is often reduced to 'an inchoate mass' in media representation (Coleman, S. and Ross 2010, p. 5); or it is limited to members of a particular class like Habermas' bourgeois public sphere. Alternatively, the public interest is assumed to be the same as the interest of the consumer in the marketplace and not constructed around the real social relations that actually link individuals into communities of interest. The public is defined as if it is monolithic when clearly it is not; it is measured by opinion polls and surveys that attempt to generalise about the public mood. Ultimately it is ideologically constructed to marginalise dissident voices. In a capitalist world, this means individuals or groups who do not measure up to normative standards, arrived at through polling techniques or media construction, can be 'justifiably marginalised and excluded' from public discussion (Coleman, S. and Ross 2010, p. 31). The public interest is not really knowable to most journalists; rather its existence is assumed and then reified into a normative ideological construct that justifies the status quo.

Journalism, ethics and ideology today

Two conceptual frameworks dominate the professional ideology of journalism today and they both incorporate elements of the key ethical concepts outlined above. One has an economic focus and one is more political in approach.

The marketplace of ideas framework is consistent with free-market economics and the fourth estate framework is consistent with bourgeois liberal-democratic ideologies; both rest on the premise that capitalism is the best possible system for organising society.

The myth of free-market news

In a perfect news world, everything that happened in any given time frame and at any given location (at least everything of consequence, impact, and interest) would be reported as news. However, because it is technically impossible to cover everything that happens everywhere, and because many things that happen are every-day and mundane, news production is a process of selection. In the free-market model, public interest is often equated with human interest, which is mainly trivia stories (colour pieces) and a summary of the important events of the day: 'market forces determine the selection of news and that news itself is [a] more or less objective portrayal of reality' (Windschuttle 1988, p. 262).

In economic terms, the free-market ideology builds on the fact that from the start of the twentieth century newspapers became more commercially oriented, and less aligned to political positions, and therefore able to appeal to a wider audience. The free-market model suggests that because the news media is also a business, it is more focused on selling, rather than preaching to the masses.

The central assumptions of the free-market model are that the capitalist market economic system is good and that the social–political status quo should be protected. It is clearly linked to the liberal-democratic myths of individuality and equal rights, and equal access to power through elections. The notion of objectivity in journalism plays to these ideological assumptions and reinforces them. These are the overriding dynamics driving the emotional attitudes of journalism today. Quite clearly, as McQueen (1977) and other political economists of communication (McChesney 2000b, 2001; Mosco 1996, 1999) have demonstrated, the intellectual dynamic of journalism – the emotional dialectic – is created and contradicted by the very nature of the news commodity. News is an important source of information, but it also has the qualities of a commercially produced commodity. It is this duality of news, and the contradiction it expresses, that drives news workers to present 'unfavourable' views of class-based issues and organisations.

On the other hand, British media philosopher, John O'Neill, argues that 'the market undermines the relations between journalism and democracy' or, in the terms of a debate about ethics, hinders the production of 'quality' news (O'Neill 1992, p. 15). This contradiction between democracy and profit is insoluble because, as O'Neill points out, 'free speech' in the 'free market' immediately runs into the legal problems of ownership, control, and access. It is precisely this property right that exerts the 'limiting' influence of economic determination over the emotional dialectic of 'ethics'. In the end, the 'hidden hand' of the free market effectively prevents 'objective' journalism from existing at all. All journalism in a capitalist market economy is compromised. Ownership, expressed through private and corporate property rights, restricts the freedom of those without property. O'Neill (1992, p. 18) himself fails to bridge this contradiction, instead suggesting that the market system encourages diversity and guarantees a 'watchdog role for the news media'.

While it is possible to express some disagreements with O'Neill's argument that media outputs are consumer-driven, it can equally be argued that the idea of a 'sovereign' consumer is a free-market myth. In our capitalist and formal democracies the real power is in the hands of those who own the means of journalistic production – which is the whole point of ownership and control – expressed as social control over the emotional dialectic of the front page. O'Neill is right to say that the market shapes news values, but producers and not consumers control this process. James Curran (1991) argues that liberal-democratic and free-market ideas have been effectively challenged in the field of journalism and media studies. Curran describes the news media as a field of ideological production in which the economic strength of capital provides a privileged position, to which subordinate social forces are denied direct, unmediated access. Ultimately it is a question of which groups have the power to influence and control news information flows.

Of course, the owners of newspapers, radio and television stations, magazines, and online news portals do have some level of influence over the news they relay to an audience. It makes perfect sense in a capitalist economy for the commercial interests of the capitalists to influence the selection of target audiences and the general editorial line to be taken by the news outlet they own. It follows, according to this logic, that the selection of news must conform to these same principles. Despite the anecdotal evidence that owners do exercise complete control, we believe that the case for direct intervention on a day-by-day basis is overstated. For one thing, it is an inadequate account of the independent role of journalists, where reporters are seen as no more than mouthpieces for owners. Most news workers would fiercely deny that they are mere pawns of the owners. Others may privately acknowledge that they do curry favour and a handful are proud of their role as interpreters and popularisers of the pearls of wisdom of their company's management. In fact, there is a common, though in our view mistaken, view that most journalists are left wing. Certainly they tend to have progressive views on some issues and some take the side of society's 'underdog', but to suggest that there is an official 'left-leaning' culture in most newsrooms is over-cooking the goose (Hanusch 2013a). In fact, we would argue that the editorial culture in most newsrooms – with one or two exceptions – is decidedly conservative. There is no doubt that editorial policy is firmly in the grip of senior reporters who agree with a conservative position on most issues, and often it is that of the major proprietor(s) too. In their provocative book, *The War on Democracy*, Lucy and Mickler (2006, p. 7) refer to the elite group of opinion-makers who work for the daily media as conservative commentators who claim to see 'leftists, radicals and extremists lurking under every bed'. Within the marketplace of ideas the news media has a specific role – in its guise as defender of the public interest – but that role too is ideological and problematic from an ethical perspective. Today, the role of the market place is to legitimise and reproduce ideas that help to sustain capitalism through economic, ideological and political crises. The fourth estate is the ideological expression of this role.

The fourth estate

The term fourth estate is attributed to the Anglo-Irish conservative, Edmund Burke (1729–97), who apparently used it to attack a 'self-important and braying' English press. In 1841, Thomas Carlyle referred to the powerful Westminster press gallery as a 'branch of government' and, by the 1850s, English newspaper editors had turned derision to their advantage. London *Times* editor, George Reeve, saw his newspaper and its peers as partners with what were, at that stage, the other three important 'estates': parliaments, courts, and, originally, the church. In 1891, Oscar Wilde referred to the fourth estate as more powerful than the government or judiciary. He lamented 'we are dominated by journalism'. The church was later replaced in the trinity by the executive arm of government. The actuality of the modern fourth estate falls a long way short of the theory (Eggerking 1998). In fact, Kitty Eggerking suggests that the radicalism and advocacy of the English press had been much moderated by the late nineteenth century. Instead, the epoch of industrial journalism saw the once radical and 'free' press become primarily commercial marketing and political process-management services for the ruling class. It is in this context that Eggerking says the problems inherent in the fourth estate mean that today it has become an 'indefensible' institution.

On the other hand, in her book, *Reviving the Fourth Estate*, former journalist, media executive, and university lecturer Julianne Schultz (1998) tries to straddle the contradiction between profitability and public interest; however, the underlying tensions of the news commodity mean that the fault lines today are very unstable. Many of them come together in undermining the idealism of the fourth estate. Schultz argues that journalism can no longer 'adequately fulfil the historic role the press created for itself ... as an institution of political life designed to act on behalf of the people'. Instead the news media has become 'a source of real and significant power and influence, an industry prepared to exercise and pursue self-interested commercial, political and cultural agendas' (Schultz 1998, p. 1). By her own admission, Schultz believes that attempting to revive the fourth estate is a thankless, even hopeless, task given the commercial pressures that dominate any democratic ideals that journalists, reporters, and editors might harbour about their work. Here we begin to examine the contradiction between the idealistic view of journalism as the fourth estate, and the competing view that the media is just another business (see, for example, Curran 1991; Hartley 1996; Stockwell 1999).

The fourth estate model has a noble heritage, related by birth to the American War of Independence and the French revolution (Chiasson 1995). However, like many young firebrands do over time, it has grown fat and comfortable in middle age, and the fourth estate today rarely strikes fear into the hearts of tyrants anywhere. In fact, as Schultz herself concedes, the tyrants have tamed the idealism of the media through control of the purse strings. The solution, according to Schultz, is for reporters and editors to rise up, *carpe diem*, and reinvigorate the fourth estate. This is a position that is in the end little different from John Merrill's existential journalism: the triumph of individual will over the social forces creates the fabric of journalism's ideological straitjacket.

There can be little argument that the concept, in practice, has shifted over time, even if the fourth estate ideal itself has remained relatively static. In terms of our fault lines thesis, these changes can be theorised as a series of discrete but related moments of interaction: thesis–antithesis–synthesis: the idea begins with a cynical and satirical use of the term 'fourth estate' (thesis); it is then co-opted by those it was meant to ridicule; they turn it to their advantage (antithesis); and it then becomes a central element of journalistic ideology (synthesis), one that we might look upon as a 'golden age' of the past. In other words, the contradictions in the ideal of the fourth estate are practical and everyday manifestations of the emotional dialectic in journalism. The operative fault lines are evident in the concrete routines of journalism today in tension with the ideals of the news media as a fourth estate.

While we agree with Julianne Schultz that we need to do something about this, we're just not sure that *reviving* the fourth estate is the way to go. The fourth estate no longer performs a watchdog role on behalf of ordinary people; the media's policing role is performed on behalf of the system as a whole – it is used to strengthen the core ideological consensus values against 'deviance' (Hallin 1994). The news media functions as a moral, political, and ideological boundary rider that keeps the worst excesses in check, but at the same time prevents any real alternative from being seriously considered through public debate. The public sphere is kept within the sphere of limited controversy (Hallin 1994). The debate does not include anyone who can be labelled an 'extremist'; only 'moderate' voices are given space and airtime. The myth of the fourth estate is an effective ideology – one that can mask the symbiotic relationship between the news media, corporate power, and the State. In addition, the journalistic ideology of 'professionalism' can blind reporters to the assumptions that underpin their daily practice and to their own objective situation as 'churners' of the dominant ideology. Thus, 'the media's real agenda – commercial success and maintenance of the status quo – is revealed' (Schultz 1998, p. 55) only when these ideologies are put under pressure by real world events that can shift the emotional dialectic of the front page (Hirst 2003). Such events are rare, for most of the time the news media's ideological role remains a hidden agenda (Pilger 1998).

Despite the shortcomings that we have identified, the free-market model and the myth of the fourth estate persist, mainly because of their ideological strength and the support they lend to the economic, social, and political status quo. James Curran, too, recognised these problems with Habermas' classic theory of the public sphere, which, he argued, 'has nothing useful to say about the way in which the media can invigorate the structures of liberal democracy' (1991, p. 29). However, like Schultz, Curran believes that the basic structures of the liberal-democratic media system, based on private market ownership and control of the means of media production, can be reformed or revived. Curran (1991, p. 48) writes that market competition can ensure diversity, if there are limits placed on monopoly. He argues that the State should impose these limits (p. 49), but this just again highlights the circularity of this argument: an independent state should regulate a market in order to ensure that the market can watch over (regulate) the actions of the state. Stockwell (1999, p. 46) also concedes this point: 'competition between different media organisations ... may produce a diversity of editorial positions'. We think this is more hope than reality. However, we agree with Stockwell that journalists have a right, and a responsibility, to seek out the 'gaps in the media hegemony where deliberation may flourish'. Further, we agree that news workers need to examine a picture bigger than notions of the fourth estate. It should be a vision that includes 'reconsidering their work practices ... beyond being mere employees', and working as advocates, consciously 'assisting in the creation of new, "active" audiences' (Stockwell 1999, p. 47).

Despite the seemingly unstoppable rise of what she calls 'junk journalism', Schultz concludes that the ideals of the fourth estate have proved 'remarkably resilient' (1998, p. 231). She argues that responsibility for maintaining the fourth estate has passed 'from the news media, as a corporate institution, to the journalists, editors and producers, who produce the content of the news media' (Schultz 1998, p. 232). In 1998, the solution offered by Schultz (1998, p. 238) seemed tokenistic and was only introduced in the very last paragraph of the book: 'If journalists were able to build more meaningful, reflective alliances with their audiences, they could become a more significant democratic force.' At the time, Schultz did not address the vital 'how' question, but today we can confidently talk about the existence of a 'fifth estate' – citizen journalism, the blogosphere and social media – none of which was in existence a decade ago. The fifth estate is a product of the digital age, set in motion by the Indymedia movement of 1999 (Hirst 2011).

We are not prone to exaggerate the impact and influence of the fifth estate, but it is important to acknowledge its existence and to engage with arguments for and against it. The old one-to-many model of broadcasting and publishing is being challenged by new interactive models of peer-to-peer information sharing and by news as 'conversation' rather than lecture. According to its supporters, the fifth estate represents a new form of public accountability (Dutton 2009), underpinned by the ability of non-journalists to critically cross-reference and fact-check the mainstream media (Jericho 2012). The digital optimists writing today argue that the Internet and the rise of so-called 'citizen journalism' represents a strong challenge to the old ways that may revive a genuine public sphere. This is a hopeful view, but it is problematic and the barriers that need to be overcome are still huge.

In the first three chapters we have explained the theoretical base for our position on journalism ethics. The following chapters look at the practical dilemmas journalists face in their daily newsgathering.

Part II

Ethics in practice

Overview and objectives

This part moves the focus from consideration of the theoretical arguments for being ethical to the very practical application of the theories in everyday journalism. Each chapter considers issues on the basis of arguments and cases which highlight ethical contradictions in journalism practice.

Chapter four covers the basic principles of honest reporting and the major transgressions that tend to occur far too often. It looks at the many facets of deception – from deceiving individual sources in order to get information they might not otherwise provide, to the use of hidden cameras and listening devices, phone hacking, plagiarism and fabrication. The argument will be made that the pressure to deceive, plagiarise or simply make up, along with engaging in chequebook journalism, are part and parcel of the dominant journalistic culture and typify the fault lines discussed in earlier chapters.

Chapter five is devoted to the complex issues surrounding chequebook journalism. We discuss the main arguments – that paying for news demeans the information and can lead to exaggeration at best and, at worst, false information, while the 'buyers' maintain that chequebook journalism is just another business expense aimed at lifting ratings or circulation and improving the media organisation's bottom line.

In chapter six we examine the very real – and very dangerous – fault lines that exist for journalists covering military conflicts. Examples are taken from the conflicts in Afghanistan, Iraq, Libya and Syria and situated against an historical backdrop. We will argue that the national interest is one of the dominant 'ideological spectacles' (Grattan 1991) that the media wears most of the time. These glasses are so comfortable that often reporters forget they are wearing them. The central dilemma news workers face in times of war is one of 'choosing' sides. As we see, this is a deep and deadly fault line. Also included in this chapter is a brief review of how the media has covered terrorism in the first decade of the twenty-first century.

After reading these three chapters, you will have an understanding of the various legal and ethical problems associated with:

- the principles of honest reporting and traps for new players
- the reasons behind the pressure to deceive in news gathering
- the ethical dilemmas associated with investigative journalism
- whether it is ever justifiable to deceive news sources 'for the greater good'
- the ethical debates for and against the practice of chequebook journalism
- the often conflicting role of the media in times of political crisis and war
- what happens when global media empires are caught up in the reporting of war
- the evolving role of the journalist in modern warfare
- the way the media has reported on terrorism this century.

4   How far do you go?

Deception and the public interest

The Fake Sheikh – the good and the bad of deception

The work of the 'Fake Sheikh', former *News of the World* investigative journalist, Mazher Mahmood (so called because of his propensity for wearing Arab robes for some of his more memorable stings), demonstrates the best and the worst of journalistic deception. It also highlights a central theme of this chapter – the 'public interest' test. Mahmood told the Leveson inquiry into British media ethics that his stories were responsible for a total of 261 successful prosecutions (quoted in Greenslade 2012b). After the closure of the *News of the World*, he joined the sister Murdoch publication, the *Sunday Times*. When his tally was called into question, the *Sunday Times* conducted their own inquiry which found evidence of only 94 individual convictions (Burrell 2012). Although he disputed the new count, Mahmood was forced into making a clarifying statement to the Leveson inquiry (Greenslade 2012b). At his first appearance, Mahmood said he usually exposed criminality, though he would also deal on occasion with cases of hypocrisy involving people guilty of moral lapses. He strongly denied that his 'stings' amounted to entrapment (Greenslade 2012d). Regardless of the precise figure, the Fake Sheikh had a formidable record of duping people. And he is still at it. In 2012, he appeared in *The Sun on Sunday* in a classic Mahmood sting over five pages in which he claimed to have exposed a former world heavyweight boxing champion, Herbie Hide, as willing to throw a title fight for £1 million (Mahmood 2013).

Let's look at four of his more memorable stings. One of the relatively recent ones involved the Duchess of York, Sarah Ferguson, the former wife of Prince Andrew, Queen Elizabeth's second son. Mahmood succeeded in getting Fergie to agree to sell access to her ex-husband for £500,000 (Reeves 2010). Media commentators differed on the merits of that scoop. British journalism professor and commentator for *The Guardian*, Roy Greenslade, gave three reasons for supporting the publication of the sting:

- It was not a fishing expedition. The paper had learned that the Duchess was already 'cashing in' on her access to Prince Andrew.
- Although it appeared the Duchess might have drunk more than was good for her, she did convict herself several times over in the video (taken as part of the 'sting') without obvious prompting.
- There is a valid public interest because, despite being divorced from the Prince, they remain close friends.

(Greenslade 2010)

Figure 4.1 'Caught! Match-fixer pockets £150k as he rigs the England Test at Lords', *News of the World*, 29 August 2010. Copyright News Syndication

Media analyst Mark Day, a veteran of more than 50 years in print and broadcast media, considered the sting entrapment 'beyond the bounds' and quite unethical (2010). In a prediction about the British media that would prove true a year or so later, Day added:

> The line is being pushed further and further towards the 'publish and be damned' end of the spectrum. Increasingly, the notion that the truth should be told at all times is threatening to overwhelm old standards that moderate the means by which the truth is obtained.
>
> (Day 2010)

The duchess apologised for her 'serious lapse in judgment' this time and, for once, the British media came out in support of her – sort of (*Day the reptiles rallied to the dopey duchess* 2010). In our opinion this one passes the 'public interest' test. As you will see in the chapter 10 discussion of privacy, the British Royal Family is very much public property, a number of them being paid from the public purse. Although Fergie is no longer on the Royal payroll, the suggestion that she could sell access to her former husband is evidence of potential criminality.

The 'Fake Sheikh' second sting involved the then manager of the English soccer team, Sven-Goran Eriksson. Mahmood posed as a rich Arab to lure the hapless Sven to Dubai where they dined on lobster and expensive champagne. Eriksson told the reporter he would quit England if the team won the World Cup that northern summer (Cozens 2006). He also criticised players, and said he could lure David Beckham to Aston Villa football club (Timms 2006). The previous year Eriksson had been caught up in another media storm when the *News of the World* broke the story of his affair with a Football Association secretary, Faria Alam (Timms 2006). While the British are fixated on soccer, and many tabloid stories involve the off-field antics of the stars of the English Premier League competition, whether this one passes the 'public interest' test is borderline. Would the British public be fascinated to know what Eriksson planned to do after that World Cup (England didn't win, incidentally, the tournament was taken out by Italy), what he thought of various players and how he thought he could lure the game's best-known player back to an English club? Does it really matter? We think not.

Another of Mahmood's sporting stings was his investigation into Pakistan cricket's spot-fixing scandal where he bribed a players' agent with £150,000 to pay three members of the Pakistan national team to bowl no-balls at a particular time in a Test match against England at 'the home of cricket', Lords, in 2010 – supposedly so that others, as the judge said at their trial, could cheat at gambling (Greenwood 2011). The three players, and their agent, were subsequently jailed and the players banned from the sport for varying periods. This one definitely passes the 'public interest' test. Mahmood was able to 'fix' part of a game to supposedly benefit illegal gamblers. Instances of match-fixing have dogged cricket for many years.

But chequebook deals can go wrong. ...

Despite his impressive stings, the Fake Sheikh hasn't always been that successful. He was involved in a case more than a decade ago where it all went wrong. 'WORLD EXCLUSIVE We stop crime of the century. POSH KIDNAP', screamed the headlines on the front page of the now-defunct *News of the World*. It was a tabloid editor's dream story. In November, 2002, the paper exposed what it said was a plot to abduct Victoria Beckham, the former Posh Spice from the famous girl band and wife of soccer superstar, David Beckham (Britain's 'other Royal Family'), and their children. The paper claimed the plotters planned to kidnap Mrs Beckham and her two sons for a ransom of $12,500,000 (Este 2003). Five men were arrested but the case collapsed when prosecutors discovered their prime witness, a parking attendant with a criminal record for forgery, was paid about $25,000 by the *News of the World* for his story (*Kidnap of Beckham Trial Axed* 2003). In our opinion, this one doesn't pass the 'public interest' test. While it is a 'ripper of a yarn', instead of seeing another group of criminals behind bars the case collapsed because of Mahmood's scoop.

By our count, that's two in the public interest and two that fail the test. All of Mahmood's stings discussed here involved the Fake Sheikh paying his various sources for the stories.

Just as one man's freedom fighter is another man's terrorist, one man's 'sting' is another man's entrapment. Are these traditional tabloid tactics – like deception, attempted bribery and paying sources for information – acceptable? If so, under what circumstances? So can we chuckle at the gullibility of a former Royal wife or gasp at the potential for Posh and the kids being held for ransom? Perhaps. A stronger case can be made for such tactics when they result in exposing a scandal the public should know about, rather than one, as we have said, that they would like to know about.

The opening clause of the MEAA Code of Ethics says it succinctly:

> Clause 1: Report and interpret honestly, striving for accuracy, fairness and disclosure of all essential facts. Do not suppress relevant available facts, or give distorting emphasis. Do your utmost to give a fair opportunity to reply.
>
> (*MEAA Code of Ethics* 1999)

Black and Roberts (2011) put it another way:

> Media practitioners and media consumers have made an implicit agreement: Media that inform and persuade have a special obligation to be truth seekers and truth tellers. Truth has a high value, and when it is diminished all of us suffer to some extent.
>
> (Black and Roberts 2011, p. 223)

As will be seen during the discussion, not everyone agrees – especially those in what we refer to as the 'investigative journalism club'. The Investigations Editor at *The Guardian*, David Leigh, told the Leveson inquiry that the use of subterfuge by journalists can be justified in exceptional circumstances in pursuing a story that is in the public interest (quoted in Robinson 2011a). He told the inquiry he once pretended to be an arms dealer in a successful attempt to prove that Mark Thatcher had entered into a business deal with a Middle Eastern businessman, arguing it was a legitimate technique because the story was in the public interest. He attacked the *News of the World* and the tabloid press in general:

> The tittle tattle is being got illegally, intrusively and sometimes cruelly.
>
> (Quoted by Robinson 2011a)

We believe strongly that journalists should be honest, accurate, fair, and should disclose all facts. The various Codes of Ethics all state that journalists should use honest means to obtain material. Like Black and Roberts say, they should be truth seekers – and that extends to how they get the information for their stories.

Much of the rest of this chapter is a litany of the practices that are at best suspect, and at worst dishonest and unethical, used by journalists to gain stories the world over.

It is our contention that it is the pressure of competition, deadlines, and individual egos in the current environment of shrinking job prospects that lead a very small minority of journalists into compromising positions that may push them to cut ethical corners. Not all journalists are so inclined. Far from it. Most journalists go about their news-gathering never once in their career being faced with a situation where they might cross the line into suspect behaviour. Others face an ethical dilemma, and take a stand against it. But a small minority give in to temptation and take others' work without acknowledging it, invent sources rather than trying that extra bit harder to find an actual credible source, fabricate information, accept a free trip or other 'freebies' that might lead to a compromising position in the future, or engage in suspect activities (like pretending to be someone they're not) in order to get a 'scoop'. In most cases of suspect actions, though, the first thing to ask yourself is whether there is a strong public interest in the story, and if there is any other way to get it that doesn't involve subterfuge.

Identifying yourself as a journalist

News journalists interview people every day. They have no problem ringing a politician, athlete, a union or business leader or simply walking up to someone in the street, identifying themselves as a reporter for whatever news organisation that employs them and seeking information for a story. Investigative journalists, on the other hand, say they couldn't do their job if they had to immediately identify themselves every time they approached sources for information. We believe that there are very few cases where journalists need to use deceptive methods – like not identifying themselves immediately – to get stories. The pivotal question in these ethical dilemmas is: Is it ever appropriate for journalists to deceive someone to get to the truth? Or as the American journalism ethicists Black, Steele and Barney put it:

> [I]s it ever justifiable for a journalist to violate the principle of honesty in order to honour the principle on which journalism is founded, a duty to provide the public with meaningful, accurate and comprehensive information about significant issues?
>
> (Black et al. 2005, p. 166)

Those who take the moral higher ground would argue that a journalist should never lie or purposely deceive anyone in the process of gathering newsworthy material. But that's too simple an answer for something as complex as the ethics of investigative journalism. Ethical decision-making in general involves deciding on a course of action after weighing up a number of options, each of which can have both positive and negative consequences.

The MEAA Code of Ethics poses problems for the investigative journalist faced with having to use deception to get that important exposé:

> Clause 8: Use fair, responsible and honest means to obtain material. Identify yourself and your employer before obtaining any interview for publication or broadcast.
>
> (*MEAA Code of Ethics* 1999)

There is a very fine line between legitimate investigative reporting and using illegitimate methods to get a story. Definitions and practices will vary from organisation to organisation but, in general, 'dubious' methods include disguising your journalistic identity and the use of undercover techniques. Some of these methods are, in fact, illegal. One of the more common methods is for the journalist to pose as someone they are not for a period of time, living undercover, and then writing the story once they are back in the office. Examples include reporters living with street kids, or in a Housing Commission flat, to get the story about hardship in those circumstances. There was the memorable – and highly controversial – case of *The Sydney Morning Herald* journalist who pretended to be a senior student to write about high school hi-jinks. Tabloid current affairs television programmes regularly use hidden cameras to get material for their stories – like the doctor who prescribes medication too readily etc. – but it is a long way from that rather tacky practice to some of the high points of investigative journalism – like John Pilger's exposé of the drug Thalidomide in the 1960s, involving months and months of work, that led to huge compensation payouts, Royal Commissions and criminal charges against 'big fish'. That's part of the problem – the daily current affairs TV programmes' readiness to 'bend the rules' for a story that amounts to little more than embarrassing someone – while the serious current affairs programmes, like the BBC's *Panorama*, ABC's *Four Corners* or SBS's *Dateline*, argue they legitimately use deceptive methods to gain their major stories in the public interest.

The justification often used by reporters for not identifying themselves at the outset is that there is no other way for them to gain the trust of the people who are the subjects of the story, or that the source would refuse access to a journalist if s/he identified her/himself before trying to get the story. Some journalists see it as a legitimate tactic in investigative journalism not to identify themselves at the start. The justification in such circumstances is the argument of the 'greater good', using the overriding principle of the public's 'right to know' to justify their deception. But isn't there an equally valid argument that by denying the 'subjects' the right to refuse (or agree) they are, at the very least, misleading them?

This is an issue on which the authors have a slight disagreement. Roger believes there are very, very few circumstances (nothing is absolute in a discussion of ethics) that justify journalists misleading sources by either not identifying themselves, or by pretending to be someone they're not. He's heard all the arguments, but still feels that stories gained by deception are 'tainted'. He acknowledges that some of the biggest investigative stories have involved some form of deception, but still questions whether the end result justifies the deceptive means that were used to get it. He knows many will disagree with him – especially those of the investigative journalism club – but that is his ethical stance.

Martin, on the other hand, believes that deception is acceptable if it leads to the exposure of a larger 'lie', such as a government deception, significant criminal activity, or corporate fraud. He says that using subterfuge to trap a lying politician or to expose a commercial scandal is obviously in the public interest, and crusading journalists are not being unethical if they use deception to gather evidence. However, Martin adds the caveat that the 'public interest' test threshold must be very high in order to avoid the gratuitous use of deception.

On one point the authors agree: deception used against ordinary people who have no chance to give informed consent to being questioned by a journalist, or might be unnecessarily embarrassed by exposure, is not justified. How would you feel if everything you said in a casual conversation with someone ended up in a newspaper? If you knew that what you were saying was being recorded for possible later use, you might answer some questions quite differently, certainly not in the often flippant way some people discuss issues. But what if the tables were turned, and the reporter was the one being secretly recorded? English actor, Hugh Grant, who has suffered at the hands of the British 'red tops' as much as any celebrity, turned the tables on a former *News of the World* reporter, wearing a concealed microphone to record the reporter alleging that the paper's former editor Rebekah Brooks 'absolutely' knew about illegal phone-hacking (Addley 2011). Grant referred to the incident as having a 'bugger bugged' (Addley 2011).

Hidden cameras and listening devices

We've mentioned the use of hidden cameras and audio recording devices in passing above, so what about their use – so popular, as we've said, with television current affairs programmes? The authors would obviously have different views on their use, too.

Roger might say, 'No, never,' while Martin might say, 'If the story warrants it and there's a strong public interest angle, go ahead.' However, there is agreement that to use hidden cameras just to trap a shoddy builder or some other minor rip-off merchant is a frivolous use of the technology. The other note of caution here is that, if you're not careful, you run the risk of being used in other forms of surveillance, some of which are clearly not in the public interest (for discussion of the surveillance society, see Hirst and Harrison (2007), particularly chapters 9 and 10).

Would you cooperate with the police?

While we are on the topic of surveillance, there's another ethical dilemma, and it involves general reporters and investigative journalists alike. Would you hand over to police video or still photographs you had taken in the course of gathering a story? Let's say you were covering a demonstration and it turned ugly, and some of the demonstrators destroyed property. The police want your coverage in order to identify the offenders. Do you hand it over? It might earn you 'brownie points' with the police that you might be able to 'cash in' at a later date – i.e. call in the favour for some information you badly need – but is it ethical to become an extension of the law? In Australia it is usually an informal request for help from the police, as it was after the ugly demonstration in Sydney in mid-September, 2012, involving local Muslims protesting about a YouTube 'trailer' for an American-made movie that mocked Muhammad and Islam. New South Wales police said they would be examining 'surveillance and media footage' to find those involved in the clashes that left six police officers injured (*Police warn of more arrests after Sydney protests* 2012). There were worldwide protests about the film, which cost too many lives. While we have no problem with the police reviewing video images that were used by the various TV channels in their regular news and current affairs programmes, they could easily have them recorded, but what about the off-cuts – the material not used? Surely the police don't see the electronic media as an extension of their evidence-gathering resources? In the wake of the major riots in a number of British cities in August, 2011, the three main TV broadcasters, the BBC, ITN, and Sky, were forced to hand over un-transmitted video of the riots after the police took out a court order against them (McAthy 2011). After the riots, the British Prime Minister, David Cameron, told Parliament that media organisations had a responsibility to hand over unused video of rioters to the police (Gunter 2011). Do they? We think not, and neither did the BBC at the time, saying they would not hand over the material without a court order (Gunter 2011), which followed a few weeks later. The ethico-legal paradox in the 2011 UK riots is that the subpoena cannot be ignored without deep pockets. After the April 2013 terrorist bombing at the Boston Marathon, police were inundated with material from members of the public who shot images and video with their mobile phones. This was helpful up to a point, but it also led to dangerous vigilante actions on Reddit and other social media as civilians posted images of innocent people who were carrying backpacks or had darker complexions.

Consider the case where a crew conceals a camera and then records some wrongdoing, like a drug sale to a reporter. You've seen the sort of thing. The reporter walks up to the camera with something suspicious in her/his hand and the voice-over says, 'See how easy it is to buy drugs of the streets of.' The reporter is only buying drugs for the story, so are they deceiving the pusher for the sake of the story? Is it entrapment? Some would say so. Is it ethical? For that matter, is it legal? The story is probably interesting in a small way, but it's not like most people that wanted to know wouldn't know where drugs were readily available in certain areas of big cities, and it's not the calibre of story that will win a national journalism award. Small-time street pushers are not the real issue, though in 'moral panic' terms they are an easy tabloid TV target. International criminal syndicates, on the other hand, are a different matter. Serious investigative journalists say hidden cameras are necessary for them to do their job in exposing major wrongdoing. But their role is not to aid in the commission of crimes by soliciting the sale of drugs in the fictitious case outlined above. What happened to the journalist as independent observer and reporter of facts? Under what circumstances should a journalist – no matter how high profile they are – take such an active (and deceptive) role in getting a story?

Black, Steele and Barney believe that journalists too often use forms of deception and misrepresentation as a shortcut in their reporting and suggest that hidden cameras or any form of deception should be used judiciously and rarely (2005, p. 167). Their American colleague, David Gordon, is even stronger in his condemnation of those who use deceptive practices:

> Journalists who say that deception is the 'only' way to get a story usually mean that they are unwilling or, in a short-staffed newsroom, unable to put in the time and effort to dig out the story properly.
>
> (Gordon et al. 2011, p. 521)

Black, Steele and Barney (2005) have provided a useful checklist of criteria, all of which need to be fulfilled, they say, to justify a lie or deception:

- When the information sought is of profound importance.
- When all other alternatives to obtaining the same information have been exhausted.
- When the journalists involved are willing to fully and openly discuss the nature of the deception and the reason for it to those involved and to the public.
- When the individuals involved and their news organisation apply excellence, through outstanding craftsmanship as well as the commitment of time and funding needed to fully pursue the story.
- When the harm prevented by the information revealed through deception outweighs any harm caused by the act of deception.
- When the journalists involved have conducted a meaningful, collaborative, and deliberate decision making process.

(Black, Steele and Barney 2005, p. 163)

This list underlines our insistence that the public interest test must be rigorously applied in any decision-making process where deception is being considered as a journalistic tool.

Phone hacking – unethical *and* illegal!

It probably goes without saying, given the coverage of the *News of the World* phone hacking scandal in the United Kingdom in 2011–2012 and the widespread repercussions in the form of huge payouts to many of those who had their phones hacked, the quick closure of the offending newspaper, the arrests of journalists and others, and the Leveson inquiry into media ethics in the UK, but we will say it anyway: phone hacking is illegal and unethical. It is gaining information by deception and involves a massive invasion of people's privacy. Here we both agree: the motives of the *NoW* in phone hacking and paying police for information do not meet the public interest test.

But is the relatively-recent case involving the *Melbourne Age* any different? They didn't hack into a phone, but rather a database. Charges were laid against three *Age* journalists accusing them with unlawful access to restricted data (*Charges against journalists 'an attack on press freedom'* 2013). The case involved the reporters gaining access to information in an Australian Labor Party (ALP) database on the eve of the 2010 Victorian state election (Ferguson, J. and Le Grand 2012). The journalists were accused of accessing the database, which contains confidential information about voters, without permission and while the paper admitted gaining access to the database, they said it was not hacking since they had been given the password to the database by a party worker (Ferguson, J. and Le Grand 2012). In August 2013 the three reporters admitted to unauthorised access of the ALP database, but escaped a conviction when they were placed in a court-ordered diversion programme (Deery 2013).

Plagiarism is theft – copyright and journalism ethics

Copyright is about protecting someone's intellectual property, particularly if it is economically valuable. It is the law of copyright that makes plagiarism an issue about stealing someone else's work. Copyright is basically a legal issue, but there are ethical aspects. An important distinction that journalists need to understand is that copyright does not exist in the idea, but in the expression of that idea (Pearson and Polden 2011, pp. 359–60). In other words, there is nothing to stop journalists from getting information or ideas for stories from other sources and then creating their own version of that information. They do it all the time. Back when Roger was at the ABC one staff member was assigned to watch the commercial TV news programmes at six o'clock (*Seven and Nine*) to ensure the ABC had the main stories that the opposition was covering. If they had missed a big story, they had the best part of an hour to match it for the main 7 o'clock ABC news bulletin. TV Current Affairs programmes are forever 'ripping off' each other's ideas for stories, if only to discredit them. So copyright does not reside in the facts of the story, but rather in their form of expression in a particular newspaper, magazine of broadcast form.

That's the case with the basic facts or idea for a story (or the circumstances), but how much of a person's original created work can you 'take', even with attribution, before it would be considered an infringement of copyright? Neither of the authors are lawyers. We suggest you seek legal advice. There is the 'fair dealing' clause, which allows the use of some part of original work for journalistic purposes. It also protects university lecturers using original material in class to make a point. It's the same clause that allows the TV stations to run excerpts from another station's programme, or highlights of various sports events in their TV news programmes, even though the 'opposition' might have paid a billion dollars for exclusive rights to the live broadcasts of a particular sport. Discussion of copyright and its possible infringement leads us to one of the more serious ethical dilemmas, which seems to have become more prevalent in recent times – at least more people are being caught out – that of plagiarism.

The MEAA Code of Ethics is clear enough:

> Clause 10: Do not plagiarise.

> (*MEAA Code of Ethics* 1999)

The US Society of Professional Journalists (*Code of Ethics* 1996) and the British National Union of Journalists (*NUJ Code of Conduct* 2011) have similar clauses in their professional codes of ethics. Plagiarism is the use of another person's work without attribution. It's copying their original material, perhaps changing a word here or there, but basically reproducing their work and calling it your own. We are amazed that it happens so frequently nowadays. With the modern technology available through the Internet, what makes a journalist think they will get away with it? University students know that if they submit their essays through a program like Turnitin that any plagiarism will be easily detected. There are plenty of members of the public who might vaguely recognise a particular sentence or phrase in a story, then type it into Google and find the original. The ABC's *Media Watch* regularly exposes plagiarists on its programme. In late 2012, it was *The Sydney Morning Herald* columnist, Tanveer Ahmed, who was accused by the programme of using the work of others without attribution (Meade 2012d). About a month later, Ahmad wrote an op-ed piece for *The Australian* in which he admitted he'd been a plagiarist 'for the past couple of years' (2012). In earlier years, various presenters of *Media Watch* have 'outed' former *SMH* computer editor, Gareth Powell, broadcaster Alan Jones (who plagiarised sections from a Frederick Forsyth novel for a column he wrote for a Sunday paper years ago), and right-wing *Sydney Daily Telegraph* columnist Piers Akerman for using slabs of an Israeli Defence Force news release (Hirst and Patching 2007, p. 222).

But they were not alone. One of the biggest plagiarism/deception cases in recent years involved *The New York Times* and the serial plagiarist and fabricator, Jayson Blair. *The Times* is one of the most respected papers in the US, yet on 11 May 2003, on page one, below their slogan 'All the news that's fit to print' was an embarrassing headline and admission (*Correcting the record: Times reporter who resigned leaves long trail of deception* 2003). The resulting four-broadsheet-page, 7,000-word investigation showed errors in half of the 73 articles Blair had written over the previous seven months (Dalton 2003). We'll revisit this case in discussing fabrication below. *The Times* had another reporter resign after being accused of plagiarism in 2010. Wall Street and finance reporter Zachery Kouwe resigned after the paper said he had 'reused language from *The Wall Street Journal*, Reuters and other sources without attribution or acknowledgement' in a number of business stories over the previous year (New York Times *reporter accused of plagiarism resigns* 2010). Another example comes from an American paper which admitted a long-time reporter had been fabricating the names of people in dozens of stories dating back to 1998. A 20-year veteran with the paper, Karen Jeffrey, admitted fabricating people in some stories, and giving others false names. An internal review in the paper had been unable to find 69 people in 34 stories since 1998, when the paper began archiving stories electronically. She no longer works for the paper (Cape Cod Times *reporter fabricated sources* 2012). We continue to be amazed at the seniority and public profile of some of the journalists who get caught plagiarising other people's stories, or passing off barely-disguised media releases as their own work. Also among the more recent offenders is the *Time* magazine writer and CNN host Fareed Zakaria, who was suspended by both employers after admitting plagiarising sections of a column he wrote for *Time* in August, 2012 on gun control (Haughney 2012). A year earlier, another respected 'journal of record', *The Washington Post*, suspended three-time Pulitzer Prize-winning reporter, Sari Horwitz, for three months for plagiarising material about the shooting of US Congresswoman Gabrielle Giffords from another US newspaper, the *Arizona Republic* (*Report Copied* 2011). *The Post*'s ombudsman, Patrick

Pexton, wrote at the time that plagiarism was 'one of journalism's unforgiveable sins' (2011). He added:

> My sympathies are with the *Arizona Republic* and Dennis Wagner, the reporter who did the initial work on the story that was most plagiarized (*sic*). But the damage is done, and it is lingering. It puts another chink in the already thin armour of journalism.
>
> (Pexton 2011)

Horwitz blamed deadline pressure for her lapse in judgment. Pexton put it down to the pressure that 'today's minute-by-minute, Web-driven, do-more-with-less news culture puts on reporters and editors' (2011). Even interns get into trouble. In July, 2012, America's National Public Radio (NPR) had to delete a story from its website – an intern's first-hand account of witnessing a public execution in Kabul, Afghanistan – after learning that parts of it were plagiarised from a story published more than a decade earlier (Myers 2012).

There are two other aspects of plagiarism that deserve mention – the verbatim use of public relations news releases without accreditation, and the practice known as 'patchwriting'. The news release issue was highlighted in 2012, when an American reporter sued his employer for defamation after being fired for publishing news releases verbatim in his column. He claimed his editors knew about the practice and that plagiarising news releases was common practice at the paper, *The Kansas City Star* (Wolper 2012). As Allan Wolper wrote at the time, lifting news releases verbatim and publishing without attribution is 'a sin against readers' and 'a violation of the public trust the media love to talk about' (2012). No public relations consultant is going to complain if their releases appear word-for-word in the paper. Reproducing them without attribution gives them the implied credibility of the newspaper. But most would expect some form of attribution (Wolper 2012). As we will see in a later chapter, much of what fills the columns of the daily newspapers in Australia originates from media releases.

According to Rebecca Moore Howard, Professor of Writing and Rhetoric at Syracuse University, 'patchwriting' is the practice where rather than copying a statement word for word, the writer re-arranges phrases and changes tenses, but relies heavily on the vocabulary and syntax of the source material (McBride 2012a). Discussion of the practice arose after an editor of the *Columbia Spectator*, the daily student newspaper of Columbia University, New York, home of the prestigious journalism school, was fired (Beaujon 2012). Three paragraphs in one of her stories were 'largely identical' to, or as the Editor termed it 'closely mirrored', those in a *New York Times* piece, and other parts of the *Spectator* version involved what was called 'clumsy rewriting' (Beaujon 2012). Professor Howard said 'patchwriting' is common among tertiary students and journalists and is often a failed attempt at paraphrasing. She said it's not quite plagiarism, but it's not original writing either (quoted in McBride 2012a). And we say it's not quite ethical, either.

One simple lesson to learn from this litany of plagiarists (and variations on the theme) is that if you do succumb to plagiarism, we can guarantee you will most likely be caught. So don't.

And you can't just make it up, either

We mentioned briefly above the so-called 'Jayson Blair Affair' in reference to plagiarism, one of his major sins. But the reporter didn't stop at taking others' material and calling it his own. He filed stories from places he never visited, quoted people he never talked to, and described details he never saw (Rosen 2003). Blair selected details from photographs to create the impression he had been somewhere or seen someone, when he had not. An African American, Blair had been a *Times* prodigy who had charmed and dazzled the right people on a rapid rise from cocky college student to national reporter – a position that enabled him to 'create' stories (Rosen 2003). By an amazing twist of fate, it was another former *News York Times* intern, Macerena Hernandez, who helped bring him down. She'd written a story for the *San Antonio Express-News* about the death of a soldier in the Iraq war, and after reading Blair's version of the story became convinced he had 'stolen' her story and dobbed him in. Before the Jayson Blair affair, the best-known case of fabrication involved the *Washington Post*. Remember it was the *Post*'s investigation into the Watergate Affair that played a major role in forcing President Nixon to resign – a high point in modern American journalism. But it was another *Post* reporter, Janet Cooke, who wrote a story in 1980 titled 'Jimmy's World' in which she looked at drug-taking among young children. Cooke claimed to have interviewed an eight-year-old heroin addict called Jimmy. The story caused a furore, and won Cooke a Pulitzer Prize. But no sooner had she taken delivery of the prize than she and her embarrassed newspaper had to announce they were returning the award – the story was a fabrication. The paper admitted there was no 'Jimmy', he represented a composite of child addicts, and Cooke's story was fiction (Hirst and Patching 2007, p. 223). Another American serial fabricator was Stephen Glass from the *New Republic* magazine. His story is told in the 2003 film, *Shattered Glass*, and is worth watching. The *Chicago Sun-Times* sacked Paige Wiser for fabrication in 2011 – she was covering a 'Glee Live!' concert and her review included details of a song that was never performed and another that she didn't stay at the concert long enough to hear (Tenore 2011a). A 17-year veteran of the paper, Wiser said she'd left the concert early because one of her children, who was at the concert with her, started to get sick.

There have been fabricated stories in Australia, too, like the one about four single mothers in Victoria each with 12 children who were supposedly being paid about $4,300 a week in the mid-90s in welfare payments. Four women with 48 children between them? That should have rung some alarm bells somewhere in the newsroom. Well, it did, not at the offending tabloid, Melbourne's *Herald Sun*, but at *Media Watch*. The Federal Department of Social Security, which made welfare payments, could find no record of the four women and wrote to the paper demanding a correction, but none was forthcoming (Hirst and Patching 2007, p. 223). Then there was the famous fabricated *Today Tonight* chase of the former corporate high-flyer and Seven Network owner Christopher Skase through the streets of Majorca, which turned out to be the streets of a distant Barcelona.

There are no excuses for plagiarising or fabricating a news item – news is fundamentally about truth and accuracy. Years ago, reporters and editors might have thought they could get away with it, but not nowadays. Someone will find the original quote or challenge the veracity of the story – online media sites nowadays welcome comments on their stories. Not so welcome perhaps would be either a comment that they pinched the story from someone else, or the suggestion that they might have made it up. One heartening thing, though, as all the examples above show, is that plenty of the 'perps' are getting caught, often in the glaring spotlight of unwanted publicity. Of course, not all of them are found out. While a degree of fame and fortune awaits the dishonest, the temptation is always there to cut corners and invent facts or sources, just to get a story. Our advice is: don't do it!

Freebies, junkets, and compromising positions, like conflict of interest

The issue of gifts and inducements offered to journalists to influence their writing is also covered in the Code of Ethics:

> Clause 4: Do not allow personal interest, or any belief, commitment, payment, gift or benefit to undermine your accuracy, fairness or independence.
>
> *(MEAA Code of Ethics* 1999)

In practice, though, the rules are regularly set and broken in-house by journalists and their editors. Many journalists see nothing wrong with accepting some 'freebies' from sources. After all, they take their sources to lunch from time to time to 'pump them' for information (if they have the luxury of time, that is) and may send them a 'bottle of something' along with the corporate Christmas card as an annual 'thank you' for services rendered. So why not let the source offer the same hospitality? And why not accept the fancy folder, pen, notepad etc. and hospitality at a conference? These 'freebies' seem petty, but there is not such a big jump between that and the free tickets to the football or live theatre, the autographed copy of the star's new book, and further down the spiral to cheap holidays or free trips. Nowadays mainstream media pay their own way, and have their own policies about accepting gifts. Basically, you can keep the pen and notepad, but anything worth more than $15 to $20 has to be handed in. What happens to the more valuable 'freebies' varies, but usually the reporter can either 'buy' it for a reasonable price, or it is auctioned in the newsroom, with the proceeds in either case usually going to charity. But what if you are offered a free trip to inspect a new mine site and the mining company says they'll put you up in a nearby city in a fancy hotel for a couple of days 'while you get a feel for the project and what it will mean for the area'? Any such offers of free flights and free accommodation are usually acknowledged nowadays in the coverage. That's not the problem. It is how do you feel a few months down the track when someone who entertained you on the visit to the mine contacts you asking for a favour, perhaps asking you to overlook an unfavourable story? We're not singling out mining enterprises; tourist destinations often offer free flights and accommodation in return for favourable coverage. Do you feel at all beholden to the source? It is an issue we discuss in relation to your dealings with sources in chapter 9.

Accepting a freebie is one type of compromising position. Another is a conflict of interest. At its very basic, it's when, say, you are asked to write a story about a problem at a service club of which you are a member. Your membership may well compromise your objectivity – particularly if the story is going to show your club in a less-than-favourable light. In such cases you need to make your Chief of Staff or Editor aware of the potential conflict of interest and let them decide a course of action. They should hand the story on to someone else who is not a member of that club.

One of the doyennes of American broadcasting, Barbara Walters, found herself in a difficult position in mid-2012 when a London paper disclosed she had attempted to use her influence to further the career of a former aide to Basher al-Assad, the President of Syria, who at the time was fighting an internal insurrection (Hughes and Sanches 2012). Walters had tried to help the girl, who was also the daughter of Syria's UN ambassador, gain a position at an Ivy League American university and an internship with Piers

Morgan on CNN (Sanchez 2012). She was not successful, but Walters said she regretted the conflict of interest her actions created (Malone 2012). The girl had helped Walters organise an interview with Assad in 2011 and when it didn't turn out the way Assad had hoped, he fired the girl and she reached out to Walters for help in finding another job (Malone 2012). If the matriarch of American broadcast journalism can find herself – in trying to help someone who'd helped her – in the middle of a conflict of interest, it is a cautionary tale for us all.

Before we leave the topic of deception, what about when the roles are reversed, and the media is the one that is deceived?

The media can be deceived, too

The 'Whitehaven hoax' in early 2013 was a timely reminder to journalists of the folly of always wanting to be first with the news without checking its veracity. A fictitious news release, purportedly from one of Australia's 'big four' banks, the ANZ, announced it had withdrawn $1.2 billion in funding for mining and explora-tion company Whitehaven Coal (quoted in Chambers and Moran 2013). Investors rushed to dump shares in the company – one of the nation's biggest coalminers – temporarily stripping 9 per cent, or more than $300 million, from the company's sharemarket value. Anti-coal environmental activist, Jonathon Moylan, created a dummy ANZ media release template complete with fictitious website, online email inbox and media contacts (including his own mobile number as the main ANZ media contact) and sent it to journalists (Swan, J. et al. 2013). The story appeared on *The Australian Financial Review* and other Fairfax Media websites after being circulated by the news service, Australian Associated Press (Chambers and Moran 2013). Mr Moylan said he received only one media call trying to verify the release – from a *Sydney Morning Herald* reporter – to whom he impersonated the fictitious ANZ media contact to give the impression the news release was real (Chambers and Moran 2013). Once the hoax was discovered and the media websites removed their stories, Mr Moylan began answering his mobile as himself and admitted he was behind the stunt. The regulatory authority, the Australian Securities and Investments Commission (ASIC), said that any prosecution of Mr Moylan could lead to fines of nearly $500,000 and up to 10 years' jail (Walker, C. and Cubby 2013). But we're more interested in the lessons to be learned by journalists. The publication of the hoax media release drew criticism from the body representing investors (*Media to blame* 2013) and Australia's share market operator (Ker 2013). The Shareholders' Association's Stephen Mayne (a journalist and founder of the *Crikey* news website), said the media needed to accept its share of the blame for the flurry of selling caused by the fake news release:

> All the selling didn't happen because of the press release, it happened because the journalists didn't check the press release, didn't check with ANZ, didn't check that there wasn't an ASX (stock exchange) announcement and that then triggered the panic selling, albeit very briefly.
>
> (Quoted in *Media to blame* 2013)

The Australian Stock Exchange's chief compliance officer, Kevin Lewis, called on the media to slow the speed at which their websites publish news to ensure the financial markets are not affected by false reports (Ker 2013). He said the media should consider 'an appropriate level of self-regulation':

> I think they may be trying to get information out too quickly, without subjecting it to the same editorial oversight and verification processes as their print cousins.
>
> (Quoted in Ker 2013)

It is a cautionary tale about news delivery in the digital age and the problems that arise when the 'rush to publish' overrides the normal information checking and verification processes that are so important in journalism.

And don't put it past Governments to try to hoax the media, too. North Korea was caught out 'Photoshopping' an image to double the number of hovercraft in a military exercise in the early stages of their aggressive posturing towards the United States in March/April, 2013 (McElroy 2013). The Iranians had been at it, too, releasing a 'doctored' image of a radar-dodging aircraft flying over snow-covered mountains a month earlier after aviation experts questioned whether it could fly (McElroy 2013).

There's a long history of media hoaxes – one involved Rupert Murdoch buying fake Hitler Diaries in 1983 (*Rupert Murdoch at Leveson: Hitler Diaries 'major mistake'* 2012). The British tabloid, the *Daily Mirror,* was hoaxed in 2004 into publishing photos purporting to be British soldiers torturing an Iraqi detainee (in the aftermath of the notorious Abu Ghraib prisoner abuse by American soldiers). The paper was forced into a humiliating front page apology (*Editor sacked over 'hoax' photos* 2004). Many others are good-natured and usually revolve around far-fetched stories on April 1 each year. The BBC had a history of hoaxing their audiences – in 1957 they aired a spoof documentary about 'spaghetti trees' in Switzerland and in 1965 interviewed a London 'University Professor' who said he had perfected 'smell-o-vision' which would allow viewers to smell scents in the studio from the comfort of their own homes! Obviously such hoaxes wouldn't last long in the twenty-first century – too many would google them. The bloggers and Twitter would have a field day. But there is a serious side to media hoaxes that should not be overlooked. Always check everything! And remember the adage, 'if it seems too good to be true, it probably is'.

Conclusion

This chapter has pulled together discussion of a number of areas where the behaviour of individuals or media organisations could be classified as either ethically suspect or simply unacceptable. We began by examining some of the memorable 'stings' by the Fake Sheikh, the British investigative journalist, Mazher Mahmood, and putting them to the 'public interest test' – were his actions justified? Discussion followed on how far the journalist should be prepared to go to get a story, and how, sometimes, it is the pressure of competition, deadlines and individual egos that cause a small minority of journalists to cut ethical corners. 'Do you always identify yourself as a journalist?' is a question that many would answer with 'it depends on the situation'. We also canvassed the ethics of using hidden cameras and recording devices in the pursuit of stories. Then came discussion of two areas that are more clear-cut ethical 'no no's – plagiarism and fabrication. The final section of the chapter dealt with the potential for conflicts of interest raised by freebies, junkets and the like. The next chapter tackles the problems associated with chequebook journalism, a practice seen by many in the media as 'just another business expense'.

Case Study 1: Johann Hari's catalogue of deception

At the height of the ongoing revelations about the *News of the World* scandal in 2011, one of the rising stars in British journalism, Johann Hari, admitted what bloggers had been suggesting for some time – he was a plagiarist and a fabricator (Hari 2011). Following in the footsteps of the serial plagiarists and/or fabricators mentioned above, Janet Cooke from *The Washington Post* in the early 80s, Stephen Glass from the *New Republic* in the 90s and, of course Jayson Blair in the early part of this century, Hari is the poster-boy for all that is bad in journalism in the first part of the second decade of the twenty-first century. He made a lengthy apology in his employer's publication, *The Independent*, in which he said he was arrogant and stupid and sought to justify his behaviour. He said that, when he interviewed someone, points that 'sounded perfectly clear when you heard them being spoken often don't translate to the page' (Hari 2011). So if the interviewee had made a similar point in their writing, or when they were speaking to someone else, he would use those words instead. He also admitted to creating a fictitious username to edit his own Wikipedia entry and to smear those of others with whom he had clashed. One he changed was that of a former Editor at *The New Statesman*, Cristina Odone, under whom he had worked and who had challenged his quotes (Foreman 2011). Initially, his supporters dismissed the claims, but eventually he came clean. His punishment? He took unpaid leave from *The Independent* to attend, at his own expense, a journalism course in the United States. He later announced he would not be returning to the paper (Urquhart 2012).

Questions for discussion:

- Why wasn't he sacked on the spot? Read some of the reaction to his apology (*The depressing tale of Johann Hari* 2011; Foreman 2011; Odone 2011) and see what you think.
- Read his 'personal apology' (Hari 2011). Are you convinced?
- He actually seems to be blaming his interviewees, not himself, for not giving him useable quotes. The *Economist* blogger, who goes under the name of Bagehot, makes the valid point that if you interview someone famous, important, witty or wise and they only say boring and incoherent things, it is mostly your fault (*The depressing tale of Johann Hari* 2011). What's been your experience?
- As part of his defence, Hari says he was 'mortified' at what he'd done to people's Wikipedia entries because 'it breaches the most basic ethical rule: don't do to others what you don't want them to do to you' (Hari 2011). Do you agree?
- In one of the articles cited above (Tenore 2011a), the writer from the Poynter Institute, Mallary Jean Tenore, asks whether newsrooms in the United States have relaxed standards and sanctions for fabrication and plagiarism. Read the article and discuss her findings.

Case Study 2: US NPR – hidden camera sting backfires and a 'shock jock' opens his mouth to change feet

The secret recording of a media sting operation in the United States in March, 2011, while it led to the resignation of a fundraiser and a senior executive of their National Public Radio, also re-opened the debate on the ethics of such techniques (Hausman 2011). In this case, a fundraiser for NPR (like the Community Broadcasting Association of Australia and reliant, partly, on raising funds from the public) was videotaped by two men posing as potential donors. Prodded on by the hoaxers, the fundraiser made disparaging remarks about the Tea Party conservatives in the US.

The Republican Presidential candidate in 2012, Mitt Romney, was secretly recorded within six weeks of election day criticising much of President Obama's traditional voter base in what became known as the '47 per cent speech', so it can happen to anyone, nowadays.

The difference here, though, is that it was a media sting, rather than the person simply 'putting their foot in it' at what they thought was a private fundraising gathering. In the United States they call it 'entrapment journalism', and various media commentators had plenty to say in the wake of that incident.

Los Angeles Times entertainment writer, James Rainey, described the NPR sting, and another earlier involving the Governor of Wisconsin, Scott Walker, as 'a load of hooey, brought to you by your friendly purveyors of "ambush journalism", secret recordings and ham acting designed to draw out the worst in others' (2011). He blames 'the influx of an untold number of new voices into journalism as computers and the Internet have lowered the cost of entry to zero' (Rainey 2011).

The *Philadelphia Post*'s Larry Mendte (2011) attacked the broadcast media for using the secretly recorded material. He said that the story was the sort of entrapment journalism that would not be tolerated by the mainstream networks, noting that CBS, NBC, ABC, CNN and Fox all have strict rules against reporters misrepresenting themselves to get a story.

Another aspect of this dilemma arose in Australia in September, 2012, when aging radio 'shock jock' Alan Jones was secretly recorded telling a Liberal (conservative) Party dinner that the father of then Prime Minister Julia Gillard 'died of shame' because of the political 'lies' his daughter told (*Jones says PM's father 'died of shame'* 2012). Advertisers deserted the station Jones works for, one of his sponsors took back his luxury car, and the broadcaster was forced into a humiliating public apology. Google it if you want to read the public reaction to Jones' comments. But we're interested in how *The Sunday Telegraph* got the comments. A News Limited journalist, Jonathon Marshall, attended the $100-a-head (for students) function and recorded the offensive comments. The comments were made in a speech at a private function, not from his usual soapbox of a breakfast radio programme. The broadcaster said he thought the function was 'private' and 'not reportable' (Leys and Kelly 2012), but it had been advertised as a public event. Marshall said he had bought a ticket for the event, like any member of the public was able to do. Organisers said the reporter had ignored a request at the start of the function for journalists to declare themselves. He denied any such request was made (Leys and Kelly 2012).

Questions for discussion:

- What rationale would the likes of NBC, CBS and CNN, etc. have used to justify using the material?
- What do you think of 'entrapment journalism'? Is it justified? When?
- Would you do it? To whom?
- Shouldn't someone feel 'safe' from the media's prying cameras at such a function?
- Did they meet the public interest test?
- What of the argument that 'it shows them like they really are'?
- Put yourself in the fundraiser's shoes – he ended up losing that job and another he was due to take up shortly thereafter (Hausman 2011) – wouldn't you feel betrayed?
- What is your reaction to Jones' comments about the PM's father?
- Should he have felt safe that his comments wouldn't make it to 'the outside world'?
- If a request is made, would you declare yourself as a journalist at such a function?
- Does it ever matter to journalists these days whether a function is 'private' or 'public'?
- Does the Jones story meet the public interest test?

5   Do you want lies with that?

The problems with chequebook journalism

The law of the market – you get what you pay for

Put simply, chequebook journalism is buying exclusive rights to a story in an effort to improve newspaper or magazine sales or broadcast ratings. It is common in mainstream media nowadays, especially on commercial current affairs television programmes and among gossip magazines and some tabloid newspapers. While it has a long history among the British 'red top' newspapers, and American so-called supermarket tabloids and, to a lesser extent, in television current affairs (especially stories of the 'kiss-and-tell', sex scandal variety), and is commonplace in TV current affairs programmes and gossip magazines in Australia, serious media in the main have resisted the temptation to 'buy the news'.

The late John Avieson, one of the founders of journalism education in Australia, put the argument against opening the corporate chequebook for exclusivity succinctly more than two decades ago. He wrote that while the media trumpets the cause of freedom of the press and the public's right to know, 'when they pay people to keep that information out of rival media, they are using their wealth to subvert the rights of the people they are supposed to champion' (Avieson 1992, p. 45).

American media ethicist John Kittross says chequebook journalism 'destroys the credibility of *all* (his italics) journalism' (Gordon et al. 2011, p. 494). He suggests an alternative to buying the news:

> If media organisations really want to spend money for news, they can always hire more reporters, pay them better, and give them more newsgathering resources.
> (Kittross in Gordon et al. 2011, p. 494)

We've talked in earlier chapters about the economic fault line in modern journalism – the quest for profit overriding the public information functions of the media. Chequebook journalism demonstrates this fault line in action and it taints the information it buys.

The biggest cheque to date …

The benchmark for chequebook journalism in Australia was set in 2006 when the Nine Network and the publications of its stable-mate, Publishing and Broadcasting, *Woman's Day*, the *Australian Women's Weekly* and the now defunct news magazine, *The Bulletin*, apparently paid Todd Russell and Brant Webb $2.6 million for the rights to the story of their 14-day ordeal underground during the Beaconsfield mine cave-in in Tasmania (*Cash for Comment* 2010). There was speculation at the time that the figure might have been as high as $3 million since the Seven Network and *New Idea* were believed to have offered $2.75 million (cited in Bainbridge 2009, p. 63). Regardless of the precise amount, and history seems to have settled on the lower figure, it's still a huge sum, when most 'exclusives' in Australia tend to go for a tenth of the lower amount, or less.

The huge payday for the surviving miners was seen as a turning point in Australian media – as confirmation of the 'increasing tabloidization and commodification of news in Australia and the impact of celebrity on news production' (Bainbridge 2009, p. 44). It was the first major demonstration of what has since become 'the norm' – the buying of news exclusives to share across multiple media platforms.

In April, 2010, it was claimed by 'other' media outlets that *New Idea* had paid the ex-wife of Melbourne gangland figure Carl Williams, Roberta, $250,000 to talk about her grief over the crime boss's murder in prison (Jackson, S. 2010b). But 'well-placed' sources told *The Australian*'s media section that the figure was 'well under' $100,000, perhaps as low at $50,000 (Jackson, S. 2010b). A 'sidebar' accompanying Sally Jackson's story chronicled some of the bigger cheques various newsmakers have supposedly received over the years. Second highest was the one million dollars paid by *Woman's Day* to tennis star Lleyton Hewitt and his former soap star wife, Bec, for a year's exclusive stories about them, including the birth of their daughter, Mia (*Cash for Comment* 2010). Australian construction engineer Douglas Wood was said to have sold the exclusive of his 47-day ordeal as a hostage in Iraq to the Ten Network, in 2005 for $400,000 (*Cash for Comment* 2010). The sidebar also listed another five stories that supposedly sold over the past 20 years for between $200,000 and $250,000. It was pointed out at the time that the main two women's magazines had weekly sales of between 330,000 and 410,000. To recoup the cost of a $100,000 interview an extra 25,000 copies would have to be sold, and a big exclusive was unlikely to bump sales more than 20,000 to 30,000 (Jackson, S. 2010b).

A media feeding frenzy ...

Few stories attract the media chequebooks faster in Australia than a person surviving a shark attack. When abalone diver, Eric Nerhus, was attacked by a three-metre white pointer off Eden in southern New South Wales in 2007, he had some story to tell:

> In an instant the shark snapped its jaws around Mr Nerhus's head with such force it crushed his face mask and broke his nose. He fought to break free but Mr Nerhus's torso was then pulled into the shark's mouth and it bit into the diver's sides.
> (Pandaram and Levy 2007)

He survived, a marine expert suggesting that the shark had mistaken the diver's wetsuit for a seal, and once the 500-kilogram shark realised its mistake, it spat him out (Pandaram and Levy 2007). Another feeding frenzy followed soon after – from the media seeking exclusive rights to Eric's story. The Nine Network and *Woman's Day* combined to buy Nerhus's story of survival (he stabbed the shark in the eye with his abalone knife and fought his way free) for something approaching $200,000 (Bodey and Ong 2007).

In another case, when a surfer claimed he'd been attacked by a shark off Mona Vale, one of Sydney's northern beaches in February, 2010, the media were again all over the story. Within an hour, the sky above the beach was 'buzzing with news helicopters, the car park thick with camera crews' (Nettle 2010). A New South Wales Health spokesman told the ABC that the man had sold his story to Channel Nine by the time his wife had driven him to hospital (Rubinsztein-Dunlop 2010). Unfortunately for the network, and fortunately for the surfer, in this case the shark turned out to be a relatively harmless wobbegong (Nettle 2010).

But the abalone diver's leap 'from the jaws of a great white to the loving embrace of a cash-happy media organisation' as it was characterised at the time (Bodey and Ong 2007), raised the spectre of another chequebook-driven current affairs television ratings war as the 2007 ratings season approached. The Seven Network's director of news and current affairs, Peter Meakin, whose network obviously lost out in the bidding, said: 'I'm worried that it's all going to get out of control again' (Bodey and Ong 2007).

Again? When has it been 'in control' in recent times? Buying stories is an integral part of the commercial current affairs television's and gossip magazines' modus operandi.

Chequebook journalism 2013 style

Three examples emerged in early 2013 that demonstrated other aspects of chequebook journalism. Australian radio and television personality, Chrissie Swan, offered to buy photos showing her smoking while pregnant to prevent them from being published in a gossip magazine. Her management was reported to have bid $53,000 before losing out to *Woman's Day* who secured the shots for $55,000. Her management said that they had tried to buy the pictures to protect Ms Swan's children from ever seeing their mother smoking as she has never smoked in front of her children or at home (Hornery 2013a). It was reported at the time that it was not the first time that the subject of embarrassing photos had spent large sums of money to buy the photos and keep them out of the gossip magazines (Hornery 2013a).

A week later photos emerged of the Duchess of Cambridge on holiday in the Caribbean in a bikini showing her 'baby bump'. *Woman's Day* was reported to have paid about $150,000 for the Australian rights to the photos (Hornery 2013b). Several other magazines around the world were believed to have paid large amounts for the photos and others in Australia were believed to have made offers. The British media were restraining themselves (as most did in another couple of instances involving the young Royals, discussed in chapter 10), honouring their 'gentlemen's agreement' not to invade the Royals' privacy. The Editor of *Woman's Day*, Fiona Connolly, offered an interesting rationale for publishing the photos. She said the Royal Family should be pleased with the photos because the Duchess looked happy and healthy after what the editor called a rocky start to her pregnancy (Woman's Day *editor defends decision to publish Catherine baby bump pictures* 2013). The magazine editor also said that the photos were taken by a 'tourist', not 'a professional photographer hiding in the bushes' (Hornery 2013b). She was suggesting that they were not the work of the so-called paparazzi, so in some way more acceptable. It's an argument we don't accept.

Finally, just to show that they are not all in it just for the money, British backpacker Sam Woodhead, 18, who was lost in outback Queensland for three days in February, 2013, sold the story of his survival to Britain's *Daily Mail* and his family said the money would be donated to the Australian search and rescue authorities (Dorsett and Seinor 2013). There is also a whiff of hypocrisy around the way news organisations treat examples of chequebook journalism by their rivals. Often they will 'pooh pooh' the story and try to spoil their competitor's scoop. But, once the story is in the public domain, they will have no qualms about running it themselves, often quoting the same sources or using the same paid-for images of the outlet they criticise.

Just another business expense …

Some media companies see chequebook journalism as just another business expense. They justify the payments because they believe exclusivity guarantees higher sales or ratings, and that improves their financial bottom line. This was certainly the case when Graham Johnson was working at *News of the World*. Payments to prostitutes or petty crims were regularly used to concoct stories and rarely challenged by the paper's bean-counters (Johnson, G. 2012). The counter argument is that the economic benefit is generally short-lived. Ratings for a particular commercial current affairs programme (or a couple of issues of the gossip magazine) might spike, but it rarely lasts. In the current economic climate, it is likely that those who hold the purse-strings might be asking serious questions before approving big payments for exclusive stories.

There are a number of other issues associated with chequebook journalism that need consideration. For instance, what effect will paying for stories have on an on-going court case? It's an issue we'll take up in the first case study at the end of this chapter, about the so-called 'Bali Boy'.

The amount paid for the 'exclusive' is rarely released publicly, but most figures quoted in the media by their opposition are educated guesses; in some cases because they had been involved in the bidding war, too, or spoke to a source that was. This is another of the murky aspects of chequebook journalism – that the money is often delivered 'under the table', the precise details unknown to the consumer (Cook 2011). Kittross says the public is among the losers in chequebook journalism – they get their news on the basis of price, not quality (Gordon et al. 2011, p. 495).

Another issue is that bought stories are often not as well researched and tested as those that result from investigative journalism or the everyday work of seasoned journalists. These stories may simply be written to the audience's perceived tastes – salacious and emotional. As Hull pointed out, there are no independent journalists there to test what the source is saying (Hull, C. 2006), just excitement in the office at the prospect of an 'exclusive' and a keenness to publish as soon as possible. While it might not pose a problem when the source is simply recounting what happened while they were trapped down a mine, or in the jaws of a Great White, it's another thing if the story has wider, perhaps political, implications. Is there an element of 'getting square' and making a packet at the same time? It is an issue we will return to in chapter 9.

What if the journalist spends months researching a major story and interviews the same person at length on a number of occasions? Does such a journalist – especially one working for a profitable magazine – really owe his sources nothing? (Boynton 2008). Should there be some leeway between the actions of the daily journalist offering money for that day's 'exclusive' and the long-form writer or essayist?

Do you want lies with that?

Whatever way you spin it, chequebook journalism compromises honest and ethical reporting. How do we know that what is being given 'exclusively' is the whole truth and nothing but the truth, as they say in those television courtroom dramas? Once a person is being paid for their story, they may feel an obligation to 'perform' to earn their fee. Who's to say they won't 'gild the lily' or exaggerate their story to give the paymaster value for money? Who's to say the reporter concerned won't 'coach' them on what might be the most quotable comments?

The *New York Times* recognised the problem in their ethics policy:

> We do not pay for interviews or unpublished documents. To do so would create an incentive for sources to falsify material and would cast into doubt the genuineness of much that we publish.
>
> (The New York Times Company Policy on Ethics in Journalism 2005)

Paying for exclusive rights is another nail in the coffin of journalistic credibility.

Unlike the United Kingdom, where anyone with a potential sex scandal can be guaranteed a big pay day, Australians seem to prefer 'worthy' people, like heroes, or someone who has survived an ordeal, to be financially rewarded by the media. Add to those mentioned above (the Beaconsfield miners and hostage victim Douglas Wood) others who have been paid handsomely for their stories – like James Scott, who survived 43 days lost in the Himalayas by living on chocolate bars (*Cash for Comment* 2010) – and you get the idea.

But there is a murkier side to the practice and it emerged in 2012 in the wake of the Australian franchise of *Sixty Minutes* paying for an interview with Gordon Wood, whose conviction for the murder of his girlfriend Caroline Byrne was quashed on appeal. The dead girl's father slammed the programme for allegedly paying Woods $200,000 for the interview (Fife-Yeomans 2012) and while his reaction may have been expected, a former New South Wales Attorney-General, John Hatzistergos, said the interview demonstrated 'the reckless indifference of Channel Nine to the suffering of the Byrne family' (cited in Maguire 2012). A similar public backlash followed *New Idea*'s decision in 2008 to pay disgraced AFL (Australian Rules Football) star Wayne Carey $180,000 to admit he had a cocaine habit and bashed his girlfriend (Byrne, F. 2008).

There is also the thought that the Nine Network paid so much to the Beaconsfield miners because they were 'ordinary Australians' that most viewers could relate to. At the same time, there was another amazing rescue – of three Torres Strait Islanders. Given up for dead, they managed to row their stricken vessel to within mobile phone range of Murray Island and send a text message for help (Hull, C. 2006). But there was no multi-million-dollar pay-day for them – little coverage in fact. While Russell and Webb were underground, about 200 Chinese miners died – and that story received scant coverage, too.

As we have seen, the main offenders in Australia are commercial TV current affairs programmes and women's magazines. Most newspapers, particularly broadsheets (or their re-born versions, compacts) don't pay for stories.

What do other codes of ethics and practice say?

The MEAA Code of Ethics covers chequebook journalism in clause 7:

> Do your utmost to ensure disclosure of any direct or indirect payment made for interviews, pictures, information or stories.
>
> (*MEAA Code of Ethics* 1999)

While the Code of Ethics does not preclude chequebook journalism, the report of the committee that reviewed the code in the 90s, and created the current version, suggested that disclosure of payments to sources should be automatic:

Whether the information bought was 'in the public interest' or merely 'of interest to the public', the audience should know the source was paid, directly or indirectly.

(MEAA 1997, p. 40)

Codes of ethics and conduct in the United States and Britain make no specific reference to paying for stories.

The code of conduct of the respected Melbourne paper, *The Age*, makes its position clear – if payment is made (and that should be avoided) it must be disclosed.

> *The Age* does not condone chequebook journalism. It will disclose any instance when it has paid for information. Payment for information should be avoided, unless an appropriate senior editor believes there is a strong public interest and there is no alternative to payment. In cases where payment is deemed by the Editor to be in the public interest, the fact of payment should be published.
>
> (*The Age Code of Conduct* 2002)

Cross-town rival, the *Herald and Weekly Times*, publisher of the highest-selling tabloid in the country, the *Herald Sun*, has a similar view:

> As a general principle, payment must not be made for interviews or information. In the event that demand for payment or other form of reward or compensation is made, agreement must not be given without the editor's approval.
>
> (*Editorial Code of Conduct* 2011)

So both the broadsheet and tabloid newspapers in Melbourne allow for chequebook journalism under certain circumstances. But it's a simple 'no' in the code of *The Age*'s sister, Fairfax publication, *The Sydney Morning Herald*:

> No payment shall be proffered to sources for interviews or access.
>
> (The Sydney Morning Herald *code of ethics* n.d.)

The latest version of the Australian ABC's editorial policies makes no specific mention of payment for stories (*ABC Editorial policies: Principles and Standards* 2011). An earlier, longer version of the ABC guidelines (*ABC Editorial Policies* 2007) said that as a matter of policy the ABC would not enter into financial competition with other media for access to news items or stories. It did note, however, that 'Interviewees whose contribution has required research, travel, a substantial commitment of time or other inconvenience may be paid a modest amount by way of compensation' (*ABC Editorial Policies* 2007, s. 5.4.2). Another clause in that section said that 'In countries where it is the lawful practice for interviewees, including politicians, to be paid, the ABC may follow that practice' (*ABC Editorial Policies* 2007).

Reporters and editors should ask themselves a number of important questions about the use of payments to sources before they head down that road:

- How important is the story and do we need it to beat the opposition? This is basically a commercial decision that should be made by the senior executives of the news organisation. Under the MEAA Code of Ethics, journalists are not obliged to accept directives they feel compromise their integrity or commitment to the Code.

- Is the source's information accurate, or is this an invitation to be ripped off? There have been instances where newspapers have paid for allegedly good stories only to find out later that they have been sold a dud, or a pack of lies.
- How much should news organisations and individual journalists be allowed to make undercover enquiries into the personal, business or political affairs of people in the 'public eye'. It's an important issue we take up in detail in chapter 10.
- Do the rights of so-called 'ordinary people' differ from those of public figures and celebrities (another major aspect of the privacy issue we explore in chapter 10).

The MEAA Ethics Review Committee considered chequebook journalism in their report (MEAA 1997, pp. 39–40), but could not reach a consensus on whether or not the practice was unethical.

One of the arguments for paying the Beaconsfield miners so much was the perception that they deserved it after what they'd been through. This is the mercenary way of viewing the issue and one, unfortunately, that seems to dominate the thinking of news executives, editors and reporters. In our view, it undermines some of the arguments against chequebook journalism because, after all, don't we all have this dubious 'right'? Chequebook journalism has also been involved in several cases where the British tabloids have tried to glean sensational and private material from sources within or close to the royal household. The case of Diana's butler, Paul Burrell, revealed how far the papers would go to secure a story on the royals (Coward 2007). It's not just royals who are subject to stories generated through payments and inducements; it is increasingly also the fate of people caught up in the news cycle inadvertently or tangentially (Amiel 2011).

So is it ever OK to pay for stories?

The committee that framed the current 12-point MEAA Code of Ethics (1999) thought there was an argument, in certain circumstances, for people to profit from their misfortune. Our view should be fairly obvious from the tone of the discussion in this chapter. We see no merit in the practice, but accept that it is a fact of life in tabloid television and gossip magazines. But while *A Current Affair* and *Today Tonight* vie for the next exclusive deal, and pull in *Woman's Day* or *New Idea* to share the financial burden, and they record audience spikes, the practice will likely continue.

But, to be balanced, here are the counter-arguments. Some people believe it is only fair that media organisations pay for stories if big stories translate into higher ratings or circulation, which in turn means increased revenue. Why shouldn't the people at the centre of the news benefit? After all, they created the increased revenue. Others argue that chequebook journalism allows people in the spotlight to tell their story in a controlled way (Haywood 2004), rather than being subjected to the chaos of 'all in' media conferences. Charities sometimes benefit from chequebook journalism when celebrities are paid for exclusive interviews and donate the money to charity.

Chequebook journalism in the UK

At the time of the big, Beaconsfield miners' payday, Crispin Hull described the difference between chequebook journalism in Australia and the United Kingdom as:

In Australia, television stations do the buying and the newspapers do not bother. In Britain it is the other way around.

(Hull, C. 2006)

He explained that the reason the papers in Australia don't bother to buy exclusives all that often is because most of them have no direct competition. With the exception of Sydney and Melbourne, Murdoch tabloids dominate most of the Australian capital cities. Additionally, many papers are home-delivered and pre-sold no matter what the content. In the UK, on the other hand, half a dozen national papers vie on the news-stands for commuters every morning and the one that offers the most sensational story will get bought (Hull, C. 2006). The so-called 'red top' tabloid newspapers in the United Kingdom have a long tradition of paying for stories – particularly those of the 'kiss-and-tell' variety involving a politician, movie star, pop icon or sporting celebrity.

A scandal involving the country's sporting 'royalty', David Beckham, was bound to see the chequebooks open quickly. Back in 2004, his personal assistant while he was playing soccer for Real Madrid in Spain, Rebecca Loos, was allegedly paid nearly $2 million (a huge amount from anyone's chequebook) for details of their affair. It was partly paid by the *News of the World* and for a tell-all television interview. Not unlike the early stages when Tiger Woods' idyllic life unravelled in 2009 (discussed in a case study below), within days an Australian model had come forward to be paid by the *NoW* to tell of her two-year affair with the soccer star that began in 2001, and yet another told the *People* newspaper she'd had sex with the soccer superstar in 2002 (*Beckham 'lover' nets $A1.9 million from claims: publicist* 2004). Like the Woods revelations, the 'kiss-and-tell' stories about Beckham temporarily shattered his image as the doting husband and devoted family man (English 2004).

Many another sporting star, politician, music, movie or film star has suffered the same fate at the hands of the British tabloids. In recent times, at the Murdoch tabloids at least, instead of paying individuals for their stories of 'sexcapades' and the like, reporters have resorted to hacking celebrities' phones to get their 'exclusives'. This led to News International – Murdoch's British arm – having to open the chequebooks again, this time paying for invading the privacy of mounting numbers of individuals.

At the other end of the importance and public interest scale, a former editor of *The Daily Telegraph* in the UK told the Leveson inquiry that the paper paid £150,000 for the information that led to the British MPs' expenses scandal (Gunter 2012).

Chequebook journalism in the USA

America, too, has a history of paying for stories but almost always in what are called the 'supermarket tabloids' – those magazine-style papers available at the checkouts, often with outlandish and unbelievable stories, like some in the infamous *National Enquirer*. But the practice has become more common in mainstream US media in recent years, particularly in the cut-throat area of television news and current affairs (does that sound familiar?). Journalism organisations that once refused to pay sources nowadays routinely write large cheques (or, as the Americans spell it, 'checks') for access to information (Moos 2011a). They call the payments 'licensing fees' and in return for the cheque they receive photos, videos, emails, or cell phone records but, as Julie Moos of America's respected ethics think-tank, the Poynter Institute, suggested: 'In the process they lose credibility and simultaneously strengthen the market for checkbook (*sic*) journalism'

(2011a). While there are legitimate 'licensing fees' paid to freelancers for photos and other material in the US, Moos says that using that label when simply paying sources for their story is a false claim (2011a). A year before Moos' article, the US equivalent of the MEAA, the Society of Professional Journalists, had issued what was called by one blogger a 'damning statement' blasting chequebook journalism (Strupp 2010). It followed the revelation that ABC News (US) had paid the family of a man accused of murdering his daughter a $200,000 'licensing fee' for videos of the dead girl. Not unlike the way the Nine Network spread the cost of the Beaconsfield miners exclusive among its stable-mate magazines, ABC News spread the videos around a number of their news, entertainment and current affairs programmes. *The New York Times* reported that the money found its way into the father's legal defence fund (Stelter and Carter 2011). ABC (US) would later announce it would no longer pay for interviews under the guise of 'licensing fees' (Moos 2011b). The Ethics Committee of the SPJ said it was troubled by how widespread the practice of paying sources had become (Strupp 2010). Writing for the prestigious *Columbia Journalism Review* the following year, after the renewed spate of payments, John Cook suggested that for American journalists chequebook journalism falls into the same moral category as paying for sex (2011). Cook told how he failed to break major stories, like the British Members of Parliament expenses scandal and the story of the former presidential candidate John Edwards having a 'love child' behind the back of his cancer-stricken wife, because others were prepared to pay sources for them (Cook 2011).

> But it's hard to argue that papers that abstain from payments are morally or professionally superior to those that do, when the latter are catching important stories that might otherwise go untold.
>
> (Cook 2011)

Maybe there is a case for some payment for 'important stories' – like the scandal involving members of the British Parliament cheating on their expenses – but they are all too often overshadowed by other stories obtained by the size of the cheque that amount to little more than audience titillation.

Conclusion

This chapter has looked at a number of issues associated with chequebook journalism. What some see as 'just another business expense' for the media, others suggest is rife with problems – like how do you ensure that the person selling their story doesn't 'gild the lily' (exaggerate) to give you value for money? We looked at various media organisations' policies on paying for stories, and found what would be expected – up-market publications rarely pay for stories and the so-called tabloid print and broadcast media are into it on almost a daily basis. We have also looked at what happens in the United States and the United Kingdom.

Case Study 1: Bali Boy

A 14-year-old Australian schoolboy from near Newcastle on the New South Wales Central Coast, was caught in late 2011 buying 3.6 grams of cannabis on a Bali street, and thus began a media frenzy in the worst traditions of tabloid journalism. He was named on Channel 9, and initially on Channel 7. He was named in the Murdoch Sunday tabloids, but not by the Fairfax papers (Dick 2011). After a few days when it had been easy to establish his name online, after radio stations carried it, as did the new-agency, AAP, he became simply the 'Bali Boy'. Seven's news director, Peter Meakin, said their first report of the arrest carried his name, then 'self-censorship took over' and the network took the view that they would not be able to name him if he had been charged in Australia, 'so why should Indonesia be any different'? (Dick 2011). However, there are legal differences between jurisdictions and this case raises the issue about which set of rules should apply. Here it seems the young man was given the benefit of the doubt and not named.

But another ethical issue arose when it was suggested before his trial ended that the Nine Network was negotiating with the family to pay up to $300,000 for the boy's story (Allard 2011). Lawyers for the boy believed word of the TV deal damaged his reputation, leading prosecutors to demand he be sentenced to three months in prison. According to its opposition, the Seven Network, Nine and its stable-mate, *Woman's Day* stitched up the deal for an interview on *Sixty Minutes* and probably a cover story in the women's magazine (Whittaker 2011). As one blogger characterised the situation: 'They (Nine) – and the boy's lamentable parents – stand accused in the court of public opinion of greed and stupidity on an epic scale' (Davis, G. 2011). The parents quickly issued a statement through their lawyers denying they had sealed any media deal that would profit from their 'son's misfortune' (Whittaker 2011). For their part, Channel Nine also denied a deal had been signed (*Channel Nine denies deal with Bali boy* 2011). One source said that the deal may have fallen through after it was leaked to the media, and when the parents realised they may not be able to keep the proceeds due to laws against profiting from crime, and that the whole grubby business may jeopardise the boy's chances of a light sentence (Whittaker 2011). Bali Boy's fine for buying the cannabis was the Australian equivalent of 23 cents, but the legal cost of fighting the drugs charges was estimated to have cost the family $100,000 (Cuneo 2011). He was also sentenced to two months in jail, but, with time served, was out within a week or so.

Questions for discussion:

- Under the same circumstances, would you name (and shame) the boy? Support your answer with your argument.
- Why do you think 'self-censorship', as Seven's Peter Meakin called it, didn't take over at other media outlets?
- Surely there are privacy issues, here, too. The impact on the teenager's future, in the short term at school, at least.
- At such a young age, should he have a right not to be shamed and ridiculed?
- What are the arguments for 'buying' the Bali Boy's story?
- What are the arguments against it?
- Where do you stand?

- Even after both Nine and the parents denied a deal had been done, do you think the 'damage' had already been done?
- Is there an argument that the parents could have used Nine's money to offset the cost of the trial?

Case Study 2: British sailors sell their story – with permission

In early 2007, 15 British sailors and marines were captured by Iran for allegedly entering its territorial waters illegally. The Iranians paraded the captured group on State television, an act said by the office of British Prime Minister, Tony Blair, to be 'entirely wrong, cruel' which 'has no place in proper international conduct' (Harding 2007). The hostages were released after 15 days. The sailors and marines were seized by Iranian forces in the Shatt al-Arab waterway between Iraq and Iran. Iran said the group entered their waters illegally. Britain said they were in Iraqi waters. The group included one woman, Faye Turney. She said, in a paid interview after her release, that she had been asked while in captivity how she felt about dying for her country and feared at one stage she was being measured for a coffin (*Freed female sailor feared death* 2007). Ms Turney, 25, a mother with a three-year-old daughter, became the symbol of the diplomatic stand-off between Britain and Iran. She told the British tabloid, *The Sun*, she feared she would be raped. Iranian television had shown the group playing table tennis and chess and watching a soccer match on TV while in captivity (*Freed female sailor feared death* 2007). Leading Seamen Turney's interview was published amid a furore in Britain over the Defence Ministry's decision to allow the 15 to sell their stories to the media. *The Sun* did not say whether or how much they paid for the interview, but *The Guardian* reported she had agreed to a joint deal with *The Sun* and ITV for close to $197,400, about four times her annual salary (*Freed female sailor feared death* 2007). Opposition politicians and defence commentators criticised the Defence Ministry for allowing the group to sell their stories. The Ministry said it had waived the rules banning serving military personnel from selling their stories because of the huge public interest in the case. A Ministry spokeswoman said the 15 would be allowed to keep any fees they were paid (*Freed female sailor feared death* 2007).

Questions for discussion:

- The British Defence Ministry obviously wanted to see the sailors' and marines' version of the events in the public arena to counter the publicity the Iran government gained from showing the captured group apparently relaxing. It was all part of a PR war, wasn't it? There were certainly two very different versions of events while the group was in captivity.
- Why didn't Defence PR just call a media conference and let them all tell their stories to all arms of the media?

- What was the significance of letting them profit from their ordeal? Is it simply so that they can get some compensation for spending about a fortnight in the hands of foreigners, or was there more to it than that?
- Was it such an ordeal, if they played sport and chess and watched soccer on TV?
- Would you want your news organisation to bid for the exclusive story?
- What would you ask Ms Turney?

6 The price of truth?

Foreign correspondence and war reporting

The price of truth

'The price of truth' was the page one headline in the London *Times* in early 2012, when the paper reported the death of the revered foreign correspondent, Marie Colvin, in a rocket attack in Syria (*The price of truth* 2012, p. 1). The reporter's mother, Rosemarie Colvin, told London's *Daily Mail* her daughter had been due to leave Syria the day she died, but 'she wanted one more story'. The 55-year-old American-born veteran foreign correspondent died alongside French photographer Remi Ochlik, 28, in the besieged city of Homs. She'd been ordered to leave the city by her long-time employer, Britain's prestigious *Sunday Times*, because the situation in the city was considered too dangerous. London's *Daily Mail* reported at the time that Syrian government forces had been ordered to deliberately target foreign journalists (Walford and Ramdani 2012). The *Australian*'s Middle East Correspondent, John Lyons (2012), a few weeks later wrote of 'a body of evidence that the (Assad) regime had been deliberately trying to kill journalists'. The *Sunday Times* editor, John Witherow, said in a statement at the time of Colvin's death that she was 'driven by a passion to cover wars in the belief that what she did mattered'. She believed profoundly that reporting could 'curtail the excesses of brutal regimes and make the international community take notice' (cited in Walford and Ramdani 2012). Ms Colvin had reported conflicts the world over for more than two decades. Her trademark eye-patch was a legacy of getting too close to the action during the long civil war in Sri Lanka. As she tried to cross back into government-held territory after spending time with the Tamil Tiger rebels in 2001, she was hit by shrapnel in four places and, despite surgery, lost the sight of her left eye (*A woman of extraordinary bravery who charmed tyrants* 2012). Her big break as a reporter came in the mid-1980s when she was in the Libyan capital, Tripoli, when America launched its biggest aerial attack since Vietnam in retaliation, US President Ronald Reagan said, for Libyan involvement in terrorist attacks aimed at Americans (*US launches air strikes on Libya* 1986). It was while Colvin was there that she was summonsed to meet the late Libyan dictator, Muammar Gaddafi. She later published an account of her many encounters with the Libyan leader under the title 'Mad Dog and Me'. Also on that *Times* front page, the paper reproduced part of Colvin's address at a service at the 'spiritual home of the London media', St Bride's Church, to commemorate war reporters who had died since the turn of the century. She spoke graphically of the dangers for the foreign correspondent in a conflict:

> Covering a war means going to places torn by chaos, destruction, and death, and trying to bear witness. It means trying to find the truth in a sandstorm of propaganda when armies, tribes or terrorists clash. And yes, it means taking risks, not just for

yourself but often for the people who work closely with you. In an age of 24/7 rolling news, blogs and twitters, we are on constant call wherever we are. But war reporting is still essentially the same – someone has to go there and see what is happening. You can't get that information without going to places where people are being shot at, and others are shooting at you.

(Colvin 2010)

In this chapter we are looking at the role of the foreign correspondent, with a particular emphasis on their role during conflicts, especially conflicts involving Western troops. Covering a war or conflict involving your fellow-countrymen and women (and those of allied nations, like the coalition of forces in Iraq and Afghanistan in recent years) poses a number of unique, ethical dilemmas. Also we will discuss the effects that reporting major tragedies, like natural disasters as well as conflicts, can have on journalists themselves.

Figure 6.1 'The price of truth', *The Times*, 23 February 2012. Copyright The Times/News Syndication

Covering conflict – a hard and dangerous job, but a vital one

Working as a foreign correspondent – reporting back to your home country on major news events around the world – is seen by many as a glamorous job, at the top of the journalistic food-chain, and is much sought-after. While the story of the final assignment in the life of Marie Colvin is a sad and sobering tale, there is a job to be done covering major conflicts around the globe. It is a very difficult and dangerous job. News camera journalist Jon Steele (2002) described his 'addiction' to 'the worst places on earth' while chasing stories in combat zones. Those words from Colvin's 2010 speech represent a mantra for the foreign correspondent. They do it because someone has to. It is a vitally important role for a journalist. Someone has to tell the rest of the world what is going on, and in Syria in recent times that has been a very dangerous occupation. A total of 65 journalists were killed around the world in the first five months of 2012, 15 of that count in Syria (Schlein 2012). Almost as many (72) died in the whole of the previous year, according to Reporters Without Borders (*2011: Journalists killed* 2012). By the end of 2012, a total of 90 journalists had died around the world, a further six media assistants and a further 47 of what were called 'netizens and citizens journalists' (*2012: Journalists killed* 2013). In 2011, the most – 10 – died reporting from Pakistan (*2011: Journalists killed* 2012). In 2012, 10 died in Pakistan, and 18 in Syria (*2012: Journalists killed* 2013). Another international organization devoted to the freedom of the media, the Committee to Protect Journalists (CPJ), was so concerned about the dangers that in 2012 they released online a Journalist Security Guide aimed at helping not only freelance journalists working in war zones, but also those involved with stories on digital security, natural disasters and organized crime (Rouse 2012).

Anyone who follows the Twitter feed from the CPJ will know how dangerous being a journalist in general, and a foreign correspondent in particular, can be in some countries. The Committee sends out almost-daily reports of journalists being assaulted, kidnapped or killed. In August 2013, the CPJ confirmed that a Sky News cameraman, 61-year-old Mike Deane, was the thousandth journalist killed since 1992. Deane was caught in cross-fire while filming the Egyptian government's crackdown on protestors in Cairo on August 14–15, 2013 (Omari 2013).

It is clear that journalists are being deliberately targeted in many conflict zones. Respected foreign correspondent, Christiane Amanpour, who reported from the front lines of war for more than a quarter of a century, said during an interview for *Vanity Fair* in 2012 'whether it's Syria, Libya, Russia or the Philippines, journalists are now being targeted. They want to shut us up. They're killing the messenger' (quoted in Heilpern 2012). The claims surfaced again a few weeks later when a Japanese journalist was allegedly deliberately shot dead by Syrian government troops (Wallace 2012). After the media attacked the Taliban's attempt to kill the Pakistani teenager Malala Yousafzai in October, 2012, for her crusade for girls to be allowed to go to school, a leader of the terrorist group ordered his followers to target media organisations that had criticized them (Greenslade 2012c).

On 10 November 2010, the same day as Colvin's speech, the head of the international newsagency Reuters, David Schlesinger, challenged the need for journalists to put themselves in danger. In a speech to the International News Safety Institute in London, Schlesinger asked whether in an age when a gunship can fire up to four kilometres, and a drone can be piloted from half a world away, journalists could justify the risks of being 'in the midst of things' (Schlesinger, D. 2010). He said that sometimes the benefits of transparency and understanding dictate that journalists 'must be right there', but added:

> Sometimes those benefits are not there and the reasons for being in harm's way are less noble: competitive pressure, personal ambition, adrenaline's urging.
>
> (Schlesinger, D. 2010)

Schlesinger also pointed to the emerging dangers for 'amateur' or 'tourist' journalists:

> With the great democratization of technology, there have never been so many people in every country on earth who have both the ambition and now the means to publish their views, thoughts and images without the structure of a large (media) institution around them.
>
> (Schlesinger, D. 2010)

The head of Reuters kept his most sobering thoughts for the end of his speech:

> We have to be ready to lose the shot to avoid being shot. We must be ready to lose some stories to avoid losing yet more lives.
>
> (Schlesinger, D. 2010)

The situation for citizen-journalists in conflict reporting

> Dirty wars attract a wide variety of odd types: Volunteers, journos, freedom fighters, NGOs, businessmen and even tourists.
>
> (Pelton, 2013)

If executives like David Schleshinger and dare-devil unilaterals like Robert Young Pelton are questioning the value of sending reporters into war zones, why would amateurs consider it glamorous or exciting to put themselves into such dangerous conditions? This is a simple question, but it seems that hundreds of young and eager photojournalists and reporters are venturing into tough conflict situations in the hope that an image or a story will bring them attention and boost their careers – or maybe it's about the 'rush'. During the 2011 Libyan civil war, experienced photojournalists were shocked at the number of inexperienced reporters who had travelled to liberated parts of the country, even though it was not safe to do so. The youngsters were accused of 'joyriding' and 'not taking the war seriously'. *The New York Times*' photographer Michael Kamber (2011) saw people 'in T-shirts and shooting with iPhones'. This is not something that we recommend – but as Kamber points out, every career has to start somewhere. But remember, bullets do not discriminate for age, gender or affiliation – if you feel the urge to travel to the world's hot spots in the hope of a career-defining image or story, then at least take every precaution you can and wear sensible shoes. The situation in Syria in 2012–13 was slightly different.

With very limited access for foreign journalists – professional or amateur – much of the frontline reporting has been done by citizen-journalists, activists with cellphones. It is not safe for them either, but they have the added advantage of being local, knowing the language and being able to blend in or move away when it is too dangerous (Arnold, D. 2012). Robert Young Pelton says the situation in Syria is 'thoroughly muddled':

> [The] positions of citizen journalists, official embeds, propagandists, counter propagandists, hackers, hoaxers, unilaterals and credentialed media are no longer discrete.
> (Pelton 2013)

The entire experience of news reporting from the Middle East has been changed by the Arab Spring. Not only is there a new fashion for war-tourism, perhaps more importantly, there is a new confident layer of young journalists emerging in Egypt and other countries in the region (Martin, J. 2006). A left-wing Cairo newspaper long-suppressed under Mubarek re-emerged on the web in 2010 to challenge repressive media laws – *Al-Badeel*, cooperatively edited and managed by a group of reporters who stand up for democratic rights (El-Hennawy, 2010). Just as newspapers played a role in the American and French revolutions 200 years ago, *Al-Badeel* was one of the many online voices of the Egyptian revolution. Today, the situation is dangerous for radical journalists in a different way. In Egypt and other countries still undergoing the revolutionary process, governments are now targeting critical journalists and media outlets. The attempt to silence the Egyptian comedian-commentator Bassem Youssef and his satirical show *El Bernameg* (The Programme) in April, 2013 is the most celebrated case, but at the same time, dozens of activist and leftwing journalists were charged or harassed by pro-government thugs. The continuing social revolutions, economic convulsions and armed conflicts that are beginning to define the early twenty-first century will no doubt further influence the dynamics of the news industry.

The war reporter through history

Throughout history, popular support 'back home' for war is often something that has to be 'prepared' according to military timetables, like battle plans and supply lines. In times of war, the media's critics often accuse it of being a government propaganda tool. Others regard support for the government as simply being patriotic. People want information and relief from the anxiety they feel about the uncertainty of a major conflict, particularly those whose relatives and friends are 'over there' defending 'our' freedom. The media can also play a vital role in any conflict by supporting one side or the other. Most of the time during major conflicts the news media plays a number of roles – sometimes simultaneously – being patriotic, critical, informative, and full of propaganda from 'their side'. It is an ethical minefield for journalists. For most of the twentieth century, news organisations were expected to 'do the right thing' and report only favourable material to the public 'back home'. Australian-born Phillip Knightley's seminal book, *The First Casualty* (2003, first published in the 1970s), provides one of the best historical accounts of early war correspondence. However, the situation has changed in recent decades. Much of the change in military–media relations can be traced to the post-Vietnam period of the late 1970s and the Falklands 'war' between Britain and Argentina over possession of a few small islands in the south Atlantic in 1982. The military considered that the foreign correspondents covering Vietnam – notably those from the major American TV networks – were given too much free rein in what they could do, see and report. The British military learned the lesson of Vietnam and restricted what the media covering the Falklands conflict could report. Primarily it was the sheer isolation of the Falklands that helped the military limit media access to the battlefield. But while that may have worked for that conflict, it would be the massive advances in technology that conspired to help journalists get closer to the action in later conflicts. Australian analysts and writers, Peter Jesser and Peter Young (1997), argue that in an age of 'limited conflict', when it is possible that 'a large part of the population might not support involvement in the conflict', journalists and editors have the opportunity to be much more critical of their own military and their political leaders. Ruling elites have always known that if they control the mass media, they can influence public opinion (and not only in times of war). Historian Carole Sue Humphrey (1995, p. 3) notes that during the American War of Independence:

> The revolutionary printer controlled the content of the paper, deciding what would and would not be published.
>
> (Humphrey, 1995)

By 1775, the gatekeeping role of the press was self-evident, and the newspapers supporting the American Revolution against the British rule would emphasize victories in battles, 'whether that was actually the truth or not' (Humphrey 1995, p. 4). During the American Civil War, a leading Republican general issued an order banning the *Chicago Times* newspaper. The order also banned several other papers, which were critical of the general, from circulating in the area under his command (Reynolds 1995, p. 85). So much for freedom of the press when the 'land of the free' was fighting to overcome the rebel Confederacy. There's a famous anecdote in American journalism that claims the newspaper and film mogul, William Randolph Hearst, actually precipitated a war between America and Spain over possession of Cuba, by planting a false report in his papers. According to the legend, Hearst told one of his newspaper artists in Havana, Frederic Remington: 'You furnish the pictures, I'll furnish the war' (cited in Wiggins 1995, p. 105). Whether or not Hearst actually sent the apocryphal cable to Remington is largely a moot point. What is clear is that Hearst and his rival in the New York newspaper industry, Joseph Pulitzer (later to have his name synonymous with the highest awards for journalistic excellence in the United States), were both strongly pro-war and used their papers to whip up patriotic and anti-Spanish sentiment among the American public. In every war since, according to former correspondent and journalism historian, Phillip Knightley (2003), the news media has been called upon to 'play their part', to live up to their 'patriotic duty', and support the national war effort. British journalist and author George Orwell (1988) recognized this in his bleakly futuristic novel *Nineteen Eighty-four*, first published in 1949. In his story, a state of perpetual warfare between 'Oceania' and its enemies required enormous domestic resources – including the production of 'hate session' propaganda and constant surveillance of the civilian population – just to keep people under a kind of ideological sedation. This is a vital aspect of modern global conflict. Without the mobilization of popular support for warfare, nations would soon run out of resources to keep fighting.

During wartime, all of these pressures have a direct impact on the minds of journalists. In Graham Greene's novel set in French-ruled Vietnam in the early 1950s, *The Quiet American* (1955), an English journalist, Thomas Fowler, tells an American that befriends him that as a reporter he doesn't have an opinion, and doesn't get involved. By the end of the story, Fowler is very much involved in Vietnamese politics, he even understands the need to choose a 'side'.

What becomes clear from an historical and contemporary perspective is that media coverage of war is, for the most part, far from objective. Journalists 'choose' sides constantly, sometimes in a conscious way (a political choice) and sometimes unconsciously (the pull of patriotism or belief in the 'national interest') (Ravi 2005). This means there is always a fine line between reporting and propaganda because all of us have a 'vested interest' in the outcome of the conflict, one way or another (Nohrstedt et al. 2000).

If the government thinks the media is not 'toeing the line', they are quick to criticize them. During the first Gulf War, Prime Minister Bob Hawke railed against what he saw as the bias in ABC (Australia) reports. During the second, John Howard's Minister of Communications, Richard Alston, levelled 68 complaints of anti-American bias against the ABC radio current affairs programme, *AM* (Holmes 2012a). As *Media Watch* presenter, Jonathan Holmes, notes in that piece, the British government has an even longer history of 'disagreements' with the BBC. The question for all media, once the troops are 'over there', is whether challenging the government policy that sent them there equates to not supporting the troops? How would they see it, reading criticism of their deployment online? Should we (as Australians, Americans or British) support our troops once they are in a foreign war zone? The difficulty is separating the political debate from support for the military. Does the media no longer challenge the government's decision to send troops into dangerous situations once the decision has been taken? It is a major role of the media to keep the public informed of such important debates and decisions.

The media legacy of the Iraq war

There were major media debates in 2003 in the US, UK and Australia over the second Iraq war which began on 19 March 2003. Did Saddam Hussein really have weapons of mass destruction and could he launch them towards Israel in about 40 minutes? The debates were long and wide-ranging, and with the benefit of hindsight perhaps they should have been even longer and more wide-ranging. Central to the debates was whether the invasion of Iraq was justified. The 'coalition of the willing' certainly thought so. We now know it was based on a series of clever deceptions of the public. The imminent threat of Saddam Hussein making and using 'weapons of mass destruction' justified the war and made it necessary. After a year of pretending to search for weapons dumps, the 'coalition of the willing' admitted there never had been evidence of WMD. The world has known for some time that this was a lie.

In late 2012, the Iraq War Inquiry Group, consisting of former generals, diplomats, academics and senior public servants, made a public call for an inquiry into why Australia joined the 'coalition of the willing'. A few months later, in April, 2013, former Australian Prime Minister, John Howard, gave a speech to the Lowy Institute, in Sydney, defending his decision to take Australia into the war as part of the 'coalition of the willing'. While protestors chanted outside the venue, Howard rejected the idea that the pretext for the invasion was based on a conscious lie as the 'most notorious' accusation made against the leaders of the allies – chiefly the US, UK and Australia. Howard attempted to shift the blame to his public service advisors who had been 'proved to be wrong' (*Former PM Howard says he didn't send troops to Iraq based on WMD 'lie'* 2012).

A former senior intelligence assessor who had worked on the WMD files came forward a few days later and said Howard and his cabinet ignored the advice of public servants that no evidence existed for Iraqi biological or chemical weapons capability

(Sweiringa 2013). Former British PM, Tony Blair, also continued to defend his actions as late as March, 2013 despite the evidence against him at a similar UK inquiry several years ago. We support calls for more public scrutiny of the decisions, then and now, about how and when and why our governments take us into disastrous military conflicts for the wrong reasons. Having followed this story for more than a decade, we are still dismayed that the news media has not yet owned up to its own role in reporting and repeating the lies of 2003 – at the time, effectively whitewashing them of government spin – and duping people into accepting the conflict against their better instincts and, ultimately, their best interests. With a few exceptions, the global news media failed to expose the lies before the war. Then, on the eve of war in early 2003, the media largely shifted support for their government's participation in the invasion of Iraq in March. We believe that this failure is a major cause of the public distrust of the media today (Hirst, 2011; Hirst and Patching 2005 and 2007).

Is the terror frame still relevant today?

In previous ethics texts we devoted an entire chapter to the ethical fault lines exposed by the launch of the 'war on terror' in response to the September 11 attacks in the United States. In 2007, it was still a prominent issue, though the focus had shifted somewhat towards 'domestic' and 'lone wolf' terror threats. The May, 2011 death of Osama bin Laden was symbolic of an American 'victory' over al-Qaida. Though we could argue the front lines of conflict have only shifted, the rhetoric of American and allied foreign policy has changed somewhat. The ability of al-Qaida and other groups to launch attacks against targets far from their limited base of operations is severely degraded. Instead, more local and regional violence is directed inward, between warring groups with various ethnic, ideological and religious differences. In Libya and other parts of northern Africa, it was British and French forces leading direct interventions and, as we argue in this book, the Arab Spring, the global financial crisis and the conflict in Syria have changed the global picture somewhat. Social revolution is always messy and unpredictable. Under the circumstances we felt an emphasis on broader conflict reporting and personal safety was more appropriate. However, it is important to note that while the 'terror frame' that we discussed in 2005 and 2007 is no longer so prominent, it is still relevant to international news reporting.

The fighting in Afghanistan and Iraq is no longer the central news issue, and our own research indicates that the global news media is losing interest in both countries as conflict zones that will generate good stories. On the tenth anniversary of the Iraq invasion, there is still some coverage of the war-ravaged nation, but in 2012 it was 20 per cent of the level in 2003 (Hirst 2013). However, the research also showed that the civilian death toll from terror attacks, including assassinations, suicide bombers, car-bomb attacks on crowds or individuals, has not slowed significantly since the carnage of Fallujah in December, 2004. The reporting has changed – alongside political analysis of the drawdown of occupation forces in Iraq and Afghanistan over the past few years, the news media has fed us a steady toll of deaths and injuries to allied forces and coverage of the larger sectarian outrages like the demolition of a mosque or the bombing of a busy street market. In March and April, 2013, the tenth anniversary of Iraq received some coverage. We read and see little of the ongoing human crisis, or the deeper political machinations behind the sectarian violence. It is generally agreed among sensible commentators – left, right and centre – that the military adventures of

Afghanistan (2001–2004) and Iraq (2003–2011) were political and policy disasters. Certainly they were humanitarian disasters littered with atrocities and war crimes, big and small. Some journalists who covered one or both of these conflicts for many years also drew the same conclusions (McGeough 2013a). As the foreign troops were withdrawn from these two devastated nations, battalions of reporters were 'un-embedded'. In the absence of a shooting war, the world's attention was drawn to other conflict zones in the region and elsewhere. Our conclusion is that despite the obvious and ongoing existence of terrorist atrocities in Iraq and Afghanistan, the fact that they target locals across a sectarian divide means that the Western media no longer feels it necessary to call them 'terrorists'. It seems that 'terrorist' attacks only occur when the intended target is Western, not when the victims are local Iraqi or Afghan civilians murdered for domestic political or religious reasons.

Embedding – then and now

War correspondents have always taken risks – typified by the attitude of correspondents like Marie Colvin and her photographer colleague. Many of the best operate on the edge, without necessarily getting the sanction of the 'allied' commanders. This freelance style has become more common as news demands increase with the 24-hour news cycle, and as the equipment has become even more portable. The laptop computer has replaced the cumbersome satellite dish of old, audio, video and pictures are easily obtained by the latest generation of mobile phones and a couple of cheap Apps. Jesser and Young (1997, pp. 14–16) earlier noted how smaller, lighter and faster digital technology 'largely made the reporter independent of the military' which 'limits even further the ability of the military to block transmissions through electronic jamming'.

By the second Gulf War in 2003, there was a new twist in the traditional media–military stand-off. The American military offered places with the front-line units to scoop-hungry war junkies. The 'embedding' of reporters with American and British military units took full advantage of the latest generation of lightweight equipment to put journalists in tanks and trucks. It might have seemed like the military was giving the reporters full access, but in reality most correspondents soon realized that 'embedding' was cleverly designed to reduce the threat of independent reporting.

Estimates varied, but it is believed that between 500 and 700 journalists were 'embedded' with individual combat units of the American and British forces in the second Gulf War (2003–2004). It seemed like a 'win win' situation for the media and the military. Journalists and camera crews were at the centre of the action, reporting on battles as the coalition advanced into Iraq. The military hoped that the embedded journalists, working alongside soldiers on whom their lives could well depend, would be more sympathetic to the coalition cause in their battlefield reporting. This certainly proved the case in many instances, such as in the book *The March Up* by reporter Bing West and his travelling companion Major General (retired) Ray L. Smith (2003), who rode with the 1st US marine division all the way to Baghdad, gleefully reporting Iraqi 'kills' and mourning the deaths of marines in the units they were with. Television audiences 'back home' were riveted to their TV screens, watching the advance through the desert or seeing a missile heading skywards from a warship in the Gulf and knowing it was probably heading for Baghdad. But reporting from the front lines has its disadvantages. Apart from being possibly shot at and killed – which has become an even bigger issue in recent times, particularly in Syria – there's the discomfort, the constant danger, and the restricted view of what's happening elsewhere in the conflict. War correspondents have to rely on information from 'head office' to flesh out their battlefield stories, with input on other aspects of the conflict from other reporters and editors. Embedded journalists do not have access to information beyond where they are located. Chris Ayres was in his late twenties and the West Coast (USA) correspondent for *The Times* when he became an embedded reporter with the US Marines during the 2003 Iraq War. His memoir, *War Reporting for Cowards: Between Iraq and a hard place*, recounts his version of the 'action':

> If truth was the first casualty of war, I thought, personal hygiene was a close second.
> (Ayres 2005, p. 186)

He soon realized what he called the 'true genius of the embedding scheme' – 'it had turned me into a Marine' (Ayres 2005, p. 242). As Ayres and his colleagues soon found out, the embedded journalist only sees what the field commanders allow them to see – from their side. They can only report back what they can deduce from what they see and what the commanders in their small area of the battlefield allow them to know. It's virtually impossible to get 'the big picture' – that's left to the reporters at Central Command Headquarters in neighbouring Qatar, in the 2003 Iraq conflict and at the Pentagon in Washington, or those trying to 'pull it all together' back in the news organisation's head office, whether that was in New York, London or Sydney.

In the epilogue to his memoir, Ayres noted that, statistically, journalists were ten times more likely to die in that conflict than coalition soldiers (2005, p. 283). An added ethical dilemma for the embedded journalist emerged in late 2004 when an American television crew filmed one of their marines shooting dead an apparently unarmed Iraqi as he was lying on the floor of a wrecked Fallujah mosque (*US Marine filmed shooting prisoner* 2004). The correspondent with the NBC (America) crew that filmed the shooting, Kevin Sites, said the mosque had been used by insurgents to attack US forces the previous week. But a wounded and unarmed Iraqi? Do you really want to show your soldiers in such a light? *The Australian*'s Media section the following day carried a cartoon showing the Iraqi pleading with the marine, 'Don't shoot' while the marine was turning back to the cameraman with the same plea (*Don't shoot* 2004).

It is an example of a wider ethical dilemma for the foreign correspondent/war reporter. There was outrage in America at news of the 1968 My Lai massacre in Vietnam and the 2004 abuse of inmates at the Abu Ghraib prison in Baghdad, but these stories have to be told, even if we would prefer it was the 'other side' committing the atrocities or abuse. It is natural to think of 'our side' as being the 'good guys' in whatever conflict, trying to free people from oppression and tyranny and fighting for justice. It is disappointing in the extreme, on a personal level, when members of 'our side' are shown to be party to such atrocities. In the early part of 2012, the American media had several more reasons to question the morals of their troops in Afghanistan. First came the video allegedly showing troops urinating on dead Taliban fighters (Bates, D. and Moran 2012) followed by the 'accidental' burning of copies of the Muslim holy book, the Koran (*Afghans protest after burning of Koran* 2012). But worse was to come a few weeks later when an American soldier went on a rampage, killing 17 Afghan civilians, including nine children (*US Soldier charged with murder of civilians* 2012). In the 'dirty' wars today in parts of Africa, the Middle East, the fringes of the old Soviet empire and in parts of Asia, truth is often the first casualty; journalists are likely to witness war crimes occurring right in front of them. This is going to be a new fault line in war-reporting: if journalists are witnesses to the truth, what role do they play in the prosecution of alleged war criminals in international tribunals like The Hague?

Operating unilaterally

As well as the two groups we've already mentioned being involved in the second Gulf War, the embeds and those reporting from command headquarters, there was another group, the so-called 'unilaterals' or 'independents'. They were the ones who chose to report from outside the coalition's protection from Baghdad or northern Iraq. In a combat situation, the attraction of being a 'unilateral' was that you were not controlled (or hampered) by military 'minders'. It could be dangerous – especially if you got caught in the middle of heavy fighting. As John Steele explained in *War Junkie*, the unilateral is free to report from wherever they please – or dare:

> Stones tore over our heads and hit well-dented police shields like bulls' eyes … The rebels fell back. Their killer faces spitting in the eyes of the militia. And me falling back with them until I tripped over something big … Pull wide and watch the old man suffer for twenty seconds, waiting for just the right look on his face, then cut. I grabbed a field bandage from my body armour. 'Here! Take this!'
>
> (Steele 2002, p. 129)

In the second Gulf War there were several incidents of the 'independents' among the Western media being killed by 'friendly fire' – i.e. by coalition forces. Of the 14 journalists killed during the actual battle phase of the war – before President Bush's premature announcement of 'mission accomplished' on the deck of an American aircraft carrier – half were 'independents' and five, possibly seven, were killed by coalition forces (Jackson, S. 2003). The most infamous case to emerge in more recent times of coalition forces taking the lives of journalists in a war zone surfaced in 2010, when Wikileaks released a 'classified' US military video from 2007 showing an Apache helicopter attacking and killing a group of Iraqi civilians (Haddow 2010). The incident rose to prominence because two of the victims were Reuters news agency staff – photographer Namir Noor-Eldeen and his driver Saeed Chmagh. The video, titled 'Collateral Murder', can be found on YouTube, for those interested. The problems of the 'unilateral' in 2003 sound very similar to the stories told by journalists involved in reporting various aspects of the so-called Arab Spring which saw several dictators and regimes fall in the early years of this decade.

The danger of being kidnapped

Another, more personal, dilemma is the possibility of journalists being kidnapped, being held for ransom, and guaranteeing publicity for the group that kidnapped them. The CPJ's Frank Smyth (2013) lists among the motivations for the diverse array of groups that kidnap journalists – militants, rebels, criminals and paramilitaries – a number of reasons why journalists are taken. They include ransom, to deliver a political message, to influence coverage, to extract information from the captive journalist, or concerns over espionage – the accusation that they might be spies (Smyth 2013). The dilemma for the journalist's superiors is do you not publicise the fact that your staff member has been kidnapped in the hope he/she will be returned promptly, or do you publicise the kidnap like you would that of any other person? It is an issue we will take up in the first case study at the end of this chapter. Here we want to mention two cases of journalists being kidnapped – one Australian and one British – both of whom spent considerable time in captivity. Australian photographer, Nigel Brennan, along with Canadian journalist, Amanda Lindhout, was kidnapped outside the Somali capital, Mogadishu, in August, 2008, and held captive for 462 days (Elliott, T. 2011). The story of Brennan's ordeal and how he was released after more than 15 months is told in the book titled *The Price of Life* (Brennan et al. 2011). Brennan's family finally raised the $1.1 million needed to secure his release, including generous donations from family members, former Australian Greens political party leader, Bob Brown, and entrepreneur, Dick Smith. His sister-in-law, Kellie Brennan, said at the time the book was released that 'we had to keep everything out of the media, because if the Somalis knew they would up the ransom' (Elliott, T. 2011). Brennan was released in November 2009. At the time he said that during his 15-month ordeal he'd been chained up and pistol-whipped and his colleague said she had been beaten and tortured (*Freed Australian describes hostage ordeal* 2009). Lindhout's family also paid a ransom for her release. In 2013, Amanda Lindhout spoke publicly about sexual abuse, including repeated rapes, while in captivity (*Amanda Lindhout talks candidly about abuse while in captivity* 2013). It was the direct opposite for the BBC's Alan Johnston, who was kidnapped in Gaza City in the Middle East in March, 2007 just two weeks before his contract was due to end. He was held for nearly four months by a Jihadi organization called the Army of Islam. The BBC mounted a major international – and very public – campaign to try to secure his release, and he was eventually freed unharmed in early July (*Biography: Alan Johnston* 2007). After his release, Johnston told his story to the *BBC* (Johnston, A. 2007) and in a book titled *Kidnapped: And Other Dispatches* (2011). As the publicity for the book noted:

> When Alan Johnston, the last western journalist to remain in Gaza, was kidnapped by religious terrorists – millions of people, from the backstreets of Gaza, to London, New York and Johannesburg, felt the need to express their anger and their determination to see him free.
>
> (Johnston, A. 2011)

Johnston had spent his 114-day ordeal largely alone in a tiny, windowless room with only a radio for company. He said he had been threatened but he was physically assaulted only in the half-hour before his freedom (Chulov 2007).

A major issue for female correspondents

As Amanda Lindhout's account of rape at the hands of her Somali kidnappers shows, sexual violence is a big issue for female correspondents. Aside from the very real lethal dangers associated with attempting to cover the various internal conflicts associated with the Arab Spring, a major danger emerged for women covering those stories – sexual assault by groups of men at the protest. Top CBS (America) *Sixty Minutes* foreign correspondent Lara Logan suffered what was termed a 'brutal' sexual assault lasting about 40 minutes at the hands of a mob of Egyptian men while covering the downfall of president Hosni Mubarak in early 2011 (*Reporter sexually assaulted by mob in Egypt* 2011). She became separated from her film crew in Cairo's Tahrir Square on the day the president stepped down and was surrounded by a mob of more than 200 men and suffered a sustained sexual assault and beating before being rescued by a group of women and an estimated 20 Egyptian soldiers (*Reporter sexually assaulted by mob in Egypt* 2011). Logan was flown out of Cairo to receive treatment in a New York Hospital. Colleagues said at the time she was so traumatized she could not speak. When she did speak out she was applauded for breaking what had been a 'code of silence' surrounding the issue of female reporters being sexually assaulted while on assignment (Stelter 2011). Within months, the Committee to Protect Journalists (CPJ) had released a report on what it called 'The silencing crime: Sexual violence and journalists' (Wolfe 2011). The issue had been rarely reported until the assault on Ms. Logan and her courageous decision to talk about it. It prompted an outpouring of commentary about the dangers that female correspondents face around the world (Mirkinson 2011). In the four months between the Logan assault and the release of the CPJ report, its author, Lauren Wolfe, interviewed more than four dozen journalists who had undergone varying degrees of sexual violence. Many said they had been worried about reporting the assaults for fear they would be reassigned or prevented from taking risky assignments in the future (Mirkinson 2011). The prestigious US media journal, the *American Journalism Review*, took up the issue about the same time, noting that women were not the only victims (Ricchiardi 2011). Sherry Ricchiardi said that journalists had traditionally dealt with the topic by 'clamming up' (2011). The *New York Daily News* interviewed Ms. Logan who said she 'still battled the demons of the horrific gang sexual assault' (Huff 2012).

Post-Traumatic Stress Disorder (PTSD)

> People don't really know that much about (post-traumatic stress disorder). There's something called latent PTSD. It manifests itself in different ways. I want to be free of it, but I'm not. It doesn't go away.
>
> (Lara Logan quoted in Huff 2012)

Respected ABC (Australia) foreign correspondent, Peter Lloyd, is an example of what can happen to a reporter who is overwhelmed by the emotional stress of covering disasters, assassinations and human misery. His friends and colleagues were shocked when Lloyd was arrested in Singapore in mid 2008 and charged with drug offences that carried up to 20 years in jail and being caned 15 times (O'Brien 2008). The charges were later downgraded and he spent 200 days in a Singapore prison. Peter recounted the awful experience in a memoir titled *Inside Story: From ABC foreign correspondent to Singapore prisoner #12988*. He talked openly about how he turned to drugs to help him sleep and to 'settle his demons'. As his lawyer explained to the Singapore court, Lloyd was not a drug abuser. He used the drugs as a form of self-medication to cope with his mental illness, PTSD (Lloyd 2010, p. 177). Lloyd recounted the cumulative traumatic effects of reporting some of the biggest stories in southern Asia in the first years of the twenty-first century. In those years, before he became the news story, Lloyd had 'stood among the gruesome human wreckage' laid out in an improvised mortuary after the 2002 Bali Bombing; joined Thailand's disaster recovery workers collecting the bloated flotsam of the 2004 Boxing Day Tsunami; and he was there for the worst atrocity in Pakistan's history, a shocking suicide bombing attempt on Benazir Bhutto's life in 2007, two months before she was finally assassinated (Lloyd 2010, back page). As he recounted early in his memoir, one of what he called the 'guilty secrets of journalism'

(p. 55) is that 'for us to have a really good day, someone else must have a very bad one', and he had seen more than his fair share of the bad ones. Peter is now back with the ABC working in radio current affairs – a remarkable recovery. We had the opportunity to ask Peter about his recovery and he said the first step was recognising that PTSD is an illness. He told us that as a 'visual' learner he needed to understand and process the science behind his PTSD, how it was affecting his brain and his moods. Peter said he now avoids doing stories that are likely to be traumatic; not becaue he can't do them but because he'd rather report on other things. Instead he concentrates on reporting stories that are interesting to him. 'I am conscious of time; I have only so many hours, days, weeks, years left in the profession and I wish to use my skill-set in other more meaningful areas,' Peter told us.

In late 2012 a Walkley Award-winning photographer sued *The Age* after she covered the first anniversary of the 2002 Bali bombings (Farnsworth 2012). The newspaper was accused of failing to provide a safe workplace and breaching its duty of care. The photographer sued for an estimated $1 million in lost earnings (Farnsworth 2012). She said she suffered depression, anxiety and post-traumatic stress disorder after covering the bombing anniversary and being involved in 21 interviews with grieving family members of bombing victims. The court was told she often ended up in tears from the assignment and went on to suffer nightmares related to the tragedy. Her mental health suffered, and since 2005 she had been 'totally incapacitated' (*Former staff photographer sues* Age *over 2002 Bali trauma* 2012). A spokesperson for the Dart Center for Journalism and Trauma at Columbia University in New York said the court case could be an international landmark as it was the first, to their knowledge, where a journalist had gone to their employer and said 'you have a duty of care around trauma exposure' (Caldwell 2012). The paper claimed it was at the forefront of staff care at the time.

Reporters are often 'first responders'

The so-called 'first respondents' at emergency situations – police, ambulance officers and fire brigade staff – were quicker than the mainstream media to realise the traumatic effects of being among the first on the scene of a tragedy. First responders have had courses for many years to teach their staff how to cope with what they will encounter at such events. Journalists, too, are considered 'first responders' – among the first to arrive at the scene of a tragedy/disaster. The major news organisations realised some time ago they had a duty of care to journalists sent to horrific events and have instituted training programmes to help them cope with traumatic events. Research by organisations like the Dart Centre shows that journalists are affected by what they witness, and need appropriate training in how to handle the awful situations they sometimes find themselves reporting on. The Dart Center has a number of useful resources for would-be foreign correspondents. Among the best is a downloadable, two-page document prepared by the Dart Centre Australasian office in Melbourne (*Self Care Tips for News Media Personnel Exposed to Traumatic Events* 2007).

While the major media employers have taken action to help their staff cope with covering traumatic events, freelancers have to fend for themselves. They often find themselves covering major conflicts – like Afghanistan – without a major news organisation behind them. They need to make special preparations for covering such events. But it is not only foreign correspondents that can suffer the effects of reporting on tragedies. One of the groups sometimes overlooked are regional journalists. Working for a non-metropolitan media organisation – the local newspaper, radio or TV station – the journalist comes to know the local newsmakers. There may be fewer than 50 major sources of news in the area, and the reporter will literally 'bump into them' professionally and privately from time to time. What happens when a familiar source is involved in a serious accident? As an example, imagine the acute loss the local Sunshine Coast (Queensland) journalists felt at the sudden death of 'Crocodile Hunter', Steve Irwin, in 2006. The larger-than-life wildlife enthusiast had provided many stories for the local media, and been a popular and valuable source. Many would have seen him as a friend and felt his loss personally. The research talks about the cumulative effect of witnessing tragedy – no better example of this than Peter Lloyd – but regional journalists, often those early in their careers, need to realise the potential to suffer the effects of witnessing repeated trauma.

The bias of convenience

Another major ethical issue for the journalist in a foreign country – and for his/her audience 'back home' – is trying to understand the local culture. The clash of media and cultural understanding was graphically illustrated in 2012 by three, what can only be described in western terms as, shocking incidents. The first, a three-minute video showing a man said to be a member of the Taliban fatally shooting a woman accused of adultery in front of a cheering crowd near Kabul, Afghanistan, was given the Western tabloid treatment by the *New York Post* (*Watch: Taliban thugs execute woman for 'adultery' near Kabul* 2012). Two months later, there were protests in a number of countries over an anti-Islam video produced in the United States (*Violence erupts as protesters burn cars and throw rocks at US military base in Afghan capital over anti-Islam video* 2012). A low-budget trailer for a movie titled *Innocence of Muslims* produced in the United States sparked furious anti-American protests across the Islamic world. The protests were initially blamed for an attack on American diplomatic staff in Benghazi, which resulted in the death of the US Ambassador to Libya, Chris Stevens (Harding, L. and Stephen 2012). It was later acknowledged as a terrorist attack. Protests at the film, which mocked Islam, spread to Australia (*Anti-Islam film protests erupt in Sydney* 2012). The reaction was similar to that in 2005 when a Danish newspaper, *Fyllands-Posten* (Jutland's Post), published 12 cartoons depicting the Muslim prophet Muhammad. The drawings had been commissioned by the paper to accompany an article on self-censorship and freedom of speech after Danish writer Kare Bluitgen had been unable to find artists willing to illustrate his children's book about Muhammad, for fear of violent attacks by extremist Muslims. While the original publication of the cartoons raised a storm of protest, it was nothing to the reaction to their re-publication in later months in Europe and around the world, including, in a couple of cases, in Australia. Muslims regarded the cartoons as deeply offensive. While there's no doubt the cartoons were offensive (google them if you really want to see them), the debate soon became 'hijacked' by extremist Muslims on the one side rioting in protest that saw lives lost in several countries and, on the other side, those who supported the 'freedom of the press' argument. The third 2012 incident, mentioned briefly in another context earlier, also involved the Taliban. They shot a 14-year-old girl in the face after she championed the rights of girls to be educated in Pakistan. The girl, Malala Yousufzai, was targeted, the Taliban said, because she was 'pro-West' (Elliott, F. 2012). She was very seriously wounded and was airlifted to the United Kingdom for specialist treatment. Malala returned to school (in Britain) a few months after the incident and vowed to continue her struggle to get girls educated.

Most western journalists, foreign correspondents included, would struggle to understand how these incidents could happen and would have no trouble writing condemning accounts. But we can't always assume that we know or understand everything about a foreign culture. While it might be hard to understand, it is part of the media's educative function to try to explain the religious or political motivation behind such actions. While in no way condoning the actions, it is important to try to understand them and put them into context. Usually such actions are those of an extremist minority and bear little resemblance to the beliefs of the majority. All-too-often journalists will carry their own cultural bias into their reporting of such upsetting stories and settle for the 'usual suspects' by way of sources for comment on such offensive stories.

A final word

The Asia-Pacific Editor for *The Australian*, Rowan Callick, has likened the foreign correspondent to the Hollywood star and the sporting hero as one of the most glamorous figures of the twentieth century, but he added:

> Some foreign correspondents have survived bombs, deadly diseases and jailing in the line of duty, only to find themselves facing a more insidious threat, that of the accountant.

> (Callick 2012)

Under the headline 'The shrinking world of news', he questioned whether foreign correspondents were becoming a rare and dying breed, chiefly because the mass media was running out of money. It's an issue – the media's budgets cuts – we have taken up in previous chapters.

Case Study 1: The kidnapped correspondent

Kidnapping has long been a tool of the terrorist, the war lord, the common criminal and, in recent times, of insurgents in the military conflicts in Iraq and Afghanistan. People are taken captive to fund their activities, or to force government action, like the withdrawal of troops or the release of prisoners. But there is another dimension to this life-threatening issue – what if the person kidnapped is a professional colleague or friend? Just as journalists are increasingly becoming the targets of gunmen, they are also routinely being kidnapped and killed in the world's trouble spots. The world was shocked in 2002 when a correspondent for the *Wall Street Journal*, Daniel Pearl, was kidnapped in Karachi by a militant group and beheaded.

As was seen in the two more recent examples earlier, the reaction of the media to a kidnapped correspondent varies.

In October, 2008, CBC (Canada) reporter Melissa Fung was kidnapped in Kabul, Afghanistan, but it would be a month before the public knew of her desperate plight and her safe release. That's because the CBC, the Canadian military, and the office of the Canadian Prime Minister, Stephen Harper,

pleaded with the western media to keep 'mum' (Kidder 2008). Fragile negotiations for her release could be instantly derailed by any publicity, the
broadcaster, military and Prime Minister's office argued. They felt that
panicked kidnappers could simply kill her to dispense with the danger of a
raid by special forces if the incident became 'big news' (Loong 2008). 'No
news story is worth someone's life' is the succinct policy of the Canadian
Press wire service, aimed at guiding the reporting of kidnapping and terrorism
stories (Kidder 2008). Journalists and their managers alike went through
much soul-searching during the weeks of Ms Fung's captivity over what's
more important – the safety of the kidnap victim or the free flow of information
(Loong 2008). July, 2009, saw *New York Times* journalist David Rohde (and
Afghan colleague Tahir Ludin) escape from the Taliban in Afghanistan after
being held captive for seven months. Although word had spread quickly in
the previous November that Rohde, Ludin and their driver had been kidnapped, *The New York Times* convinced news organisations around the
globe to keep a lid on the story with a simple appeal: the kidnappers had
demanded silence. By defying them they could be signing the reporter's
death warrant (Hoyt 2009). They were even able to keep any word of the
kidnapping off Wikipedia for the entire time (Perez-Pena 2009). The paper's
Public Editor at the time, Clark Hoyt, wrote that some readers and even some
journalists 'see hypocrisy when a news organisation subordinates its fundamental obligation to inform the public to its human impulse to protect one of
its own' (2009). The Poynter Institute's Kelly McBride said the paper's
defence of the total news blackout 'made the job of every free journalist in the
world harder' and accused the paper of putting their 'loyalties to a few in front
of the larger journalistic principle of truth telling' (2009). She said that the
paper had indicated that when a life was in danger, journalists should avoid
reporting the truth until the life is secure, setting a standard journalists
couldn't possibly uphold. 'By telling the story of Rohde's escape, we've
already violated it, compromising the life of the driver who was left behind'
(McBride 2009).

[The driver did not escape with Rohde and Ludin.]

Questions for discussion:

1. Put yourself in the position of a kidnapped journalist. What would you want
   your bosses to do? Publicise your kidnapping widely, like the case of the
   BBC's Alan Johnston, or keep quiet and negotiate?
2. Now put yourself in the position of the news organisation's Editor. Debate
   how you would reach your decision? Publish or shut up?
3. The Australian engineer Douglas Wood was kidnapped by insurgents in
   Baghdad in 2005. His plight was covered in newspapers 'back home' for
   the six weeks of his captivity before his rescue by the American military.
   What's the difference?
4. You're reporting from Kabul and a colleague is kidnapped. What would
   you do? Is there any difference when it's a friend, and not you?

5. Nigel Brennan and Amanda Lindhout were freed after their families raised a ransom of more than a million dollars and paid it to the kidnappers in Somalia. How do you feel about paying kidnappers? Does a political motive differ from a purely financial demand?
6. An Australian parliamentary inquiry in 2012 into 'official emergency response measures when Australians are held hostage abroad' recommended that under 'exceptional circumstances' the Foreign Minister should allow money to be sent overseas to save the life of an Australian citizen (Flitton 2012). Do you agree?
7. The Foreign Affairs Department rejected the recommendation saying changing the relevant policy (banning the practice) would undermine Australia's no-ransom policy, and indirectly result in Australians overseas being targeted. Do you agree?
8. Where does that leave Brennan's relatives?

Case Study 2: The heroes that weren't

The US fetes its mythical heroine – Private Jessica Lynch

Among the first American soldiers taken prisoner by the Iraqis in the 2003 Iraq War was 20-year-old supply clerk, Private Jessica Lynch. Pt. Lynch was captured near the southern city of Nassiriyah. Eleven other US soldiers were killed and nine wounded in the incident. An early report quoted unnamed US officials as saying she fought fiercely before being captured. They claimed she was shot and stabbed in the engagement. It was also reported Lynch had emptied her weapon in a fire-fight with the enemy while her colleagues lay dead nearby. In the land of Hollywood blockbusters, the Jessica Lynch 'story' was the stuff of legends, and the media lapped it up. She became a symbol of American heroism. US commandos later 'rescued' Lynch from an Iraqi hospital. The Army made sure television stations around the world received the official video of the rescue. After it was too late to stop the 'heroism' story, a military investigation established a different story to the popular myth. Her convoy had taken a wrong turn, resulting in the Iraqi attack. Pt. Lynch suffered multiple fractures and spinal compression when her military vehicle rammed the one in front after being hit by a rocket-propelled grenade. Apparently her weapon had jammed (Monaghan 2003). The BBC's John Kampfner called the Lynch story 'one of the most stunning pieces of news management ever conceived' (2003). But America badly wanted to believe the original version of the heroine from rural West Virginia. When Pt. Lynch returned home in a wheelchair after 102 days in a Washington military hospital, she was greeted by cheering crowds wearing 'Welcome Home' T-shirts and waving American flags (Kampfner 2003). Other awkward facts were to emerge, like how she had survived partly due to the care she received at the Iraqi hospital. While the story of her heroism had been eroded as far as the rest of the world was concerned, to Americans she was a hero. US Government officials had described Lynch as a Rambo-like heroine, but in a *Sixty Minutes* interview with celebrity reporter, Diane Sawyer, Lynch said: 'I would have been the only one … able to say, "Yeah, I went down shooting." But I didn't. I did not … My weapon jammed and I did not shoot, not a round, nothing' (quoted from Sawyer 2003).

The sad tale of Pat Tillman

Pat Tillman was the heroic face of the War on Terror – a star of American football (NFL) who left a multi-million-dollar contract and a new wife to fight for his country after the 9/11 attacks. He became one of the most high-profile soldiers in the American military. When he died in Afghanistan in April, 2004, the Army told his family he'd been killed by enemy fire after courageously charging up a hill to protect his fellow Army Rangers (Couric 2009). The Army awarded him a Silver Star for his 'gallantry in action against an armed enemy'. But that version of the story didn't hold up. He had actually been killed by 'friendly fire', shot accidentally by his fellow soldiers (Couric 2009). Later investigations would reveal that Tillman was shot in the head in a confusing fire-fight (Bronstein and McIntyre 2006). It wasn't until 26 days after a memorial service for America's latest war hero – more than a month after his death – that the Army would publicly acknowledge what the Rangers that were with him at the time knew almost right away – he had died after US soldiers mistook him for the enemy (Bronstein and McIntyre 2006).

Questions for discussion:

1. You can understand why the American military would try to get the most positive publicity from each incident, can't you?
2. What do you think went through the minds of the American military when they received the first reports of the Jessica Lynch and Pat Tillman incidents?
3. Do you think the American military deliberately misled reporters, or did it just not know or simply got it wrong in the heat of the battle?
4. It's virtually impossible to check some of these stories at the time, so you have to go with the 'official line', don't you?
5. The American public wanted to believe Jessica was a hero and that Tillman had died a hero. In a time of war, would you want to be the one to burst the bubble?
6. What lessons can the media take from the Jessica Lynch and Pat Tillman stories?
7. Can you blame the military for not wanting to admit that they'd killed a hero?

Part III

Dealing with the law – ethically speaking

Overview and objectives

Reporting crime and court cases is the bread and butter of local news for all forms of mainstream media. Serious crime might attract national or international attention, but neighbourhood crime will always get a big run in local media. It is important that journalists understand the legal limitations and the ethico-legal paradoxes that impact on the reporting of crime, especially from the time someone is charged with an offence until the end of any subsequent trials and appeal processes. It is another area where the rise of social media has been a 'game-changer' in recent years.

Chapter 7 looks at the ethical problems journalists face covering the courts and the legal issues that can arise from time to time. Everyone deserves a fair trial and we'll look at several recent cases where there have been appeals to the public (as well as the media) not to jeopardise an accused's trial. We examine the phenomenon of 'trial by media' from the point of view of the coverage of criminal or civil matters that are, or might be, before the courts. In this context, trial by media refers to the pre-judging by the media of an accused person before, and possibly during, the so-called *sub judice* period – that is, after a suspect has been charged, and before their case has been decided.

As will be seen in chapter 8, there's a more common, and less legal, 'trial by media' where no charge has been laid against the person at the centre of the media's attention. There may never be criminal charges laid in the particular incident, but the media – either individual media outlets, commentators, radio 'shock jocks' or even bloggers and social media users – decide to 'try' the person in the 'court of public opinion' and often, in the process, all but destroy the person's reputation. It is another of those grey, ethico-legal areas where legal stipulations and ethical considerations might overlap or come into conflict.

The final chapter in this section on 'dealing with the law' looks at the ethical problems for journalists in their dealings with sources, without whose co-operation in the provision of information there would be no serious investigative journalism. While shield laws offer some protection for sources against court-imposed directions to the journalist to reveal them, there are jurisdictional variations which, in some cases, mean there is no guaranteed legal protection of source confidentiality. We also look at the strongest of the source relationships, between public relations practitioners and journalists, and some of the problems associated with that.

After reading these three chapters, you will have an understanding of the various legal and ethical problems associated with:

- guaranteeing everyone gets a fair trial
- what constitutes contempt of court

- why justice must be seen to be done
- justice and the celebrity
- the media as judge, jury and executioner
- long-running inquiries that become media 'trials'
- dealing with sources, and their importance
- how the law and ethics treat source confidentiality
- shield laws and protecting whistle-blowers
- the relationship between public relations and journalism.

7   Covering the courts and legal issues

The law v. the *Gold Coast Bulletin*

It wasn't the first, and it probably won't be the last, but the Queensland regional daily, the *Gold Coast Bulletin*, caused a trial to be aborted in early 2008 after a district court judge called the paper's coverage of the hit-and-run case 'mischievous' (quoted in *Judge orders mistrial* 2008). Six months later, when a second re-trial began, another judge relocated it to Gladstone, about 600 kilometres away, again blaming coverage in the *Bulletin* for the decision (Redmond 2008). In the original trial of the 2006 case, a man aged 30 was charged with dangerous driving causing death after allegedly hitting a 20-year-old woman on the Gold Coast and driving off. Judge Deborah Richards said the paper's coverage of the trial had been deliberately placed alongside two separate stories reporting on other drivers accused of killing people with their cars (*Judge orders mistrial* 2008). One of the two other reports inside the paper, and on the same page as coverage of the trial, concerned the case of a Mildura man accused of killing six teenage pedestrians and the victims' families anger at the jury not being told about the man's traffic history (*Victims' families 'betrayed' by verdict* 2008). The judge described as 'mischievous' the paper's editorial that day that referred to the Mildura case and called for laws to be changed to allow jurors to be informed of defendants' prior convictions and traffic history. The judge had earlier warned jurors to ignore what they read in a newspaper, but said she had 'no option' but to order a mistrial, saying if she gave the jury a second warning about media coverage 'the first thing they will do is go home and read it' (*Judge orders mistrial* 2008). The second trial was set for later in the year, but it, too, was aborted on factors, according to the Crown, other than media publicity. The third time around, District Court Judge, Warren Howell, decided to relocate the trial hundreds of kilometres away saying:

> Gladstone is much further away from ... what's the paper called? The *Gold Coast Integrity*?
>
> (Quoted in Redmond 2008)

The man's defence counsel referred to other coverage in the paper – notably a front-page headline 'You Coward' referring to a separate hit-and-run on the Gold Coast the previous Sunday. The paper made no reference to the trial in that story. Judge Howell decided it would be preferable to move the trial:

> Not only would we be walking on eggshells, but we would dread looking at tomorrow morning's paper.
>
> (Quoted in Redmond 2008)

Judge Howell noted he'd had problems with the Gladstone paper's reporting, too. He said a well-known trial in that city had been aborted because of the local news-paper's coverage – 'if it was in Gladstone I would have the journalists in first' (to warn them), the judge said (quoted in Redmond 2008). The *Gold Coast Bulletin* ran two editorials on the judge's decision – a small one alongside the coverage of the relocation decision (*Editorial – The Bulletin* 2008), and the main editorial of the day (*Editorial – We must be allowed to report freely* 2008). In their comment alongside coverage of the relocated trial, the *Bulletin* said it 'was quite within long-held expectations of the judicial system to report on a recent spate of hit-run accidents on the Gold Coast even though, as a pure coincidence, litigation about a 2006 hit-run case happened to commence in the District Court on that day' (*Editorial – The Bulletin* 2008). In its main editorial, the paper said the decision to blame it was set-ting 'a very dangerous precedent' (*Editorial – We must be allowed to report freely* 2008). The paper said that the trial was stopped on the basis that the paper had reported the previous day on five hit-run incidents in the previous 10 days and published an associated cartoon.

> The unfortunate corollary of this view is that a newspaper should not be allowed to report on any spates of crime – involving murder, assault, robbery or fraud – if there happens to be any case under those subjects coming before a jury in this city.
>
> (*Editorial – We must be allowed to report freely* 2008)

While the judge wanting to guarantee the accused a fair trial is as it should be, the unintended consequences would appear to limit the media from doing its job. This is a good example of the ethico-legal paradox in action, where conflicting rights compete for attention and priority. What should come first or take precedence: the right of the accused, or the right of the press (representing the public interest)?

What is 'trial by media'?

Covering crime and court hearings, as we have noted earlier, is the bread and butter of many mass media organisations. It is also an essential component of the transparency of the legal system. The media is granted access to all but the rarest of cases so that, as a representative of the public at large, they can see justice being done, and report on it for their respective audiences. Fair and accurate reports of the proceedings of court hearings are covered by qualified privilege – meaning an accused cannot sue for defamation if the journalist writes a fair and accurate (and for fair, read balanced, too) account of the court case. A lot of what journalists write defames someone – not only the evidence given in a trial. Any story that shows someone in a bad light (or, in legal terms, 'lowers them in the minds of right-thinking people' or 'lowers their reputation') is defamatory. Like those stories so beloved of the commercial current affairs programmes from the dodgy landlord to the exposé of the corrupt politician. They are defamatory, so how do the media get away with it? Because they are true (the legal defence against defamation) and, many editors would argue, in the public interest. However, in some cases, as we will see later in this chapter, the courts will protect the names of some people, and they do that in the name of public interest, too. Before a person is charged, there is little about a crime that cannot be reported, since the *sub judice* rule has not kicked in. Law academics Elizabeth Green and Jodie O'Leary (2012) summarised what tends to happen in this way:

> Trials are often conducted subsequent or parallel to the publication of information about an offence, the victim's life story and suffering, details about the suspect and any prior offences, the opinions of family and neighbours, and the likelihood of the suspect's guilt or innocence.
>
> (Green, E. and O'Leary 2012, p. 101)

Such information is published under the principles of freedom of the press and is justified by the public's right to know and the principles of open justice. While UK, Australian and US laws are similar, common law and jurisdictional differences create exceptions and situations in which these principles collide in practice. The key aspect common to all jurisdictions is the difficulty in defining the public interest – particularly when two competing interests are in play.

There are two distinct types of 'trial by media'. In this chapter we concentrate on the interaction of the news media and the legal system (police and courts). In this sense, 'trial by media' is also bound up with issues of contempt of court and, while we will mention some examples in passing, we leave it to media law experts and the legal texts to inform you on that topic. Journalists and news organisations sometimes tread a fine line between what they report, fair comment on legal matters, the *sub judice* rule and contempt of court. 'Trial by media', while multifaceted, often amounts to the media taking on the roles of judge, jury, and executioner before a charge has been laid, if it ever is, and that aspect of the phenomenon will be examined in the next chapter. However, it is more usual for the media to assume 'guilt' and then to vilify the accused, regardless of the legal niceties, like 'innocent until proven guilty'. The issue represents a very clear fault line – one that exists between the news media and the police – and one that gets blurred regularly.

Contempt of Court

The most common contempt of court occurs when something is published that is seen by legal authorities as having the potential to adversely affect the accused's chance of a fair trial. Journalists know from their media law training at university, or refreshers in the office, that they need to be very careful about what they say in the so-called *sub judice* period – i.e. after a person has been charged, and before their case and any appeals are concluded. A media law text, like Pearson and Polden (2011), is a good starting point for sound advice. But the mainstream media's efforts to inform the public about high profile crimes sometimes lead to poor judgment on the part of reporters and editors. The Australian *sub judice* laws were pushed beyond the limit in early 2006 by none other than *The Age*, the respected Melbourne newspaper, in a story about the Mildura road deaths referred to above. On Saturday night, 18 February 2006, six Mildura teenagers died after being struck by a car driven by Thomas Towle. The broadcast media was saturated with coverage of the tragedy all Sunday, and on Monday *The Age* reported extensively on the tragedy on their front page (Tippet et al. 2006). The following day, though, they took the highly unusual step of publishing Towle's prior convictions. Remember the *sub judice* rule prohibits the publication of material relating to a pending legal proceeding which has a 'real and definite tendency' to 'interfere with the course of justice'. Breaching the rules can lead to possible imprisonment and the abandonment of the trial. So it is brave reporters and editors that test the system. A little over a week after the accident, *Media Watch* (*Media and Contempt* 2006), in commenting on *The Age*'s controversial coverage, gave two other examples where broadcast and print media had published material that led to trials being postponed. Publishing material about an accused's background has long been a grey area for the media – like the police 'parading' the accused in front of TV cameras on their way in and out of police headquarters or the courts.

Police are quite willing to provide background material to reporters, and there seemed to be a consensus among the media that in cases like the Mildura road deaths, the trial would be so far off that a story appearing at the time would have little effect on the later trial. But, about 10 months later, the media were given a severe wake-up call. *The Age* was convicted of contempt of court and fined $75,000 in the Victorian Supreme Court (Age *found in contempt* 2006). Justice Philip Cummins said the paper's publication of the accused's prior convictions before his trial was a serious contempt because it had the potential to prejudice jurors and the man's right to a fair trial. The judge said the information had not been previously in the public domain, and the fact that the convictions were directly relevant to the offences the accused was charged with meant the information was unlikely to fade from readers' minds (Age *found in contempt* 2006). In March, 2008, Towle was found guilty of six counts of dangerous driving causing death (*Victims' families 'betrayed' by verdict* 2008). The victims' families had hoped for convictions on the more serious charge of culpable driving which would have carried a heavier penalty (*Victims' families 'betrayed' by verdict* 2008).

Another case that had a high profile, because of the infamy of the central figure, proved a legal nightmare for the media. Australian underworld figure, Carl Williams, was killed in prison in 2010. According to legal writer Sally Jackson (2010c), reporters were having to use extreme caution in their stories about Williams' death 'as they pick their way through a maze of court suppression orders controlling what they are allowed to reveal'. She said that certain key facts that would have added context to his bashing to death in Barwon Prison could not be reported in Victoria or online, while others were suppressed nationally (Jackson, S. 2010c). The Victorian Director of Public Prosecutions at the time was investigating *Who* magazine for breaching those suppression orders and possible contempt of court over a cover story (*Death of a gangster* 2010). Newsagents in Victoria were instructed to remove the issue from sale (Petrie 2010). Sixteen years earlier, the same magazine under a different title, *Who Weekly*, was fined $100,000 plus costs, and the editor another $10,000, for contempt of court for publishing a cover story on serial killer Ivan Milat titled 'The Accused' (Hirst and Patching 2007, pp. 178–9). The front page photo of Milat clearly identified the now-convicted serial killer, but at the time it was found to be in contempt because it could prejudice or influence a jury since the question of the suspect's identity was to be an issue at the trial. *Who Weekly* was forced to withdraw the issue and re-release it with Milat's face covered with a non-removable sticker (Hirst and Patching 2007, p. 179).

Contempt and the Family Court

In 2012, Brisbane's *Courier Mail* was charged over its coverage of an international family custody case involving four young sisters whose mother was challenging an order to return them to their father in Italy. The mother had brought the girls to Australia for a holiday in 2010 and stayed, breaking a shared custody agreement to return to Italy (Byrne, E. 2012). *The Courier Mail* published on its front page on both May 15 and 16,

2012, the names and a photo of the mother and the four girls, who at the time were 'on the run' from authorities with their great-grandmother while their mother appealed the court decision to send them back (Jabour 2013a). Under Australian law, the identities of people involved in Family Court proceedings cannot be published (Bavas 2013). Judge Colin Forrest said at the time that the non-publication law existed to protect 'the people who matter most in this case, the children' (Owen, J. 2012). It was suggested by a sister publication to *The Courier Mail* in the Murdoch stable that the journalists involved faced potential jail sentences (Owen, J. 2012). A former Brisbane Family Court judge, in a newspaper opinion piece, said irresponsible sections of the media had helped 'orchestrate and feed a media frenzy with the children placed front and centre' (Jordan 2012). Former judge, Brian Jordan, said in 40 years in the law, he had 'never before witnessed such irresponsible and harmful reporting of children's matters before a court' (2012). He added *The Courier Mail* had also published sensitive letters between the children and their father. *The Courier Mail* was not the only media outlet criticised by the former judge. He said the children had been interviewed by reporters and video of them criticising their father was shown on television (Jordan 2012). After emotional scenes at their Brisbane home, where the girls were shown on the TV news being dragged away screaming, and later calling to their mother at the airport, the girls were finally flown back to their country of birth, where they remain (as of April, 2013) with their father. Eight months after *The Courier Mail* published the girls' names and photo, the Australian Federal Police handed a brief of evidence to the Commonwealth Director of Public Prosecutions (Jabour 2013a). Two *Courier Mail* editors faced court in early April, 2013, charged with breaching the Family Law Act, and the paper pleaded guilty to the charges in August 2013 (Elks 2013; Calligeros 2013).

The issue had arisen a year earlier in the Sydney hoax-bomb case involving high school student Madeleine Pulver, who we will discuss later in the context of the invasion of her privacy by the media. Again it demonstrated what the journalist and media academic, Margaret Simons, characterised as the way 'the media often treat contempt law with contempt' (2011a). This time it had to do with pictures of the businessman Paul Peters, accused of fixing a fake bomb around the teenager's neck in a failed extortion attempt. It was a huge story at the time – a teenager spending 10 hours with a bomb strapped around her neck, not knowing if it was real. All the Australian newspapers covered Peters' later arrest in the United States, and published photos of the accused – while some obscured his face, others didn't. As we mentioned in relation to the Ivan Milat case earlier, it is contempt to publish a picture of an accused person where identity is going to be an issue at the trial. But at that early stage after Peters' arrest, how would the media know if identity would be an issue? Margaret Simons (2011a) showed how differing approaches by different newspapers demonstrated they must have had differing legal advice about how sensitive the case would be in the state in which any eye witnesses or jury members might be drawn, and different levels of caution:

> The *Herald Sun* [Victoria] ran the picture with no suppression. *The Daily Telegraph* [New South Wales] pixelated it. *The Australian* [national] used a big black box over the eyes – which were the only part of the face that Maddie Pulver could see, according to news reports. *The Sydney Morning Herald* [New South Wales] ran a picture of Peters unobscured, but oddly obscured the faces of the people he was photographed with.
>
> (Simons 2011a)

We added the home states of the various newspapers in square brackets, for added clarity. Peters was sentenced to at least 10 years in jail for the extortion attempt and what the court was told was the 'unimaginable terror' he had inflicted on Miss Pulver (Dale, A. 2012). There is no hard and fast rule in this area and every day we see different news organisations taking different approaches to pixelating or covering the identity of people in legal difficulties. On the same story one outlet will pixelate and others won't. It is a difficult area of the law, and one in need of change in light of those differences, and problems associated with Internet bloggers and social media, as we will see later.

Everyone deserves a fair trial

Everyone, regardless of who they are, what they are alleged to have done and what anyone thinks, deserves their day in court and the chance to face their accuser(s) – in other words, to have a fair trial. It is a cornerstone of the British system of common law in use throughout most of the English-speaking world.

How a trial can affect the media in a different way was demonstrated when *The Weekend Australian* magazine accompanying the May 22– 23, 2010, issue of the paper was circulated in all Australian states except Victoria. The Victorian Supreme Court late on the Friday had granted an injunction against publication (of the cover story in the colour magazine). The injunction stopped Victorians reading the particular story that the rest of Australia was allowed to read (Overington 2010b) until the end of a high profile trial (*Judges ban story of unrelated murder* 2010). On page two of the paper proper, Peter Faris (2010), a Melbourne criminal barrister, explained to readers outside Victoria, under the headline 'Silenced by "risk of unfair trial"' why Victorians wouldn't be allowed to read the feature article – or his story either – for the time being. The former head of the Murdoch group in Australia, John Hartigan (2012), later told a media and the courts symposium on the Gold Coast that 70,000 copies of the magazine were withdrawn from circulation at a cost of hundreds of thousands of dollars. 'Little wonder it became known as the "stupid juror rule",' he added (Hartigan 2012, p. 19).

We have highlighted these past cases to show the difficulties the media faces in reporting crime and court cases. You could be writing a story and be unaware that it could be affecting a current trial – like the *Gold Coast Bulletin* cases that began this chapter. Most editors tend to group stories on similar topics together (rather than scatter them through the paper or news bulletin). *The Age* and *Courier Mail* cases are perhaps more clear cut, but with the lead-time associated with the production of *The Weekend Australian* magazine, how could they possibly predict that a particular trial would be on at the time of publication? These cases are relatively rare but serve an educative and cautionary purpose.

A fair trial in the digital era?

A bigger threat to an accused receiving a fair trial nowadays comes from the Internet and social media. Whenever there is a high profile crime, like a murder, a Google search will alert anyone with access to a computer, tablet or smartphone to any number of Internet forums, social media sites and blogs 'where rumour is taken as fact, opinions stand unchallenged and any knowledge of the law as it applies to defamation or contempt is ignored, if known at all' (Remeikis 2012). While traditional media, as we have already seen, are held accountable for what they publish, and are bound by law and their Code of Ethics, the law is struggling to keep up with new media. Publishers on the Internet, like bloggers and social media users, seem untouchable. This is the techno-legal time-gap (Hirst and Harrison 2007), which means that legal and regulatory regimes may lag behind the functionality of new technologies in the communication field.

The problems associated with the unregulated Internet first came to the attention of legal authorities in Australia in a major way after a multiple murder in Kapunda in South Australia in 2010. The identity of the man accused of murdering three family members in the township, about 80 kilometres north of Adelaide, was suppressed from mainstream media publication by the court, but many people knew who he was from postings on Facebook (*Kapunda murder trial prompts Facebook alarm* 2010). One media website called it 'Facebook justice' while the State Attorney General said reg-ulation of the social media site was the responsibility of the federal government (Littlely et al. 2010). Twenty-year-old Jason Alexander Downie was jailed for 35 years for killing teenager Chantelle Rowe, and her parents, Andrew and Rose. He had stabbed the three at least 112 times (*Justice for Chantelle as jealous killer jailed for 35 years* 2012). Earlier in the year, police in Queensland were calling for calm after the death of a young girl in Bundaberg and the appearance in court of the man charged with her murder. The case generated hate posts on social media sites with experts warning the information in the messages could 'pervert the course of justice' (Bourke and Binnie 2010). It is now common when any major story erupts involving public outrage – think of the Boston bombings of April 2013 – for social media to go feral with spiteful and hateful commentary, or even conspiracy theories. We call this phe-nomenon the 'witches of Facebook' (Hirst 2009) because it often resembles a witch-hunt in which innocents and perpetrators are often confused, or vigilante-style calls for severe punishment (the death penalty, for example) are demanded by ignorant people who hide behind false identities and manufactured moral outrage. Police in many jurisdictions now routinely call for people not to use social media in this way because it can lead to trials being aborted.

The issue led to the Law Commission in the United Kingdom issuing a 'consultation paper' in late 2012, about whether social media were making contempt of court laws unworkable, in which it suggested tightening the existing laws (Rozenberg 2013).

In 2011–2012, there were three, high-profile cases in Australia where authorities pleaded with social media users to be careful not to threaten the various accuseds' chances of a fair trial. We discuss two of the cases here, and use the third as a case study at the end of the chapter. The first concerned the man accused of the murder of Queensland teenager Daniel Morcombe in 2003. Initially, it was a case where the Queensland Police social media strategy, in the opinion of one journalism academic, 'came seriously unstuck' (Knight, A. 2011). Their Facebook site had announced the breakthrough in the eight-year investigation into disappearance of Daniel, aged 13, from a bus stop on the Sunshine Coast north of Brisbane. It was to be the biggest missing-person investigation in Queensland Police history. When police announced on Facebook they had arrested a 41-year-old man on several charges, including murder, it generated hundreds of comments, mostly praising the police. But some made angry and speculative claims which, according to journalism academic Alan Knight, 'might be seen to influ-ence a court case which had not even begun' (2011). The police quickly posted a warn-ing of the dangers of such posts on their Facebook page. Media law expert, Professor

Mark Pearson, said at the time that the police should be concerned about the comments on their site as they could jeopardise a trial:

> It may be counterproductive for a conviction or it may cause a delay. Either way it's a huge cost to the community.
>
> (Pearson 2011)

Criminal defence lawyer, Bill Potts, said it was inevitable lawyers would attempt to delay or abort trials because of what was said about their clients on the police Facebook page (cited in Gough 2011). Weeks later, after a court appearance by the accused and the day before the lifting of a suppression order on his name, legal experts were still warning social media users that anyone who posted about the possible guilt, identity or history of the accused could jeopardise the trial and face hefty penalties (Dickinson 2011). *The Australian* provided an example of responsible mainstream media coverage on 15 August 2011, the day before the renewed warning to social media users. It ran two versions of the latest Morcombe story. In states outside Queensland, the paper included details of the alleged murderer's identity, while online and on the newspaper service Press Display the stories were missing. On Press Display, the far right column is blank, save for the comment 'Content has been suppressed for editorial and/or legal reasons' (Crook 2011). *The Australian* told *Crikey* the action was taken in order not to affect the legal proceedings taking place in Queensland, noting that the story could be published outside that state, but not in the state where legal action was taking place or online (Crook 2011).

An equally high-profile case in Melbourne, the tragic death of ABC employee Jill Meagher, in September, 2012, highlighted both the benefits and dangers of social media involvement in criminal investigations. Both police and Jill's father praised the positive role social media like Facebook and Twitter had played in the investigation (Posetti 2012). Social media networks helped search for the woman, to trace her last steps and helped identify the person seen on CCTV approaching her, the one who was later charged with her murder and who would lead police to her body (Silvester 2012). The level of social media engagement with the case was described by one expert as 'unprecedented other than [during] natural disasters in Australia' (Lowe 2012). There was a massive outpouring of grief after her death was announced but then the social media posts turned ugly. An expert on the relationship between the media and social media, journalism academic, Julie Posetti, said 'speculation grew in inverse proportion to the available evidence' (2012). There were judgments about the accused's guilt, speculation about his history, and links to pictures of him, which led police to follow their Queensland colleagues in the Morcombe case and warn of the effects such posts could have on presumption of innocence and a fair trial (cited in Posetti 2012). Victoria police had to make repeated requests before Facebook removed several hate pages targeting the accused killer (*Facebook bows to police demands over hate pages related to the killing of Jill Meagher* 2012). The police identified six Facebook pages they said could jeopardise the accused's right to a fair trial, one that had more than 44,000 'likes' and included posts inciting violence and sharing details of the man's background. Jill's husband, Tom Meagher, called a media conference to plead with people to stop posting comments about the accused (Russell 2012). In June 2013, Jill Meagher's killer, 41-year-old Adrian Ernest Bayley was sentenced to life in prison with a minimum term of 35 years (*Adrian Bayley to serve at least 35 years in jail for rape and murder of Jill*

Meagher 2013). At the time of writing (early April, 2013), controversial Australian journalist Derryn Hinch had been charged with contempt of court (again) over suppressed material he allegedly published on his website (Russell 2013a). He faces trial in late 2013 in what he claims is a 'test case for social media' (Akerman 2013).

Social media activity around the Jill Meagher case kick-started renewed calls for federal action on national guidelines to counter social media's adverse effects. Australia's attorneys general met in Brisbane (as the Standing Committee on Law and Justice, formerly the Standing Committee of Attorneys-General) on the day of Ms Meagher's funeral and decided on a working group to make recommendations on how to regulate the spread of prejudicial material on social media, including warnings for users and protocols for social media companies. The group would also propose directions that courts could give to juries on social media, examine laws that detail juror offences and assess what research was needed to determine how social media affected jurors' decisions (Lee, J. and Oakes 2012). At the time, many commentators felt that enforcing contempt laws in cyberspace was nearly impossible. Bond University law professor, David Field, had said earlier in the year that he didn't think a fair trial was possible in the digital age, while University of Technology Professor of Law and director of the Communications Law Centre, Michael Fraser, was more optimistic, saying balancing the digital age with the right to a fair trial was a challenge for the legal system, but not a hopeless case (both quoted in Remeikis 2012). However, when it comes to high-profile trials – and massive media involvement – no one beats the United States.

Justice and celebrity – the media trial of the twentieth century?

They called it 'the media trial of the twentieth century' when American footballer, actor and media personality, O. J. Simpson, was accused, tried, and acquitted of murdering his wife and her friend in a very public trial in Los Angeles, California in the mid-1990s. In a civil case brought by her family Simpson was subsequently found to have materially contributed to his wife's death and was ordered to pay the family millions of dollars in compensation. The media circus began with the police chasing Simpson through LA with television station helicopters overhead beaming the action live around the world. When the trial got under way, a virtual television city was built outside the court. Throughout the trial the major players – defence and prosecution lawyers, potential witnesses and judge Lance Ito – were not only the subject of media speculation, they often gave their opinions freely in media conferences and arranged media statements. Every minute of the trial was broadcast on 'Court TV' in America and was covered extensively in the international media. In the end, the public verdict was divided on Simpson's guilt, but the jury found him not guilty. In December, 2008, Simpson was jailed for 15 years over a botched attempt to recover sports memorabilia that became an armed robbery (Tran 2008). In mid-2013 Simpson was seeking a new trial (Glionna 2013).

Another celebrity media circus

What was described as the largest concentration of US media outside Iraq (at the time, the 'coalition of the willing' were 'over there') descended on the small Colorado town of Eagle in August, 2003, for the first court hearing of a rape charge against Los Angeles Lakers basketball superstar, Kobe Bryant. Hundreds of reporters and television news crews were there to record the brief court appearance by Kobe, who was charged with raping a 19-year-old woman while staying at a local hotel the previous June. He publicly admitted having sex with the woman, a hotel employee, but claimed it was consensual. The sports star stood to lose millions in endorsements, and if found guilty could have faced life in prison. As the US judicial system slowly ground along, ethical dilemmas emerged for the media. A tabloid published the name and photo of Bryant's accuser in what one media ethicist called the 'anything-goes-as-long-as-it-sells contest' (McBride 2011). After the criminal case collapsed in mid-2004, the woman sued for unspecified damages for mental injuries, public scorn and the humiliation she had suffered since the alleged rape. The civil lawsuit was settled on undisclosed terms (*Bryant settles rape damaged claim* 2005). One lawyer said the case was too complex to estimate a settlement amount but offered an opinion:

> In Kobe Bryant terms, the check will be small. In her terms, the check will be gigantic. Kobe just bought her a home.
>
> (Quoted in O'Driscoll 2005)

Chasing the 'King of Pop'

The mantle of 'OJ Mark 2' settled firmly on the first trial of the 'King of Pop', Michael Jackson. In late 2003, the eccentric entertainer was charged with child molestation. His appearance to plead not guilty to the charges in the equally-small Californian town of Santa Maria in early 2004 was another media circus, with the late pop star jumping onto the roof of his limousine to greet his fans (McKenna 2004). Vendors sold hot dogs, steaks, and t-shirts. Many fans had come in chartered buses and cars in a 'caravan of love' from Los Angeles and Las Vegas. After the court appearance – he was scolded by the judge for being 21 minutes late – Jackson invited the fans back to his Neverland Ranch for refreshments. Court appearances don't get much more bizarre. Forests of paper were devoted to every detail of the long trial. Lurid accusations were levelled at the singer. There were delays caused by the star's back pain (*Wacko wobbles* 2005). It all dragged on through much of the first half of 2005. He was found not guilty on all 10 counts after the jury had deliberated for seven days, having heard 140 witnesses and seen some 600 items of evidence. Hundreds of fans outside the court cheered the verdicts. Jackson himself was reported to have dabbed his eyes with tissues (Shovelan 2005). Three months after the end of the trial two of the jurors told a TV interviewer they believed the singer's young accuser had been sexually assaulted (*2 jurors say they regret Jackson's acquittal* 2005). Jackson died in 2009.

Another OJ-style trial in the US

Americans faced another potentially-high profile case in 2013 involving the killing of African-American Trayvon Martin, 17, who died at the hands of a white armed guard, George Zimmerman. Zimmerman appeared in court charged with second-degree murder more than six weeks after admitting he killed the unarmed schoolboy (*Zimmerman faces court* 2012). The case sparked a national uproar about race relations and the right to self-defence in the United States (*Shooter charged over death of US teen* 2012). Zimmerman told police he shot the teenager in self-defence, having earlier told them by phone that he had noticed a suspicious-looking black teenager wearing a hoodie.

Under Florida law the 28-year-old had no case to answer (Kennedy 2012). As the (Australian) ABC's Stephanie Kennedy reported at the time, 'anger and outrage swept through the US' (2012). It soon became another demonstration of what the Poynter Institute's Kelly McBride called the new tools of media power and justice (2012b) – how a story of a teenager's killing went from barely rating a mention in local newspapers to a major national issue. McBride said that a decade earlier Martin's family would have had a hard time getting the attention of the national media, but with the help of a few bloggers and social media, they managed to pressure the local police in Sanford, Florida, into charging their son's killer (McBride 2012b). There was massive American and international interest in the trial, which ended with Zimmerman's acquittal on all charges (Millar 2013). As in the Simpson case previously mentioned, at least one juror later said publicly that she did not feel comfortable with the decision. Several days of protest followed Zimmerman's release from custody.

Suppression orders

One of the major hindrances to court reporting in the eyes of both media employers and journalists is the readiness of courts to suppress names and information, preventing the mainstream media from reporting various aspects of cases. Reporters and editors question the impact suppression orders have on the concept of open justice – the public being able to see justice being done. It has been an ethical issue for some courageous journalists who, in the past, have breached suppression orders on the principle that the public had a right to know the suppressed information – usually the identity of a particular accused – and paid the legal price. The former head of News Limited in Australia, John Hartigan, noting that colleagues at the Murdoch stable's colourful American tabloid, the *New York Post*, had not seen a single suppression order in the previous five years, estimated in early 2011 that their legal counsel in Australia had faced more than 500 in the previous 12 months – 270 in Victoria alone (2012, p. 18). And he said, 'they were just the ones we knew about'. Former Victorian court media officer and journalist member of the Australian Press Council, Prue Innes, summarised the dilemma for the media:

> The problems with suppression orders are that many are far too wide, poorly worded and effectively last forever because they are worded 'until further notice' (which is rarely made).
>
> (Innes 2012, p. 83)

Hartigan described suppression orders as the media's 'bugbear' (2012, p. 18).

Take the case of one of Australia's 'most wanted', drug trafficker Tony Mokbel, as an example. Sydney media lawyer, Nicola Shaver (2011), pointed out that more than 40 suppression orders were made in relation to his 2011 trial. The orders even prevented Victorians from watching the same version of the Channel Nine crime series, *Underbelly*, as everyone else (Shaver 2011).

One of the key arguments for suppression orders is that research suggests that media coverage of criminal suspects can influence the opinions of prospective and eventual jurors (Green, E. and O'Leary 2012, p. 102).

The MEAA, in its 2012 report on the state of press freedom in Australia, said research by the Right to Know Coalition found a total of 1077 suppression orders were granted in Australia in 2011, 644 of them in Victoria (*Kicking the Cornerstone of Democracy* 2012, p. 58). Tasmania and South Australia had no formal notification process, meaning that it was not possible to accurately report the numbers of orders granted in those states. The Right to Know Coalition, in a submission to a Senate Standing Committee, articulated the problem as the media sees it:

> The fundamental problem with suppression and non-publication orders in Australia is that there are too many unjustifiable and unnecessary orders which act as a gag on the media's ability to report on the justice system.
>
> (*Kicking the Cornerstone of Democracy* 2012, p. 60)

One of Australia's best-known journalists, Derryn Hinch (we mentioned his latest run-in with the law earlier in this chapter), who named his autobiography *Human Headlines* (2010) after his nickname, the 'Human Headline', spent five months in home detention in 2011 for breaching suppression orders by naming sex offenders (*Defiant Derryn Hinch vows to continue campaign to name sex offenders* 2011). He was banned from broadcasting on any medium as part of the sentence. He had earlier lost a High Court challenge to the Victorian law preventing the public naming of child sex offenders (Harrison 2011). Hinch is no newcomer to challenging the law – he spent 12 days in prison in 1987 and was fined $10,000 for revealing the prior convictions of a priest who was on trial for other sex offences.

New Zealander Cameron Slater, who blogs at Whale Oil Beef Hooked, has crusaded for changes to that country's suppression laws for years. He was fined nearly $8000 in mid-September, 2010, after being convicted on nine out of ten charges of breaching suppression orders (*Whale Oil may appeal convictions* 2010). Some of the charges related to blog posts containing pictures that revealed the identities of a prominent New Zealand entertainer and a former NZ Olympian who were both charged with sexual offences (*Blogger on trial for breaching suppressions* 2010). He said before the hearing that he thought NZ's suppression laws were out of date (*Blogger to defend suppression breach charges* 2009). Outside court, after his conviction, he said that he had 'copped a flogging as best they can with a wet bus ticket' (quoted in *Whale Oil may appeal convictions* 2010).

In response to widespread complaints from Australian journalists that they were often unaware of what information was subject to non-publication orders, a proposal was put before the Standing Committee on Law and Justice for a national register of suppression orders canvassing two options – a publicly available register or one with access restricted to authorised persons, with the MEAA supporting the alternative that it be publicly available (*Kicking the Cornerstone of Democracy* 2012, p. 60). The Commonwealth Director of Public Prosecutions has developed a National Register of Suppression Orders made in Commonwealth prosecutions, but their guidelines do not indicate that the register is available to the media (*Suppression Orders* 2012).

Suppression orders are another area where social media are leaving the law behind. We've seen earlier in this chapter that police and the families of victims have had to plead with bloggers and users of Twitter and Facebook not to jeopardise criminal proceedings. Social media over-riding suppression orders was demonstrated in what *Crikey* reporter, Andrew Dodd (2011b), dubbed 'suppression-happy' South Australia in 2011. A state MP was charged with child pornography offences and Dodd said that although the man's name had been suppressed by the court, meaning the mainstream media could not name him, 'If you use social media (and who doesn't) you might already know [who he is] because the man's identity is all over the net – particularly in South Australia' (Dodd 2011b). The suppression order stayed in place for about 17 months while a Google search at any time would have revealed his name (Dowdell 2012). In September, 2012, his name was released temporarily after a magistrate found he had a case to answer on six charges relating to child pornography (Marcus 2012). Four months later the Supreme Court ordered the magistrate to reconsider (Fountein 2013). While the man's identity was published widely after he was committed to stand trial, the Supreme Court decision meant it was automatically suppressed again (Fountein 2013).

Suppression orders, or injunctions to stop media reporting of high-profile cases, are a threat to media freedoms but, thankfully, courts are not always disposed to grant them. In a famous case involving Australia's richest woman, Gina Rinehart, a judge refused a suppression order on the grounds that there was public interest in the case and that it would set a bad precedent, leaving the way open for anyone in the public spotlight to suppress news about them that was unfavourable to their reputation (Wells 2012). In the UK, until recently, suppression orders were easier to get and their very existence was subject to secrecy. So-called 'super injunctions' issued to football celebrities like Manchester United's Ryan Giggs not only suppressed reporting, but also suppressed the reporting of the injunction itself. This system was eventually smashed when British newspapers refused to go along with the super injunctions in the Giggs case and blew the lid on what was essentially a legal racket to keep the rich and famous out of the newspapers, even when there was legitimate public interest in their case (Ackland 2011; Cohen 2011).

Case Study 1: The Baden-Clay murder and the media

Brisbane mother, Allison Baden-Clay, 43, went missing on 23 April 2012, and her husband, Gerard, was charged with her murder on 14 June. For the weeks following her disappearance, speculation about what had happened was rampant in mainstream and social media. The Queensland Police Facebook page, whose fan base of 290,000 exceeds the circulation of Brisbane newspaper, *The Courier Mail*, was used to announce the arrest. Then began a pre-trial 'trial' on Facebook. Media law expert, Professor Mark Pearson, characterised the postings on the Police's Facebook page as the work of a 'lynch mob'. Just as had happened after the arrest of a suspect in the Daniel Morcombe case the previous year (discussed above), the site was inundated with comments – some of them offensive and prejudicial. More than 1,500 people reacted to the Facebook announcement, many posting inflammatory comments, forcing the police to appeal to users not to undermine the case (Christensen 2012). Professor Pearson found that in the first 21 hours after the announcement of the arrest, more than 500 posts were made to the Police's Facebook page, and as he noted, those were the ones that survived the moderation process after officers checked and deleted the inappropriate ones (Pearson, Mark 2012).

[Early in 2013, Baden-Clay was committed for trial for the murder of his wife (Kyriacou and Murray 2012)].

Questions for discussion:

1. You might think this case study of little interest in a journalism ethics text, but wait. The media organisation you might work for probably has a Facebook page or invites comments on stories on their website. Who has the responsibility for what is posted in either area?
2. Wouldn't it have been easier for the Queensland Police to call a news conference – they do that often enough on other matters – and tell the mainstream media of the arrest, rather than run the risk of soliciting comments from 'armchair detectives'?
3. Do you have a Facebook page? Many people do. Perhaps you comment on the news of the day. Are you responsible for what your friends post in reaction to what you 'announce'?
3. The husband, now charged with Ms Baden-Clay's murder, was seen regularly on TV, and quoted in newspapers, during the period between her being reported missing and his arrest. What implications might that have for potential jurors in the trial?
4. Can mainstream media report any of the adverse comments on the Queensland Police's Facebook page after Mr Baden-Clay's arrest?
5. Does it make any difference that the trial might be years off (because of the backlog of serious cases)?

Case Study 2: Amanda Knox – guilty on the website, but not in court

It was a case that attracted massive media attention on both sides of the Atlantic for years, with the lurid details of sex games gone wrong and the eventual death of a British girl allegedly at the hands of an American girl and her Italian boyfriend (Alberici 2011). Both girls were university students studying abroad in Perugia, Italy. Amanda Knox and boyfriend Raffaele Sollecito were initially found guilty (along with a small-time drug trafficker from the Ivory Coast) of the 2007 murder of Knox's flatmate in Perugia, British university student, Meredith Kercher, and spent four years (of a 26-year sentence) in jail before being freed on appeal (Kissane 2011). The media coverage of the trial was at all times emotive and, with the benefit of hindsight, biased. The international media (outside America) had variously reported during her many court appearances that Knox was a drug-taking, sex-crazed she-devil and a spell-casting witch (*Amanda Knox: 'satanic whore' or saint?* 2011). As soon as Knox was arrested, her family employed a public relations company specialising in crisis management as part of an effort to counter her portrayal by prosecutors (and much of the European media) as a 'she-devil' (Cooper and Raftery 2011). The British tabloids labelled her 'Foxy Knoxy', a nickname she used herself on her Facebook and MySpace pages (apparently referring to her prowess at soccer), while the US media portrayed her as 'a nice young woman' consistently protesting her innocence (Cooper and Raftery 2011). The case showed how differently international news is reported in various countries and raised serious questions of objectivity, when the story involves, in this case, an American citizen abroad being accused of a serious crime against a British citizen (Ballard 2011). After being freed, Ms Knox, then 24, flew home to America to field multi-million-dollar media and book deals. About four months later, Knox, who had not publicly discussed her ordeal beyond a brief expression of gratitude on her release, was reported to have signed a big book deal (*Amanda Knox signs '$US4 million' book deal* 2012). While the media coverage of the initial trial and the appeal could be described as a classic 'media circus', the case is remembered by media ethicists for a classic case of 'not wrong for long'. As the Leveson inquiry sparked by *The News of the World* scandal was holding its first hearings into the British press in London, several news outlets there got the Knox appeal result wrong. While the hundreds of British, American and Italian journalists scrambled to report the verdict, Britain's *Sky News* mistakenly flashed across its screens that the appeal had been dismissed, confirming the guilty verdict (Wilson 2011). The reverse was the truth – the appeal had been upheld, thereby freeing Knox and the others earlier convicted. Other British outlets quickly followed confirming the wrong verdict. London's *Daily Mail* reported the wrong result on their website, but quickly deleted it, but not before screenshots of the story circulated on the Internet (Wood 2011). Part of that initial report read:

> As Knox realised the enormity of what Judge Hellman was saying, she sank into her chair sobbing uncontrollably while her family and friends hugged each other in tears.
>
> (Wood 2011)

The *Daily Mail* website even had 'sources' commenting on the verdict:

> Prosecutors were delighted with the verdict and said that 'justice has been done', although they said on a human level 'it was sad two young people would be spending years in jail'.
>
> (Quoted in Wood 2011)

So that we won't be accused of singling out one paper, the London Murdoch tabloid, *The Sun*, and *The Guardian*, which played such a major role in bringing the *News of the World* phone-hacking scandal to light, also got it wrong (Wilson 2011; Wood 2011).

[In late March, 2013, Italy's Supreme Court overturned her acquittal and ordered Knox and her co-defendant Raffaele Sollecito to face a retrial (*Italy's court order retrial for Amanda Knox in murder case* 2013)].

Questions for discussion:

1. Google the Amanda Knox case and read reports from the US and UK. What's your reaction? Do you agree the coverage favours one side or the other?

2. Isn't it understandable that the American media would favour one of their own – remember the Australian coverage of the Schapelle Corby case in Bali years earlier – especially a young University student studying overseas who protests her innocence?
3. Put yourself in Amanda Knox's shoes. How would you feel about being called some of the names the European media labelled her?
4. Surely if she is called a 'she-devil' by an Italian lawyer (for the man Knox falsely accused of the murder) (Babington 2011), the media has every right to describe her as such, don't they?
5. How do you justify Sky News (UK) getting it so wrong? (Surely their reporter understood Italian?)
6. What of the other media outlets rushing to repeat the mistake? Are they even more at fault for plagiarising another outlet's story?
7. Is this the price we pay nowadays for 'instant' news?
8. Charles Feldman, co-author of the seminal work on the problems associated with modern newsgathering (*No Time to Think: The Menace of Media Speed and the 24-hour News Cycle* (Rosenberg and Feldman 2008)) told a conference of journalism educators in Melbourne in December, 2012 (Feldman 2012), that, given the impact of social media, he now refers to it as the 24-second news cycle. Is it up to bloggers and Twitter to highlight the media's errors?

8   Trial by media

Trial by media – a nightmare on mainstream

The tragic suicide in late 2012 of a nurse in Britain involved in the prank call from two Australian radio announcers pretending to be the Queen and Prince Charles and seeking information about the condition of the pregnant Duchess of Cambridge, revived memories of what the journalist involved later described as 'one of the most despicable pieces of journalism in Australia' 15 years earlier (Hansen 2012). In 1997, *A Current Affair* reporter, Jane Hansen, produced a typical consumer protection 'sting' involving a Filipino television repairman in Sydney who was charging for work not done. After a weekend of promotion on the Nine Network, the story ran on the Monday and the man took his life several days later. Calling on the public not to blame the young announcers involved in the royal prank call, Hansen recounted her own spiral into post-traumatic stress disorder following the man's suicide:

> I can now write that for years I did not sleep, I woke with nightmares, I stifled panic attacks in media conferences when all my colleagues were there, perhaps casting a judgmental eye. I threw myself into the most dangerous pursuits in journalism – coups, wars, you name it – to regain some of the credibility I had lost. A few years later, I finally sought help.
>
> (Hansen 2012)

Mention was made in the preface of the relatively low standing of journalists in the eyes of the public – somewhere near the bottom with advertising people and used car sales staff. It is our contention that much of that mistrust can be put down to the way some sections of the media – most notably the nightly commercial television current affairs programmes and tabloid newspapers – treat members of the general public and people the public admire. Part of Rawls' theory of the veil of ignorance suggests one way of looking at an ethical issue is to 'walk in the other person's shoes'; in other words, to ask yourself how would you feel if what you were writing was said about you, your parents or a close friend? We believe that the general public, perhaps unknowingly, do just that on a regular basis – certainly more often than the media thinks. It is not only the proverbial 'man in the street' that is publicly humiliated by often petty TV and tabloid entrapments. Other times it is someone whom the public admires that is subjected to a 'hatchet job'. Commercial current affairs programmes rate very highly, and some of the output of these programmes is commendable. But some is not, compared to the investigative journalism undertaken by, say, the ABC's flagship current affairs programme, *Four Corners*, or the investigative team at *The Age* in Melbourne.

Stories about the latest celebrity match-up, break-up, make-up, punch-up, or booze-up are guaranteed to see celebrity junkies rush to their favourite websites and send the 'twittersphere' into overdrive. Journalists' credibility is also not helped by the so-called 'shock jock' radio commentators who are paid handsomely to give their views on any-thing and everything. And they do, often inflaming public reaction to an individual, issue or event. It is not only the broadcast media that humiliate members of their 'audience' – the tabloid media must take some of that blame, too. How often have you seen a headline like 'Is this the worst mother in Australia?' on a tabloid front page or website, accom-panied by a photo of a woman trying to shield her face? As if she isn't already feeling bad because of being involved in a court case, the tabloids, in the form of both print and commercial broadcast media, are there to pile on the humiliation. She may not be identi-fied, but her relatives and friends – and the 'tut-tutting' gossips in her neighbourhood – will all know who she is. You may be watching the local news on TV or reading the morning paper, and there's a report of a colleague or friend accused of a serious crime. One of the authors (Roger) had just this experience towards the end of 2012 when a long-time friend, originally a source when the author worked for the ABC in the 1970s, and later a university colleague, appeared on the front page of the local paper accused of sexual abuse (Wuth 2012). It would be months before his case came to court and, regardless of the result, his reputation had been irrevocably damaged. While one of the major roles of the media is to bring such cases to light, and rightly so, you can't help feeling for someone who protests their innocence but has to wait months for their day in court. Then who is to say that if they are found not guilty the verdict will attract the same coverage as the original allegations? In many of these cases, the person at the centre of the story has been 'tried' by the media long before they appear in court, if they ever do.

Court reporting often brings into focus one of our key themes – the fault line that exists when competing ethico-legal principles collide. The legal system requires that the media observe particular rules in reporting, basically respecting the autonomy and dig-nity of the courtroom and officials, including judges. It also requires that accused per-sons get a fair trial. But the media will counter with the demand that it should be allowed to fulfil its own professional and ethical duty to deliver on their promise to audiences to honour their right to know. Trial by media crosses the line, driven in part by the profit motive and, increasingly by the role of social media and the 'witches of Facebook' that we described in the previous chapter.

What is 'trial by media'?

In this chapter we examine 'trial by media' from the point of view of its ethical, rather than legal aspects. In the previous chapter, trial by media referred to the pre-judging by the media of an accused person during the *sub judice* period – that is, after they had been charged and before their case had been decided. But there's a more common, less legal, 'trial by media' that we discussed in the introduction to this chapter where no charge may have been laid against the person at the centre of media attention. There may never be criminal charges laid, but the media (or individual media outlets or wri-ters/commentators) 'try' the person in the 'court of public opinion'. This chapter focuses on this, another of those ethico-legal grey areas.

This 'trial by media' involves the media taking on the roles of judge, jury, and executioner in much the same way as it does in the instances of invasion of privacy that are recounted later in chapter 10. In this form of 'trial by media', the stories take on a life of their own. The media may defend itself by saying it reports the facts, but once they are 'out there' the stories are subjected to the constant rewriting and updating of the 24/7 news cycle, churned in the social media 'rumour mill' and further 'enhanced' by the utterances of radio's 'shock-jocks'. If caught out the media will usually offer corrections where stories are proven wrong, but rarely with the same prominence as the original story. And who is to say that those that read the original story or stories will ever read the correction? After their media 'trial', the audience largely believes 'there is no smoke without fire' (to use a cliché) and a person's reputation is all-too-often ruined before they have their day in court, if they ever do.

Before detailing examples of 'trial by media' and considering their ramifications, we must repeat what we have said in other contexts in this book – ethical issues are never black and white (unlike the law). There are only varying shades of grey. If the issue was clear cut, it wouldn't pose an ethical dilemma. A story that one media outlet considers to be in the public interest another might decry as 'trial by media'. Journalists differ on what they think is acceptable to report in a given circumstance. While it might appear that we are 'picking' on various media outlets and suggesting all they do is unethical, this is not our intention. The mainstream media has much to be proud of. Most journalists rarely encounter major ethical dilemmas in their everyday reporting. But there are some cases where the media has clearly crossed the line and taken on the role of judge, jury and executioner. We have already mentioned one recent case in the Preface where one of the most admired broadcast organisations in the world, the BBC, got it wrong in a big way in their investigation of a Conservative Party peer over allegations he'd been involved in paedophilia in the 1980s (Kissane 2012).

Two classic 'trial by media' cases, both involving a missing daughter

Australia's most famous 'trial by media' case involved the disappearance of baby Azaria Chamberlain and the later sentencing of her mother, Lindy – amid massive media coverage – to life in prison. In the United Kingdom it was the disappearance, just days before her fourth birthday, of Madeleine McCann while on holiday with her parents in Portugal. The Chamberlain case goes back to August 1980 and the McCann case to 2007. The fact that we are still talking about them shows their importance and impact on media ethics.

Barely nine weeks old, baby Azaria Chamberlain was snatched by a dingo from her parents' tent during a family camping holiday to Uluru (also known as Ayers Rock, a huge sandstone rock formation, and major tourist attraction), south of Alice Springs in the Northern Territory on the night of 17 August 1980. The baby's disappearance sparked massive public and media interest. Within days, rumours were circulating, some in the media, suggesting alternative theories on what had happened to baby Azaria. It was falsely reported that 'Azaria' meant 'sacrifice in the wilderness' when Lindy said the name meant 'blessed of God' (*Rumours and Facts* n.d.). Much was made of Lindy not reacting to the loss of her child as would be expected of a grieving mother. Lindy and Michael Chamberlain were devout Seventh-day Adventists and said it was their faith that gave them strength (Godfrey 2012). The case polarised the nation. The initial conoroner's inquest supported the parents' claim that a dingo stole their baby. Such was the interest in the case that the finding was broadcast live on television – a first for Australia. After further police investigation and a second inquest, Lindy Chamberlain was tried for murder and sentenced in 1982 to life in prison. Michael was convicted as an accessory and given a suspended sentence. The Chamberlains appealed all the way to the High Court without success, but it was the chance finding of a piece of Azaria's clothing in an area frequented by dingoes in 1986 that led to Lindy's release from prison. The Chamberlains' convictions were overturned, but it would be three decades after the tragedy before Lindy received justice – to hear a Coroner finally say that a dingo had sneaked into the family's unzipped tent and snatched Azaria (Brown, M. 2012). Finally, in 2012, the Chamberlains heard a Coroner agree with their account of what happened to their baby (Godfrey 2012).

Following the disappearance of Madeleine McCann, one antipodean blogger (and at the time, a judge's associate) characterised the media treatment of Maddy's mother, Kate, as being 'sickeningly familiar to any Australian who remembered the anguished case of Lindy Chamberlain' (Dale, H. 2008). She added:

> Like Lindy, Kate McCann is characterised by her strong religious faith and her determination to find her missing child. Like Lindy, Kate has not behaved in the manner expected of a grieving mother. Although – to use poet Les Murray's phrase – her fault is not 'a defect in weeping'; rather, it is apparently unseemly to use the media to publicise Madeleine's disappearance.
>
> (Dale, H. 2008)

The ongoing nightmare for the McCanns began during a holiday in Portugal in 2007 when, while dining with friends at a nearby restaurant, their three-year-old daughter Madeleine disappeared from their holiday apartment. It was one of the biggest stories in the United Kingdom in years, regularly topping the lists of most-read stories on newspapers websites. One tabloid editor was quoted as saying: 'Put it on page one and sales soar by 30,000' (Button 2007). *The Age's* Europe correspondent at the time, James Button, described the media frenzy surrounding coverage of Madeleine's disappearance as 'unsourced British reports of unsourced Portuguese reports' which created 'a perfect storm: huge media fascination with almost no facts to feed it' (2007). The McCanns appeared before the Leveson inquiry in late 2011 to discuss their treatment by the media. They said that press coverage of their daughter's disappearance was initially sympathetic but soon changed, with some articles implying the parents were 'hiding something'. One story said the couple had sold their daughter into slavery, another that they had killed her and hid her body in a freezer (*The parents of missing British girl Madeleine McCann have appeared before the Leveson media inquiry* 2011). Kate said the family felt powerless to do anything about the adverse coverage – 'when it's your voice against a powerful media, it just doesn't hold weight' (quoted in *The parents of missing British girl Madeleine McCann have appeared before the Leveson media inquiry* 2011). She told the inquiry she felt violated when extracts from her private diary appeared in *The News of the World* (Murphy, D. 2011). The McCanns successfully sued several British newspapers over suggestions that they had caused their daughter's death and covered it up. Two of the papers, the *Daily Express* and the *Daily Star* (and their Sunday stablemates) were forced to take the almost-unprecedented step of printing front page (and on their respective websites) apologies to the McCanns and pay £550,000 damages (*Statements in full: McCann case* 2008). Journalism academic and media commentator, Roy Greenslade, in one of his *Guardian* blogs (2008) reproduced some of the front page headlines the *Express* papers published: 'We can prove the parents did it' – Portuguese police; Madeline (*sic*) was 'killed by sleeping pills' – sensational new claim; McCanns 'are hiding a big secret' – speculation by John Stalker; and 'McCanns or a friend must be to blame' – interview with a waiter (quoted in Greenslade 2008). Many of the stories were followed a day later with articles carrying denials. In mid-2013 Scotland Yard announced it was re-opening the case, saying they believed Madeleine may still be alive and that they had 38 suspects (Miranda 2013).

Trial by media can have wide ethical ramifications

The long-running saga of union-official-turned-Australian-federal-politician, Craig Thomson, is a classic 'trial by media'. If ever anyone has been subjected to an on-going campaign of media allegations, it has been the former Labor, later Independent, member for the New South Wales Central Coast seat of Dobell. Thomson is accused, as the national secretary of the Health Services Union (HSU) before he entered Parliament, of mis-using up to $500,000 of union funds to, among other things, pay for prostitutes (Packham and Vasek 2012). At the end of 2012, Fair Work Australia, the national work-place relations tribunal, was pursuing 37 charges against him in the Federal Court (*Thomson's loophole closes* 2012). It is no surprise that this case has attracted massive media coverage in Australia. It has all the ingredients of a classic political thriller: the government in Canberra clinging to power by a thread, including reliance on Thomson's vote; allegations of sordid liaisons with high-class and high-priced prostitutes; and intrigue within a large and faction-ridden trade union. In late January, 2013, Thomson was charged with more than 150 counts of fraud in what turned into another media 'event'. The media had obviously been tipped off to his pending arrest and television crews and journalists were at his office as he was led away by a group of detectives – a classic 'walk by' for the media. It prompted a furious response from his lawyer, Chris McArdle:

> We repeat our outrage that this has turned into some sort of reality TV show for the benefit of Channel Seven. It's absolutely disgusting. This is not reality television, this is someone's life.
>
> (Quoted in Cullen 2013)

Thomson pleaded not guilty at a brief court appearance. It emerged the following day that Thomson had been strip-searched after his arrest in what his lawyer said was a case of 'humiliation and intimidation' (*Thomson strip-searched by 'goons': lawyer* 2013). The New South Wales Premier, Barry O'Farrell, said the strip search was 'standard procedure' and then added:

> I think Mr Thomson and his lawyer need to calm down a bit – after all, the allegations surrounding Craig Thomson are that he was all too ready to take his clothes off in front of strangers in exchange for money.
>
> (Quoted in Higgins and Packham 2013)

Mr McArdle called for an apology from the Premier or Thomson would sue for defamation (*Thomson lawyer threatens to sue O'Farrell* 2013). Whether it was defamation or not would depend on the results of the fraud charges against Mr Thomson, but it raises questions about a State Premier pre-judging his guilt.

Thomson had said in his long-awaited explanation to Parliament in late May, 2012, that in the court of public opinion he had already been tried and found guilty. He admonished both the Parliament and the media saying they had no right to pass final judgment on anyone. Respected Canberra Press Gallery journalist Lenore Taylor (2012) agreed but offered her reasons for the public's opinion:

> … because the evidence against him appears so damning, the allegations so tawdry and the explanations so far fetched that in the front bars and lounge rooms around the nation people have already made up their minds.
>
> (Taylor, L. 2012)

In his lengthy Parliamentary defence, Thomson accused the opposition and the media of unleashing a 'lynch mob on his family and staff'. While acknowledging that some journalists were professional and 'responsible', he hit out at a Seven Network reporter who he claimed was 'hovering beneath the bathroom window' while his pregnant wife was having a shower (Leys 2012a; Wright 2012). He also criticised the Fairfax, saying that 12 stories had been written about him without any attempt being made to contact him for comment, something he saw as a requirement of the MEAA Code of Ethics. Both Seven and Fairfax rejected the embattled politician's claims (Leys 2012a).

Rarely in these instances does the media think about the effects of such stories on the family of the person accused of wrongdoing. Thomson's wife, Zoe Arnold, was expecting the couple's first child at the time the allegations first surfaced (about three years before her husband's explanation to Parliament) and a few months after his parliamentary statement gave Australia's top-selling magazine, *The Australian Women's Weekly* her side of the story (2012). As a former journalist-turned-political adviser she had loved reading newspapers and keeping up with the news:

> Not anymore. I can't tell you the last time I read a paper or checked a news website online. I'm too anxious that there will be yet another story about my husband, more misinformation instead of truth and more nasty comments posted by anonymous 'trolls'. I can't stomach it any more.
>
> On the weeks of bad media, I just want to run away. I hate it. I hate the photographers and so-called journalists at my front gate. I hate the pressure it puts on our parents, who are worried sick. I hate that I can't think of anything else.
>
> (Arnold, Z. 2012, p. 34)

Arnold's magazine piece confirms her husband's story about a TV reporter standing outside her window as she showered while pregnant – 'like any entitlement to privacy was gone' – adding that not long after, photographers pursued her in her car as she headed off for a routine checkup – 'I arrived in tears' (Arnold, Z. 2012, p. 34).

Her article provides a rare insight into the often-untold side of major scandals – how the loved ones (and friends) try to cope in such circumstances.

Thomson was due back in court in late 2013.

Regardless of any legal outcome(s) and aside from the politician's very pubic trial by media, there are several ethical issues raised by this case that illustrate unexpected ramifications of a media 'trial'. At one stage, Thomson pleaded with the opposition and the media to be left alone while a series of inquiries continued into his conduct, declaring 'enough is enough' (Packham and Vasek 2012). At the same time, a number of Federal MP's said they felt Thomson was 'being pushed to breaking point' and feared he may self harm (*MPs voice concern for Thomson's wellbeing* 2012). At that 'enough is enough' media conference Thomson hit out at reports that *A Current Affair* was to pay a prostitute $60,000 for an interview in which she identified Thomson as a client, describing it as 'chequebook journalism at its worst' (Wright and Ireland 2012). Thomson said the media were 'collectively' to blame for a scenario where an escort was being paid 'more than 10 times as much money as it has been alleged to have been used on the HSU credit card for prostitutes' (quoted in Wright and Ireland 2012). *A Current Affair* ran the woman's allegations against Thomson, but stopped short of using their interview with her. A week later the programme said they had given the interview and her statutory declaration to Victorian police (Vincent and Bainbridge 2012). The Nine Network would have their reputation tarnished further when the prostitute concerned revealed – on the opposition Seven Network's current affairs programme, *Today Tonight* – that Nine had aired her allegations after she told them she was an unreliable witness and wanted to retract her story (Murphy, K. 2012). She told Channel Seven it had been a case of mistaken identity and she had been in New Zealand on the date on which she was supposed to have had sex with the union-official-turned-politician (*Media standards: a Tawdry TV tale* 2012). The woman said she had not been paid by Nine or Seven (Murphy, K 2012).

The Federal Government at the time was considering tougher media regulation and a proposed Privacy Tort after inquiries in Australia that followed the *News of the World* revelations. Their suggested changes to media regulation failed to pass the Federal Paraliament in March, 2013, and the proposed Privacy Tort was referred back to the Australian Law Reform Commission (whence it had come some years before) for 'further consideration'.

A union official accused of mis-using union funds is a serious allegation and the media is justified in pursuing the story, especially since the union official had later become a federal parliamentarian. The difficulty with this case is that every accused person deserves their day in court and Thomson has consistently protested his innocence, even after being charged with multiple counts of fraud. But as we saw above, and will see again in the second case study at the end of this chapter, many members of the public appear to have already made up their minds.

While the media can quite rightly justify pursuing alleged wrongdoing by a politician on the grounds of public interest, various arms of the media have not emerged from the affair without their reputations tainted – like the TV reporter who allegedly invaded the accused politician's wife's privacy as she showered and the TV network that chased down a prostitute and offered to pay her handsomely for saying she had sex with the politician and ran the story even after she said she was mistaken. The print media didn't emerge unscathed, either, with the Fairfax papers being accused of unbalanced reporting. And what if the politician had self-harmed as some of his colleagues feared might happen? The case demonstrates the multiplicity of ethical considerations that can emerge in a serious ongoing story, especially when competing commercial current affairs programmes are battling for ratings supremacy.

The Hey Dad! *scandal*

Celebrity scandals often emerge after police have been called in to investigate. Such was not the case with what's known as the *Hey Dad!* scandal. After 17 years of silence, Sarah Monahan, one of the child stars of the popular 1987–1994 Australian family situation comedy, *Hey Dad!,* took her story to the gossip/tabloid media first and then, when the allegations had been in the public domain for more than two weeks, agreed to make a statement to police. After what was reported as 'months of negotiations', Monahan was paid by the gossip magazine *Woman's Day* for her story accusing an unnamed member of the cast of 'Hey Dad!' of sexual abuse (Jackson, S. 2010). Within days, Monahan made a paid appearance on *A Current Affair* to name her father on the show, actor Robert Hughes, as the alleged offender (Hornery and Jacobsen 2010). Monahan's on-screen sister, Simone Buchanan, alleged Hughes made unwanted sexual advances towards her, too (Tovey 2010). *A Current Affair's* Executive Producer at the time, Grant Williams, said his team had amassed an 'overwhelming' amount of evidence against Hughes, which it had made available to police, but only after going to air with it (Hornery and Jacobsen 2010). *Woman's Day* revealed Monahan had been 'relentlessly bombarded with hate mail from doubters and fans of the show' after making the claims (cited in Tovey 2010). Hughes maintained his innocence, initially instructing defamation lawyers. But as Hornery and Jacobsen (2010) noted:

> [T]he barrage of claims from Monahan and others, strategically timed to fit around media deadlines, have sparked accusations of trial by media.
>
> (Hornery and Jacobsen 2010)

Outspoken opinion writer at *The Australian,* Janet Albrechtsen, described the media frenzy sparked by Monahan's allegations as 'the worst kind of Australian journalism' and a 'textbook case of irresponsible media conduct'. She said the actions of *Woman's Day* and *A Current Affair* may have hindered a fair trial for the former sitcom star.

> [I]f Hughes is innocent, the media has damaged his reputation beyond repair. Defamation damages cannot compensate for the cloud of paedophilia that will always hang over him.
>
> (Albrechtsen 2010)

Albrechtsen's colleague at *The Australian* at the time, Caroline Overington, weighed into the controversy, suggesting there was a real risk that if charges were laid that Hughes could argue that his exposure on *A Current Affair* meant he could not get a fair trial.

> After all, he's been described, on the highest rating programme of the week, as a dirty old man.
>
> (Overington 2010a)

Tasmanian lawyer and prisoner advocate, Greg Barns, writing on the ABC's commentary website, *The Drum*, suggested – tongue-in-cheek – that police investigation units, prosecutors, defence lawyers and courts could be abolished and *A Current Affair* allowed to do the job of all of them:

> They can be investigator, judge, jury and prosecutor of all causes and it won't cost the taxpayer a cent. The punishment for those found 'guilty' by *ACA* can be a hounding by the media, and a very public campaign of vilification.
>
> (Barns 2010)

He went on to say the programme had undermined the right of Hughes to be presumed innocent and shown once again 'the dangers of allowing the media to conduct its own criminal investigations':

> It is not the business of the media, when serious criminal allegations are made against a person, to conduct its own trial.
>
> (Barns 2010)

New South Wales police soon began investigating the allegations made by Monahan and others saying they expected a protracted investigation (*Police set up* Hey Dad! *strike force* 2010). Nearly a year later, Monahan announced she planned civil action against the Seven Network and Robert Hughes, saying her anger at what happened to her extended beyond her on-screen father to the television executives she believed knew of what was happening (Hey Dad! *scandal: child star to launch civil action* 2011). At the time of the original 2010 allegations, Hughes, and his celebrity agent wife Robyn Gardiner, lived in Singapore. By September, 2012, 30 months after the original allegations surfaced, the now 64-year-old was living in London when the British government authorised his extradition to Australia to face 11 child-sex charges (Wilson 2012). At that time he accused Australian police and media of orchestrating a 'trial by media' against him. His lawyer, Robert Katz, read a statement outside the court after the extradition hearing saying police had not needed to arrest Hughes and have him held in jail for a night pending the hearing. The statement added that, contrary to media reports, the lawyer had been in touch with police over the matter on numerous times in the previous two years. The statement by Mr Katz added:

> Mr Hughes is shocked and perplexed as to why he is being extradited and police knew he was willing to return to Australia of his own accord to answer their questions if he had been asked. Rather than continue to suffer a trial by media, my client is keen to defend the allegations, which he vehemently denies.
>
> (Quoted in Wilson 2012)

Hughes arrived back in Australia in early December, 2012, and was granted bail on the charges, which date back to the 1980s (Ralston 2012). After a brief hearing in mid-2013 at which he pleaded not guilty to all charges, Hughes' trial was set for early 2014 (*Media coverage may hurt Robert Hughes' chances of a fair trial: lawyer* 2013).

Long-running stories like the Madeleine McCann disappearance, Craig Thomson saga and the *Hey Dad!* scandal demonstrate the problems for mainstream media in the era of the 24/7 news cycle of covering even slow-moving stories ethically. Neither Thomson nor Hughes has yet (as of early April, 2013) had their day in court, both strongly deny all charges against them and yet both have probably been found guilty in the 'court of public opinion'.

The Duke University rape case

An international example of a 'trial by media' that blew up in the media's face was the case of three student lacrosse players at the prestigious Duke University in the United States who were accused of kidnapping and raping a stripper after an off-campus team party in 2006. As the American *60 Minutes* programme reported some time later (Schorn 2009), the case put one of country's top tertiary institutions under intense scrutiny and pushed issues like race, gender, politics and privilege onto the national agenda. The lacrosse players were white, from wealthy families. Their accuser was black. The American media portrayed the case as an example of the racial and class tensions in the North Carolina town where the university is located (Cherry 2007). The town was characterised as being divided between the elite university and the mostly black locals (Coultan 2007). The case started to unravel when no trace of the defendants' DNA was found on the accuser and amid charges that the original prosecutor had played up the case because he was facing re-election (Cherry 2007). The State Attorney General took over the investigation and his inquiries 'led us to the conclusion that no attack occurred' (*Lacrosse rape case collapses* 2007). The three men and their lawyers accused the media (and the public) of disregarding their presumption of innocence and portraying them as thugs. The exonerated players wondered what would have happened to them if they had not come from rich families who could afford the best legal advice. According to *CBS News*, their families spent between $3 million and $5 million defending them (cited in Coultan 2007). The then Public Editor of *The New York Times*, Byron Calame, wrote at the time that the announcement that the three men had been declared innocent had triggered a flood of critical emails to the paper. Many criticised *The Times'* coverage suggesting it favoured the woman and suggested the paper apologize to the accused. Others called on *The Times* to name the woman – some seeing it as 'good journalism', while others seemed to be more interested in retribution or punishment for causing the falsely-accused university students so much grief (Calame 2007). As part of a longstanding policy of not naming victims of sexual assault, no mainstream media outlet had published her identity before prosecutors dropped the rape charges (Dadisman 2007). When the rape charges were dropped, kidnapping and sex-offence charges were still pending, but several major media outlets, including *The Chicago Sun-Times*, *The New York Post* and *60 Minutes* decided to part with their policy and name her. The *American Journalism Review*'s Sally Dadisman noted that:

> As the Internet's influence grows, some also worry that the protection the media are trying to offer becomes ineffective.
>
> (Dadisman 2007)

One of America's leading voices on media ethics, the Poynter Institute's Kelly McBride, in a column titled 'Winners and Losers in the Duke Lacrosse Story' (2007), concluded there were no winners in the sorry saga, just losers, and the biggest loser was the media. She said journalists had tripped over each other to tell the story and in their attempts to shed light, had 'lit a fire of public scorn' (McBride 2007).

> The story we all thought was true: A bunch of privileged white college boys at an elite school took advantage of a poor black woman. Over the ensuing months, the coverage of the story took another, equally distorted shape: An unstable messed-up stripper and an out-of-control prosecutor ruined three young lives. (T)he reporting has failed to demonstrate that either of those stories was ever completely true.
>
> (McBride 2007)

What was true was that the boys had been convicted in the 'court of public opinion' long before all the evidence was in. It seems that, globally, social media continues to race ahead of both the law and the mainstream media in undermining legal and ethical protections against undue exposure of identity in controversial cases of 'trial by media'.

Did Neil Mitchell do the right thing in naming AFL players questioned by police?

Neil Mitchell, talk show host at Melbourne's 3AW, caused a major stir in late 2010 when he named two members of AFL team Collingwood who had been interviewed over an alleged sex scandal on Grand Final night. Collingwood had beaten St Kilda for the premiership flag in a grand final replay after the teams played out a draw the previous

Saturday. While the Melbourne media had been carrying stories about two footballers being interviewed for several days, and their names were known to journalists and editors (and had been revealed on the Internet), no one in the mainstream media had named them before Mitchell's broadcast the following Thursday (Crook 2010). The nation's biggest-selling weekday newspaper, the *Herald Sun*, told its readers at the outset it had chosen not to name them (Dowsley and Harris 2010). There was no legal reason why the players could not be named – they had only been interviewed. The *sub judice* rule only applies after charges have been laid. Mitchell, a former journalist and news executive at *The Age*, and also a current columnist for the *Herald Sun*, told his listeners he thought the names should be made public for several reasons. Among the reasons was that every one of their team-mates could have been considered to be the ones talking to the police, and that was not fair to the other players; the precedent that other clubs had gone public with the names of players before they were charged; and the names were being whispered around and were on the Internet (Mitchell 2010). He added that he'd been told several names he knew were wrong. The controversial broadcast brought a stinging rebuke from opposition Triple M radio host, Eddie McGuire, who is also the President of the Collingwood club. Calling Mitchell a self-appointed, self-important windbag, McGuire added:

> He gets on every day, he bangs on how he wants footballers to be treated like everyone else but then bangs on that 'No, they are special people' and names two young men who have not been charged or done anything wrong so far as the police are concerned yet.
>
> (McGuire 2010)

After Mitchell named the two footballers, other media outlets followed. But why did they wait so long? As journalism academic and media critic Margaret Simons suggested, everyone was watching everyone else.

> Inevitably somebody would break ranks and others would follow. ... As soon as Mitchell named the names, every other media outlet in the nation ran them big, sometimes while banging on about how they were too holy and ethical to do what Mitchell had done.
>
> (Simons 2010)

Under a headline reading 'Radio host went too far' Mitchell's colleague at the *Herald Sun*, the controversial opinion writer, Andrew Bolt, asked what was to be gained by naming the two players? In Mitchell's case, he wrote, it was 'ratings and audience share'. Noting that Mitchell said he was only being 'fair' to other Collingwood players by naming the two being interviewed by police, he added:

> It's only fair to other innocent radio hosts that I now name the one who is accused of being a sanctimonious, self-important hypocrite. Good heavens! It's Neil Mitchell.
>
> (Bolt 2010)

The two players, including one from the Premiership-winning team, were later cleared of any wrongdoing (Dowsley 2011).

This example, and others like it, also demonsrate the hypocricy of the news media over ethical dilemmas. Some editors will argue there is a strong public interest in knowing the names, or that not naming them throws suspicion on others. Outlets that choose not to name them either a) go on the attack and claim the moral high ground, or b) reverse their original opposition to naming and shaming them on the grounds that the others have already let the cat out of the bag. It highlights the ethico-legal paradox: there was, in this case, no reason *not* to name them, but ethical considerations were used to justify both options.

Would you have named the footballers?

Another case where the pressure to name and shame finally got the better of British tabloid editors was that of an 83-year-old Australian entertainer who lived in Berkshire, England and who had been arrested (but not yet charged) on suspicion of sexual offences in the wake of the Jimmy Savile revelations. The mainstream British media was camped outside his house and their conversation centred around the fact that they would not, unless someone broke ranks, publish two words – the name of the instantly-recognisable man they were pursuing (Miller 2013). Halfway round the world, in Australia, media commentators were asking why? Were they just being kind to a legend in the entertainment industry and waiting for him to be formally charged? Were they worried they might be risking contempt of court, or were they still worried about the final form of the new media regulation regime they face in the wake of the Leveson inquiry? It's not as if his name was hard to establish and the reporters camped outside his house knew who he was. Author Roger guessed correctly (he only knew of one person who fitted the description) and Google confirmed it. Several bloggers were not so sympathetic, wasting no time 'spilling the beans'. Yet another case where the 'citizen journalists' on the internet and social media are having an impact. Eventually, *The Sun* named the man as the famous singer and friend of the Queen, Rolf Harris. Harris denied the allegations against him, but it didn't matter; within minutes of *The Sun* naming him, every other media outlet on the planet was following suit. In mid-May, 2013, one of Harris's accusers gave paid interviews to an Australian gossip magazine and commercial television current affairs programme detailing her encounter with the entertainer, leading to suggestions the interviews could prejudice any potential criminal trial involving Harris (Ralson 2013). At the end of August 2013, Harris was finally charged; a gaggle of TV crews remained camped outside his house, only to report that he wasn't there at the time (*Rolf Harris charged with indecent assault on girls* 2013). This is a clear example of how hypocritical the media can be: a hollow silence is maintained, but when the dam wall bursts, everyone else piles on and the person at the centre of the maelstrom has no way of stopping the flood.

Media coverage of paedophiles

Few issues stir emotions and cause more moral panic in a community than a paedophile being re-located into their suburb or town. In many parts of the world, including the UK, Australia and the US, various news media have actively campaigned for the naming and shaming of child sex offenders from time to time. In the UK it was (unsurprisingly) the *News of the World* that led this practice. In June 2000 it named 49 alleged or convicted paedophiles, leading to vigilante style attacks on several men. One of the most notorious paedophiles in recent Australian criminal history was Queenslander, Dennis Ferguson. Ferguson was jailed for 14 years in 1988 for kidnapping three children and violating them in a motel. He served all 14 years and on release was hounded out of a number of towns by outraged locals (Lappeman 2008). Typical of the almost hysterical coverage at times was

The Gold Coast Weekend Bulletin in early July, 2008, after Ferguson had been forced out of the western Queensland town of Miles. Under emotive headlines (*No Rest For The Wicked: Disguises of a monster* 2008), the paper noted that the convicted paedophile had 'gone back into hiding' so they published a head-and-shoulders photo of Ferguson in six possible disguises the paper suggested he might use to keep out of the public eye. Then it said: 'If he turns up in your suburb, call *The Bulletin* on ... , SMS ... , email ... or go to our website ... ' (*No Rest For The Wicked: Disguises of a monster* 2008). The release of Ferguson turned into a debate about the public's right to know if paedophiles were living in their neighbourhood (Lappeman 2008). At the time, Ferguson had been on remand for an alleged child sex offence for two-and-a-half years (Oberhardt and Odgers 2008). On two previous occasions, he had been scheduled for trial (Nyst 2009). On the second occasion, a Queensland judge found Ferguson's notoriety after widespread media coverage meant all or some of the 12 jurors would be incapable of delivering a 'dispassionate judgment' (quoted in Oberhardt and Odgers 2008), but the decision was overturned on appeal (Barns 2009). On the third occasion Ferguson opted to forgo a jury trial, and have a judge determine his case. The notorious child sex offender was found not guilty (Nyst 2009). The prisoner advocate Greg Barns said it was the 'gross irresponsibility, harassment, and hysteria generated by the national media about Ferguson' that led to him choosing a judge-only trial. Here, too, Barns said, the Internet and social media had an impact:

> The rise of the Internet, social networking sites like Facebook and sensationalist media with no regard to privacy or legal principle has meant that it is getting harder and harder to ensure that jurors come to the case they judge without in some way being tainted.
>
> (Barns 2009)

Ferguson relocated to Sydney, only to have the NSW State Government pass legislation to allow them to lock him out of his suburban public housing unit (*Paedophile saga to end badly* 2009). Ferguson died late in December, 2012 (*No tears for death of child sex fiend* 2013).

Conclusion

While the media can be justifiably criticised from time to time for 'overstepping the line' and all but destroying a person's reputation despite their denials and before they have had a chance to defend themselves in court, equally, journalists can rightly claim there is public interest in what they do. Australia has a rich history of investigative journalism. Stories like the May, 1987, *Four Corners* exposé of politics and criminality in Queensland titled *The Moonlight State* (Masters 1987) by acclaimed investigative journalist Chris Masters, which contributed, along with the work of *The Courier Mail*'s Phil Dickie, to the establishment of the Fitzgerald Royal Commission into police corruption in that state in the late 1980s, which resulted in the jailing of three former cabinet ministers and a police commissioner, who also had his knighthood revoked.

Another *Four Corners* investigative journalist, Sarah Ferguson, produced a seminal episode titled *Code of Silence* (2009a) which looked at sexual misbehaviour by footballers, and detailed an instance of group sex in New Zealand by a number of Cronulla (Sydney) rugby league players, including the high profile player-turned-commentator (and comedian) Matthew Johns. The programme led to much soul-searching in football circles about players' attitudes towards women. Ferguson told the annual George Munster forum in Sydney later in the year she had been amazed by the mostly negative reaction to the programme's revelations (Ferguson, S. 2009b).

Case Study 1: *Herald Sun* front page: 'We don't believe you'

On the day the member for Dobell, Craig Thomson, finally gave his long-awaited explanation to the Federal Parliament in late May, 2012, the biggest-selling weekday tabloid in Australia, Melbourne's *Herald Sun*, conducted a readers' poll (which they called a 'readers' jury') and gave the result front-page treatment the next day along with a digitally-altered photograph of the politician with a Pinocchio-length nose (*We don't believe you* 2012). There were three other, smaller headlines on the issue on the paper's front page, but the page is dominated by Thomson's elongated nose and the 'We don't believe you' headline (see Figure 8.1). The Australian Press Council received a number of complaints about the paper's coverage of Thomson's Parliamentary explanation (*Adjudication No. 1556: Debra Creevy and others/Herald Sun (November 2012)* 2012). The adjudication said the principal criticism was that the material unfairly pre-judged Mr Thomson and constituted 'trial by media'. The Council upheld the complaint, concluding that the overall impact of the front page and other coverage on page seven of the paper was 'highly unfair to Mr Thomson by seeking to convey too close an analogy with a courtroom conviction on criminal charges, especially at a time when the laying of such charges was being widely demanded and anticipated'. The newspaper responded that the trustworthiness of parliamentarians was of crucial importance in a democracy and required very close scrutiny by the media, especially when there were such strong grounds for concern (*Adjudication No. 1556: Debra Creevy and others/Herald Sun (November 2012)* 2012). The *Herald Sun* breached press standards more than any other newspaper in 2012. The Press Council handed down five adverse judgments against the *'Hun'* during the year, compared to three for their News Limited stablemates, *The Advertiser* in Adelaide and the *Daily/Sunday Telegraph* in Sydney (Knott 2012a). As we have consistently suggested, there is a legitimate public interest in the Thomson case and it deserves the massive coverage it gets. But here we can't help thinking that the Pinocchio image and provocative use of the readers' 'jury' result as the dominant headline goes too far.

Questions for discussion:

1. What's your initial impression of the front page illustration and dominant headline?
2. Isn't it the media's role to be impartial or balanced?
3. Doesn't a politician deserve his day in court before a paper effectively calls him a liar?
4. Does it matter since everyone has already probably made up their mind about his guilt or otherwise long before he made his statement to the federal parliament?

5. Research the rest of the *Herald Sun* coverage on an online research site like Factiva. What's your impression of their stories?
6. After all the media coverage could Thomson ever expect a fair trial before a jury?
7. Is the *Herald Sun's* digitally-altered photo any different to a *Daily Telegraph* front page that showed Federal Parliamentary Speaker Peter Slipper with a rat's ears, whiskers and tail? You can see a version of the digitally-altered image in Hildebrand's story (Hildebrand 2011).
8. A year later, new media rules were announced for covering Federal Parliament which banned newspapers and TV stations from digitally-altering images of MPs (Johnston, M. 2012). Which side of the argument do you support – maintaining the dignity of the parliament, or suggesting that our 'pollies' are being a bit precious?

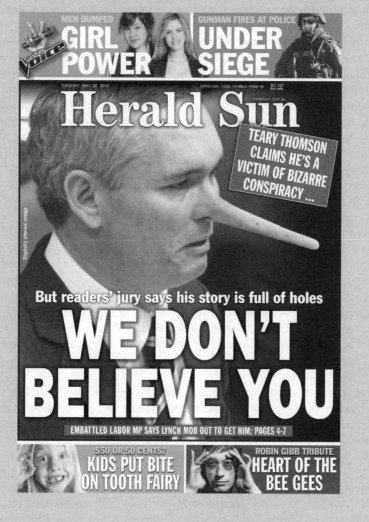

Figure 8.1 'We Don't Believe You', *Herald Sun*, 22 May 2012. Copyright Herald Sun/ Newspix

Case Study 2: The 'outing' of politician David Campbell by Seven

A 'trial by media' case that never made it to court, and never would, was the 'outing' by the Seven Network of New South Wales Labor Minister, David Campbell, in late May, 2010. The politician quit his cabinet post literally minutes before he was shown on Seven News walking out of a gay sex club in Sydney's east (McDonald 2010). Reaction to the story – mostly critical of Seven and other media, like *The Daily Telegraph* that followed suit next morning with a huge front-page headline 'Minister quits in sex club scandal' (Jones, G. and Kamper 2010) – quickly followed. Seven initially defended the story on the basis that Campbell had used his taxpayer-funded car to visit the club, suggesting that he was misusing taxpayers' money, but that was quickly retracted when it was shown that government regulations allowed for private use of Ministers' vehicles. The Seven reporter concerned, Adam Walters, told *Media Watch* (Holmes 2010) the story was in the public interest because Mr Campbell had previously campaigned strongly as a family man. Walters' boss, Seven's Head of news and current affairs at the time, Peter Meakin, said 'a minister who carries on like this … is very much open to, you know, the danger of blackmail' (quoted in Holmes 2010). Seven said they had a right to broadcast the story because the private life and conduct of the Transport Minister (and former Police Minister) was at odds with his personal persona (McDonald 2010). *Sydney Morning Herald* journalist and former host of *Media Watch*, David Marr, described Seven's action as 'just a very nasty, prurient intervention in a desperately sad private business' (quoted in Edwards 2010). *The Australian*'s media commentator, Mark Day, told the same ABC *PM* reporter the story wasn't in the public interest, but it definitely was of interest to the public (quoted in Edwards 2010). One blogger said:

> With complete insensitivity towards David Campbell's family, and his mental well-being, Channel 7's 'investigative reporting' has single-handedly destroyed this man's career and seen him publicly humiliated nationwide.
>
> (Fiasson 2010)

Journalism educators from around Australia took the rare step of sending an open letter rebuking Walters, Meakin and Seven's owners. The letter, signed by more than 50 journalists and academics (including author Roger), said in part:

> We know that sometimes the private lives of public figures need to be exposed for public good, in the public interest. But you exposed this man for no public good; nor was it in the public interest. It was shameful and hurtful – not just for Campbell and his family; but for all of us. It demeans journalism.
>
> (Quoted in Price 2010)

The broadcasting watchdog, the Australian Communications and Media Authority (ACMA) investigated the Seven story and exonerated the network (O'Brien 2011). The media watchdog concluded that Seven was justified in invading Campbell's privacy to explain why he had resigned, even though the reason he resigned was that the network was about to 'out' him on national television (Dodd 2011a).

Questions for discussion:

1. Would you have broadcast the story? If so, why? If not, why not?
2. Politicians give up the right to any privacy once they enter public life, don't they?
3. Hadn't he been living a double life for his entire marriage of some 25 years, and didn't he deserve to be 'outed' for, if nothing else, being a hypocrite?
4. Was it an issue for public debate or for private discussion between Mr Campbell and his wife and children?
5. Would you enter public life and invite such scrutiny of your private life?
6. Look up David Penberthy's 2010 article on *The Punch* website (http://www.thepunch.com.au/articles/why-david-campbell-has-a-lesser-right-to-privacy). Do you find his arguments convincing? Why? Why not?
7. What's your reaction to the public stand by journalism educators?
8. Campbell may have been secretly visiting legal gay sex-on-premises venues, but is there a public interest in this matter if it has no direct bearing on the MP's official duties?
9. What about visiting such private clubs while Police Minister?
10. What about the argument that as a 'family man' Campbell was being hypocritical by visiting a gay sex venue and therefore a public interest in his behaviour is warranted?

9   Fair dealing – sources, shield laws and PR

'Collateral murder' – WikiLeaks and source confidentiality

> 5 April 2010 10:44 EST WikiLeaks has released a classified US military video depicting the indiscriminate slaying of over a dozen people in the Iraqi suburb of New Baghdad – including two Reuters news staff.
>
> (WikiLeaks 2010a)

The release of the 2010 'collateral murder' video shot WikiLeaks and its editor-in-chief, Julian Assange, to international notoriety. The 'gunsight' camera view from an Apache helicopter and the chilling commentary from its crew drew outrage and attention on US military practices in occupied Iraq. But Assange and WikiLeaks were not finished. In October, 2010 the group released the first batch of secret communications between American embassies and officials in Washington that blew the lid off many aspects of military and political intelligence gathering. Scores of other governments and many leading international figures were implicated, being spied upon or complained about by the Americans. Everyone was embarrassed and some dirty secrets exposed. WikiLeaks collaborated with prominent newspapers around the world to cover the dramatic story. More than 250,000 documents were released in what has become known as 'Cablegate' (WikiLeaks 2010b). It remains an outstanding piece of collaborative journalism and is a model for much of what is following in terms of new investigative and 'data' journalism. The WikiLeaks story and the drama surrounding Julian Assange is ongoing as we write this. We are strong supporters of transparency and of WikiLeaks. In our view, it is shameful that the Australian government has not helped Julian with his contrived legal difficulties in the UK and Sweden.

If anything typified the dilemmas posed by the use of anonymous sources in stories in recent years, it has been the controversy surrounding the release of literally millions of confidential documents by the whistle-blowing website, WikiLeaks. The international organisation, which has been publishing largely-classified information from anonymous sources since 2006, was founded by Australian, Julian Assange, who, at the time of writing (April 2013) had been holed up in the Ecuadorian embassy in London for many months trying to avoid extradition to Sweden to face questioning over sex charges (*UK threat to storm embassy to take Assange* 2012). The WikiLeaks exposés highlight a number of ethical issues that will be discussed later in this chapter. In particular, this case highlights the dangers faced by public-spirited whistle-blowers like Bradley Manning, the young, gay American soldier who was given 35 years in prison for releasing thousands of classified documents to WikiLeaks (McGeough 2013b).

For starters, though, ask yourself, if your organisation were to obtain secret, newsworthy documents that might damage your country's national interest and perhaps endanger the lives of individuals, would it publish them? Would you? That was the ethical dilemma facing editors at *The New York Times*, *The Guardian*, Germany's *Der Speigel*, France's *La Monde* and Spain's *El País* in 2010 when they gained access to thousands of American diplomatic cables ahead of their release by WikiLeaks (Adams and Vascellaro 2010). The papers concerned wrote extensive background reports about the cables between the US and countries like Pakistan and South Korea and discussions with other countries on how to close the Gunatanamo Bay prison in Cuba. Some attached examples of the cables to their websites. Media around the world followed suit, so clearly they had no problems with the anonymous source of the cables. WikiLeaks has divided the public; some see it as a 'radiant shaft of light, cutting through official obfuscation and sharing vital information every citizen deserves to know', while others see its publication of classified documents as a 'treasonous breach of confidentiality, seizing up the well-oiled protocols of international negotiation and endangering the lives of military, diplomatic, and intelligence operatives around the world' (Kidder 2010). Bradley Manning, who was at the time 25, was court-martialled on multiple charges of downloading US war logs, cables and video clips from Iraq and Afghanistan and sending them to WikiLeaks in what has been described as the 'biggest leak of government secrets in US history' (*Judge upholds charge against Bradley Manning in the Wikileaks case* 2012). Just as WikiLeaks divides the public, so does Private Manning. To anti-war campaigners, he's a hero making a stand for free speech and transparent government; to others, he's a traitor who betrayed his country and its military by releasing government secrets (Evans 2011). Appearing at his court martial in late February, 2013, Manning said in a 35-page statement that he read to the court that he had tried to leak the documents to *The Washington Post*, *The New York Times* and the website *Politico*, before approaching WikiLeaks (Pilkington 2013b). Admitting to 10 of 22 charges, he said he leaked the documents 'to make the world a better place' (Savage 2013) and because he believed the American people had a right to know the 'true costs of war' (Pilkington 2013a). Bradley Manning's disclosure of secret cables was followed up in 2013 by a young contract spy who worked for the National Security Agency (NSA). Edward Snowden released thousands of documents that showed the extent of illegal domestic and international spying by the American security state apparatus. At the time of writing, Edward Snowden was 'enjoying' political asylum in Russia after being helped by Wikileaks. Snowden is also facing a lengthy jail sentence if he ever returns to the US. A leading American investigative journalist, Glenn Greenwald, has been harassed by the US government since helping to reveal Snowden's secrets in *The Guardian* and other newspapers (Fonseca 2013). The Manning and Snowden cases highlight aspects of the journalist–source relationship that are either problematic or downright dangerous.

Sources – the life-blood of serious journalism

Serious journalism is about getting information into the public sphere that those in power would prefer was kept secret (Hurst and White 1994, p. 151). Exposure can lead to inquiries, resignations, and even bring down governments. At another level it can lead to police investigations, court cases, and the jailing of offenders. At the very least, disclosures can spark serious public concern and debate that forces governments, private corporations or individuals into action. But it is not beyond governments and corporations to take measures that might protect them from exposure, such as invoking 'national interest' or 'commercial-in-confidence' arguments to counter whistle-blowers' revelations and leaks.

The MEAA Code of Ethics Clause 3 (*MEAA Code of Ethics* 1999) says: ' Aim to attribute information to its source. Where a source seeks anonymity, do not agree without first considering the source's motives and any alternative attributable source. Where confidences are accepted, respect them in all circumstances'.

The American Society of Professional Journalists (*Code of Ethics* 1996) and the British National Union of Journalists (*NUJ Code of Conduct* 2011) have similar clauses in their ethics codes. The AJA (Australian Journalists' Association) Code of Ethics Clause 3 [1984] (MEAA 1997, pp. 122–3) of the time said: 'In all circumstances they shall respect all confidences received in the course of their calling'.

Some critics believe the current clause on source confidentiality is weaker than the one in the former Code. Where would journalism be if there was no trust (and mutual respect) between reporters and their sources? The first requirement in answering those questions is to look at the importance of confidentiality for sources in journalism.

The source relationship – vital for both journalist and source

The relationship between journalists and their sources is a two-way street. The journalist needs sources to get those elusive 'scoops', and the sources need the journalists to get their messages to the wider community. Such relationships are built on trust and reliability, often built up over many years. Much of that trust on the source's part comes from their belief that if they pass on information and ask for anonymity, then the guarantee will be honoured by the journalist. The quality of journalism around the world would be the poorer if stories based on information gained from sources that need to remain anonymous were eliminated. But before we delve too deeply into the ethical (and legal) dilemmas associated with source confidentiality, it should be noted that not every source demands anonymity. In fact, few do. Most of the work of the everyday newsroom journalist involves ringing their sources – those with whom they have probably had countless dealings – and talking about potential stories and what they can add to what the reporter already knows. Often they provide information that 'fleshes out' the story and gives it valuable depth and perspective. Other times they will initiate information that leads – after checking with other sources – to a story. It is certainly not all 'guarantee me confidentiality or I won't talk to you' negotiations.

The 'two-way street' means that the sources are usually just as keen to get their information into the media as you are in writing it. It is here that you and the source need to realise the conditions under which you are talking – whether what they say is 'on the record', 'background' or 'off the record'. There might be degrees of 'background', but these are the three main categories of the source–reporter relationship. It is important that both reporter and source have a common understanding of the meaning of these terms to avoid confusion and possible embarrassment. 'On the record' means that anything the person says can be quoted directly (or paraphrased) in a story, and directly attributed to the source. This happens every day at hundreds of media conferences around the world – a VIP calls the media in to make an announcement and expects to be quoted. Or in thousands of conversations between journalists and their regular sources. It is the most common source–reporter relationship. 'Background' means that the information is being offered to help the reporter put the story into context; it is intended for publication, but not to be directly attributed to the source. It might be used without attribution in a story, it might be used carrying a descriptor of the source, without directly identifying them, or it might provide another thread of inquiry for the reporter to follow. The most controversial is 'off the record'. This means that the source is giving you information confidentially, perhaps as a favour, and it is not intended for publication, certainly not in any way identifying the source. It amounts to the source giving you a 'heads up' on a potential story, but they don't want to be associated with the final publication. Sometimes there is confusion between 'background' and 'off the record', with some sources thinking they mean the same thing. Former Australian Treasurer, Peter Costello, ended up with a problem when he initially said that a 2005 dinner conversation with three journalists, in which he attacked PM John Howard's chances of winning the 2007 federal election and said he planned to destroy his leadership, was 'background', only to have his media adviser plead with the journalists the next day that the conversation was 'off the record' (Franklin, M. 2007). The three journalists reluctantly agreed (Muller 2007), but Costello later denied planning a leadership coup as early as 2005, so the journalists – among them the ABC's Michael Brissenden – decided to recount the earlier dinner party discussion because Costello's denials, Brissenden said, 'go to matters of credibility for the man who still holds hopes of one day leading the nation' (cited in Bolt 2007). They still broke the 'off the record' rule, didn't they? If you agree that something is 'off the record', aren't you agreeing that if anyone asks you need to deny it was ever said? There's a multi-layered, ethical dilemma involved in source–reporter relationships. The best advice is to always seek advice 'on the record' and where possible confirm it with another source.

Source anonymity – a difficult fault line

> Democracy cannot work when secrecy exceeds its proper limits. The press cannot work when important information is suppressed.
>
> (*Journalistic sources and the law: blowing the whistle on truth-tellers* 2013)

Anonymous sources are important in investigative journalism, but they also create something of a trust problem for journalists whose hard-won credibility can be undone by a problematic and secret source (Franklin, B. and Carlson 2011). The problems associated with anonymous sources were demonstrated in stories that started running in late 2011 and continued through to late February, 2012 'talking up' the likelihood that former Australian Prime Minister, Kevin Rudd, who had been replaced as PM in mid-2010 by Julia Gillard, would challenge for the 'top job'. Many of the political journalists knew that a challenge was 'on' – they had been briefed by senior members of the Rudd camp on the basis their source(s) remained anonymous. Some political journalists, radio commentators, and probably the general public – those obviously not 'in the know' – were suggesting that the Canberra press gallery, who love a good leadership brawl, were 'beating up the story'; after all much of it was during the so-called 'silly season' – the Christmas holiday break – when the nation's political leaders are out of the national capital and political stories are usually 'thin on the ground'. When the leadership challenge did eventuate early in 2012, there was some gloating along the lines of 'we told you so' from those who had been predicting the (ultimately unsuccessful) attempted leadership coup. But the media was accused, by one newspaper blogger, of being 'complicit in creating the circumstances' for a leadership challenge by reporting in a way that was designed to 'generate a feeling of inevitability' (Brent 2012). When the journalists claimed vindication, the blogger, Peter Brent, wrote:

> But can you claim vindication for a situation you helped create? Encouraging something to happen and then saying 'I told you so' does not quite pass the logic test.
>
> (Brent 2012)

Crikey's Canberra Correspondent, Bernard Keane, addressed what he called the public frustration with what many people perceived as the media's preoccupation with Labor's leadership. He said the frustration seemed to take two forms – that the media were substituting leadership speculation for covering actual news and issues and that the media had become players in the leadership contests (Keane 2012a). They were players in the sense that they were reporting what their sources were telling them – that Rudd would challenge, and soon – but were unable to say who was telling them because they guaranteed their sources anonymity in return for the scoops.

Source protection – an ethical principle to die for?

Protecting the sources of important information is a fundamental tenet of journalism, a principle on which serious journalists should be prepared to end up in court. A few brave souls have spent time in jail for protecting sources and many more have rallied to support colleagues who have been jailed. When *Courier-Mail* journalist, Joe Budd, was convicted of contempt and sentenced to 14 days in jail in March, 1992, his editor, Des Houghton, spoke at a rally in his support: 'The day journalists get into the witness box and spill the beans is the day that people will stop giving us vital information about wrong-doing in public office' (quoted in Hurst and White 1994, p. 150). Sources need to be certain that the journalist will not reveal their name under any circumstance, otherwise there will be far fewer willing to 'blow the whistle'. David Burnet (1992) argued that without some protection in law for journalists and their sources, if they are faced with a legal challenge, reporters 'would be well advised to destroy the material in question' (p. 59). Three journalists ended up in jail before the turn of the century because they refused to identify the sources of their stories. In the late 1980s and early 1990s, four journalists – Deborah Cornwall, Tony Barass, Chris Nicholls and the aforementioned Joe Budd – were all found guilty of contempt for refusing to name a source. The three men spent time in jail for standing by their journalistic principles, and Ms Cornwall had her sentence suspended on condition she undertook 90 hours of community service. Guaranteeing a source confidentiality is not an action to be taken too readily.

Would you go to jail to protect a source?

Melbourne *Herald Sun* reporters Gerard McManus and Michael Harvey were the last journalists in Australia to be charged and face jail for refusing to name their source for a story that federal cabinet had planned to adopt only five of 65 recommendations from a review into veterans' entitlements before a backbench revolt changed their mind (*Journalists avoid jail over contempt* 2007). Senior ministers wanted to know who'd leaked the story that they intended to short-change veterans, and when the two senior political journalists were called before Victoria's County Court in August, 2005, in a pre-trial hearing ahead of a trial of the senior bureaucrat accused of the leak, they refused to divulge the name. In February, 2007, McManus pleaded guilty to five counts of contempt of court, and Harvey to four and they would wait another four months – with the real threat of jail time over their heads – before being fined $7000 each (*Journalists avoid jail over contempt* 2007). At their trial, the chief judge of the Victorian County Court, Michael Rozenes, said the *Herald Sun* reporters had put their ethics above the law in refusing to name their source and added that journalists who refused to name sources saw convictions for contempt as 'a badge of courage' (quoted in Berry 2007). The public servant had been convicted in early 2006 of releasing a confidential memo to the journalists without authorisation. Journalists and news organisations around the country expressed outrage at the suggestion the two might be jailed. The vehemence of the media's reaction to the possibility of jailing two senior journalists put reform of the contempt laws (as they affect journalists and their sources) onto the political agenda again, as is discussed later in the chapter. In our view, this ethico-legal paradox is almost impossible to resolve. The black-and-white law says reporters are in contempt of court if they refuse to divulge sources when legally required to do so. The grey-area, ethical principle that a journalist never reveals confidential sources is often seen as a 'line in the sand' by journalists and editors.

Confidentiality and the law

The court system has long felt it has valid reasons for demanding reporters 'give up' their sources in certain cases. The MEAA Ethics Review Committee listed some of them as partial reasons why the 'absolute' nature of the 1984 confidentiality clause should be amended in the revised code of 1999. The legal contexts in which a court might demand names from journalists include:

- When a potential plaintiff is attempting to discover the name of a source so they can sue for defamation or civil damages.
- A civil or criminal trial when a source's identity may be sought from a journalist who is giving evidence on oath.
- A trial where the source is being sought in order to give evidence on their own behalf.
- In a situation where the source might be able to lend assistance to an investigation by a Royal Commission or similarly authorised body.

(MEAA 1997, p. 57)

The Committee suggested that the 'key test' was whether disclosure of the source's identity was necessary 'in the interests of justice' (MEAA 1997, p. 57). The fractures over confidentiality go to the heart of journalistic ethics because the keeping of promises and trust are crucial for the reporter seeking the honest pursuit of 'truth', 'fairness', and 'balance'. Here we truly have fault lines with consequences. At the time of writing, although shield laws (to protect confidential sources from having their names revealed by journalists under threat of legal sanction) have been enacted federally in Australia, and the States are slowly following suit, there are still cases where courts are demanding journalists reveal their sources.

In September, 2012, Fairfax Media appealed against a decision by the New South Wales Supreme Court's Justice Lucy McCallum, which required three reporters from *The Age* to reveal to businesswoman Helen Liu their confidential sources for a series of stories in 2010 about her relationship with federal Labor MP, Joel Fitzgibbon (Hall 2012a). *Age* editor-in-chief at the time, Paul Ramadge, said: 'We pledged to protect them and we will' (quoted in Hall 2012a). The judge said that the right of the three journalists to protect their sources was outweighed by the 'interests of justice' and Ms Liu's right to sue for defamation (Shanahan 2012). One of the stories claimed that former defence minister Fitzgibbon had been given $150,000 by the Chinese business-woman (Shanahan 2012). The articles also alleged the payment was part of 'a campaign to cultivate him as an agent of political and business influence' (Hall 2012b). They lost that appeal, and at the time of writing the reporters faced contempt of court charges and possibly terms of imprisonment if they continued to refuse to divulge their sources. The NSW shield law protecting sources came into effect after Ms Liu began her efforts to establish the identity of the source (Ackland 2013).

About the same time, Fairfax Media was fighting another legal demand that they reveal their confidential sources for another big story. Two of the three *Age* reporters involved in the case above had been subpoenaed to take the witness stand in the committal hearing of a former executive of a Reserve Bank subsidiary accused in what's become known as the banknote bribery scandal (Beck 2012). The accused's lawyers wanted to know the source of a report that an alleged bagman would testify against the accused (Beck 2012). The legal move came after laws to protect journalists from revealing their sources had passed the Victorian Parliament the previous September but, again, before they took effect. The Fairfax lawyers lost the fight against the summons to give evidence and appealed to the Victorian Supreme Court which ruled the reporters must take the witness stand (Beck 2013). The Victorian Court of Appeal later upheld an appeal by the journalists and set aside the summonses requiring them to give evidence (Russell, 2013b).

In the most recent case, Australia's richest person, mining magnate Gina Rinehart, a major shareholder in the Ten TV Network and Fairfax newspapers, took legal action against two journalists – one a Fairfax employee – seeking to expose confidential sources behind articles and books the two journalists had written about her. Rinehart lost her action against Perth-based journalist Steve Pennells in August 2013 (Jabour 2013b). But it is not likely that Australia's richest woman will stop attempting to silence reporters who produce damaging stories about her, her family or her extensive business and political interests.

In all, at the time of writing, five Australian journalists were facing legal action – which could result in fines or jail sentences – to reveal sources, a situation that prompted the journalists' union to call for a national legislative approach to protect journalists and their sources. The union pointed out that while most states already have shield laws, as we will see later, they vary in the extent of their coverage (Caldwell 2013).

Protecting sources is not an issue unique to Australia, as you will see in the second case study at the end of the chapter. Consider the thoughts of a British journalist caught in the same dilemma:

> If journalists do not protect their sources, they might just as well shut up shop and become propaganda sheets for government or official bodies.
>
> (*Just Bloody mindedness* 2004)

The London *Daily Telegraph's* former Ireland correspondent Toby Harnden had just heard a tribunal into the 1972 Bloody Sunday shootings had finally decided, after four years, to drop contempt charges against him for refusing to name two British soldiers he interviewed about their part in that infamous day of carnage (*Just Bloody mindedness* 2004).

There are many issues that need to be considered before a journalist agrees to grant confidentiality to a source – a course of action that could conceivably lead to the journalist spending time in jail, although that is far less likely in Australia now that most jurisdictions have introduced various forms of shield laws. The question of maintaining confidences, it can be argued, relies on the 'public good' defence. In this context, using information provided by a source on the basis that they won't be revealed is a 'greater good' than not using the material because the source refuses to be named. On the other hand, some might argue that if a source does not have to reveal his or her identity, they might be inclined to make things up, or 'embellish' the story to make it more appealing to the reporter. Because journalists are reliant on sources, and some sources are reluctant to go on the record and be named, this relationship of dependence has consequences for the reporter. The same is true for the source – if the reporter 'burns' them they, too, may suffer consequences. It is a difficult fault line to straddle safely.

Are you authorised to leak that leak?

We need to make a distinction here between the different ways confidential information is released by a source to a reporter. The practice is called 'leaking' a story. There are 'authorised' and 'unauthorised' leaks.

As a tragic example, the British scientist, Dr David Kelly, was 'unauthorised' to 'leak' information to the BBC in 2003, but he thought the public should know of his reservations about the British Government's reasons for going to war against Iraq as part of the so-called 'coalition of the willing' led by the United States and including Australia. The scientist was used to talking to journalists 'behind the scenes' but he became a key figure in the row between the government and the BBC over claims Downing Street had 'sexed up' a dossier on Iraq's weapons capability (*Dr David Kelly: Controversial death examined* 2011). On the other hand, the British Ministry of Defence (MoD) media officers were 'authorised' to 'leak' (confirm) Kelly's name, if it was suggested to them by a journalist. After he was named in newspapers, Dr Kelly gave evidence to a British parliamentary committee in which he said he did not think he was the main source of the story. Two days after giving evidence, the 59-year-old was found dead near his home, apparently having taken his own life. His wife later told an inquiry into his death that her husband had been 'utterly dismayed' by the media frenzy that had erupted around him (*Dr David Kelly: Controversial death examined* 2011).

'Authorised' leaks, though, usually involve someone in authority in an organisation – for example, a company CEO, a Cabinet Minister, or Opposition Shadow Minister (or their chief media adviser) – taking a journalist aside and telling them something by way of 'background', which in journalism jargon means 'information that can be used, but not attributed to the source by name'. It is used every day in Canberra, Washington and London to get the Government's and Opposition's messages out when the source doesn't want to be publicly named in the story. It's just another form of media manipulation, and often involves the idea of payback – 'Use this material and next time we have something good, you'll be (among) the first to know.' Or it may be what is called a 'selective leak' – the source hopes to ingratiate him/herself with a journalist (or small group of journalists) by leaking an important story. It appears to be a 'win–win' situation. The journalist gets exclusive access to a story in a highly competitive environment and the source can virtually guarantee favourable treatment for their story. Often it will involve the prior announcement of a policy initiative that amounts to no more than a politician 'testing the water' to gauge public reaction. If there's an adverse reaction, the politician drops the idea, knowing his or her name has not been publicly associated with it. It is up to the individual journalist whether they play that game, and to what extent.

Quality, motivation, or a means to an end?

One of the important issues to consider before agreeing to confidentiality with your source is the quality of the information. Is it an important story? Is it something that the public really needs to know about? Does it justify anonymity for the source or could you get it from other sources without having to betray the originating source? Can you get the same information on the record from somewhere or someone else? Does the story pass the 'public interest' test to a standard that warrants confidentiality? If you can't answer 'yes' to all these questions, then there are other issues to consider before agreeing to guarantee your source's confidentiality.

For instance, what is the motivation of the source? Ask yourself: 'What's in it for them?' Are they motivated by the highest ideals of a whistle-blower – seeing that important information gets into the public arena – or are they simply after revenge against an institution or individual? Is the source trying to hide behind the journalist's ethical stance that they won't reveal his/her name to ensure that they can evade any responsibility for what they have said?

As part of the process of deciding whether to agree to grant the source confidentiality, you must assess the source's motivation. If you are at all concerned, you need to weigh up the decision on confidentiality, probably in consultation with your superiors. A second issue is the validity of the information – is it true? Could the source be lying? Could they be putting the best 'spin' they can on the story by ignoring relevant facts? You must always do your best to verify the information by cross-checking and trying to corroborate it with other sources. Another problem arises here – you might 'tip off' someone strongly associated with the story if you delve too far for verification, and that person might attempt to deflect the impact of the story by releasing a similar story to your opposition, thereby possibly negating your 'scoop'. It's a ploy sometimes used by political media advisers. Confidential sources have even been known to plant misleading information. A recent example is the second case study at the end of this chapter.

It is common practice for those affected by leaks to try to establish the identity of the confidential source by saying: 'Reveal your source or we'll know it's not true'. We have mentioned all-too-often that journalists in general don't enjoy high credibility among the public at large, and the repeated use of 'confidential sources' probably doesn't do much to enhance that reputation. You can imagine a reporter on the phone pleading with a sceptical public servant. It might go something like this: 'You can trust me, I'm a journalist.' And then in a conversation with a sceptical reader: 'Here's the information, there is a source, scout's honour, I just can't tell you who it is.' What a dilemma for everyone: the source, the journalist, and the audience. Why should the source, or the public, believe you if your credibility isn't much better than that of a used-car salesman?

The ethical issues that came to light at the time of the 2010 WikiLeaks document 'dump' are also worth mentioning in this context. Melbourne media ethicist, Denis Muller, identified five major issues raised by the WikiLeaks cables release: What should be done with material that is reasonably suspected of having been unlawfully obtained? What can be done to verify the genuineness of the material? What harms might be done by publication? What can be done to minimise those harms and what public interest is served by publication? (Muller 2010). If you can answer those questions positively in the broader context of any material that comes your way from a source that demands confidentiality then go ahead and publish, but be prepared for a backlash, especially from anyone embarrassed by the release of the information.

Before we move on from the discussion of a reporter's relationship with a source, there's another point to be made. That's the issue of getting too close to a source. The reporter who covers any round on a regular basis, from politics to courts and sport, gets to know the important sources at more than just a professional level. They might exchange small gifts at Christmas (in the case of the reporter often paid for by the office) and share the odd drink or three. It becomes an ethical issue when the source becomes the story (or a major part of it) for the wrong reasons, and you feel sorry for your friend on a personal level. Is that likely to influence how you write the story? It shouldn't – the source should realise that you have a job to do – but if you think it might, discuss it with superiors or colleagues in the newsroom.

Shield laws – a double-edged sword?

The protection of sources is an ethico-legal paradox that highlights serious areas of conflict between the media and the law. It is one of our 'grey areas' and fraught with contradictions. Areas like defamation are covered by specific legal frameworks that set out quite clearly what reporters can and cannot do. However, in the area of a journalist's relationship to her/his sources, legal source protection is still not universally accepted, as demonstrated by the cases outlined above and the call for a uniform approach. A shield law is a specific piece of legislation that applies protective conditions to the journalist–source relationship. Unlike whistle-blower legislation, which specifically protects a source, the shield law can also apply to a reporter. As of early 2013, the majority of Australian states had either passed shield laws or were in the process of enacting them. South Australia and Tasmania were the only states (with the Northern Territory) where shield laws were not imminent (Lidberg 2012). The South Australian government announced in late 2012, that they could not consider shield laws to protect 'journalists, professionals and whistle-blowers' because of the pending national Royal Commission into child sex abuse (Owen, M. 2012). But, as the union has pointed out, and as will be explained below, the laws that have been passed in the different jurisdictions lack uniformity, especially when it comes to what they define as a 'journalist' and where they publish.

In the United States, journalists have the Constitutional protection of the First Amendment and in about 40 of the states there is specific 'shield law' legislation. In the wake of the WikiLeaks document 'dumps' and the NSA release by Edward Snowden, a federal shield law in the US would appear to be some time away (Policinski 2012). In the UK there have been calls to establish shield laws, or at least offer some legal protection to journalists who protect sources or whistle-blowers (Halliday 2012b). *The Guardian* was one of several British newspapers which called for a review of source protection in the wake of the *News of the World* scandal (*Journalistic sources and the law: blowing the whistle on truth-tellers* 2013). According to the editorial, the ability to protect sources is a vital aspect of the media carrying out its democratic functions.

The debate in Australia

Serious debate about the need for shield laws began in Australia in the mid-1990s. It was in the news then because of a number of court cases involving journalists mentioned above.

These cases drew attention to the sometimes weak defence that reporters had when it came to the forced disclosure of confidential sources. The journalism profession was divided along interesting fault lines by the debate. A number argued for some form of legislative 'shield' to protect journalists, but others were equally convinced that it could have the opposite effect, creating an offence of non-disclosure in all but the most restricted circumstances. A number of points were raised at the time in relation to the proposed shield laws:

- Should there be special privileges for journalists similar to those applying to doctors, lawyers, and priests? This again raises the professional fault line argument from previous chapters.
- Unscrupulous journalists might take advantage of shield laws to make unsubstantiated or malicious allegations.
- Shield laws are only partial protection. They are legislatively applied and can be legislatively removed, allowing prosecution of journalists in some circumstances, or forcing disclosure on certain terms.

The MEAA, and an unlikely coalition of the proprietors, through their pressure group, the 'Right to Know Coalition', continued to pressure federal politicians (especially after the *Herald Sun* reporters were fined in 2007 after months of not knowing if they'd be jailed or not) until they introduced legislation after the federal election in 2010 (which had resulted in a hung parliament). Both Houses passed a shield law in early 2011 that saw source protection in federal cases extended beyond the traditional news media. The new law defined 'journalist' to include anyone 'engaged and active' in the publication of news in any medium. This would include bloggers, citizen journalists, independent news organisations and, presumably, tertiary journalism students (Alysen et al. 2011, p. 132; Stilherrian 2011). But the same broad definition of what constitutes a journalist, and their publication, is not to be found in the state shield laws. The legal expert who writes under the pen-name Stilherrian for the *Crikey* news website (and his colleagues) would have been very interested in the views of the New South Wales Attorney General, Greg Smith, when asked at a budget estimates hearing why the NSW shield law didn't cover bloggers. The Minister said they weren't subject to the same sanctions and responsibilities as journalists, who could be sacked for publishing 'something that is inappropriate' (*Crikey 'gossip' dismissed in shield debate* 2011). Bloggers, or those 'who just want to have an opinion', he said, didn't deserve the same protections (quoted in *Crikey 'gossip' dismissed in shield debate* 2011). It would seem that the minister didn't think much of the content of the daily email from *Crikey*, either, given the headline. Similar definitions of 'journalist' appear in other states' laws (McArthur 2012; Trenwith 2012).

Protecting whistle-blowers – it's about secrecy, not privacy

Shielding the identity and protecting the careers of so-called whistle-blowers is closely related to the issue of protecting sources, as WA politicians decided when they chose to deal with both at the same time (Trenwith 2012). People who risk their relationships and livelihood to expose official corruption have often been hounded when their cover is blown, even when they consistently protest their innocence, as we shall see in the first case study at the end of the chapter. It is argued that potential rackets and wrongdoings might not be uncovered if informants are silenced by fear of retribution. Throughout the 1990s, a number of legislative measures were adopted by various Australian state governments to address the issues of whistle-blowers and allegations of public corruption. Legislatively-mandated whistle-blower protection regimes aim to protect people from reprisal if they report illegal, improper, or wasteful conduct to the authorities. However, experience in Australia shows that the 'proper authorities' may be incompetent, ineffective, or corrupt themselves and hence not the best people to investigate allegations made by whistle-blowers. This is why special commissions have been established at arm's length from governments with a broad mandate to investigate matters in the public interest. Can it be left to the legal system, or to politicians, to determine what is in the public interest, given that the very definition of public interest is in fact controlled by the State? Do corporations represent public interest? Equally there are a number of contradictions in the argument that what is in the interests of the Government of the day is also in the interests of the body politic.

As we mentioned in the earlier discussion in this chapter, it was the prospect of two senior *Herald Sun* political journalists being jailed for refusing to reveal their sources in a story embarrassing to the Australian government that gave renewed life to moves to introduce shield laws for journalists' sources. Leaks by federal public servants are punishable under the Crimes Act with two years in prison. The Tasmanian independent federal MP, Andrew Wilkie, himself a former whistle-blower, and one of the prime movers in the introduction of federal shield laws, is also pushing for federal whistle-blower protection (Merritt 2012a). In 2003, Wilkie had resigned from the Office of National Assessments (ONA), an Australian security agency, over the advice to government that it produced to justify the second Iraq war. He publicly exposed the paucity of government arguments for invasion (Forbes 2004), further detailed in his book, *Axis of Deceit* (2004). Surveys in 2012 suggested that about 80% of private employees and public servants would feel obliged to report wrong-doing to someone (Brown, A. 2012). Wilkie introduced a private members' bill in late 2012 (Keane 2012e), drawing an immediate response from the government that it would introduce whistle-blower legislation early in the 2013 parliamentary year. It introduced the proposed federal whistle-blower protection legislation in late March, in the midst of the heated debate over proposed changes to media regulation – most of which failed in the federal parliament. The proposed whistle-blower legislation was initally criticised as inadequate window dressing, and as only 'a step in the right direction' (Dreyfus 2013; Knott 2013; Merritt 2013).

There is no doubt that the protection of sources – often from persecution, or even murder – is a cornerstone of journalistic ethics. At the same time, the legal status of 'privacy' is itself another of our 'grey areas'. Legal protection of individual privacy is unevenly available (as you will see in the next chapter), as are civil remedies if personal privacy is breached. In most English-speaking countries, it is further complicated by local conditions, such as America's First Amendment free speech guarantee, and also cultural attitudes towards public figures and celebrities. Some private information is protected by statute, such as tax files. Others, like medical files, are supposed to be 'confidential', but courts and other tribunals can get access. On the other hand, in the name of 'transparency', a mix of state and federal Freedom of Information (FOI) laws cover statutory and corporate information. This makes it theoretically available to anyone who can pay the access fees. But editors and reporters have frequently complained that FOI laws have proven to be freedom 'from' information laws as far as investigative journalism is concerned. As the prosecution of Bradley Manning and the hounding of Edward Snowden both demonstrate, the protection of whistleblowers is problematic and continues to be an area of dispute between governments and the news media.

The increasing role of public relations in the news-gathering process

The relationship between journalists and public relations staff is complex. We've already looked at some of the issues in relation to dealing with sources, but there are a number of other aspects raised by the ever-increasing role public relations practitioners are playing in the provision of information nowadays. The two-way relationship between journalists and their sources we discussed earlier is even more relevant with the physical two-way traffic between the two professions – journalists becoming public relations consultants or advisers, and public relations people moving into mainstream media jobs, although probably more journalists move into PR than vice versa. In the realm of politics, it is common for journalists to work for a media organization and then move into a public relations advisory role for a politician and then, after a few years, move back to mainstream reporting, particularly after a change of government. Long gone are the days when colleagues would invoke the *Star Wars* mythology and refer to someone entering PR as going 'to the dark side of the Force'.

Journalists deal with PR people every day, whether it is an inquiry seeking background information for a story they are working on, or in response to a news release or 'news alert' that a PR department has circulated, right up to the sometimes hostile interaction between journalists and political media advisers in the political capitals, like Washington, London and Canberra. Just as there is a range of interactions, there is a range of approaches taken by both sides. The student journalist will be familiar with dealing with (without being at all offensive) 'lower level' public relations people in gathering stories for university assignments and possible wider publication. The majority of interactions between journalists and public relations people are friendly and mutually satisfactory – the journalist gets the information they want, and the PR person gets their message out – like the source relationship discussed above.

One important difference between the everyday news source and the public relations consultant/officer/adviser is that the latter is a paid employee – paid to advocate the best interests of their employer, which might involve not giving the reporter all the information they are seeking. They will rarely volunteer, for instance, information damaging to their organization. That's why public relations staff are often referred to – especially in political reporting – as 'spin doctors', putting the best 'spin' they can on the information they release. At the time of the major retrenchment announcements by both Fairfax and News Limited in Australia in 2012, Melbourne-based PR academic, Noel Turnbull, noted that the US military was the biggest employer of PR people in the world and in his home town PR people outnumbered journalists (Turnbull 2012). On the latest available figures, Australian taxpayers spend more than $150 million a year on spin doctors to sell the federal government's policies to voters (Berkovic 2012). A total of 1,600 staff is employed by government departments and agencies in media-related roles. The highest number – 271 – were in the Taxation office, followed by Defence and Defence services with 175 staff (Berkovic 2012). Government spin is almost enough to overwhelm news organisations and there have been several cases worldwide of news organisations unknowingly running what is essentially government advertising in their news bulletins. Government departments and corporations are increasingly using video news releases (VNRs) to get their message out to the public. Carefully disguised as complete news stories, these VNRs make it into news line-ups when busy editors do not check closely enough the provenance of the material that comes into the newsroom. The system works best when the company or agency places the VNR into the news flow via a third party. In one well-publicised case, government VNRs were being 'cleaned' of PR traces by being released through a news wholesaler who was paid to carry the VNRs, but stripped out signs of their origin before on-passing them to its own clients (see Hirst 2011 for details).

A darker side of the political journalist–spin doctor relationship was demonstrated during the 9/11 terrorist attacks in the US when a British Labour aide, Jo Moore, circulated the now-infamous email suggesting it was a good time to 'bury' controversial or 'bad' news stories (Sparrow 2001). The memo was written within an hour of the second plane flying into the World Trade Center, before either tower collapsed. It was described at the time as 'tasteless beyond belief' (*Aide apologises for 'attacks memo'* 2001).

There was a similar media reaction in Australia when a publicist argued that the big journalism job cuts mentioned earlier were 'great news for our clients' (*Aide apologises for 'attacks memo'* 2001). From her perspective, Tina Alldis saw the job losses as resulting in improved PR campaigns, with stories running across multiple platforms and extending out into social media (2012). She said that fewer journalists meant publications would be looking for content they could syndicate across their networks. Within hours, both Alldis and her Managing Director had updated the opinion piece, apologizing to anyone offended by her remarks. Her boss labelled the article 'insensitive' (Alldis 2012). *Crikey*'s Tom Cowie characterized the comments as opening up 'fresh wounds in the ongoing cold war between journalists and their public relations cousins' (2012). A survey by *Crikey*'s Matthew Knott about six months later found that the public relations industry had been 'the big winner' from the newspapers' redundancies. Confirming the point about the two-way traffic between PR and journalism already mentioned, Knott found a number of reporters, especially from the Fairfax group, had moved into communications roles (Knott 2012b).

Journalism relying heavily on PR-generated material

Surveys in recent years have shown an increasing use of PR-generated material in the mainstream media. The practice gave rise to the concept of an 'information subsidy', first espoused by Oscar Gandy (1982) more than three decades ago. He said the provision of pre-packaged material (like media releases and news conferences, video news releases, media briefings etc.) by public relations practitioners reduced the costs of production for media outlets by providing them with 'free' content. British researchers (Lewis et al. 2008) in an article titled 'A compromised fourth estate?' found that at least 41 per cent of print articles and 52 per cent of broadcast items examined in their survey contained PR material which played an agenda-setting role or where PR material made up the bulk of the story. They also found that if the stories in which PR involvement seemed likely, but could be verified, were included then a majority of stories – 54 per cent of print stories and 58 per cent of broadcast news stories – were informed by PR (p. 10). The survey concluded that the British news media 'has been significantly affected by its increasing reliance on public relations and news agency material: and for the worse!' (p. 10). The researchers suggested that the relationship between journalists and their sources was 'too cosy' and they needed to establish their independence from sources 'or risk the fourth estate being driven by the fifth estate of public relations' (p. 18). Nick Davies, the British journalist largely responsible for uncovering the *News of the World* scandal, commissioned independent research for his book *Flat Earth News* (Davies, N. 2008) and found 80 per cent of the stories in Britain's quality dailies were either rewritten wire copy or news releases. He called the practice 'churnalism' (Jackson, S. 2008), a word that has come to symbolize the high usage of PR-generated material in mainstream media. Another, more recent, survey concluded that 'items totally free of PR involvement are an exceptionally rare phenomenon' (Reich 2010, p. 811). A joint survey of Australian newspapers by the Centre for Independent Journalism at the University of Technology, Sydney and *Crikey* found that more than 50 per cent of stories analysed in 10 Australian newspapers were 'driven by some form of public relations or promotion' (Bacon and Pavey 2010). Top of the list for PR-driven content, not unexpectedly, was Sydney's *Daily Telegraph* with 70 per cent, followed by the Hobart *Mercury* (67 per cent) and Melbourne's *Herald Sun* (65 per cent). At the bottom were *The Age* (47 per cent) and *The Sydney Morning Herald* (42 per cent) (Bacon and Pavey 2010). But even at 42 per cent, that's approaching half their content.

The question we often pose about the journalism–public relations nexus is: Who stands to gain the most? Your initial answer might depend on which side of the revolving door you happen to be standing at the time. Journalists might say that PR gains the most because clients get free publicity when a media release is run as if it were news. PR people might say that the news media gains because public relations does all the work of finding – and often writing – the story; it's cheaper than hiring reporters. We believe the relationship is parasitic; but often students are surprised when we say that news is parasitic on PR, not the other way around. Newsrooms' dependence on PR material is a sign of sickness (downsizing of staff, for example) and also further weakens the news organism by outsourcing the gate-keeping function to PR operatives.

Conclusion

This chapter examined the traditional arguments about the protection of sources. Source protection, like the issues of privacy discussed in the next chapter, involves that grey area of legal, ethical, and philosophical issues. In ethical terms, there are a number of issues to be considered before agreeing to confidentiality. As we explained, source protection is a very important issue for journalists, one that still has not been fully resolved in some Australian states and one that has the potential to open up existing fault lines and perhaps create some new ones. Discussion in this chapter also looked at 'shield laws' for journalists and the important companion issue of the protection of whistle-blowers. Among the sources that reporters contact on a regular basis are the public relations staff of various organisations, individuals and governments and we looked at that relationship and how more and more content in this age of 24/7 news and reduced staffs at media outlets is being directly sourced from public relations releases.

Case Study 1: The tale of Alan Kessing

Allan Kessing remains (as of early 2013) a convicted whistle-blower who has consistently protested his innocence. He worked for the federal Customs department for 15 years, mostly at Sydney Airport. In the wake of the 9/11 terrorist attacks, he wrote a report that detailed abuses of Customs regulations, theft, smuggling and systematic criminality at the nation's premier airport (Kessing 2009). He was then asked to write a risk analysis of the private security staff employed at the privatized airport. The report (and his recommendations) was forwarded to his superiors in early 2003 and, in his own words, 'was met with shock and horror at the implications and rejected out of hand as impossible to implement for a number of commercial and operational reasons' (Kessing 2009). He prepared another report on the workings of the airport that are beyond the public view, the so-called 'sterile areas' restricted to those with an appropriate ID. He took a random cross section of persons holding these IDs and the report that followed was also rejected. The report said that 20 percent of staff in Sydney Airport 'sterile areas' had criminal convictions and others were living in Australia illegally (Kessing 2009). Kessing retired in May, 2005, and the following month *The Australian* published details from his reports outlining serious security flaws at the airport (Levy 2012b), much to the embarrassment of the federal government. While the government rushed to assure the public that Australia 'had the safest airports in the world', it quickly commissioned a review. Within weeks, according to Kessing, the head of the review, Sir John Wheeler, endorsed Kessing's reports and Prime Minister Howard pledged $200 million to implement the suggested reforms (Merritt 2009a). In September, 2005, Kessing was charged with leaking the reports to *The Australian*. In 2007, he was convicted and sentenced to a nine-month, suspended sentence (Kessing 2009). The former Customs officer had applauded the leaking of the reports, mainly out of frustration that nothing had been done about their findings, but always maintained he was not behind it (Merritt 2009a). A representative of Mr Kessing's professional association described the investigation that led to his being charged as 'disgraceful', adding: 'The man was stitched up' (*'Victimised' whistle-blower loses appeal* 2008). Kessing's conviction (and loss of the subsequent appeal) saw renewed calls for federal whistle-blower protection (Merritt 2009a). In December, 2012, came the revelation that Australian Customs and Border Protection staff had been involved in alleged corruption and drug trafficking (Merritt 2009b). A few months earlier there had been another call for a pardon for Kessing on the basis that if he did leak the reports then his actions probably saved lives; if he didn't, as he has consistently stated, the reason for a pardon was even more compelling (Levy 2012b).

Questions for discussion:

1. Reports such as those penned by Kessing, when leaked, are said to 'have fallen off the back of a truck'. However you came by them, would you publish?
2. Would you give a second thought to what might happen to the person who leaked the documents? Or who might be blamed, even though he claims it wasn't him?
3. If it wasn't him/her, would you say so?

4. What if you knew they were stolen – like so many of the WikiLeaks cables? Is there any ethical debate to be had about reproducing stolen documents?
5. What about academic Denis Muller's five ethical issues cited above?
6. More than five years on, and Kessing is still a convicted whistle-blower, who says he is innocent and has 'wasted', as he put it (Merritt 2012b), more than $70,000 defending himself. Would you pardon him? Why? Why not?
7. If there are whistle-blower protection laws in the Australian states, why is the federal government dragging the proverbial chain?

Case Study 2: The outing of Valerie Plame

Much of the intrigue in domestic politics in the United States in the immediate post Iraq invasion years centred on the investigation into who 'outed' a CIA spy to *New York Times* reporter Judith Miller and others. It ended up being a senior member of then Vice President Dick Cheney's staff, Lewis 'Scooter' Libby (*Cheney's aide was spy source* 2005). Miller, 57, was jailed for 85 days from early July, 2005, for refusing to identify 'Scooter' as her source. 'I went to jail,' Miller said in a statement on her release, 'to preserve the time-honored principle that a journalist must respect a promise not to reveal the identity of a confidential source' (*Cheney's aide was spy source* 2005). She'd spent more time in jail for her stand than any American journalist in history (Schmidt and VanderHei 2005). Miller only agreed to identify 'Scooter' as her source after he released her from her confidentiality agreement with him (Borger 2005). But here's where the story gets a bit difficult. It's been suggested that she really didn't need to go to jail in the first place, since Libby had apparently released her, and others, from their confidentiality agreement about a year earlier (Schmidt and VanderHei 2005). At the centre of the political storm was the contention that the woman (Valerie Plame) had been 'outed' as part of an effort by the Bush Administration to counter criticism of the president's justification for the war in Iraq. It's suggested Plame's name was leaked to punish her husband, Joseph Wilson, for publicly suggesting that the Bush Administration had stretched evidence about Saddam Hussein's nuclear arsenal in order to justify the war (McClellan 2005). Wilson, a diplomat in the former Clinton administration, had attacked President George W. Bush over evidence he had presented to justify the assault on Iraq (Duffy 2003). No sooner had Ms Miller been released from jail than *The New York Times'* public editor (readers' representative) and a prominent columnist argued in print that her presence in the newsroom damaged the credibility of the paper (*US reporter jailed in CIA trial* 2005). Three months in jail, and then your colleagues start calling for your sacking? The paper's editor sent a memo to staff claiming Ms Miller misled him about her involvement in the CIA story. Ms Miller had come to prominence at the *Times* for her controversial coverage in what's called America's 'journal of record' reaffirming the presence of weapons of mass destruction. Stories about journalists and political heavyweights and Iraq's weapons of mass destruction just wouldn't go away, would they? As one commentator noted at the time, 'embedded with the US military, she was blowing the clarion call of their existence much louder and more assiduously than most of her colleagues, to the point where her critics claimed she was merely a mouthpiece for the war' (Younge 2005). Perhaps that's why she got access to people like 'Scooter' and stories like the CIA leak. One commentator called Miller a 'woman of mass destruction' for her role in further lowering the credibility of one of, if not the, most respected papers in America. While the events occurred upwards of a decade ago, it raises important issues about source relationships. The issues prompted two Hollywood films. The first, released in 2008, *Nothing but the Truth*, was loosely based on the case and involved a young Washington-based reporter going to jail for not revealing her source for a story revealing the identity of a covert CIA agent (*Nothing but the Truth* 2008). The second, *Fair Game*, was 'inspired by the experiences of real-life CIA officer Valerie Plame' (*Fair Game* 2010), and starred Australian actress Naomi Watts as Plame. Both are worth watching.

Questions for discussion:

1. While accepting this is a very complex case, the principle remains, doesn't it, that if you value the profession of journalist, you must be prepared to go to jail (assuming you are not covered by shield laws) rather than give up the name of a confidential source?
2. You have to respect Ms Miller's integrity, don't you?
3. Or is she 'tainted' by her enthusiasm for the 'weapons of mass destruction' story that was really suspect from the start?
4. How does a series of events get that far before someone in senior management starts asking serious questions? (You could ask the same question of the *Times* senior management over the Jayson Blair case).
5. Who is really at fault here – the over-zealous reporter, or the senior management that didn't seem to want to rein her in?
6. It seems like journalistic martyrdom, but would you really be prepared to spend time in jail (or pay a hefty fine) rather than reveal the name of a confidential source?
7. What if it could be shown that your source lied to you?

Part IV

The big issues in media ethics

Overview and objectives

This final part begins by looking at arguably the most contentious ethical issue facing journalists today – the constant balancing act between the public's right to know and the individual's right to privacy. The dilemma ranges from celebrities trying to keep their 'affairs' out of the mainstream media to an individual suddenly thrust into the media spotlight. The right to privacy versus the right to know represents the most public of the fault lines in journalism ethics and is without doubt the one most likely to cause public outrage. It is a clear ethico-legal paradox that seems difficult to resolve.

Chapter 10 looks at how privacy of various types is 'invaded' in unequal ways, depending on privilege, power and circumstances. The news media can sometimes seem quite callous in its disregard for the privacy of individuals.

This leads to what we call the 'privacy rich' – those who have the resources to defend their privacy, in the courts if necessary – and the 'privacy poor' – the average citizen who in most cases just has to 'cop it' when the media decides to invade their privacy.

Chapter 11 looks at the ethical dilemmas that can arise with images, both still and moving. With the rise of citizen journalism and smartphone Apps, this is another area where social media has had a big impact. Nowadays cameras are everywhere. Anyone with a smartphone can record still and moving pictures and upload them to their Facebook page or sell them to the media. We also look at other aspects of images, like their manipulation.

Chapter 12 is devoted to the media game-changer of recent times – social media. There have been examples of the impact of social media in almost every practical chapter so far, but there are a number of other issues associated with social media that justify a stand-alone chapter. We consider the protocols for using Twitter and the vexed question of dealing with Facebook content as a source material.

The final chapter canvasses how you can handle the types of problems we've been discussing once you find yourself in a busy media newsroom, it suggests some possible ethical fault lines in the future, and discusses a possible way forward for journalism.

After reading these chapters, you will have an understanding of the various legal and ethical problems associated with:

- the balancing act between the public's right to know, and the individual's right to privacy
- privacy and secrets
- celebrity and fame and 'public' versus 'private' privacy
- how the media chronicles history in pictures
- the ethics and legality of using pictures from social media sites
- the manipulation of images – the good, the bad and the ugly
- the pros and cons of media organisations' social media policies
- how to resolve an ethical dilemma
- emerging fault lines in journalism ethics.

10 Do we need to know?
Privacy and the press, an ethico-legal fault line

The Milly Dowler story – a sickening tale of deceit and false hope

> "She's picked up her voicemails, Bob, she's alive!"
>> Milly Dowler's mother falsely thinking her daughter was still alive soon after her disappearance in March, 2002, and while the search for her was still under way.

The name Milly Dowler is synonymous with the worst of the illegality uncovered in the *News of the World* phone hacking scandal. But what did the popular British Sunday tabloid do, and what made it so terrible?

Milly, a 13-year-old English girl, was abducted on her way home from school in Surrey in March, 2002 and later murdered. Her disappearance was a time of excruciating anguish for her family as Surrey police hunted for clues to her fate. *The Guardian*, which had pursued the phone hacking scandal for years, published a story in early July, 2011, alleging that a private investigator employed by the *NoW* had not only listened to the missing girl's phone messages in search of a scoop, but also deleted messages from the phone (Leigh 2011). The appalling result of the illegal phone hacking and deletion of the messages was that Milly's parents were given false hope that their daughter was still alive. The tabloid's theory – gleaned from a hacked message that they misunderstood – was that at the time they hacked her phone, Milly was still alive, and they sought police support for their theory. According to *The Guardian*, the behaviour of the paper helped neither the Dowlers nor the police. Milly's mother, Sally, and father, Bob, were the first witnesses at the Leveson inquiry into the ethics of the British media. Sally told of her elation at being able to leave a message for her daughter – 'it clicked into voice mail, so I heard her voice and it was just like, she's picked up her voicemail, she's alive' (*Milly hack gave Dowler parents false hope* 2011). After her disappearance, Milly's voice mail had quickly filled and prior to the deletions all Mrs Dowler heard was a recorded message saying a message couldn't be left. Part of Rawls' veil of ignorance theory suggests 'walking in another's shoes', in other words, putting yourself in their position. Can you imagine how you would feel under the circumstances? Little wonder Rupert Murdoch closed the *News of the World* in the wake of *The Guardian*'s repulsive revelations. Murdoch authorised the payment of £2 million in compensation to the Dowlers and a further £1 million donation to six charities chosen by the family (Gayle 2011). Murdoch said he made the donation to underscore his regret for the 'abhorrent' hacking of the schoolgirl's phone (Gayle 2011). It would emerge later that police could not be sure that the paper had been responsible for deleting the girl's phone messages (*We may never know how Milly Dowler's voicemails were deleted* 2012). Milly's body was discovered more than six months after her disappearance. Serial killer, Levi Bellfield, was found guilty of her murder in 2011 and sentenced to a 'whole life tariff', meaning he will never be released (Rayner 2011).

Figure 10.1 'News of the World hacked Milly Dowler's phone during police hunt', *The Guardian*, 5 July 2011. Copyright Guardian News & Media Ltd 2011

An all too familiar experience for 'victims' of the media

Few people will ever endure the pain that the thoughtless pursuit of a scoop by *News of the World* caused the Dowler family, but all too many suffer to lesser degrees at the hands of an unthinking media. The media usually justify intrusion into a person's private life by saying the story is 'in the public interest'. The authors believe that in many cases 'the public interest' actually means 'what the public is interested in' or more accurately, what editors think the public wants. In many cases it amounts to little more than voyeuristic pleasure at seeing a 'tally poppy' cut down and, in other instances, mere titillation. An argument can be made for privacy invasion in the case of a politician if the incident is suggestive of the morals they would bring into their public life – but what public interest is there in what happens between two consenting adults in the privacy of a hotel room, even if one of the participants is an international film star, music icon or sporting celebrity? This is one of those 'shades of grey' that we have referred to in other chapters. What one might see as not in the public interest – between them and their spouse, for instance – another might say shows the person concerned is cheating on their spouse and deserves public condemnation.

The *Australian's* media commentator, Mark Day, put the journalist's position on privacy succinctly about a decade ago during debate over a smear campaign against the current Labor leader Mark Latham:

> It's now a fact of life that if there's dirt to be dug, particularly in the political arena, it will be dug. One way or another, fairly or unfairly, deliberately and with malice, or inadvertently by accident, truth will out.
>
> (Day 2004)

Sadly, the truth is that journalists can't do their job of informing the public on matters of importance without invading some people's privacy. But it is a balancing act – the individual's right to privacy versus the public's right to know, not simply what the public might like to know. After all, we all like a good bit of juicy gossip, don't we? But the reporting of gossip has no place in mainstream media. Although few will agree with us, we believe it has no place in the so-called gossip magazines, either. You need go no further than the Internet or follow social media for plenty of gossip, if that's what you want.

So what does the public have a right to know about? This is where you need to apply the public interest test. What is the public benefit in what you're about to report? Is it critical for the public to make an informed decision in an election, for instance? Is it a major breakthrough in medical science that might bring relief to millions? Or does it demonstrate a person's hypocrisy – do they flaunt their family in front of the TV cameras when it suits them for publicity purposes while privately cheating on their spouse? Does a former, very high profile, cricketer accept sponsorship from a nicotine patch producer to stop smoking and still 'light up' when out of the public gaze? The test is not 'would the public be interested in this?', but rather does the public need to know the information for an important reason? If it fails that test then the ethical journalist should consider ignoring the story. We know news has to have some entertainment or pleasure value to readers in order to sell and be palatable. After all, variety is the spice of life (to borrow a cliché). But that does not mean replacing worthy stories with entertaining fillers, nor does it always justify embellishing stories with frivolous or irrelevant incidentals. To do so is the journalistic version of 'sexing up' a story to make it more saleable.

One of the bigger ethical constraints on the media involves individuals' and groups' moral rights to privacy and confidentiality. Privacy is another of those ethico-legal paradoxes we have referred to in other contexts. It simply means that there are legal, or quasi-legal, limits on what the media can, and cannot, do in relation to matters of privacy, and that these constraints can (and often do) conflict with what the media is willing to do in chasing a story. In Australia it means the media cannot access or publish some information covered by privacy laws, like medical and taxation records, for instance. There's no general privacy law in Australia – hence the renewed push for a tort on privacy in Australia in the wake of the revolting revelations of privacy invasion by the *News of the World*. In early 2013, the federal government had just announced it was referring the issue of a privacy tort back to the Australian Law Reform Commission for 'detailed examination' (Conroy 2013) meaning, in effect, in an election year, nothing will be done in the relatively-near future.

In the United States, the right to privacy (or perhaps more correctly, the legal remedy for the invasion of privacy) as a legal concept has developed into four distinct torts allowing the aggrieved to seek damages (Prosser 1960), but American courts have tended to side with the media, citing the overriding claims of the First Amendment rights of the US Constitution, which guarantee freedom of the press. Across the Atlantic, the United Kingdom passed the Human Rights Act in the late 1990s, taking in the European Convention on Human Rights, including Article 8 (a right to privacy) and Article 10 (freedom of expression). While the British courts have held back on developing a specific tort on privacy, they have instead used the already-established breach of confidence as a legal remedy for those who believe their privacy has been invaded. It's been used in a number of high-profile celebrity privacy invasion cases.

Public and private privacy

In terms of the news media's rights, a number of clear distinctions need to be made between 'public' privacy and 'private' privacy and between 'privacy' and 'secrecy'. Andrew Belsey (1992, pp. 82–3) says secrecy differs from privacy in terms of its 'moral status' – secrets per se are morally neutral and only take on significance in particular contexts. For example, there's a big difference between 'innocent' secrets, like personal details, and 'guilty' secrets, such as when governments or corporations lie to the public. In such circumstances, it is not considered legitimate for government agencies, politicians, or business figures to claim 'invasion of privacy' in order to conceal matters that should be available to the public.

In the media context, 'public' and 'private' privacy concerns the differences and difficulties the news media faces in respect of the privacy of public information – that is the levels of privacy accorded to public figures versus the taken for granted everyday privacy 'enjoyed' by 'ordinary' citizens. In these circumstances, the issue of 'consent' is also important. A person can give informed consent to be involved in a news story, and there is implied consent if people agree to talk to you once you have identified yourself as a reporter. In effect, by identifying yourself as a reporter you are giving them the chance to say 'go away' or 'I don't want to talk to the media', and if they do say something like that, then you are obliged to go. This situation may well arise when you seek a 'death knock' interview and the grieving relative, for instance, is too upset to talk and asks for privacy. If they don't ask you to leave them alone, then you can fairly assume 'consent' unless you are dealing with children, in which case you need to seek permission from a person in a position to give it, like a parent or legal guardian. The issue of consent is important when making the distinction between the 'right' of the average citizen to say 'no', and to have their privacy respected, and public figures, who, to a greater or lesser extent, rely on publicity and exposure for their own gain (through, for example, election to high office, or through sales of DVDs and books, or film or concert ticket sales). As you will discover shortly, 'celebrity' has taken on a life of its own as both a news value and a commercial value in the media.

Belsey made three distinctions between cases involving breach of privacy that are worth keeping in mind:

- For public figures 'consent can be assumed' for all but a small protected personal domain.
- In matters of criminality or unethical behaviour by a public figure, 'consent is not needed' because if a law has been broken then the perpetrator deserves public exposure.

- In cases concerning 'ordinary people' suddenly thrust into the public eye, 'consent should be a requirement'.

(Belsey 1992, p. 89)

Privacy intrusion – the grey shades of an ethico-legal paradox

Privacy has always been an issue and the media has been accused of invading privacy for at least 100 years; the early American press first debated whether it could invade the implied privacy of public officials in the late eighteenth century (Burns 2006). Today, ubiquitous social media has only complicated matters even further. Everything on Twitter is public, but Facebook is a grey area when it comes to privacy. Theoretically, everyone can control who gets to see the content they post on Facebook, but in practice most of us rarely restrict access very much, if at all. As we will discuss in chapter 12, journalists are very adept at finding ways around privacy settings and won't hesitate to do so in pursuit of a story.

We also need to look at privacy in relation to autonomy, because without some degree of privacy a person's autonomy and individualism are undermined. As we have seen in the examples already mentioned, unwarranted invasions of privacy have the potential to cause enormous harm, and would break several of the ethical philosophies, to say nothing of various Codes of Ethics and editorial charters. Privacy is also at the core of our own personal esteem – it protects us from 'ridicule and scorn', allows us to preserve our reputation, and it regulates social interaction by keeping other people out of our 'personal space' (Retief 2002, pp. 152–3). Some qualifications to the universal right to privacy are based on the fact that an individual is a public figure or otherwise in the public sphere. Another qualification is predicated on the public's need to know about certain issues that might affect them.

The ethical dilemma here, in essence, is where do you draw the line between telling all, and minding your own business? The discussion in earlier chapters on the relationship between freedom of the press, its commercial imperative, and the public's right to know, creates privacy – or the invasion thereof – as one of the most serious fault lines in media ethics, certainly as far as the public is concerned. The Australian journalists' code of ethics (*MEAA Code of Ethics* 1999), the code of the American Society of Professional Journalists (*Code of Ethics* 1996) and the British equivalent of the National Union of Journalists (*NUJ Code of Conduct* 2011) all address the issue of individuals' privacy to varying degrees.

One of the most unpopular aspects of invasion of privacy – both with the public and with many journalists – is the aforementioned 'death knock' interview. The journalist seeks an interview with someone who has suffered a tragedy in their lives – a loved one may have been killed, for instance. The public is interested in the feelings of family or friends about the tragedy, but the reporter needs to approach people in such a traumatic state with the utmost tact. Often, nowadays, a relative, family friend, or a member of the clergy, will agree to speak on behalf of the grieving. The MEAA Code addresses the issue in Clause 11:

> Respect private grief and personal privacy. Journalists have the right to refuse to intrude.
>
> (*MEAA Code of Ethics* 1999)

So, ethically speaking, you can refuse such an assignment. There will always be other reporters in the office that will do it. Former students have told the authors of the practice of 'grass knocks' – meaning tapping on the lawn in front of the person's home, rather than knocking on their door, then reporting back to the office that no-one was home. While it's an easy way out of what could be a very difficult interview, it's also unethical because you are failing in your duty to your employer by not completing the assignment.

The price of fame is the invasion of your privacy

The ABC's former Director of Editorial Policies, Paul Chadwick, a Walkley-Award-winning journalist and former Victorian Privacy Commissioner, teamed with a colleague at the Communications Law Centre in the late 1990s to develop what they called 'The Taxonomy of Fame' (Chadwick and Mullaly 1997, pp. 5–6). It is a useful starting point for a discussion of fame, and the all-too-often price of fame: invasion of privacy. Chadwick and Mullaly identified five kinds of fame:

- fame by election or appointment (politicians, judges and others in public office)
- fame by achievement (film stars, TV presenters, sporting heroes and business leaders)
- fame by chance (previously anonymous people randomly caught up in tragedy, disaster or good fortune)
- fame by association (anyone close to the rich and famous – like the children or relatives of a leading politician, film or sports star)
- and Royal fame (a category reserved for those born into, or who marry into, a royal family).

(Chadwick and Mullaly 1997, pp. 5– 6)

Media law expert, Professor Mark Pearson, has suggested there are several key factors a journalist or editor should consider in weighing up the intrusion into someone's privacy – the nature of the private material, the means of intrusion, the fame of the individual and the potential damage caused by the intrusion (Pearson 2005).

What follows is a catalogue of some of the more outrageous invasions of individuals' privacy in recent times. We'll be looking at what some sections of the media – notably tabloid press and television – have done, but we should repeat the point we make several times elsewhere, that the majority of journalists go through their careers making minor and sometimes major ethical decisions that never come to the public's attention. While their decisions decide how a particular story will be told, they are not seen as invading an individual's privacy in a major way and, if they do, they are seen by the public as justified. The worst of the examples that follow are the work of a small minority of the profession.

Royal privacy – fit for kings and princes?

Let's start with the last category first – royal fame. The British royalty seem to suffer most from what many see as the unwarranted attention of the tabloid media, Internet bloggers and gossip sites, and social media. Every public move (and some very private ones) of the Royal Family is snapped by an 'army' of photographers, the much-maligned paparazzi, who rely on saleable photos of 'the Royals' – usually the younger ones doing something stupid – for their livelihood. Nowadays, anyone with a smart phone could capture a member of the Royal Family off guard, and profit financially from their luck. Not only in the Commonwealth, but in countries the world over people seem to be fascinated by Britain's Royals. And the media love them! The Royals are paid from the public purse, so the argument goes that they are fair game. They will often agree to the obligatory 'photo op' when they are on holidays, on the understanding that after 15 minutes of posing for the gaggle of photographers/camera operators and responding to reporters' often-shouted questions, everyone is happy and they will be left in peace to enjoy the rest of their holiday. But let there be the slightest hint of controversy or scandal and the media pack will hound them to ground – not unlike a royal fox hunt of old. That's why the photographers were outside that Paris hotel on the night Princess Diana died in 1997. She had a new lover – and a very rich one at that – and pictures of them were selling for 'top dollar'. That sort of unwarranted attention is nothing new to the British Royal Family, but it is not always embarrassing (just more often than not).

On the plus side, remember the massive coverage afforded the lead-up and wedding of Prince William and Kate Middleton in 2011, and the Queen's Diamond Jubilee a year later? Aside from the odd complaint from William (*Prince and the paparazzi: William to adopt zero tolerance* 2010) and the in-laws (*Middletons shop the paparazzi over 'press intrusion'* 2011) about invasion of their privacy, the media enjoyed the events, even heeding pleas from Buckingham Palace to leave the newlyweds alone on their honeymoon (Bates, S. 2011). Why intrude, when Australian women's magazines were chalking up record sales for their 'straight' coverage of the wedding (Jackson, S. 2011)? But 15 months after the wedding, the Aussie gossip magazine, *Women's Day*, earned the displeasure of the latest royal couple with their 'world exclusive photos!' of the newlyweds strolling along a secluded beach – William in swimming trunks, the new Duchess of Cambridge in a skimpy black bikini (*Wills and Kate: Our Island Paradise* 2012). Inside, the magazine published another three pages of the royal couple in their swimwear, and a montage of various 'royals at play', including a bikini shot of Diana (*Wills and Kate: Our Island Paradise* 2012). Some London newspapers knew the location of the honeymoon – a beachside bungalow in the Seychelles costing $5,000 a night – but agreed not to send photographers at the request of the Palace (Sykes 2012). While the second in line to the British throne and his wife were representing his grandmother on the other side of the world as part of the Diamond Jubilee celebrations of Queen Elizabeth's coronation, a huge invasion of privacy scandal broke with a French magazine publishing topless photos of the Duchess taken while she was relaxing around a pool during a brief holiday prior to the tour. The Duke and Duchess were furious, describing the action by the French magazine, *Closer*, as 'grotesque and totally unjustifiable' (Ravens 2012). A spokesman for the couple described the magazine's behaviour as 'reminiscent of the worst excesses' suffered by the Prince's mother (Lydall et al. 2012). The threat of legal action failed to stop an Irish newspaper publishing some and another magazine in the *Closer* stable, *Chi*, announcing a 26-page special on the photos (Lee, K. 2012). The Editor of the *Irish Times*, Michael O'Kane, resigned in the wake of the furore caused when he published the topless photos. Swedish and Danish papers would follow despite a French court blocking *Closer* from publishing further photos (*Magazine 'proud' to publish Kate photos* 2012). Both *Closer* and *Chi* are owned by the former Italian Prime Minister, Silvio Berlusconi. *Chi* has a history with the British Royal Family. It was the only media organisation to publish a black and white image of Diana, as she lay dying in the wreckage of the car in 1997 (Miranda 2012c). The editor of *Closer*, Laurence Pieau, insisted there was nothing degrading about the photos of Kate – 'They show a young woman sunbathing topless, like the millions of women you see on beaches,' he added (*Royals sue magazine over nude pictures of Kate Middleton* 2012). The British tabloids, one of which had a few weeks earlier published nude photos of Prince Harry (discussed below), perhaps realising that Lord Leveson was soon to release his recommendations on their future, variously labelled the editors of the magazine as 'grinning perverts' and the photographer a 'peeping tom' (Levy 2012a) and did not publish any of the topless shots. In late April, 2013, the publisher of the French edition of *Closer* and the photographer who took the topless photos were being 'formally investigated' for invasion of privacy (Batty 2013). Up to that stage in her marriage, the main interest in Kate, particularly in the gossip magazines, had been whether she was pregnant. On the day after the topless scandal broke, the *Gold Coast Bulletin*'s main coverage contained four shots of the Duchess that included her stomach and posed the question (*Is this woman pregnant? Decide for yourself* 2012). A week earlier, one opinion-writer had made the prediction:

> ... there's little doubt as soon as the euphoria and furore of the Olympics dies down, Britain's attention will turn to Kate's ovaries.
>
> (Lette 2012)

It didn't happen quite that fast, but Kathy Lette did get her wish a few months later when it was announced that the Duchess was indeed pregnant after she had been rushed to hospital with severe morning sickness (Miranda 2012a). *Media Watch* noted that the 'joyous news' had been announced 10 times in the previous 15 months by the Australian gossip magazine, *New Idea* (Holmes 2012b). We've already mentioned in Chapter 6, in the context of chequebook journalism, the hefty price paid by *Women's Day* for pictures of the four-month-pregnant Duchess (Hornery 2013b). Unfortunately, anything to do with a pending royal birth is big news, especially for the gossip magazines.

Coverage of the royal couple's 2011 honeymoon was not the first time that an Australian women's magazine had earned royal displeasure in recent years. In a more serious breach of royal protocol, *New Idea* scooped the world media in February, 2008, when it leaked details that William's younger brother, Prince Harry, was fighting the Taliban in Afghanistan (New Idea *slammed for Harry story* 2008). The Prince, at the time third in line to the British throne, was quickly recalled 'for security reasons' (*'No Hero' but Harry wants to go back* 2008). The magazine later apologised for breaking the global media blackout on the Prince's deployment (New Idea: *regrets 'lapse of judgment' over Prince Harry story* 2008). The argument against publication was that if Afghan insurgents knew where Harry was, he might become a high profile target for kidnap or assassination. We find this excuse absurd. The Afghan Taliban has much better ways of gathering intelligence in the war zone. To argue that publication of a photograph in a gossip magazine thousands of kilometres away would create extra danger for the prince is not credible.

The British Royal Family – particularly the young Princes William and Harry – have a long history of providing fodder for the British tabloids – the so-called 'red tops'. While there was general agreement in the years immediately following their mother's death that they should be 'left alone', relatively speaking, as they grew up, less than a decade later, interest in their every move escalated. Prince Harry made plenty of headlines – one of the more embarrassing involved him wearing a Nazi uniform to a fancy dress party two weeks before the 60th anniversary of the liberation of Auschwitz, the Nazi concentration camp where more than a million Jews were killed (Jones, S. 2005). Big brother William disgraced himself at Harry's military passing-out ball in 2006 by being what one paper called 'drunk and out of control' (Pilling 2006). A sub-editor at the *Gold Coast Bulletin* couldn't resist the temptation for a right royal dig at the second in line to the throne giving the story the headline: 'Prince Swills' Shame' (Pilling 2006).

Most of the 'shock, horror' exposés about the Princes' behaviour, while embarrassing to their grandmother and the Palace PR machine, have amounted to little more than youthful enthusiasm for living life to the fullest – the sort of behaviour every parent regrets, but probably expects from time to time. But after behaving himself impeccably during his grandmother's Silver Jubilee in 2012, and then being part of the cheer squad for 'Team GB' at the London Olympics, nude photographs of Prince Harry taken during a party in his Las Vegas hotel suite appeared on the American gossip website, TMZ (*Flash Harry: Prince's 'strip billiards' photos spark a right royal row* 2012). To put the story into context, the pictures surfaced in late August, as the British media awaited the judgment of the Leveson Inquiry, which they expected would establish a stronger regulatory regime on the recalcitrant British tabloids. Initially, the Prince's minders at St James's Palace were selling the story not as a sex scandal, but as the Prince 'letting off steam' between representing the Queen at the closing ceremony of the London Olympics and returning to duty as a captain with the Army Air Corps. The palace also raised concerns over the prince's security (how did someone smuggle a camera or smart phone into the Prince's suite?), the risk of blackmail, and the return of his 'Party Prince' reputation (Schlesinger, F. and Malvern 2012). Dai Davies, a retired chief superintendent, who was head of the royal protection squad for three years, said that the naked young woman pictured with the prince 'could also be an IRA sympathiser, a Muslim extremist or a fixated nutter' (Schlesinger, F. and Malvern 2012). The ethical issue here, though, was would the infamous British tabloids publish the photos after the attacks on their professionalism that followed the *News of the World* scandal, and pending the release of the recommendations of the Leveson Inquiry? Initially, the papers refrained from using the photos of the cavorting Prince after royal officials had contacted the Press Complaints Commission, the media watchdog, and sent letters to British newspapers urging them not the use them, suggesting that it would be an invasion of the Prince's privacy and could lead to court action. That first morning the country's scandal-loving tabloids devoted many pages to the story of Prince Harry's naked romp, but didn't run the pictures (*'Terrified of their own shadow': Nude Harry photos give British tabloids a headache* 2012).

The country's top-selling daily paper, the Rupert Murdoch-owned *Sun*, came nearest to upsetting the Palace when they front-paged a staff member conveniently named Harry, aided by one of the paper's female interns, re-creating one of the Prince's naked poses under an appropriate heading (*Harry grabs the family jewels* 2012). But that wasn't enough for *The Sun*. It announced on its website later that day that it would be publishing the actual photos the next day because its readers had a 'right to see them' (*The Sun defies royals to publish naked Prince Harry photos* 2012). Sure enough, there on the front page the next day was the now familiar full length shot of Harry with his hands strategically placed in what *The Sun* touted as a 'souvenir print edition' (*Heir it is! Pic of naked Harry you've already seen on the internet* 2012). The move was seen as sending a message that the Murdoch tabloid would fight expected tougher media regulation. Other papers had been wary of taking the risk – and printing naked photos of British royalty would have been a big one – for fear of provoking a much tougher set of rules to govern the British media than the current system of self-regulation. *The Sun's* Managing Editor, David Dinsmore, in a statement on the paper's website, said that the issue had become one of 'the freedom of the press' (The Sun *explains decision to print naked Prince Harry pictures* 2012). He added:

> This is about the ludicrous situation where the picture can be seen by hundreds of millions of people around the world on the internet, but can't be seen in the nation's favourite paper read by 8 million people every day.
>
> (The Sun *explains decision to print naked Prince Harry pictures* 2012)

It was also about guaranteeing record sales, a cynic might suggest. The bandwagon effect also kicks in, once again exposing media hypocrisy. The 'nude prince' story could be lavishly reported by all media outlets thanks to *The Sun*'s boldness. Everyone else can feel morally smug by pointing out that they are only reporting on *The Sun*'s ethical breach – while still using the offending images. Australia's papers took their lead from their British counterparts (all publishing before the 'real' photos appeared in *The Sun*), although at least two included the mock-up *Sun* front page – *The Courier Mail* (*Law denies what readers want (and can get)* 2012) and Adelaide's *Advertiser* (Miranda 2012b) under the headline: 'Brits turn the other cheek for Harry'. No sooner had interest waned in royal nudity than the media was full of coverage of Harry back in Afghanistan. This time the PR machine at the Ministry of Defence decided on a different approach. They permitted coverage of the Prince within days of his arrival, and then allowed both print and broadcast media access to the Prince on three separate occasions during his four-month stint in the war zone on the understanding that the stories would not be published until his tour of duty was over (Hopkins 2013). One paper characterised the approach as a gamble 'to keep Prince Harry safe – from reporters' (Hopkins 2013). The stories that emerged, aside from leading with the angle that he had killed Taliban during his tour, also revealed, hardly unexpectedly, his hatred of the media (*Scathing Harry reveals 'anger' at press intrusion* 2013).

While William and Harry have dominated royal scandal news in recent years, there have been other instances of people connected with 'the Palace' making the news. The BBC was forced into an embarrassing apology to the Queen when it issued promotional footage for a programme which wrongly implied that she had walked out of a photo shoot (Sherwin 2007). Chalk one up for Her Majesty. The most embarrassing 'not-Will-or-Harry' scandal in recent times involved the Duchess of York, Sarah Ferguson, former wife of Prince Andrew. She was caught in another sting by the 'fake sheikh', Mazher Mahmood, discussed, along with other Mahmood stings, at the start of Chapter 4. One of the rare victories for the Palace was the jailing in 2007 of the *News of the World*'s royal editor, Clive Goodman, and one of the paper's private investigators, Glenn Mulcaire, for hacking hundreds of telephone voicemail messages intended for staffers at Buckingham Palace (*Who's Who in the U.K. Phone-hacking Scandal* 2011; *Profile: Glenn Mulcaire* 2012). The paper insisted for years that they were the only two involved in phone hacking, referring to Goodman as a 'rogue reporter', but persistent investigation by *The Guardian* led to the uncovering of the depth of the *News of the World*'s illegal activities. Both men have also been arrested in connection with the wider scandal.

Fame by achievement – the heat of the spotlight

Following a close second to the royals in the 'unwanted attention of the tabloids' stakes are the A-list celebrities – those at the top of their respective sports, pop idols, and film and television stars. Although an argument could be made for including various politicians and business leaders in this group because of their public profiles, we're leaving discussion of invasions of their privacy to the next group, fame by appointment. In most cases, the relationship between celebrities and the media is such that one cannot exist without the other, but does that necessarily make them 'fair game'?

For many years, the British media's A-list was headed by 'Britain's other royal family' – soccer superstar David Beckham, his wife Victoria (the former 'Posh Spice'), and their children. But interest in them waned slightly when David accepted a huge contract to play in America. They were quickly replaced in the eyes of the paparazzi by other sports stars, rock, TV and film stars. For an idea of who had their privacy invaded by Britain's top-selling tabloid of the time, look up the list of those who have settled grievances with the *News of the World* after the scandal broke in mid-2011. A natural for close attention was the captain of the national soccer team, John Terry. An attempt to protect the privacy of those who could afford to seek it from the media saw the institution in the UK of the super injunction. Super injunctions prevent the media from reporting not only details of a story but even the existence of the injunction. There are said to be between 200 and 300 super injunctions in existence at any one time in the UK (Reidy 2010). Terry applied for one when he learned a Sunday paper was going to publish details of his extra-marital affair with the ex-girlfriend of his English team-mate Wayne Bridge, only to have it lifted because the judge felt he was not concerned about privacy, but rather about protecting his reputation in the eyes of his sponsors (Rayner and Evans 2010). British media lawyer, Mark Stephens, estimated the cost of a super injunction at about £100,000, putting them out of the reach of most (*Twitter outings undermine 'super injunctions'* 2011). But, as the previous headline infers, social media have thwarted the intent of the rich and famous. In mid-2011, a Twitter user posted details of six instances of what they said were injunctions obtained by celebrities to cover up affairs or prevent publication of revealing photographs (Rayner and Evans 2010). We won't repeat their names, except to say they include the 'likely suspects' – film and TV stars and sporting personalities.

In the United States, a couple of states have introduced laws aimed at guaranteeing celebrities some privacy. Not surprisingly, California (home of Hollywood) passed a law in 1998 (after the death of Princess Diana) and updated it in 2009 allowing lawsuits against media that 'pay for and make first use of material they knew was improperly obtained' (Hofschneider 2013). Rock legends Steven Tyler and Mick Fleetwood appeared before the Hawaiian Senate's Judiciary Committee pushing for a similar law in that state and the Hawaii Senate had approved the legislation named the Steven Tyler Act after the Aerosmith rocker (McManus 2013).

All celebrities have to learn to live with the often-unwanted attention of the paparazzi. They are willing enough to call in the media when they are publicising their latest tour or film, so they have to accept that if they openly court the media's attention for promotional purposes, then the public – through the media – is going to be interested in their private life, what they do when they are not on the field, stage or screen. At the height of the *NoW* scandal, the editor of the British media industry publication, *Media Week*, Jeremy King, put the case succinctly:

> (I)f you court the media in the first place and don't like it when they say something nasty, then unfortunately once you push the toothpaste out of the tube it's hard to get it back in.
>
> (Quoted in Hassan 2011)

Put another way, if you use the media, you can't complain too much when the media uses you (Hassan 2011). Sometimes the celebrities are in league with the supposedly-dreaded paparazzi stalkers. Sydney's *Sunday Telegraph* reported in mid-2012 on what they headlined 'FAKE-arazzi: celebrity set-ups' (Marshall, J. 2012) where the celebrities work with the photographers and pocket handsome fees in return for exposing private moments. Some were reported to have been taken on all-expenses-paid trips to overseas 'love nests' for the photo shoots. The paparazzi were in the news in early 2013 when one of their number was struck and killed by a passing car while trying to get shots of pop star, Justin Bieber's white Ferrari. It led to renewed calls in the United States for tougher laws to rein in the photographers (*Justin Bieber calls for crackdown after paparazzo death* 2013). Previous calls for action over the dangers posed by the paparazzi to themselves and the celebrities they pursue have been stymied by the US First Amendment protection of the freedom of the press.

As has been mentioned before, Australia effectively has no real privacy safeguards, giving the media virtual 'open slather' to invade the privacy of celebrities. There are any number of cases of the invasion of an individual celebrity's privacy by the Australian media. Google names like Wayne Carey (in the wake of him having to stand down as captain of the North Melbourne AFL club after it emerged he was having an affair with a team-mate's wife, but more controversy would follow), Shane Warne (for any number of exposés of his private life), and Nicole Kidman (who once complained the paparazzi in Australia made her life unbearable (Murray 2009)) to see how their private lives have been reported.

Not long after the Convergence Inquiry presented its final report to the Australian federal government (Boreham 2012) and a couple of months after the Finkelstein Inquiry recommended a News Media Council covering all media (Finkelstein and Ricketson 2012), the oft-mentioned *A Current Affair* embarked on one of the more sleazy invasions of privacy in recent times, promising in their promos: 'An Affair to Remember. One of Australia's most famous celebrity wives ... the Aussie superstar, known worldwide ... their eight-year secret exposed' (*The shameless airing of an un-current affair* 2012). It revealed the affair between Leanne Edelsten (former wife of Dr Geoffrey Edelsten, medical entrepreneur and one-time owner of the Sydney Swans AFL team), and writer and TV personality Clive James. The programme flew Ms Edelsten to England where she confronted an ailing James and regaled him with titbits about their eight-year relationship, and how they enjoyed sharing a certain popular chocolate bar. Aside from the expected tabloid follow-ups, typified by the coverage in the Murdoch media (*I loved Clive James, Leanne Edelsten tells* A Current Affair 2012), most other print media coverage attacked the tabloid current affairs programme.

Journalist, publisher and lawyer, and a former presenter of *Media Watch*, Richard Ackland, noted:

> This little kiss-and-tell was broadcast in Australia, so James really can't sue for breach of privacy, as he could if the show had gone to air in Britain.
>
> (Ackland 2012)

The *Australian*'s media writer, and former editor of their weekly *Media Diary*, Amanda Meade, blogged the programme was 'just like the worst of the scandalous tell-alls in the UK press', titling her critique 'A Current Affair's dirty new low' (2012a). *The Daily Telegraph*'s Miranda Devine, known for her forthright views, also blogged on the tawdry exposé, describing Ms Edelsten's ambushing of her former lover as 'cringe-worthy' and added that Edelsten 'stooped to despicable when she confronted James in London with a camera crew' (2012). She added:

> Befuddled, frowning and frail, James, who has leukaemia, smiles, looks embarrassed and tries to shuffle away.
>
> (Devine 2012)

It was an example of what media critics refer to as 'the race to the bottom' as far as ethics and taste are concerned.

Fame by appointment – public office, public life

The category of 'fame by appointment' includes politicians, appointed officials like judges, and the so-called 'captains of industry'. Leading politicians are consistently in the news and have to accept they will have little of what the average citizen would classify as a 'private life'. They are also able to stand up for themselves, particularly if they are a government or party leader. If they want to react to an attack by a certain newspaper, current affairs television programme or 'shock jock', there are plenty of alternative media sources quite happy to give them a voice. Former head of the Australian Greens, Bob Brown, described the Murdoch press in Australia as the 'hate media' in part because of their treatment of him and his party's policies (Grattan 2011). But that was in the cut and thrust of political debate, and to be expected from time to time. Former British Prime Minister, Tony Blair, in a parting shot at journalists after a decade in power in the UK, made a more general attack describing the British media as 'a feral beast, tearing people and reputations to bits' (*Blair attacks 'feral' media* 2007).

The news media has been grappling with these issues for two hundred years as it creates tensions and fault lines connected to the 'fourth estate' role of the news media to be a check on the probity of those in public life. In the eighteenth century American editors were divided over the line between the public and private lives of politicians. Some felt that their role was not to practise 'ad hominem' journalism – that is attacking the private foibles of public figures; others, notably William Cobbett's *Porcupine's Gazette* believed it OK to fiercely attack an opponent's private life in the service of truth (Daniel 2009). The same divided opinion runs through the news media today.

We've already mentioned a serious invasion of a politician's privacy in recent times – the 'outing' of NSW cabinet minister, David Campbell – as a case study in chapter 8. At the time, prominent political commentator and former Labor federal cabinet minister, Graham Richardson, said politicians in Australia didn't have a right to any sort of private life:

> And I don't think they've had that right for 20 years; it's been eroded steadily over time but now anything goes.
>
> (Quoted in Moore 2010)

A current senior politician was quoted in the same article suggesting that media figures, among others, should be held to the same standard that they were applying to politicians. Australia's former Foreign Minister, Bob Carr, a former journalist and former Labor Premier of New South Wales, suggested:

If parts of the media want to adopt a new (privacy) standard in respect of politicians, it's a standard that should now be applied to other people in the public eye, including business leaders, media figures, sports figures and judges.

(Quoted in Moore 2010)

When another federal cabinet member, Workplace Relations Minister, Bill Shorten, asserted in 2012 that his private life and his family were 'off limits' to the media, at least one print media commentator reacted by insisting that politicians' families were fair game 'because what they do in their private lives matters' (O'Brien, S. 2012). It matters, Susie O'Brien contended, because: 'We pay their salaries and so have a right to know how they live their lives when it influences how they do their job' (2012).

One of the more controversial politicians in recent Australian history is the right-wing Queenslander, Pauline Hanson. A fish and chip shop-owner, who held the federal seat of Oxley as an independent after the 1996 federal election, Hanson formed the One Nation party. She was known for her right-wing, some would say racist, views. Hers has been a turbulent political career, including being jailed temporarily for alleged electoral fraud, charges which were subsequently quashed (Hanson n.d.). But it was her attempt to win the state seat of Beaudesert in the 2009 Queensland election that saw her in the public eye again. The weekend before the vote, several Murdoch Sunday papers published what the *Sunday Herald Sun* front-paged as 'raunchy photos of Pauline Hanson taken in the 1970s' (*Uncovered* 2009). Raunchy indeed – one showed the young woman topless.

Leaving aside the embarrassment when the Murdoch media discovered the photos were fake, debate initially centred around whether such photos of a political candidate – albeit a very controversial one – qualified as being 'in the public interest'. The public would certainly be 'interested' in seeing topless photos of a very young Pauline Hanson, but were obviously private photos of the woman legitimately 'in the public interest' many years later in the context of an attempted political comeback? Ms Hanson maintained from the start that the pictures were not of her. The *Sunday Telegraph* had negotiated to buy the photos from a person who claimed to have been her lover in the mid-1970s (cited in *Hypocrisy Unlimited* 2009). Its editor at the time, Neil Breen, later admitted that he 'did not check the facts enough' before rushing to publish (MacBean 2009). Before it was shown to be a hoax, some defended the publication as being in the public interest (Riley 2009), while a former political adviser of Hanson's suggested it might help her campaign (*Nude photos 'a help for Hanson'* 2009). How, you might ask? Private photos of a young woman barely out of her teens, obviously taken during intimate moments with a boyfriend? Would you consider entering public office if you thought foolish things you did in your youth would be published more than 30 years later for all to see?

Fame by association – family and friends become fair targets

This category is reserved for those whose news value rests almost entirely on their relationship with someone noteworthy. If you are the father of star English premier league soccer player, Wayne Rooney, and you get involved in an alleged betting scam, it is bound to be widely reported – and not reported by your name in the lead to the story, but rather as 'Wayne Rooney's father' (Hull, L. 2011). Six months later, police announced Wayne Rooney Senior would face no charges, but he's still his son's father in the headline and lead of online versions of the story (*Wayne Rooney's father faces no further action on betting scam claims* 2012). Is he only newsworthy because of his famous son? Would he receive such close attention from the media if he was a pro-verbial 'man in the street'? An Australian instance of the same issue emerged in 2010, when the nephew of media icon, Ita Buttrose, was jailed for up to 16 years on drugs charges. Ita had been among a large contingent of family and friends that had supported her nephew, Richard, during the trial, but the Sydney tabloid *Daily Telegraph*, led their online version of his sentencing with 'Media identity Ita Buttrose watched on in anguish today as her nephew ... ' (Davies, L. 2010). Google 'Ita Buttrose's nephew' and there are hundreds of references to the story, all beginning with the same description of the accused. It was a serious series of drug-supplying offences – one carried a maximum sentence of life imprisonment – but the lead paragraph invariably began by referring to his famous relative. Does the media believe that we wouldn't be interested in a drug supplier sentenced to 16 years, regardless of his famous relative?

[Ms Buttrose was named Australian of the Year in 2013 for her contribution to the media and charity work.]

Fame by chance – sorry about your loss, but we'll put you on the front page anyway

This category has been deliberately left to last because it stirs the most emotion from the public. This is where a person is suddenly thrust into the limelight because they have been randomly caught up in a tragedy, disaster or good fortune. Let's dismiss the final part first. Someone wins a big lottery. The public – most of whom dream of being in that person's shoes – are interested in the person who has had the sudden windfall. What will they do with all that money? How often do you read about someone who bought their ticket on the way home that night, only to win enough that they wouldn't have to work again unless they wanted to? It's one of those all-too-rare good news stories that we read about from time to time. That's the pleasant side of 'fame by chance' – the one in many million chance that the person's numbers 'come up'.

Unfortunately, there are far more examples of the controversial side of this category of fame – where someone finds the media pack on their doorstep because they have become involved in a tragedy or disaster. This is where our 'man in the street' can relate to the person in the news. They know how they would feel if they were suddenly in the same position – grieving for a lost loved one and the seemingly callous media wanting them to comment on the tragedy. We've already briefly mentioned a couple of instances where the media has invaded the privacy of people suddenly thrust into the news – the bomb hoax victim Madeleine Pulver, and the mother of teenager Molly Lord, who died in a quad bike accident.

The insensitive handling of the quad bike story drew reaction from the media. The paper criticised for the graphic photograph it published of the dead girl, the *Illawarra Mercury*, had apologised to the family on its website (Meade 2012c), and the Australian Press Council announced it was strengthening its guidelines covering the use of images of dead and dying people and those relating to journalists interviewing patients in hospitals and nursing homes (Jackson, S. and Bodey 2012). Press Council chairman, Julian Disney, said even before the death of Molly Lord, concern had been expressed to the Council over the issue (Jackson, S. and Bodey 2012). The family wanted the federal government to legislate to curb media intrusion (Meade 2012b). Molly's parents, Peter

Lord and Linda Goldspink-Lord, had a private meeting with Communications Minister, Stephen Conroy, to push their case (Meade 2012b). They wanted the government to implement 'Molly's Law' to prevent the media from intruding on 'the most private and grief-stricken moments that any family could ever experience' (Lord, 2012). The petition mounted by family and friends of the Lord family proposed restricting media contact with families within 48 hours of the deceased's passing, banning publication of photos and names of the deceased for that period, and photos of deceased children under 18 could only be published with the permission of the parents (Azzopardi, 2013). At the time, the government was considering its response to the Convergence and Finkelstein inquiries on media regulation and moves for a privacy tort for serious media privacy invasions. Nothing came of either.

Before the Milly Dowler case became the epitome of everything wrong with the way the *News of the World* did business, one of the more repulsive cases of offensive reporting in the UK centred around the media's handling of the family of another missing girl – Madeleine McCann. We discussed the McCann case in the context of 'Trial by Media' in chapter 7. But, to refresh your memory, Madeleine's parents, Kate and Gerry McCann, both medical practitioners, were on holiday in Portugal with their three children when on 3 May 2007, a few days before Madeleine's fourth birthday, she went missing from their holiday unit while her parents dined with friends nearby (Overington 2011b). What followed was a parent's worst nightmare. It would be more than a year before the parents were cleared as suspects in the disappearance (*Maddie's parents cleared as suspects* 2008). The *Australian*'s respected European correspondent, Peter Wilson, characterised the media's treatment of the case as 'one of the most heavily reported, and most irresponsibly reported, personal tragedies in memory' (2007). He said that the coverage had been able to convince millions in Britain and Portugal that the McCanns were behind their daughter's disappearance (Wilson 2007).

We would argue that ordinary people caught up in a big story should generally not have to face the onslaught of the media pack without a very high level of real public interest in the story. The McCann case was one such episode – Madeleine's still unexplained disappearance and possible murder is a big story – but the media's unfounded speculation about the parents' involvement in the case was clearly out of order.

Protecting privacy? What can the reporter do about it?

In this chapter we've detailed cases of how some sections of the media cover people who, for one reason or another, and whether permanently or fleetingly, fall into one of those five categories of fame. One of the reasons the media give for covering 'the rich and famous' is that they made their fortunes from the public watching their television show, going to their movies, watching them play whatever sport they excel at, or buying the merchandise they endorse or CDs they produce. So the public, in a way, 'owns them' and therefore has a right to know every little detail about their lives. But do we really? If it were you, how would you feel about people reading or seeing the sort of material we've been talking about in this chapter? What would your parents or children think? It might not be an issue for the average university journalism student, but stories have a very long 'shelf life' on the Internet. Google one of your favourite lecturers and see what it tells you. One of the authors was told that as soon as students learned he was about to join their university, 'we jumped online to check you out'. Employers nowadays not only google potential employees, they check their Facebook pages, too. This is a good time to revisit Rawls' veil of ignorance, behind which 'it is possible to walk in the shoes' of the person whose privacy is about to be breached. According to Patterson and Wilkins (1994, p. 118), behind the veil of ignorance 'freedom of the press ... becomes equal to freedom from unwarranted intrusion into private life'. Is this a proposition that, as journalists, we can live with? We think not. We have a problem with the veil of ignorance. It suggests that all people should be treated equally, which clearly doesn't happen, simply because of the news value of prominence. The Mayor of a city, for instance, is a far more newsworthy person than our long-suffering friend, the man in the street. The former will appear in the local paper far more often than the latter.

As we mentioned earlier, the US, UK and Australian codes of journalistic ethics deal with privacy to varying degrees, but what does the Australian Press Council and ACMA, the broadcast regulatory authority, say?

The Australian Press Council's privacy principles (*Statement of Privacy Principles* 2011), fortuitously updated as the full extent of the *News of the World*'s gross invasions of privacy was emerging, notes that:

> Journalists should not unduly intrude on the privacy of individuals and should show respect for the dignity and sensitivity of people encountered in the course of gathering news.

ACMA issued its revised privacy guidelines in December, 2011, after considering public submissions (*Privacy Guidelines for broadcasters* 2011). 'The general principle' of the national Code of Practice enforced by ACMA 'protect against the broadcast of material that:

> Relates to a person's personal and private affairs – for example, by disclosing personal information; or
> Invades a person's privacy – for example, by intruding upon his or her seclusion.
> (*Privacy Guidelines for broadcasters* 2011, p. 2)

It also notes our oft-mentioned distinction – 'Not all matters that interest the public are in the public interest', adding that 'it is unlikely to be in the public interest if it is merely distasteful, socially damaging or embarrassing' (*Privacy Guidelines for broadcasters* 2011, p. 6).

Those are some of the formal industry guidelines, but when faced with a decision about potentially invading a person's privacy, a journalist needs to consider a number of ethical blueprints mentioned earlier in this text. Which best fits the case – the public benefit, Aristotle's Golden Mean? Rawls' veil of ignorance? Does it pass the 'public interest' test? Is it fair to all concerned?

Suicide reporting – journalism and mental health collide

Half a century ago, when one of the authors was a cadet journalist at the now-defunct Adelaide afternoon tabloid, *The News*, the word 'suicide' was never used in a news story. Such stories were avoided, and where they had to be published (perhaps because of the high profile of the victim), the phrase 'there were no suspicious circumstances' was used by both the police and the media to denote that the victim had taken their own life. Nowadays, there is not the stigma that attached to the word 'suicide' decades ago, but caution is still needed in covering such tragic events. Part of the Mindframe website, set up by the Hunter Institute of Mental Health with the help of journalism educators and medical professionals, provides a mass of information about issues to be considered when reporting a suicide. It also looks at similar issues for those covering stories about mental illness, self-harm, and eating disorders. Among the advice offered in the suicide section of the Mindframe website is to consider whether the story needs to be written at all. It also discusses the language to be used in suicide stories, suggests reporters not be too explicit about the method used to commit suicide and raises other issues like the reporting of celebrity suicides, where the story should be placed in the paper or broadcast bulletin, interviewing the bereaved, placing the story in context and suggesting helpline numbers be included in every story. There is also useful information about the latest statistics on rates of suicide (it is going down), material on the phenomenon of copycat suicides, and suggested 'experts in the field' that reporters might contact for comment. The Australian Press Council released its new standard on suicide reporting in August, 2011 (*Standard: Suicide Reporting* 2011) and gives similar advice to that offered at the Mindframe site.

Reporting a suicide, or attempted suicide is difficult enough, but when it is 'one of your own' it is even more difficult. The Australian media was saddened to hear of the death of popular Network 10 Sydney newsreader, Charmaine Dragun, in November, 2007. Her inquest was told she had long fought depression (*Smile hid newsreader's 10-year depression battle* 2010). The Coroner found that her death was 'probably preventable', if her mental condition had been properly diagnosed (Taylor, P. 2010).

A major ethical dilemma arose with the shock news in early December, 2011, that respected ABC cricket commentator, and *SMH* writer, Peter Roebuck, had taken his life in Cape Town, South Africa (Badel 2011). The story was complicated for his colleagues by the news that he was about to be detained over an alleged sexual assault (Stein 2011). Colleagues grappled with discussion of Roebuck the private man with his 'demons' while praising his contributions to the game and cricket journalism (Baum 2011; Marks 2011). Others were not so generous. *Herald Sun* columnist Andrew Bolt asked if Roebuck were a Catholic priest, would there have been the silence?

> The silence I mean is the hush by his employers and some close colleagues over what drove him to jump from the sixth floor of his South African hotel on Saturday.
>
> (Bolt 2011)

A raft of allegations would follow to further taint the cricket writer's memory. This is one of those sad cases where you think you know the person – 'they wouldn't do that, would they?' The authors shared an admiration for Roebuck, the writer and commentator, and were saddened by some of the accusations made against the man, even though there had been isolated incidents reported in the past.

When it is OK to breach privacy?

While journalists will differ on whether many of the instances mentioned above qualify as breaches of an individual's privacy, and to what degree, there are instances where breaches are justified. One case that focused attention on moral behaviour and its professional implications was the resignation, in late 2012, of the director of the United States' Central Intelligence Agency (CIA), David Petraeus, after admitting an affair with the woman who wrote his biography (*Petraeus mistress feels devastated* 2012). His job meant there was a high level of public interest in the former military leader. There was speculation at the time that he resigned because the four-star general had violated a military code that condemns affairs, while others suggested there was a strong stigma attached to extramarital affairs in intelligence circles because such behaviour, and its potential revelation, could lead to blackmail and the compromising of State secrets (*Petraeus Resignation Highlights Moral No-Man's Land at Intersection of Private Lives and Public Responsibility* 2012).

A final word ... here come the drones ...

We've seen them for some time giving us a bird's eye view of the action at sporting events, but privacy advocates are pointing to the increasing use of aerial drones as the next frontier of privacy invasion. Major retailers will apparently sell you a remote-controlled aerial device equipped with a camera for as little as $350 (Moses 2013). The use of such devices has moved from their 'big brothers' being used in the War Against Terror to a backyard near you. While TV stations are already using drone-mounted cameras for some stories, there are fears they might replace the prying long lenses of the paparazzi. It is even being suggested that the day is fast approaching when a small, personal drone will be a part of the tool box for journalists, photographers and bloggers (Moses 2013).

Case Study 1: A tiger on the course, a cheetah in the bedroom

The idyllic world of the world's most recognised sporting figure, golfer Tiger Woods, started to unravel after a minor road accident around the Thanksgiving holiday weekend in 2009. Since he turned professional in 1996, Tiger Woods had crafted a larger-than-life persona with the help of the media. As sexual indiscretion after sexual indiscretion emerged, the media started putting that persona in a different light. It became obvious that the squeaky-clean image of the sporting superstar, adored by millions the world over, who had become the first athlete to earn more than a billion dollars, may have glossed over personal faults (Jonsson 2009). Everything about the 'Tiger Woods' affair' was big. It was alleged he had cheated on his wife with more than a hundred women during their five-year marriage (*Tiger Woods' 120 affairs* 2010). The story finally became public when Woods crashed his luxury car outside the family's palatial home. Some reports suggested his wife had attacked Woods' car, or even the golfer himself, with a golf club during an argument that preceded the crash. His 'public' apology was a huge media event (*Tiger Woods apology biggest media event since Bill Clinton's Monica confession* 2010) while some didn't believe his sincerity (*Forgive me sponsors for I have sinned: Tiger slammed over 'staged' apology* 2010). By anyone's measure it was a big story. One blogger noted that at one stage Tiger appeared on the front page of the Murdoch tabloid, *The New York Post*, 21 days in a row – one more than coverage of the 9/11 terrorist attacks (Stableford 2010). Apparently, Woods had used his wealth and a clique of loyal friends to conduct and conceal his adulterous lifestyle, lavishing his mistresses with gifts to keep them quiet (Crawford 2009). As British journalism academic, Roy Greenslade, wrote in the *London Evening Standard* at the time, 'if you ever wanted a demonstration of a media feeding frenzy, then the treatment of Tiger Woods since his car accident has been a classic example' (2009). Television advertisements featuring the golfing superstar were quickly dumped, and while some sponsors stood by him, others fled (Shovelan 2009). While all arms of the mass media gave the revelations blanket coverage, bloggers had a proverbial 'field day', too. One tried to explain the massive coverage:

> This sequence of events was unheard of 50 years ago. Not because transgressions didn't occur then – there have been philanderers throughout the history of mankind – but because coverage of this type did not occur in reputable publications.
>
> (Spratling 2010)

However, even media outrage has a shelf life. Five years after his very public marriage split and career meltdown, Tiger Woods is back on the golf course and fronting advertising campaigns for expensive watches and other luxury goods.

Questions for discussion:

1. Do so-called 'reputable publications' (as referred to in the final quote above) have a higher calling than to report the seedy indiscretions of sporting celebrities?
2. Given that celebrity gossip is part of the daily diet of all arms of the media nowadays, what has caused formerly reputable newspapers to join the so-called 'race to the bottom'?
3. Do huge celebrities, like Tiger Woods, deserve any privacy at all? Why or why not?
4. What about the effects of the coverage on his family?
5. Is there a case for sympathy for the wife, while still covering what was the biggest sporting scandal of 2009–10?
6. If the media is so all-pervasive nowadays, how was Tiger able to get away with his philandering for so long? Was the golfing media in some way complicit?
7. Faced with Woods' litany of indiscretions, where do you draw the line and say 'enough is enough' and ignore further revelations? Or do you just keep on publishing everything, 'warts and all'?

Case Study 2: Lara and Michael

One of the authors (Roger) completed his doctorate on how the Australian print media has covered the private lives of five cricketers in the years between 1945 and 2010. One of his case studies involves the then Australian vice-captain Michael Clarke (later to take over as captain of the national team) and the break-up with his bikini-model fiancée, Lara Bingle. For the two weeks being researched their story was the most-mentioned in all mainstream media (*Media Monitors* 2010a; *Media Monitors* 2010b), in one case outstripping the second-most-mentioned story of the week by about 50% (*Media Monitors* 2010b). Eight daily newspapers – from Brisbane, Sydney, Canberra, Melbourne and Adelaide – were researched from March 9 to 21 (inclusive). In that 13-day period, a total of 129 news stories, 74 opinion pieces, 14 cartoons, one set of 'voxpops', two polls and seven 'letters to the Editor' were published on the couple's breakup in those eight newspapers (Patching 2011). Almost every commentator had an opinion on what the 'captain-in-waiting' should do at this critical time in his private life. Google (or look up Factiva) for that fortnight in mid-March, 2010, to get an idea what some of the commentators – not only cricket commentators, but the bevy of 'know-it-all' commentators who give their opinions on anything and everything at the proverbial 'drop of a hat' – were suggesting how the young cricketing superstar should handle his private life.

Questions for discussion:

1. Lara and Michael were the nearest Australia had to sporting royalty – the 'down under' equivalent to Posh and Becks – surely their break-up was a big story that deserved blanket coverage?
2. Can an argument be made that the person who is in line to assume what some people regard (tongue-in-cheek) as the country's most important job (behind that of the Prime Minister), leading the national cricket team, and who is paid handsomely for his work on and off the field, has given up any right to privacy in his personal life?
3. Were Lara and Michael so high profile that they deserved what they got? They openly courted the media when it suited them, so they then can't plead for privacy when publicity doesn't suit them, can they?
4. Both were relatively young people – Lara hardly older than the average recent university graduate. How would you feel if 'everybody' was publicly giving you advice on your private life?
5. Don't even the most publicity-hungry celebrities deserve some degree of privacy – particularly at such a difficult time in their lives?

11 The ethics of the image

To save a life or take a picture – the worst of dilemmas?

> If they're just trying to hold up a mirror to society, then how do they escape their responsibility as members of the public to help helpless children?
>
> (Bartholet quoted in Paterno 1998)

One of the hardest choices a reporter has to make is whether or not to intervene when they witness horror in the course of their reporting duties. Do you maintain professional detachment, or do you forget your role as witness and enter the story as a participant from that point forward?

This dilemma was brought into stark relief in early December, 2012, when the Murdoch tabloid, the *New York Post*, carried a front page photo of a man moments from death (*Doomed* 2012). Under that huge headline, the sub-heading read: 'Pushed on the subway track, this man is about to die' over a full-page photo of the train only metres from the man (*Doomed* 2012). Ki Suk Han, a 58-year-old married father of one from Queens, was pushed onto the tracks by a man who had been hassling other commuters on the platform (Manker 2012). The photo raised many issues, like why didn't the people on the platform try to pull him to safety? Why didn't the photographer put down his camera and try to help? What purpose did publishing the photo serve? Freelance *New York Post* photographer, R Umar Abbasi, was waiting on the platform (after attending another job for the paper), when he saw Mr Han fall. He started running towards him, firing his camera's flash in an attempt, he said, to warn the driver of the approaching train (*'This man is about to die': anger over photographer's role in subway death* 2012). But his attempt to justify taking the pictures was dismissed by most of the public. Abassi was denounced on the *Post*'s website as 'horrible ... greedy ... a spineless coward ... a selfish bastard who thought only about getting the pictures ... a useless, worthless human being' (quoted in Allen-Mills 2012). One Tweeter questioned why someone's first instinct would be not to help the man, but instead to 'snap a photo of him about to die and sell it to the NY *Post*' (Pearson, Michael 2012). He stood accused of prioritising 'capturing the photos over helping save the man's life' (Zhang 2012). Abbasi insisted that others were closer to the man than he was and could have helped. Others on the platform at the time were said to have quickly started filming the aftermath of the fatality on their mobile phones (Allen-Mills 2012). Abbasi showed police the photographs he had taken and left the camera's memory card with editors at the *Post*. He said he was not part of the decision to publish the photos (Moos 2012). Defending his decision to take the pictures, Abbasi said:

> I had no idea what I was shooting. I'm not even sure it was registering with me what was happening. I was surprised at the anger over the pictures, of the people who are saying: Why didn't he put the camera down and pull him out? But I can't let the armchair critics bother me. They were not there. They do not know what they would have done.
>
> (Quoted in Moos 2012)

While the public was critical of the photographer's decision to keep his camera flashing, some in the industry and media ethicists identified with his dilemma. One industry blogger asked what the reaction would have been if he had 'simply said he was doing his job rather than using his camera flash to warn the train operator?' (Zhang 2012). It is one thing to take a picture. It is quite another to publish it, and with such prominence. The *Post* came in for heavy criticism for printing the chilling image. The coverage was condemned as insensitive and sensationalist (Petrecca and Eversley 2012). Members of the public took to Twitter to express their outrage – a 'misuse of humanity' one called it, 'snuff porn' said another (quoted in Collins, L. et al. 2012). The paper's media critics wanted to know what purpose publishing a photo of a person moments from death served. It is hard not to think that the *Post*'s purpose in publishing was to maximise sales of the paper that day with a sensational front page. The Poynter Institute's Kelly McBride is one commentator who saw no clear 'journalistic purpose' to publishing the image. 'There has to be a journalism purpose behind the decision to run an horrific photo,' she said (quoted in Petrecca and Eversley 2012). David Carr of *The New York Times* was particularly critical of the paper's coverage:

> The *Post* cover treatment neatly embodies everything people hate and suspect about the news media business: not only are journalists bystanders, moral and ethical eunuchs who don't intervene when danger or evil presents itself, but perhaps they secretly root for its culmination.
>
> (Carr 2012)

For a range of other perspectives from media commentators, photographers and media ethicists and photography professors, read the initial wrap-up by the Poynter Institute's Julie Moos (2012).

The New York Post is no newcomer to controversy. A few years ago they published a book of their most memorable stories, with probably their best-known headline as its title (*Headless Body in Topless Bar* 2008).

The graphic image – when too much pain is barely enough

In this chapter we will look at the ethical dilemmas that photographers (and video camera operators) face when telling stories through the lenses of their cameras and those faced by editors 'back in the office' in deciding whether to publish a particularly graphic image. The photographer is almost always close to the action of any story, trying to capture its essence in one still or a sequence of moving images. They have front-row seats at the most important events of their time. They record the moment history is made – often in terror and confusion. Without the professional photographer, these historic moments would be lost. We'll be mainly concentrating on the ethical dilemmas presented to still newspaper/magazine photographers, but the points are equally valid for television news camera operators. The public reaction to the subway death photos (there were others inside the paper), highlighted above, raises a major ethical dilemma for a journalist: Do they intervene in the story they are covering? If so, at what stage? Are they there to cover the story as an observer, or to become a partici-pant? Every photographer/journalist will have a story about how they once took off their 'journalist's hat' and became a member of the general public to help someone in desperate need. Photographers are criticized from time to time for taking pictures that are 'too graphic' or intrusive. Then they win national and international awards for their powerful and often emotive efforts. We'll shortly discuss that dilemma further. Social media have rated a mention for varying reasons in almost every chapter and this will be no exception. In this context, though, we're defending the intellectual property rights of the owners of Facebook pages and those who post photos on Twitter, and debating the media ethics of the practice of republishing them without permission. Finally we'll look at something that has become commonplace in recent years. It's that aspect of the ethics of images that allows – with the digital technology now available (even on your phone) – the manipulation of any image. We made a case study of one such unflattering manipulation – the extending of a politician's nose, Pinocchio-style, in chapter 8.

Images chronicle history – without a witness, we don't know

Images – still or moving – from news events around the world are etched in our mem-ories. Journalists, and photo-journalists in particular, will often recall a momentous event as much from their memory of the images that accompanied it as the precise details of the story. If you think of any recent major event or conflict, your mind will probably recall a particular image (or TV news sequence) that illustrates it for you. They don't have to be major catastrophes or life-threatening events, either. Some of our fondest memories are from human interest stories – of people who 'beat the odds' or are victorious over 'City Hall' (over any authority for that matter). And who doesn't like a good animal story – a birth at a zoo, or the latest pictures of the annual whale migra-tion off the Australian eastern seaboard?

Sadly, the images most remembered are probably associated with the major tragedies of recent times – 9/11, the Asian Tsunami of 2004, the London terrorist attacks of 2007 (often referred to as 7/7, like 9/11, because of the date they occurred), the 'Black Satur-day' Victorian bushfires of 2009, the Christchurch earthquakes (2010– 2011), the Bris-bane floods of early 2011 and the Japanese earthquake/tsunami a few months later. It is the powerful, emotive and sometimes intrusive images that create controversy.

In January, 2013, when bushfires ravaged vast areas of Australia, a photograph of a grandmother, huddling with her five grandchildren in chest-high water under a jetty to escape the firestorm that destroyed their home in Dunalley in southern Tasmania, made the front page of the local paper, the Hobart *Mercury* (*Reluctant Heroes* 2013). As well as being published in other Australian papers, it became the international face of the state's bushfire disaster, appearing in many overseas newspapers, including the *Interna-tional Herald Tribune*. In the days following the family's story of survival, one popular news website reported 20 million hits on the story and media outlets in France, Ireland and Canada were reporting it (Dawtrey 2013). More than a hundred homes were lost in the Dunalley area in that bushfire, but it was that one image of six people that captured the emotion more than any statistic.

Many opposed the Vietnam War because of the 'napalm girl'

One of the defining images of the Vietnam War was the 1972 photo of 'napalm girl', nine-year-old Kim Phuc, running naked down the nation's main highway – Route 1 – in agony after a US air attack on suspected Viet Cong rained blobs of sticky napalm on her that melted her clothes and layers of her skin. That image, taken more than 40 years ago, polarised American opinion about that unpopular war and won the nation's highest journalism award, the Pulitzer Prize, for Associated Press photographer Nick Ut, who took the iconic shot (*The 'napalm girl' image that haunted the world turns 40* 2012). Other distressing images have won many media awards since, including the 2012 Pulitzer for the best breaking news photography for the picture of a screaming girl standing amid the carnage of an Afghan suicide bomb attack (Blake 2012). Covered in blood and standing amid a pile of dead mothers and their children, the picture of the screaming 12-year-old brought home to the world the reality of a war that has devastated the lives of ordinary people across Afghanistan (Blake 2012). Agence France-Presse (AFP) photographer, Massoud Hossaini, was nearby when a bomb ripped through a crowd in the Afghani capital, Kabul, killing 63 (Blake 2012).

The one thing that the examples mentioned so far have in common is that in each case the photographer 'just happened to be there' to freeze the moment in time. That's their job – to be there to capture those iconic images. Such emotion-charged pictures (and others discussed below) put a human face on tragedy and have moved nations to action – over political issues, over famines in developing countries, over examples of cruelty in times of conflict – and they have also led to soul-searching by the public and those who took the pictures.

'The most famous photograph no one has seen'

That's what Associated Press photographer, Richard Drew, calls his iconic photo from the 9/11 attack on New York's twin towers – the photo simply known as 'The Falling Man'. Drew had been preparing to photograph a fashion show (because it was to feature pregnant models) when he was sent to what became the most photographed event in history. It is believed up to 200 people took the decision to jump rather than die in the flames engulfing the twin towers, or simply fell from the higher floors of the World Trade Center on September 11, 2001. One image came to symbolise their awful fate. It was published on page seven of *The New York Times* – and in countless American newspapers and others around the world. The picture shows a man, frozen in mid-air, perfectly vertical, plunging headfirst from the North Tower (*9/11: The image of The Falling Man that still haunts 10 years on* 2011). It was one of a 12-frame sequence Drew took of the man falling to his death. He would recount later how he captured a number of sequences of people falling from the burning buildings on that day no one will forget (Howe 2011). The photo of 'The Falling Man' caused a furore, with readers complaining it 'exploited a man's death, stripped him of his dignity, invaded his privacy, turned tragedy into leering pornography' (Junod 2003). Others questioned the media's sense of decency, calling the photo 'tasteless, crass and voyeuristic' (Anderson 2011). Most letters of complaint to American papers stated the obvious: someone seeing the picture had to know who he was. Many papers responded to the wave of criticism by wiping the image from their online records, and although the *Times* ran it again on the front of their book review section in 2007, it has rarely been seen in print since 2001 – the reason for the photographer's description that headed this section (Anderson 2011). Tom Junod, in his seminal piece on 'The Falling Man' for *Esquire Magazine* (2003), said 'the images of people jumping were the only images that became, by consensus, taboo – the only images from which Americans were proud to avert their eyes'. Junod's article was adapted for a documentary of the same name (Singer 2006). The identity of the man remains a mystery, but relatives believe it to be Jonathan Briley, who worked in the restaurant, Windows on the World, which occupied floors 106 and 107, the top two floors of the North Tower (Junod 2003). In the minds of many it remains one of the defining images of the biggest news event since the turn of the twenty-first century.

The photo that 'made the world weep'

We touched on the ethical dilemma in times of tragedy in discussing the *New York Post*'s controversial coverage of the 'doomed' commuter at the beginning of the chapter and briefly in the introductory remarks. It is the major ethical dilemma that will face both the journalist and the photojournalist – when does the professional duty of the journalist to witness and report give way to the compulsion to help? Any number of famous press photographs could be used to illustrate this dilemma. We have chosen Kevin Carter's, Pulitzer-prize winning, 1993, photograph of a malnourished toddler under the menacing gaze of a vulture in southern Sudan. One blogger called it 'the most iconic photograph of the century' (Oberei 2012). A close colleague of Carter's labelled it the 'picture that made the world weep' (Macleod 1994). It was characterised as a 'metaphor for Africa's despair' (Oberei 2012) and an 'icon of Africa's anguish' (Macleod 1994). Carter reportedly waited 20 minutes before taking the photo, hoping the vulture, which was seemingly poised to devour the child, would spread its wings. When it didn't, he took the photo and chased the bird away, and the toddler resumed her attempt to reach an emergency feeding centre, apparently only 100 metres away (Knight, E. 2012). The response to the emotive photo was huge, and multifaceted. It not only ignited efforts to send aid to the famine-ravaged country, it also, while it brought the South African-born photographer fame, drew criticism. *The New York Times* bought the photograph and published it on 26 March 1993. It was picked up by other papers around the world. Because of the reaction of the American public – they wanted to know what happened to the child – *The New York Times* later took the unusual step of publishing an Editor's note saying the girl had enough strength to walk away from the vulture, but that her ultimate fate was unknown (Ryan 2006). Why not, the public asked – wasn't she close to the safety of the food distribution centre? Journalists on assignment in Sudan had been advised not to touch famine victims, for fear of spreading disease, but Carter was criticised for not helping the little girl. 'The man adjusting his lens to take just the right frame of her suffering,' said the *St. Petersburg (Florida) Times* in an editorial, 'might just as well be a predator, another vulture on the scene' (cited in Macleod 1994). Carter had been watching 20 people starve to death every hour in the Sudanese village near where he encountered the little girl (Freund 1999). Should he have carried this one little girl to safety? He'd been surrounded by hundreds of starving children. His supporters contended that the one picture he sold to *The New York Times* did more good for the starving people of Sudan than anything he could have done for any individual at a personal, humanitarian level. *The New York Times* then Executive Editor, Bill Keller, wrote in 2011: 'Any photographer who has snapped memorable images has had the experience of being damned for it, and it is something the most thoughtful of them take to heart' (quoted in Knight, E. 2012). He also said that photographers were 'more exposed' than journalists covering a story for two reasons:

> They need a sustained line of sight to frame their photographs; a reliable source is never enough. And they cannot avert their eyes; they have to let the image in, no matter how searing or disturbing.
>
> (Keller 2011)

Carter was a member of a group of four photographer friends who covered the violence of the dying days of the Apartheid era in South Africa in the 1980s and early 90s. The four became so well-known for capturing violence, particularly in the black townships, that a Johannesburg magazine, *Living*, dubbed them 'the Bang-Bang-Club' (Macleod 1994). Two members of the group (Greg Marinovich and Joao Silva) later told their story in a book named after the 'club' (2000) and a film followed (*The Bang Bang Club* 2010). Carter's colleague, Scott Macleod, told the story of his friend (Macleod 1994), detailing a troubled life that ended in suicide two months after he received the Pulitzer for the iconic image of the Sudanese child. The fourth member, Ken Oosterbroek, was killed in crossfire in a South African township near Johannesburg in the same year.

Hussein, Gaddafi and Bin Laden – death pictures that created controversy

The death of one was a YouTube sensation, the final moments of another were considered 'not too graphic for television', while at the time of writing an American court was deciding if the public would see the photographic proof of the death of the third. Proof of the deaths of two of the world's last dictators, and of the world's most wanted man, would always be demanded by the public. Each case, in its own way, raised ethical issues for the media.

Saddam Hussein – grisly images on phone – who would do that?

The hanging of the Iraqi dictator, Saddam Hussein, took place before dawn on 30 December 2006 (Santora et al. 2006). Iraqi state television broadcast video of part of the execution, showing the former dictator being led to the gallows and ending after his head was placed in the hangman's noose (*Saddam Hussein executed* 2006). Newspapers showed restraint, publishing various stills of the execution, mainly head and shoulders shots with the noose in plain view. But it was an unauthorised dark, grainy mobile phone recording of the execution showing Hussein falling through the trap door of the gallows that created a sensation on YouTube. The video had been leaked soon after the execution but the mainstream media ignored it. US President George W Bush, who had ordered the troops into Iraq in 2003, was said to have been upset after seeing the video, likening it to how he had felt after seeing the photographs of Iraqi prisoner abuse by American military personnel at the notorious Abu Ghraib prison near Baghdad (*Officials: Bush upset by Hussein hanging video* 2007). Even today, when you google any variation of 'Hussein hanging', the citations are dominated by references to the YouTube video.

Muammar Gaddafi – witness to a bloody execution

Video and still photographs of the former Libyan leader, Muammar Gaddafi, wounded, bloodied and beaten, shortly before his death in October, 2011, were widely published.

As the media rushed to provide visual proof that the dictator was dead, critics complained about the publication of explicit pictures of his demise (*Muammar Gaddafi photos: did media go too far?* 2011). The BBC defended its decision to broadcast images of Gaddafi's final moments after it received hundreds of complaints (*BBC defends Gaddafi death images* 2011). The Head of the BBC's newsroom at the time, Mary Hockaday, said in a blog on the corporation's website that the images were an important part of the story:

> We thought very carefully about the use of pictures – which incidentally we used more sparingly than many other UK media – and I believe that overall they were editorially justified to convey the nature of yesterday's dramatic and gruesome events. We do not use such pictures lightly. There were sequences we did not show because we considered them too graphic.
>
> (Quoted in *BBC defends Gaddafi death images* 2011)

Coverage in the British tabloids was graphic, one showing a half-naked Gaddafi lying in a makeshift morgue and caked in dried blood, while others carried earlier photos of the wounded and distressed dictator being carried on top of a rebel car. The *Sun*'s front page carried a large picture of a battered Gaddafi under the headline 'That's for Lockerbie. And for Yvonne Fletcher. And IRA Semtex victims', highlighting some of the tragic events Gaddafi had been accused of having been associated with (Halliday 2011). American newspapers were apparently more restrained, with only seven of more than 400 surveyed using large images of Gaddafi's corpse on their front pages, while many international papers published photos of his body (Moos 2011c). The Poynter Institute's Al Tompkins said editors could be justified in using gruesome photos if they raised or supported critical questions of public interest – for example the issue of how Gaddafi died (*Muammar Gaddafi photos: did media go too far?* 2011). The British broadcast regulator, Ofcom, apparently agreed, announcing that it would not investigate complaints about the coverage (Halliday 2011). It ruled that the coverage was 'not too graphic to broadcast', despite nearly 500 complaints about the BBC coverage and more than 100 complaints about coverage on commercial TV news services seen in Britain.

Osama bin Laden – death comes by chopper

There have been calls for the release of photos of Osama bin Laden's body since he was killed in a raid by US special operations forces on his compound in Abbottabad, Pakistan, in May, 2011. President Obama announced at the time that gruesome images of the slain al-Qaida leader would not be released because it was feared that they would incite violence and lead to a national security risk. The President told a TV interviewer: 'That's not who we are. We don't trot out this stuff as trophies' (quoted in *Fearing incitement of violence Obama vetoes pix release* 2011). US officials had been debating whether to publish the pictures to counter conspiracy theories that the architect of the 9/11 attacks on America, and other atrocities, did not die in the raid. Photos purporting to be of the slain terrorist leader are available on the Internet. At the time of writing (August 2013), the Supreme Court in Washington was considering whether photos of bin Laden's body should be released (Kravets 2013). Judicial Watch, a conservative legal group, argued that the Freedom of Information Act required the government to release the pictures or they should explain why the release of specific images would damage national security (Levs and Cratty 2013). They asserted that the Central Intelligence Agency (CIA) had failed to demonstrate how images of the terrorist leader – specifically those of him cleaned and ready for burial – would harm national security or reveal classified intelligence strategies (Schoenberg 2013). A lower court judge had sided with the government and dismissed Judicial Watch's lawsuit in April, 2012 (Schoenberg 2013). The court was told there were 52 images of bin Laden taken just after his death and when his body was aboard the USS *Carl Vinson* prior to burial at sea (Levs and Cratty 2013). In late May 2013, the court ruled that the government did not need to release the photos (Ingram 2013).

Why have we detailed various aspects of the deaths of these three? Because it raises again the ongoing ethical dilemma of when to use shocking images. If the American court had released the photos, ask yourself, if you were a newspaper editor would you publish them? Which ones? Would you be prepared to publish a photo of the man who was the western world's 'most wanted' for more than a decade with a bullet hole in his head (assuming the court had gone so far as to release those photos)? What about a photo of the former terrorist leader ready for burial? Someone may well have to make those decisions in the future. As one commentator said about the images: 'Just to use the images because you can is not a good enough answer' (quoted in *Muammar Gaddafi photos: did media go too far?* 2011).

The ethics – and legal implications – of using images from social media

It is now accepted that social media – particularly Twitter and Facebook – beat mainstream media with the news on a daily basis. In fact, the raid that resulted in the death of Osama bin Laden was first mentioned on Twitter (*Bin Laden raid was revealed on Twitter* 2011). Authorities in Australia are now regularly using social media to alert the public to the latest emergency and social media was used extensively during the 2011 floods in Brisbane and the 2012/13 bushfires in several Australian states. One of the best-remembered Twitter scoops was the first picture of the US Airways flight that crash-landed into the Hudson River, New York, in 2009 (Deards 2009). It is the speed with which so-called micro-bloggers can upload pictures to their sites that has captured the attention of the mass media. As we have commented in various contexts in other chapters, social media has transformed the way mainstream media cover breaking stories, forcing them to develop policies to cover a range of associated issues.

In this context, social media is giving journalists quicker access to pictures from the scene of news events than their traditional means. When a helicopter crashed in central London in mid-January, 2013, killing two people, Twitter again beat traditional media to the story with brief eyewitness accounts, pictures and video. Radio stations were quoting from Twitter feeds, but by the afternoon the *London Evening Standard* had covered their front page with a photo from Twitter capturing the blazing scene and the convoy of emergency service vehicles heading for the scene (*Helicopter horror crash* 2013). While it is understandable that newspapers would use such material – the Tweeter most times is on the spot long before the paper's staff photographers – it raises the issue of copyright. *The Daily Mail*, *The Sun*, *The Guardian*, the *Evening Standard*, Sky News, the Press Association and Caters News agencies all used Twitter pictures of the fatal helicopter crash (O'Carroll 2013). Under the law, the photographer owns the copyright to their pictures, even ones uploaded to Twitter. An *Evening Standard* pictorial executive told *The Guardian* that in the heat of the moment they could not find the man who took the photo,

Craig Jenner, but if he contacted them about payment, they would oblige (O'Carroll 2013). Is that enough? Put yourself in Craig's shoes – he shares his photo on Twitter only to see his efforts on the front page of a national newspaper. Literally the day before the accident, on the other side of the Atlantic, a judge in New York was deciding the legality of the situation, finding that two news organisations had improperly used images that a photo-journalist had posted on Twitter in what was one of the first cases of intellectual property involving social media (Smith, E. G. 2013).

Agence France-Presse and *The Washington Post* were found to have infringed the copyright of photographer Daniel Morel in using pictures of the aftermath of the Haiti earthquake in 2010. The case was important because it was believed to be the first that addressed the issue of how images that users make available to the public through social media can be used by third parties for commercial purposes (Smith, E. G. 2013). AFP had argued that once the pictures had appeared on Twitter they were freely available, a position rejected by the judge (Smith, E. G. 2013). While lawyers can debate the specifics of the arguments, we're more concerned with the ethical aspects of the issue. For instance, is it ethical to download for publication someone's photo off Facebook? Former students often tell the authors that the first thing they do once they learn the identity of someone suddenly in the news is to check if they have a Facebook page and what they can establish about the person from that. The issue arose in late 2007, when an Australian soldier was killed by a roadside bomb in Afghanistan (*Soldier David Pearce killed after just 15 months in army* 2007). At the time of his death, the Department of Defence issued a statement saying that the family had requested their privacy be respected and noted that they would not be conducting any media interviews (quoted in *Filleting Facebook* 2007). Newspapers and broadcast news services found photos of the dead soldier (and his family) on Facebook and downloaded them for publication. The *Sydney Morning Herald* titled the story 'Snapshot of a soldier, a fisherman, a dad' above a photo of the soldier and his family captioned 'Online family album ... a photo downloaded from Facebook shows Trooper David Pearce with his wife and girls' (Collins, S-J. 2007). Another paper referred to Trooper Pearce and his wife as being prolific users of Facebook and another headlined their story 'Facebook's story of loving husband, father'. Legal issues aside, there's the issue of privacy. Was the media respecting the privacy of the grieving family when they downloaded pictures from their Facebook pages? As *Media Watch* asked at the time: does privacy also mean not having your online photographs raided for the front pages? (*Filleting Facebook* 2007). The Madeleine Pulver extortion attempt in 2011 (see chapter 7) saw the issue raised again when media outlets used photos of her and her father taken from social media sites (Christensen 2011). The Australian broadcast regulator, ACMA, addressed the issue in late 2011 in relation to a Seven network news report in Perth which contained photographs of a woman and her family sourced from a Facebook tribute page (*ACMA considers privacy of material sourced from Facebook* 2011). They found that because of the open nature of the tribute page, the TV station had not breached privacy provisions (*ACMA considers privacy of material sourced from Facebook* 2011). Earlier that year ACMA had released a major research report on the public's expectations of media content (*Digital Australians – Expectations about media content in a converging media environment* 2011).

Among the research findings relevant to this discussion were that many of the Australians interviewed considered that online content (like Twitter, Facebook and You-Tube material) published by mainstream broadcasters represented the ultimate loss of control of that material, and they were aware that 'once content was posted online very little control existed over what happened to it' (p. 65). Another ACMA research report released a few months earlier found that most of those surveyed felt it was 'very intrusive' to broadcast personal material from online social media sites where access had been restricted to online friends (*Australians views on privacy in broadcast news and current affairs* 2011, p. 7). Just over three-quarters (76%) of media users believed it was 'very intrusive' on a person's privacy. So the Australian public has strong views on the media lifting material for publication from social media sites, regardless of the legal position.

Facebook is problematic for journalists because it is becoming harder and harder to claim that what is on the social networking site is 'public'. Variable privacy settings allow users to restrict access to the material posted to their Facebook timeline and, in an ethico-legal sense, surely this implies a level of restriction and privacy? Journalists who bypass a user's privacy settings to access what they regard as newsworthy material are at least on ethically-suspect ground. Very likely they are also breaching copyright law by using images without the permission of the person who took them.

Distorting the image – that's what editors do, right?

Anyone with a computer program like Photoshop knows how easy it is to manipulate images. Microsoft's Publisher allows users to 'add' to images, like digitally placing the photographer into a composite family photo for the annual, Christmas happy snap. The latest smartphones also allow photo manipulation. But that's all harmless fun, a far cry from 'enhancing' a picture for mainstream media publication that introduces distortion or blatant fabrication like the previously-mentioned 'photoshopping'of images by the North Korean and Iranian government publicity machines.

Even before the technology improvements of recent decades, 'wire photos' as they were called – pictures sent to newspapers using telegraphy from overseas, or interstate, of news events – often had to be 'enhanced' by office artists so the detail in the picture could be seen. It was common practice to remove any potentially-offensive material, like graphic images of bodies at crash scenes. Physical manipulation of images has been around a long time. Australia's cricket legend, the late Sir Donald Bradman, talking to Ray Martin on the Nine Network two decades ago (*87 not out* 1996), said a photo of him walking with King George during one of his tours of England had been 'doctored' to omit others, who, like him, were walking with the King. 'The Don' drew criticism for 'insulting' the King by walking alongside him with his hands in his pockets and, as they say in royal circles 'he was not amused' (*87 not out* 1996). The *Gold Coast Bulletin*'s coverage of Prime Minister Howard's announcement in 2003 that he would 'bat on' past his 64th birthday in the nation's top job was a very obvious case of photographic manipulation. Under a banner headline 'Colossus of Canberra' on page 1, the paper depicted the Prime Minister, a self-confessed cricket tragic, in national one-day cricket gear, astride Parliament House with bat over his shoulder, having (it would appear) hit the ball either for a boundary or six. The sub-head on the front page said: 'John Howard 7 years, 2 months ... Not Out, No declaration in sight'. The paper reported that the Prime Minister had gone walking in an Australian cricket team tracksuit before his dramatic announcement (*Colossus of Canberra* 2003). This can be defended as a 'bit of fun' and a clever representation of the essence of the story, given the Prime Minister's love of the 'gentlemen's game' (*Colossus of Canberra* 2003). The *Bulletin* example might seem harmless, but what about more serious issues of digital manipulation, for example inserting people into a photograph to make a more interesting or emotive news photograph?

War throws up many ethical dilemmas, as you will have seen in chapter 6, but we've saved this one for this chapter because it has to do with photo manipulation. *Los Angeles Times* photographer, Brian Walski, while covering the 2003 war in Iraq, was fired for deliberately altering an image to enhance its impact. The *Times* unknowingly published the photo of a British soldier near Basra directing Iraqi civilians (one a male clutching a young child) to take cover. After the photo was published on 31 March 2003, it was noticed that several of the civilians in the background appear twice (Gordon et al. 2011, p. 239). Walski admitted he used his computer to combine elements of two photos to provide a more newsworthy image. Other members of the Tribune group, of which the *Times* was a part, had access to the photo via the company's internal distribution service (Irby 2011). Both the *Hartford Courant* and the *Times* used the photo prominently on page one. Walski, by telephone from southern Iraq, admitted that he had combined elements of two photographs, taken moments apart, to 'improve' the photo. On Tuesday, April 1, the *Los Angeles Times* posted an editor's note on its web site notifying readers of the breach of its photographic ethics policy, the investigation, and the subsequent sacking of the photographer. All three photos, the two originals and the altered composite, were published by both papers the following day (Irby 2011). The three photos, and the editor's note, can be seen at www.sree.net/teaching/lateditors.html (Gordon et al. 2011).

Martin Bryant – 'wild in the eyes'

On the afternoon of Sunday, April 28, 1996, a man in his late twenties opened fire in a crowded café in south-east Tasmania. By the end of the day, 35 people were dead, dozens more wounded. That day at the site of the historic Port Arthur penal colony, a quiet and 'strange' local, Martin Bryant, became Australia's most deadly mass killer. He was taken into custody after an all-night siege at a farmhouse near the site of the colonial ruins (*The Suspected Killer – Young, Rich And Wild* 1996). Bryant had set fire to the house in which he was holed up, randomly firing at the surrounding police. In the days following the atrocity, there was a media-initiated debate over Bryant's 'state of mind'. Bryant quickly became the 'world's worst killer' and he would hold that dubious distinction until Norwegian, right-wing extremist, Anders Behring Breivik, killed 77 people and wounded 242 in 2011 (Townsend 2012). It wasn't until two days after his shooting spree, that the first picture of Martin Bryant was splashed across front pages around Australia and the world. Tasmania's director of public prosecutions, Damien Bugg, threatened legal action against media organisations for publishing the photograph identifying Bryant, accusing them of prejudicing his trial (Conroy and Ryle 1996). In the context of this discussion, there was one photograph that stood out. *The Australian* 'enhanced' the image of Bryant to emphasise the whiteness of his eyes. This had the effect of giving him an eerie, 'spaced out', 'mad' look that fitted a favoured media image of the killer. *The Australian* quickly apologised (on its front page) for the photograph which it admitted had been 'processed in such a way as to distort the appearance of Bryant's eyes' (quoted in Conroy and Ryle 1996). It was suggested at the time that the first photographs were taken from Bryant's house by journalists, while their police guard was distracted.

With advances in digital technology available to the media today, there is virtually no limit to what can be done to an image – often with the best of intentions. But when you add something to an image that wasn't there originally, you cross the ethical line between recording history for posterity, and fabricating it. Several photo-journalists working in the Middle East have been sacked or exposed for faking images, including by making a bombing raid seem worse than it was by adding extra smoke to the image and also to make individual soldiers seem more heroic by cutting two or more images together (Hirst and Patching 2007).

The death of the Blade Runner's girlfriend and a tasteless front page photo

On Valentine's Day, 2013 world news was dominated by the tragic story of the shooting death of model Reeve Steenkamp, the girlfriend of South African sporting superstar, Oscar Pistorius. Early reports suggested Pistorius, Paralympic gold medal-winner and the first double amputee to compete in an Olympics, at the London Games, and known worldwide as the 'Blade Runner', shot the cover-girl and aspiring reality TV star, mistaking her for an intruder. It had all the ingredients of a major story destined for front pages the world over – the international sporting icon, the girlfriend named twice in men's magazine *FHM*'s '100 Sexiest Women in the World' and the traditionally romantic day on which the tragic death occurred (Voorhees 2013). Pistorius was charged with murder and given bail, and, at the time of writing, his trial was many months away. Here we're interested in the coverage given the story on that first day by the world's media – and in particular one front page, the cover of Rupert Murdoch's top-selling British tabloid, *The Sun*.

While the page one headlines were pure tabloid and tasteless enough (3 *shots. Screams. Silence. 3 more shots. Blade Runner Pistorius 'murders lover'* 2013), it was the photo that accompanied the coverage that caused widespread uproar. It was an almost full-page, provocative shot of Steenkamp in a bikini appearing to be unzipping her top. The reaction on Twitter was swift, with comments like 'disgusting' and 'despicable'. One suggested it 'glorified domestic violence', and another asked whether it was 'the most inappropriate picture ever of a murder victim?' (Mirkinson 2013). *Guardian* columnist, Suzanne Moore, tweeted that the front page coverage represented 'lechery over a corpse' (cited in Greenslade 2013). Former United Kingdom deputy Prime Minister under Tony Blair, John Prescott, tweeted to Rupert Murdoch that the coverage represented 'a new low' for the paper (*Prescott hits at Sun's 'titillating' Reeva Steenkamp cover* 2013). Prescott claimed that *The Sun* had paid £35,000 for the picture. Other tabloids showed photographs of the model in revealing clothing, usually lingerie shots, but none chose to put the images on the front page, next to news of her death (Dunt 2013).

One media commentator under a headline that read in part 'when the profit motive turns ugly', likened *The Sun*'s coverage to 'retailing domestic violence as popular entertainment' and 'turning a horrific tragedy into a money-spinning sensation' (Bryant 2013). Journalist and media law consultant David Banks (2013) suggested the widespread comments on Twitter highlighted 'the difficulty of enforcing rights to a fair trial in the age of social media'. He said readers need their newspapers to provide background and context to a story, 'which they will go looking for on the web if they cannot find it in print'. 'We had verdict, mitigation and aggravating circumstances all wrapped up in a morning on Twitter' (Banks 2013).

The Sun front page raises several issues canvassed in this text – primarily, though, the tasteless approach to reporting the news by the 'tabloid' media, and in that group we include commercial television's daily current affairs programmes. The pursuit of sales and ratings often leads to bad decisions. Sometimes you are just left shaking your head and asking: 'What were they thinking?' Whoever decided to put a near full-page, bikini shot of a shooting victim on the front page alongside a very graphic description of her murder needs to put themselves in the shoes of those who admired or loved both Steenkamp and Pistorius and ask themselves how they would react to that front page? It's probably not contempt of court – it was published outside South Africa and they don't have trial by jury, judges decide the fate of an accused. Certainly some of the Twitter comments could be libellous, depending on the outcome of the trial, and if the offending Tweeters can be traced (Banks 2013).

Case Study 1: *The Independent on Sunday* defends using pictures of dead Syrian children

The Independent on Sunday was one of three British papers that published graphic pictures of Syrian children killed in the Houla region in late May, 2012. The paper's editor, John Mullin, told *The Guardian* he felt he had a responsibility to use the harrowing image (which appeared to show the badly beaten bodies of at least nine children laid side by side) despite Press Complaints Commission (PCC) guidance on their potential intrusion into grief and shock (Halliday 2012a). The PCC received one complaint – about similar pictures published by the *Mail on Sunday*. *The Independent on Sunday* printed the picture on page three, rather than page one, they said, to avoid distressing children. The page one pointer read in part: 'More than 90 people were massacred in Houla late on Friday, 32 of them children under the age of 10. Many had their throats cut. To convey the full horror, we publish a shocking image of the defenceless victims on page three' (cited in Halliday 2012a). Mullin told *The Guardian* he saw the pictures as a 'game changer' and he thought it would pressure the United Nations to intervene in the Syrian conflict. He added: 'They (the pictures) were of such awful proportion that they spoke not just 1,000 words, but 2,000 words, 10,000 words and I wanted to use them immediately' (quoted in Halliday 2012a).

He said that the whole point of publishing the pictures was that they were a challenge to the international community. *The Independent on Sunday* editor, Mullin, said he wanted them also to be a challenge to his readers (Halliday 2012a). He conceded that some readers might think the paper guilty of bad taste, but rarely, 'we need to be shocked' (quoted in *Newspaper Review: Syrian children massacre image shown* 2012) The *Mail on Sunday* said they published the photo to 'illustrate the depth of revulsion that may lead to UN intervention' (*Newspaper Review: Syrian children massacre image shown* 2012).

Questions for discussion:

1. You are the editor of a major newspaper, and pictures of a graphic nature come into its possession. What do you need to consider before publishing them?

2. Does the MEAA Code of Ethics offer any help? Compare it with the Press Complaints Commission's Code at http://www.pcc.org.uk/cop/practice.html.
3. Where do you draw the line with distressing images?
4. Do you accept the editor's reasoning that the UN needed to be shocked into action?
5. Or are you a bit cynical and think the front page pointer is a sales pitch – 'buy the paper and be shocked'?
6. Shocking coverage is sometimes labelled as 'grief porn'. Could publication of these photos be seen as an example of that?

Case Study 2: Would Diana have got along with Kate, and do we care?

We discussed 'royal privacy' at length in the previous chapter, but now we're looking at a particular case where an image of Diana was aged and manipulated to make it appear she was walking and talking with her daughter-in-law. It was the cover story for a July, 2011 edition of *Newsweek*, titled 'Diana at 50: If She Were Here Now'. Some of the content is available at the magazine's online site, thedailybeast.com (Brown 2011). Most of it was the opinions of Tina Brown, the editor-in-chief of the magazine, and author of *The Diana Chronicles* (Brown 2007). Released four months before the tenth anniversary of the Princess's death, her book was headlined in one review as 'The most savage attack on Diana EVER' (their capitals) (Churcher 2007). While her book raised some eyebrows, so did her *Newsweek* article, featuring the 'digitally-aged' photo of Diana on the cover. The *Newsweek* cover story speculated, among other things, that by age 50 Diana would have had 'strategic botox shots' to her chin, been married twice more, while 'retaining a weakness for men in uniform, and a yen for dashing Muslim men', be living mostly in New York, and would have 'enjoyed some elegant schadenfreude' over the *News of the World* scandal (Brown 2011). In keeping with the dominance of social media by that time, Brown's 'think piece' suggested the Princess would have been a Facebook friend with her arch-nemesis in life, Camilla Parker-Bowles, and have 10 million Twitter followers (Oliver 2011). A mock Facebook page reproduced as part of the article showed Diana having 107,623 friends, including U2 singer Bono, Chelsea Clinton, David Beckham, J. K. Rowling and Rafael Nadal (Oliver 2011). There was another 'doctored' photo inside the magazine of the Princess holding an icon of the first decade of the twenty-first century, a smartphone. One online news site ran a poll asking readers whether the story was 'kind of cool', 'a bit much', or whether they were 'unsure' (Moss 2011). When one of the authors checked the figures (in early 2013), more than half of the respondents (53 per cent) thought it was 'a bit much', about a third (30 per cent) thought it was 'kind of cool' and the rest – nearly 16 per cent – weren't sure what they thought (Moss 2011).

A gossip website asked another question (*'Princess Diana' Walking with Kate on Newsweek Cover – Cool or Creepy?* 2011).

Questions for discussion:

1. Gossip Cop said they'd rather look at pictures of William and Kate 'happily living in the actual present' than digitally introduce Diana to 2011. What do you think?
2. Given the author's track record (her book on Diana), she was always going to have a few digs at the Princess, wasn't she? Is that fair?
3. Look up the *Huffington Post* article (Moss 2011) and vote – that's the only way you see the latest figures. Are you in the majority or the minority?
4. Explain why you voted the way you did – i.e. do you approve of the general thrust of the *Newsweek* article or not?
5. It is relatively harmless speculation or 'over the top'?
6. No one really thought the photo wasn't 'doctored' did they? Does it really matter?
7. Can you think of other examples of such photo manipulation that you consider might have gone too far?

12 Social media: the game-changer

M'lud condemns 'trial by Twitter'

We mentioned the 'witches of Facebook' phenomenon in a previous chapter – the propensity for online crowds to turn into a lynch-mob at the click of a mouse – and it is likely that there will be more vigilante-style calls for online 'justice' as more and more of us embrace social media. Social media also raises a number of ethical issues for journalists and editors. In December, 2012, Lord Leveson, whose inquiry into the British print media in the wake of *The News of the World* scandal was the catalyst for change, visited Australia shortly after his report was released. At a $950-per-head symposium on privacy in Sydney, the retired British judge highlighted the dangers to individuals' privacy from what he called 'trial by Twitter': an unending punishment, with no prospect of rehabilitation, forever notorious on Google (Jackson, S. 2012). He said the resulting harm was 'both permanent and disproportionate':

> It takes but a minute to record someone doing something in a public place and to upload it to the Internet. Once on the Internet the episode, the behaviour, is there for the world to see and is there permanently at the click of a mouse.
>
> (Leveson 2012)

Lord Leveson was not the first to draw attention to the dangers of social media – the communication revolution of the first decade of the twenty-first century. While millions use Facebook and Twitter on a daily basis to keep in touch with friends, relatives and contacts, authorities are grappling with the 'down side' of the phenomenon, like how to handle cyber-bullying among children and the 'hate mail' some celebrities and other newsmakers attract from time to time. And how to prevent social media from jeopardising an accused's right to a fair trial. Cases from around the world highlight problems and ethical dilemmas that come up when grieving social media friends, or legally-ignorant vigilante groups, interfere with legal processes. This is a clear ethico-legal paradox of the digital age. Then there's the sad stories – like the twins who found out that their younger brother had died in a car crash when they opened their Facebook page on their 20th birthday expecting to read well-wishes from friends (Cuneo 2012). It becomes an even more tangled web of ethical contradictions when social media collides with the 24-hour, continuously-present, news cycle.

While, initially, social media may have been scoffed at by journalists, it is now an essential tool of the trade – one of many used by reporters for news-gathering and connecting with an audience. Social media offers mainstream journalists new ways to gather information and for their employers to expand the reach of their content

(Hermida et al. 2012). They are best considered as part – and only a part – of a reporter's toolkit, along with the long-standing methods of gathering news. Social media present their own ethical challenges; many of them occur because legal codes and our ethical frameworks have not kept up with the speed of the digital revolution (Hirst 2011).

The techno-legal and techno-ethical time-gap

While many of the ethical issues for journalists raised by social media have already been canvassed in the earlier chapters, there are a number of other issues associated with social media that reporters need to keep in the back of their minds. Many of these are to do with the time lag between the arrival of new applications and the setting up of appropriate regulatory and self-regulatory apparatus. It has long been the case that anyone with a computer could publish their thoughts in blogs, on Facebook and through Twitter – and many do, including co-author Martin (@ethicalmartini) – for the rest of the world to read. But the advent and explosion of social media has been a 'game-changer' for mainstream media. We have made the point before that anyone with a smartphone is now a reporter, if only to their Facebook 'friends', but sometimes their efforts receive much wider exposure. It is widely accepted that Twitter users regularly beat traditional media in being first with the news, especially with pictures of accidents or other emergency stories. We highlighted some of those instances in earlier chapters – like the first photo of the 'miracle on the Hudson River' plane crash in 2009, and the mainstream media using Twitter photos of the fatal helicopter crash in central London four years later. Presidents, Prime Ministers and celebrities use Twitter from time to time – some more often than others – to share their thoughts and opinions on anything and everything. Pope Francis has eight or more Twitter accounts in various languages and within days of being elected had millions of faithful followers. Hundreds of journalists now tweet on a daily basis alerting their followers to the latest news flash or to material coming up in an attempt to draw an audience to their writing or broadcasting. Political journalists, as well as tweeting their opinions and providing the latest political headlines, will probably follow hundreds of other political tweeters – local representatives, national leaders, political advisers and lobbyists – and, of course, watch what their colleagues are saying on their Twitter feeds. Journalists on other reporting rounds will follow those appropriate to their area of interest. For the general reporter they will be many and varied. The authors follow a number of their favourite journalists, media academics and media executives. The ABC's Managing Director, Mark Scott, is a prolific tweeter, highlighting upcoming ABC programmes, sharing information about developments in the mass media generally, about various on-air personalities and alerting his followers to the latest news – and directing them to the appropriate ABC outlet for more. Rupert Murdoch is a regular, too, but his tweets are often, but not exclusively, about American, British or Australian politics, rather than media-related topics or the latest news. He did, however, take to Twitter early in 2013 to alert his followers that Chinese hackers were targeting his American media outlets (*News again targeted by Chinese hackers: Murdoch* 2013). That relatively brief story was an example of what some see as an emerging trend in reporting in recent times – journalists trawling tweets for a 140-character comment around which to build a story. One comment from a newsmaker, a few paragraphs of background, and there's an update for the 24/7 news cycle. The needs of a busy and skeleton-staffed newsroom intersect with the new high-speed circulation of information, inaccurate or inappropriate social media comments, to produce a sometimes confusing picture. Hoaxing, deception and baiting of 'marks', or opponents, is much easier on social media. For many reasons, journalists need to be careful. In some instances legal protections for journalists are dated and more suited to an analogue environment; privacy is being redefined and new ethico-legal fault lines are emerging. The law is playing catch-up in many different national, regional and global forums – on copyright and copy theft; over patents on Apps for download and storage devices. At the same time people are finding ways around some restrictions by off-shoring or using encryptions tools like Tor or Bitcoin. The updating of laws and reg-ulations governing journalism in the digital age recommended in both the Leveson and Finkelstein inquiries came as a direct government response to the techno-legal time-gap. What made the editors and proprietors of news media in both the UK and Australia baulk at the changes was, in part, driven by their opposition to more State sanctioning of the news media and a desire to exploit the legal and commercial opportunities offered in the digital and networked global media economy (Hirst 2011).

A 'deepening penetration of digital and social media' in newsgathering

> Print journalists in particular no longer have the luxury of putting off until deadline what can be published immediately.
>
> (Clayfield 2012)

The desire to be first with news online – even by a few seconds – has created an unhealthy taste for speed among news organizations, leaving us with 'no time to think' (Rosenberg and Feldman 2008). So, too, has competition between reporters and tradi-tional outlets to have the biggest social media following. News has always been com-petitive; social media increases reach, but also risk. A key risk is that in the rush to be first, truth becomes the casualty (Hermida 2012). A 2012 global survey into how news was being sourced found a 'deepening penetration of digital and social media into all areas of newsgathering and reporting' (*The influence game: How news is sourced and managed today* 2012, p. 2). The survey found that providing there was a pre-existing relationship with the source, or the source was recognised by the journalist as trust-worthy, social media were 'a key element of the journalistic arsenal'. Globally, more than half (54 per cent) of respondents used social media like Twitter and Facebook and 44 per cent used blogs by people they already knew, to source angles for new stories. More than 600 journalists in 16 countries took part, mainly from Europe and North America, including New Zealand, but not Australia. It seems gone are the days when you have to actually talk to a potential news source to quote them in a story. Hopefully, reporters still see face-to-face interviews as the best way of gathering newsworthy information. Another trend is emailing potential news sources with a list of questions and writing a story from their replies. It is common practice in magazines, notably sports magazines with their long lead times, where the results are often published as 'Question and Answer' (Q & A) pieces. There's an argument for emailing questions to someone who is not easily contactable by phone, Skype or in person, but the building of a story by mainstream media journalists around one or two Twitter comments seems like lazy journalism to us. Journalists who use the practice would probably argue that it is the 'pressure to produce' that leads to such reporting short cuts.

In many newsrooms nowadays, staffs are so small, and productivity expectations so high, that journalists avoid face-to-face interviews because of the time they take. At the same time, social media has had an impact on journalism (Stassen 2010). Experiments in 'crowd-sourcing' stories, a 'real time' reliance on social media uploads and creating social media as a legitimate space for all kinds of 'journalism' are to be applauded and encouraged. There is a role for citizen journalism and news-like content from a variety of sources. We support the citizen journalists, bloggers and tweeters who provided invaluable information to western media during the Arab Spring, and who continue to provide news about conflicts like the tragedy in Syria. We see the public benefits of crowd sourcing social media to provide journalists with otherwise unavailable information, as well as alerts from the emergency services in times like the 2011 Queensland floods or the 2013 Tasmanian bushfires and any number of other major news events. However, it is rare that one 140-character comment alone could a story make, even if it is a tweet from 'the Boss'. As will be shown later in the chapter, information from social media which cannot be verified, but is published anyway on a fast-moving story, has led to some bad decisions by journalists in recent times.

Mainstream media v. social media

> ... a campaigning journalist who publishes via a website. He campaigns against political sleaze and hypocrisy. He doesn't believe in impartiality nor pretend to it.
>
> (Staines 2004)

'Guido Fawkes' is the influential and unashamedly rightwing avatar created by English-Irish blogger, Paul Staines. Guido's self-penned bio declares he is a journalist with a political mission. Staines is a celebrity blogger with a brash and irreverent routine and he is now famous enough to regularly be used as a commentator on global news channels. In a decade 'Guido Fawkes' moved from being a lone character on the fringes of English political journalism to being a global brand. Staines' website has employed a news editor and a reporter since 2010 and there is plenty of advertising real estate on offer too. The success of Guido Fawkes is measured in awards received and the blog's reach within the UK political and media establishments. The added irony is that this once *enfant terrible* is now a Westminster insider. Staines has a colourful history and tells his story shamelessly on the 'about' page of his blog created in 2004 – very early in the development of blogging. He says the Guido Fawkes character was initially created purely to make mischief at the expense of politicians and for 'the author's own self-gratification'. Staines has had commercial success as a social media entrepreneur and without any journalism background says he is an investigative reporter who breaks news that the mainstream media then picks up. The Guido Fawkes story is an insight into the 'fifth estate', with its mix of professional stirrers, political junkies, zealots, ex-journos and independents, busybodies, serious amateurs, commentators, committed tweeters and casual uploaders. 'Guido Fawkes' is just one example of amateur and alternative journalism that produces a range of user-generated news-like content (Atton and Hamilton 2008; Hirst 2011). The question is: Does this new field of amateur and alternative journalism compete with or complement the mainstream news media? There is certainly friction and tension between the two and this also spills over into the ethical influence each might have over the other. This is the digital expression of fundamental dialectical pressures. Social media and journalism exist in mutual constitution. It is a *pas de deux* of embrace and contradiction pushing the boundaries of news ethics in interesting directions.

Guido Fawkes is one of many independent brands that have flourished within the blogosphere and on the fringes of political journalism. In the United States there are dozens; most famously *Politico* and *Slate*. Others have become successful and then made business deals with old media. In 2010, an unlikely alliance developed between *Newsweek* magazine and Internet start-up aggregator The *Daily Beast*. The following year, Ariana Huffington's eponymous *Huffington Post* did a deal with the giant AOL group (*AOL agrees to acquire the Huffington Post* 2011). In Australia, political blogging is not so lucrative and online-only news start-ups are rare. The *Global Mail*, backed by a philanthropist's $5 million has survived for over two years without advertising; *The Guardian* launched an Australian edition in 2013 and several smaller independents make small amounts from their online commentary work.

The Australian blogger 'Grog's Gamut' was able to parlay a moment of notoriety into a new career. Greg Jericho was a public servant in Canberra and Grog's Gamut was a sharp take on politics and political personalities. In September, 2010, *The Australian*'s James Massola (2010) identified Jericho as Grog's Gamut and suggested he might be breaching public service guidelines for what the paper described as 'pro-Labor' views and attacks on opposition figures. But what really got up the noses of the Canberra press pack was an attack on their coverage of the 2010 federal election campaign:

> In the post that made Mr Jericho a public figure he wrote news editors should 'bring home your journalists following Tony Abbott and Julia Gillard, because they are not doing anything of any worth except having a round-the-country twitter and booze tour'.
>
> (Massola 2010)

Greg Jericho is now well known and publishes widely. Grog's Gamut is still an active blog and Greg's commitment to tweeting tennis matches is legendary. In his 2012 book, *The rise of the fifth estate*, Jericho describes the Internet and social media as a 'cyclone ... spinning control away from the ... forces of the establishment'. He clearly sees it as a dialectical challenge in which one side seeks to 'manage and formalise' the blogosphere and the other seeks to extend the freedom of the network beyond the control of 'the centre'. Jericho argues that from 2007 – the birth year of Twitter – bloggers and social media commentators began 'breaking down the gate-kept world' of politics. But the key is that it only happens 'in a fluid and messy way' (Jericho 2012). Each side was feeling its way in 2007. Today there are still grey areas, but the processes of capital consolidation, impending tighter regulations and the small income streams generally available to freelance bloggers are clear indicators of the current political economy in the digital mediasphere. With these clashing economic, social and cultural forces in play there are bound to be ethical and philosophical issues, including about age-old concepts like freedom of speech, or freedom of the press.

Aside from the ethical dilemmas associated with the social media already discussed, there are several other issues for mainstream media and individual journalists raised by the all-pervasive nature of the Internet and social media. The first is the still-evolving relationship between mainstream media and the emerging 'fifth estate' – the bloggers and social media users.

In the wake of criticism of the Australian news media's poor initial coverage of Prime Minister Julia Gillard's anti-sexism speech in late 2012, pioneering Australian political blogger, Tim Dunlop, contended that members of the public were no longer passive observers in the news process. Writing under the emotive heading 'The gatekeepers of news have lost their keys', he suggested that the public were 'no longer dependent on the mainstream media to interpret and explain important events' (Dunlop 2012). He said audiences were no longer prepared to accept the media's interpretation of events:

> In a world where we can watch things unfold in real time and then chat about them among ourselves, we simply don't need journalists to explain and analyse them for us.
>
> (Dunlop 2012)

It was the issue taken up to the ABC's Jonathan Green a few months later in response to the ongoing debate on how mainstream media could find relevance in the digital era. He said that the debate was beside the point:

> The big change to the flow of information in the past decade has been to liberate it from journalistic mediation. Blogs, social media … all of that: we now have a conversation that exists in parallel to the mainstream media and in many instances dwarfs it in the seriousness of its intent.
>
> (Green, J. 2013)

'Fightin' words' for some in the mainstream media. All over the world, daily newspapers consider themselves to be the real newsmakers and opinion leaders. Newspapers continue to set much of the daily news agenda, often followed by radio and television. There is competition for attention across all platforms and social media is no exception. The main game is still the political economy dynamic of monetising the clickstream (Hirst 2011). Despite enormous growth in social media and mobile usage worldwide over the last decade, it is still only a relatively small number of people who are heavily involved in watching what's happening around the world, blogging about it or joining Facebook and Twitter conversations. There is a correlation between affluence and access. Not all members of the broad global public are that 'switched on' to the possibilities of the digital world, or have the time needed to be that 'switched on'. They still rely on various mainstream media platforms for their daily dose of news and information. About a month before Dunlop's 'gatekeeper' piece appeared on the ABC's discussion site, *The Drum*, research was released showing just one per cent of Australians surveyed nominated Twitter as the social media or communications platform they used the most. Email topped the list with 37 per cent of respondents, followed by Facebook with 33 per cent. Blogs were down with Twitter on 1 per cent (Keane 2012d). Another survey, commissioned in the United Kingdom by the Reuters Institute for the Study of Journalism gave a stronger result for social media with more people there sharing news by email (33 per cent) than Twitter (23 per cent), but substantially more (55 per cent) sharing news on Facebook. Overall, though, only one in five respondents to the UK survey said they shared news stories every week by email or social media networks (Marshall, S. 2012). A 2013 survey by the Pew Research Center showed that Twitter was often not representative of public thinking. The year-long study, which looked at reaction on Twitter and compared it to the results of national polls in the United States, found that the Twitter conversation was at times more liberal, at other times more conservative, but it was tweeters' overall negativity that stood out (*Twitter Reaction to Events Often at Odds with Overall Public Opinion* 2013).

On April 15, 2013, America (and the rest of the world) was rocked by a terrorist attack that claimed three lives and left more than 100 injured, some seriously, after two bombs exploded near the end of the popular Boston marathon. In the context of the discussion in this chapter, many of the problems associated with social media would emerge in the immediate aftermath of the tragedy. It was the first major terrorist attack on American soil in the age of smartphones, Twitter and Facebook. But, as the *Los Angeles Times* reported, what could have been a watershed moment for social media 'soon spiralled out of control':

> Legions of Web sleuths cast suspicion on at least four innocent people, spread innumerable bad tips and heightened the sense of panic and paranoia.
>
> (Bensinger and Chang 2013)

Users of the popular news aggregator Reddit and other social media sites began to post their own images of potential suspects in the bombing. The man-hunt soon became an online witch-hunt. It was a matter of good fortune, rather than good police work, that no one was seriously injured or killed after being falsely identified as the bomber on social media. There was also an element of racism in the online wanted posters; most of the wrongly-identified 'suspects' were non-whites.

Tweet as I say, not as I do – media organisations' social media policies

In recent years, the major global news media organisations have devised policies for how their staff will interact with social media – how they will use material from the likes of YouTube, Facebook and Twitter and how they will interact with it – i.e. the rules for individual journalists wanting to blog or tweet. Before the end of the first decade of the twenty-first century, media executives seemed wary about allowing their journalists to engage with social media or to use material from blogs or social media, but they soon realised they needed policies to cover the use of such material for news-related purposes, and to protect their 'brand' from over-zealous staff tweeters. If you googled 'News Limited and social media policy', in early 2013 you were directed first to the policy of the Melbourne-based *Herald and Weekly Times* arm of the group (*Editorial Code of Conduct: Social Media Policy* 2011). Google 'Fairfax Media social media policy' and the first recommendation was to a News Limited site which contained a document appropriately headed 'Fairfax Media Group Social Media Policy' (2011). In line with other such policies, like those from the ABC (*Use of Social Media Policy* 2011) and the BBC (*Social Networking, Microblogs and other Third Party Websites: BBC Use* n.d.), the News Limited and Fairfax policies cover similar areas. They acknowledge that the use of social media plays an important role in the professional and personal lives of their staff, and while they are seen as efficient platforms for them to deliver content to audiences, they need policies governing their two-way use. They don't want staff to use social media in a way that would embarrass the employer, disclose any confidential information obtained while at work, break any law, or imply that the organisation approves of the personal views they express on social media sites. This is a common element in social media policies across the MSM. The *New York Times* was among the first to issue a policy and it is clearly aimed at protecting the brand of the newspaper than the rights of its journalists (Hirst 2011).

No matter how complex a news organisation's social media rules are, there will always be blind spots, loopholes and contradictions to be overcome in practice. The policies are constantly evolving, responding to the techno-legal time-gap. One key issue is the expression of 'personal' opinion on official accounts. A case exposed on the *Media*

Watch programme (Holmes 2013) highlighted how an Australian journalist got into trouble over a careless tweet. The confusion in this case, as pointed out by then *Media Watch* host Jonathan Holmes, is that the ABC's social media policy made no clear distinction between personal or corporate accounts. The dimensions of a possible breach of the ABC code are broad and ill-defined:

> Do not mix the professional and the personal in ways likely to bring the ABC into disrepute.
>
> (ABC Use of Media Policy)

The ABC told *Media Watch* that in its opinion even if the inappropriate comments had been made on a personal account, the fact of the tweeter's employment with the ABC could make it a breach of this policy. Holmes called this a clear case of 'individual censorship' by the broadcaster. It highlights the ethico-legal paradox very well too. When does an obligation to an employer override a right to freedom of expression? Can it ever? The *New York Times* seemed to think so when it codified its social media policy in 2009. The *NYT* was then encouraging reporters to lift information from Facebook because it could be considered public property, but not to be social media friends with politicians in case it was interpreted as support for their policies. The code also had clauses about bringing the *NYT* into disrepute through social media actions: 'do nothing that might cast doubt on your or *The Times*' political impartiality in reporting the news'. The justification for this, from the newspaper's point of view, was that: 'readers will inevitably associate anything you post on social media with *The Times*'. It seems this is a lesson the newspaper's reputation management gurus take to heart. Google the phrase 'New York Times Social Media Policy' and you might expect a link to the company's ethical guidelines or some similar corporate destination. Instead, the top item is a news story from 28 March 2013, headlined 'Police Dept. Sets Rules for Officers' Use of Social Media' (Goodman and Ruderman 2013). Serving police are 'warned' to clean their social media profiles. Apparently it was in response to the son of a fire chief posting a 'racially inflammatory' tweet. The *NYT* described the police action as defusing 'lurking social media landmines'.

It is actually worth quoting at length from the *Times*' article to make a simple point:

> The three-page order dated Monday details online behavior that could land officers in trouble, including posting photos of other officers, tagging them in photos or putting photos of themselves in uniform – except at police ceremonies – on any social media site.
>
> Members of the department are also "urged not to disclose or allude to their status" with it. Doing so could make that person ineligible for certain sensitive roles.
>
> Other regulations were more straightforward: Do not post images of crime scenes, witness statements or other nonpublic information gained through work as a police officer; do not engage with witnesses, victims or defense lawyers; do not "friend" or "follow" minors encountered on the job.
>
> (Goodman and Ruderman 2013)

If we remove references to uniforms, the prescribed behaviours are not that dissimilar to those which media employers are demanding of journalists. Like the ABC's policy, the police order also related to personal accounts. The second item prioritized by Google, from January 2013, has a headline defending an employee's right to freedom of expression on social media: 'Even if It Enrages Your Boss: Social Net Speech Is Protected'

(Greenhouse 2013). A US government agency, the National Labor Relations Board, ruled that the right to discuss working conditions and aspects of one's job on social media was worth defending. The Board chairman told the *NYT* that his organization was 'applying traditional rules to a new technology'. However, a newspaper employee was not so lucky. The NLRB found against him:

> The N.L.R.B. had far less sympathy for a police reporter at *The Arizona Daily Star*.
>
> Frustrated by a lack of news, the reporter posted several Twitter comments. One said, "What?!?!?! No overnight homicide. ... You're slacking, Tucson." Another began, "You stay homicidal, Tucson."
>
> The newspaper fired the reporter, and board officials found the dismissal legal, saying the posts were offensive, not concerted activity and not about working conditions.
>
> (Greenhouse 2013)

Like we said earlier, 'Be careful.' John C. Merrill might well be spinning with delight at such an elegant working example of the dialectic of journalism in action. The Labor Relations Board also said that it was 'merely adapting the provisions of the National Labor Relations Act, enacted in 1935, to the twenty-first century workplace'. Employers were not impressed. This is the most recent example of the ruling class arguing that freedom of expression is not required in the workplace. One bosses' representative told the *NYT* reporter that disgruntled staff were only 'venting', not engaged in union-related activity by discussing their workplace situation on Facebook (Greenhouse 2013). Hardly encouraging signs for the future.

One final example is necessary to really confirm the problems with attempting to write and police a workable social media policy. The third-ranked *New York Times* article in the Google search was headlined 'It's a Good Policy to Have Rules in Writing' (Gomes 2013). The author was a senior public relations operative in a large New York firm. The opening line expresses the contradictions of the techno-legal and techno-ethical time-gaps perfectly:

> Absolutely, employees should face consequences at work for what they say on social media – sometimes ... Business in the information age is, in large part, governed by Industrial Age rules intended to restrain J.D. Rockefeller, J.P. Morgan and so on – bit-and-byte realities wrestling with concrete and steel legacies.
>
> (Gomes 2013)

Confusion and contradiction in social media policies is not uncommon. It is still really 'early days' when it comes to fine-tuning them and there still has to be a big question mark over their real value. Common sense and good manners should certainly guide all social media conversations, but companies could be stepping over the line legally and ethically by trying to bind their employees' use of social media. There is no doubt that an organisation or individual has the right to control a social media account that appears under their name. Official accounts should also reflect the values of the corporation, like the *New York Times*, or public body like the ABC. Some guidelines and editorial direction are also important where several individuals might tweet on behalf of an organization. However, we do not think that organisations have a right to censor or edit personal opinions. Making rude comments about your boss on Facebook is not common sense because they are published and repeatable and therefore defamatory. It is much better just to tell your family and friends in a conversation. But, if you want to express an opinion under your own name on social media, your boss should not be able to stop you. Rules that prohibit employees from commenting on working conditions also undermine the right of workers to organise their union via social media.

Should reporters tweet breaking news first?

One of the early debates on the use of social media involved whether reporters should tweet breaking news before it could be published on their employers' various platforms. As we mentioned in the Preface, one British news-reader saw tweeting a major news story as leading 'the information thirsty to water' (Snow 2012). It's a marketing tool from Managing Director down. Senior and trusted staff have use of official accounts to promote their own reporting or other work – fronting a high profile current affairs programme, for example. Celebrity or noteworthy and respected media personalities have large social media followings. Barring the odd blunder, these figures can set the terms for public debate or pronounce on issues with some influence. They are effectively a new cadre of digital gatekeepers, across both mainstream and social media. Media companies are now competing by substituting the personalities of their stars for the credibility of their stories in social media marketing. Their interests and differences do not always coincide and credibility is still a live issue. Are we all now our own gate-keepers – with all the ethical baggage that implies – as the still hopeful believe? Former editor, Steve Buttry, argues that the fences have 'blown away' and an 'endless selection of blogs' renders the gatekeeper of old as redundant. Instead, he argues, on major stories like the unlawful killing of teenager Trayvon Martin, it was social media that brought a traditional 'justice' story to the fore. The MSM largely ignored it as just another black teen death. The old media had to play catch-up (Buttry 2012).

Lower down in the editorial food chain, the use the social media is more tightly regulated. The *Herald and Weekly Times* policy specifically addresses one aspect of that issue when it directs reporters wanting to disclose breaking news on social media to check with their editor 'if there is any doubt over whether the story is breaking widely or exclusive' (*Editorial Code of Conduct: Social Media Policy* 2011, p. 5), suggesting you might hold on to an exclusive, rather than alert the opposition. The American news agency, the Associated Press, changed its policy in mid-2012, to allow their reporters to tweet breaking news even if the news was not yet on their wire service, providing they had informed the news-desk of the information and provided them with the story (*Social Media Guidelines for AP Employees, July 2012* 2012). The change demonstrates how the policies of media organisations are constantly shifting in response to the impact of social media. Another version of their policy, released six months earlier, told staff: 'Don't break news on social networks that we haven't published in AP's news services' (*Social Media Guidelines for AP employees, January 2012* 2012). Similarly, BBC reporters were told in early 2012 not to break news stories on Twitter before they told their newsroom colleagues, to ensure the story was fed into the organisation's various news platforms without the delay of an update on Twitter (Plunkett 2012).

Be careful what you tweet, tell your Facebook 'friends' or blog about

The first of 20 'Tips for Tweeting Journos' circulated by Julie Posetti (2009), an Australian journalism academic and researcher into the journalist/Twitter relationship, reads: 'Think before you tweet – you can't delete an indiscreet tweet!' Technically, you probably can, but Google may have stored it somewhere before you do, or someone may have re-tweeted it or taken a screen shot for future embarrassment. The same goes for Facebook entries and what you say on your blog. While news-makers' indiscreet tweets are all too often fodder for mass media, like politicians' ill-considered remarks, or sporting personalities 'sounding off', here we're talking about journalists falling foul of the tools of the digital era. While there have been any number of examples of senior journalists and commentators 'putting their foot in it' in recent years (*Columnist sacked over Logies Twitter 'jokes'* 2010; *Tweet like you mean it* 2012; Jackson, S. 2010a; Leys 2012b; Power and Hall 2012) there are a couple that deserve brief mention.

The editor of a northern New South Wales newspaper was stood down after a tasteless remark on his personal Facebook page (*Editor said policeman's death would boost sales* 2010). The policeman, who was fatally shot during a drug raid in Sydney, had grown up in the region in Glen Innes. The *Glen Innes Examiner* was the first outlet to name him, and it was its editor that made the offensive remark. What was he thinking? While it was not a tweet, is it a classic example of that 'first tip'. It shows the danger of 'thinking out loud' on social media sites. Black humour has always been a part of the high-pressure environment of a working newsroom, for many it is a coping mechanism for some of what they see and hear, but it doesn't translate to the world of social media.

The second example is in the tradition of 'not wrong for long'. When former Australian Prime Minister, Kevin Rudd, challenged PM Julia Gillard for the leadership in late February, 2012, most political journalists had predicted the inevitable outcome, so the real contest, as far as the waiting Canberra press gallery journalists were concerned, was who would tweet the result first? The contest was won by *The Sydney Morning Herald*'s chief political correspondent at the time, Phillip Coorey, who first tweeted 'Gillard wins 73 – 29'. The only problem was that it was wrong (Christensen and Meade 2012), but he wasn't far out – the real margin was 71 – 31. Other press gallery journalists re-tweeted the wrong figures while they waited for the official announcement. While it might be considered trivial, does it matter – the former Prime Minister was soundly beaten, what if Coorey's tweet was slightly off the mark? He corrected it soon after. It demonstrates the problems associated with the rush to be first with the news on the one hand, and using material that has not been verified on the other.

One aspect of social media that we think creates an ethical trap for reporters is the need for speed. The race to publish first has always been problematic as the rush to scoop rivals can lead to shortcuts in reporting. This is where mistakes creep in and, when the mainstream news media is down-sizing and cost-cutting, the temptation to cut corners can lead to bigger errors. Add to that the split-second speed of the Internet and the probability of 'screwing up' increases. The damage – to reporters and lives – can also be greater because tweets and Facebook go global as soon as you hit the 'Send' key.

Verification is important – think twice, tweet once

Sure, we have to be a bit careful, but what of all the information that floods into media offices (or, probably more correctly, into reporters' Twitter feeds) in times of major emergency, like the aforementioned Arab Spring, or during bushfires or floods? Or journalists soliciting information from the public about what is going on in a particular story? How do you verify the information before publication? In November, 2010, a new Qantas A380 plane was involved in an incident when one of its engines exploded over Indonesia. It landed safely back in Singapore, but not before reports on Twitter that it had crashed were being picked up by mainstream media (Stilgherrian 2010). It's difficult to imagine how news like that would be received by anyone with friends or relatives on the particular flight.

At the time of writing, information and communications technology researcher Manuel Cebrian (2013) was 'crunching the numbers' on all Twitter messages reacting to super-storm Sandy which battered the east coast of the United States in October, 2012, to assess the amount of misinformation and its impact. While he said it would take months to get an accurate picture, 'I am prepared to wager that at least two of every three tweets will prove to be inaccurate to some degree' (Cebrian 2013). What does that say for news-hungry journalists wanting to inform their audiences of the latest developments?

After the horrific mass shooting at the Sandy Hook elementary school in the American state of Connecticut in December, 2012, the media wanted to know who would gun down 20 children and six of their teachers before turning a gun on himself? Early reports quoted a local law enforcement officer identifying the killer as a 'twenty-something' from the local area called Ryan Lanza. Unfortunately the information was wrong – the mass killer was Ryan's brother, Adam. But a number of news organisations tweeted links to Ryan's Facebook page. For several hours, based on media speculation, and an easily-available Facebook page, Ryan Lanza was vilified on social media before he posted on his Facebook page: 'Everyone shut the f*** up it wasn't me' (Serwer 2012). The frantic posting came shortly after he discovered his mother was dead, and his brother was a mass murderer (Levy 2012c). It was not the only thing the media got wrong that day – the boys' mother, Nancy Lanza, was reported to be a teacher at the school where the shootings took place (Farhi 2012). She wasn't, although dozens of media organisations reported it as fact. Within hours of the tragic shootings, one of the 'big three' American commercial TV stations was reporting she was a teacher at the school and many of the victims were her students. An American communications studies professor, W. Joseph Campbell, suggested at the time that the widespread reporting of the teacher angle highlighted the media's tendency to fill in blanks on initially confusing and tragic stories (cited in Farhi 2012). In other words, the race to report often introduces incorrect information. It is a real ethical fault line: Do I go with what I've got, believing my source, or wait until it is confirmed? This tendency is accelerated in the digital age. The speed of information circulation is so quick, and the volume so great, that we sometimes seem hopelessly confined to the continuous present with no time to consider historical precedent, context or future repercussions. Journalists under the pressure of an almost continuous deadline can feel this pressure acutely (Hirst 2012b).

Another ethico-legal dilemma involving social media emerged during the mid-February, 2013, police manhunt for accused murderer and former Los Angeles Police Department officer, Christopher Dorner. It was alleged that Dorner, a police officer sacked from the LAPD for misconduct, was on a rampage of revenge against former colleagues he believed had lied, leading to his dismissal. Police appealed to the media to stop tweeting the latest news as they closed in on the fugitive. Some complied and others were skeptical of the LAPD's motives. Police claimed the tweets were endangering officers at the scene of the final stand-off (Sottek 2013). Major news outlets agreed with the police's unusual request, suspecting Dorner might be following the coverage on Twitter and watching the police operation. But theories soon emerged that the police might have wanted to create their own version of events, trying to block journalists from accessing the scene to confirm how events unfolded. The LAPD did not respond to requests to explain why they wanted a Twitter blackout and later deleted their tweeted request (Porter 2013). They also temporarily turned off their police scanners to prevent journalists or other interested parties from listening in. While Twitter was alive with conspiracy theories at the time of writing (some cited in Porter 2013), the request does highlight a long-term problem for the media. In the past, police and elite armed services in many countries have complained about direct television coverage of crimes, like hostage-taking, fearing that the criminals/terrorists could watch the events unfold on television and thwart police rescue attempts. This is the modern-day digital or social media version of an older problem. Journalists rely on police, emergency services and other official State sources for routine and exceptional news breaks. As we discussed in reporter–source relations (see pages 145–149) getting too close can lead to journalists being captivated by sources – a kind of Stockholm Syndrome in which news becomes hostage to the official line.

Tweeting from court – is your phone out of order?

Another area that deserves brief mention is 'live' tweeting from court. Again there are legal and ethical aspects to consider. Ethically speaking, you'd need to virtually tweet every few minutes if you were to adequately cover a complex case. Legally, you could run the risk of causing a mistrial. That was the reason an Australian magistrate decided to ban tweeting from a committal hearing in 2011 (Christensen and Akerman 2011). At the time of writing, the New South Wales government was acting to formalise arrangements to allow mainstream journalists to tweet from courts (Smith, G. 2013). The journalists' union, the MEAA, pointed out that the legislation appeared to disadvantage emerging media by defining journalists as those 'engaged in the profession or practice of reporting', or in other words, traditional, mainstream media personnel (Colley 2013). Few Australian courts have specific policies on the use of social media to report on cases, so it is the responsibility of the reporter to establish whether the particular court allows the tweeting of proceedings. Tweeting from court is becoming a common practice in the era of the 24/7 news cycle. Since the advent of the Internet, mainstream media organisations have needed frequent updates on stories. The problems arise when they report or tweet something that is later suppressed, thereby threatening a mistrial and a potential contempt of court charge. The Law Institute of Victoria's Kerry O'Shea summarised the situation in this way:

> Court reporters no longer file one story for the next day's paper – they blog, they tweet, they do live updates from the steps of court. Social media, as one of my colleagues has described it, is just *regular media on speed* (his italics). Its use and misuse is not just a risk for court reporters – anyone with a smart phone or iPad can blog or tweet.
>
> (O'Shea 2011)

A trial in the United States in 2012 was aborted after a reporter tweeted a photo of the jury (Alfonso 2012). A tweet is a publication in the eyes of the law (Tenore 2011b).

In 2011, an Australian journalist and academic was warned against tweeting from a Melbourne court during a hearing involving allegations of senior police leaking information to a newspaper. Meg Simons was covering the case and a representative from the newspaper alerted court authorities to her tweeting. The judge told Simons that it was 'inappropriate' and that she should stop. The following day His Honour exercised judicial discretion and ruled appropriately:

> His Honour Peter Mealey raised the matter, said he had been informed that "there is something called Twitter" and said that any tweeting from his court would be regarded as contempt.
>
> He clarified that the reason for the restriction was that in this sensitive case, concerning matters of national security, live reporting could make any necessary suppression orders pointless.
>
> (Simons 2011b)

Many in the Australian media scene regard *The Australian*'s subsequent and frequent attacks on Meg Simons as a form of harassment. *Media Watch* presenter Jonathan Holmes (2012c) called it a 'habit' of the paper to launch personal and 'vitriolic' attacks on its critics. The paper called on Melbourne University to review Simons' recent appointment to a senior post. The details of the argument between Simons and *The Australian* – personified by editor-in-chief Chris Mitchell – are complex and involve several groups of warring factions of state and federal police; a thwarted alleged terrorist raid; an ethical oath by a journalist not to reveal a source and a long-running political feud between Simons and Mitchell. To complicate matters further, the source in the original story – a serving officer named Simon Artz – had signed a waiver releasing *The Australian*'s journalist, Cameron Stewart, from his bond of source confidentiality. Holmes was highly critical of *The Australian*'s attacks on Simons' integrity as a journalist and as director of Melbourne University's Centre for Advancing Journalism. In 2010, another journalism academic was threatened with a defamation action by Chris Mitchell for tweeting unflattering comments made about his editorial style by a third party who was a former staffer on *The Australian*. Nothing came of the #twitdef matter, but it did raise some concern that the lecturer, Julie Posetti, was also on Mitchell's hit list.

Discretion is required, particularly when a seemingly innocuous tweet can cause grief. Journalists have been fired for inappropriate tweets, mostly referring to controversial political topics that seemed to be a conflict of interest with their role. High profile victims include CNN's senior editor for Middle Eastern affairs, Octavia Nasr, fired for tweeting she was saddened by the death of Sayyed Mohammed Hussein Fadlallah (Walker, P. 2010). The Imam was described in the tweet as 'One of Hezbollah's giants', and Nasr wrote he was someone 'I respect a lot'. Nasr was the victim of political censorship – respecting a leader of Hezbollah is not a good career move for someone at CNN. She was not the first and won't be the last journalist sacked for social media indiscretion.

The right to be forgotten

> ... the Internet records everything and forgets nothing.
>
> (Rosen, J. 2010)

The 'right to be forgotten' is an 'old' European idea, dating back to before the Internet, when people wanted to delete their criminal pasts from the public record after a period of several years and no re-offending. In France it is called *droit d'oubli* – the right to oblivion.

You can understand the argument: why shouldn't a person have the right to have their past misdeeds forgotten? They've paid the price, they're trying to move on, to build a new life. But google their name and what do you find? At the time of writing, the European Parliament was debating legislation that updates 'the right to be forgotten' for the digital era. The proposed legislation would give everyone the right to rectify and even erase personal information about them held by a commercial organisation. The issue is complex, and the debate has been lively. However, a number of legal and ethical experts are concerned that the law would place unfair restrictions on third parties, such as the news media, that would have the effect of limiting freedom of speech (Rosen, J. 2012). The questions raised in the European Union are important because privacy in the digital age is such a big issue. Who should be compelled to remove online data, for example, is a fraught area of both law and ethics. Should the right be limited to the takedown of information I post about myself, or can you be ordered to delete material about me that you post or re-post from my own feed? Journalists are worried that, if passed, the European 'right to be forgotten' could result in the wholesale purging of news information that is unflattering to someone, particularly public figures who can afford expensive legal action. Supporters of the law also make a valid point: companies and governments should delete information held about individuals when it is no longer relevant to the purpose it was collected for. Oxford Professor of Internet Studies, Viktor Mayer-Schönberger, says that stored data should have an expiry date, after which time it is automatically removed from databases (Connolly 2013). In a related move, Spanish officials took Google to the European Court of Justice in early 2013 in a bid to force the search engine to delete information that breaches a person's privacy after a complaint that a Spanish man googled himself and found an old story that said his house was being auctioned because he hadn't paid his taxes (*EU judges to hear Google 'right to be forgotten' case* 2013). The legislation and the decision of the European Court of Justice will have wide implications for freedom of information and the protection of individual privacy. There is a large fault line opening up in the area of digital privacy and the right to be forgotten. One element is about the political economy of the surveillance economy – based on so-called 'big data' and reliant on the gathering, sorting, storing and commodification of information about us. None of us has control over this process and we are unlikely to ever get it; there is too much money at stake in advertising, marketing and monetizing our preferences and habits in the surveillance economy (Hirst and Harrison 2007).

Some valuable advice

Not so long ago, the American Society of News Editors commissioned James Hohmann (2011) to research best practice in the use of social media and to provide guidelines for news organisations. The 10 key points to emerge from the research – although some might consider at least one is already out-of-date – are:

- traditional ethics rules still apply online
- assume everything you write online will become public
- use social media to engage with readers, but professionally
- break news on your website, not on Twitter
- beware of perceptions
- independently authenticate anything found on a social networking site
- always identify yourself as a journalist

- social networks are tools not toys
- be transparent and admit when you're wrong online
- keep internal deliberations confidential.

(Hohmann 2011, p. 3)

You won't go far wrong if you adopt that as your personal code for social media practice.

Case Study 1: The 'Kony 2012' social media campaign

The power of social media to bring something to the attention of the world was demonstrated by the 'Kony 2012' campaign. Within a few days, this little-known Ugandan warlord was a household name. The fugitive rebel leader, Joseph Kony, stood accused of kidnapping and enslaving 30,000 children to his Lord's Resistance Army of child soldiers (Marcus and Domjen 2012). Some put the figure as high as 60,000 (Atherton 2012). The warlord had eluded capture for more than 20 years. He was indicted by the International Criminal Court in 2005 on 33 charges, including 12 of crimes against humanity (Atherton 2012). A 30-minute film on Kony created by a US charity was uploaded to YouTube and became the fastest growing viral phenomenon in the history of the Internet, being viewed more than 80 million times in the first six days after its release (Orden and Steel 2012). By the end of that first week, 50,000 Australians had signed a pledge calling for Kony to be captured by the year's end and brought to justice for his crimes. One newspaper characterised the phenomenon as 'obscurity to instant infamy' (Marcus and Domjen 2012). Australian social media commentator, James Griffin, said the campaign would be seen as a 'turning point where people understood the power of social media' (quoted in *11m views in two days: a social media super power* 2012). As a direct result of the campaign, Kony became Yahoo's most searched international category of 2012 (*International Affairs: #1 "Kony 2012"* 2013). The story of the amazing success of the campaign was covered extensively by media across the globe. But the campaign divided opinion. While millions signed on to the campaign to hunt down Kony, some were concerned that the viral video painted Africans as helpless and could stop money going to what were termed 'more effective' aid efforts (*Another 30m watch Kony film ... in a day* 2012). Others questioned the motives of the campaign organisers. Others asked whether the whole thing was just a slick campaign that was 'vacuous, superficial and long on feel-good sentiment, where kiddies and hipsters got to feel like revolutionaries because they have "disliked" on Facebook or written a tweet with the search tag #stopkony' (Penberthy 2012). Respected commentator and journalist, David Penberthy, referring to Kony in a Sunday paper opinion piece as 'a beast of a man', supported the social media campaign: 'Kony 2012 is one of the first times when it [social media] has been used in the West to get behind a genuinely good cause in such remarkable numbers'.

While at the time of writing (March 2013) Kony was still at large, a recent report suggested a senior member of his entourage had been killed (*Joseph Kony top bodyguard killed* 2013).

Questions for discussion:

1. There's no doubt the campaign was a success on several fronts, but did it really achieve anything? Kony is still at large (more than a year after the campaign was launched).
2. What did you think when it swept the social media in early March, 2012?
3. Did you sign the pledge?
4. What is the news value of this story?
5. What were the positives about the 'Stop Kony' campaign?
6. What are the negatives?
7. What role should the mainstream media play in such campaigns?
8. Was the media duped by this clever, viral marketing campaign?
9. Could such campaigns pose a threat of a conflict of interest for journalists?
10. Would it matter what you thought?

Case Study 2: The St Kilda nude photo scandal

In late 2010, a Melbourne teenage girl uploaded nude pictures of several members of the St Kilda AFL club to Facebook, including one of the team captain, Nick Riewoldt. The club quickly sought a court order, and the site was shut down to prevent further publication of the images, but by that stage the pictures had gone viral. The girl said she was a former girlfriend of another St Kilda player, but it didn't stop there. Aspects of the wider story would make headlines for months and draw one of the biggest names in AFL football into a tawdry sex scandal. Google 'St Kilda schoolgirl' if you don't know the details, we want to stop short of a blow-by-blow description of what happened, before and after the nude photos appeared, and concentrate on the ethico-legal aspects of the sorry saga. The major issues for us centre on the news media's naming of the girl and consideration of her mental well-being. For months, mainstream media did not mention the girl's name, referring to her as the 'St Kilda Schoolgirl' as they reported allegation after allegation and various counter allegations. Her name – like so much, as we have noted in different contexts elsewhere – was easily available on the Internet. Some mainstream media said they did not initially name her as much for ethical reasons as legal ones. She was only 17, and obviously had medical issues. Then on 6 March 2011, *Sixty Minutes* not only named the girl, but showed her face, thereby revealing her identity, something the rest of the media had been avoiding (Jennings-Enquist and Kodila 2011). *The Age* alleged that *Sixty Minutes* had contravened a court suppression order dating back to the time of the original incident of the uploading of the nude photos (Beck and Khokhar 2011). Nine denied they had broken any laws. Other legal advice suggested the original suppression order had been lifted in late January, meaning the mainstream media could have named the girl for about five weeks prior to the *Sixty Minutes* segment (Overington 2011a). The media were full of stories during that February about the girl's alleged affair with high profile football manager, Ricky Nixon, who numbered among his clients the aforementioned Nick Riewoldt. In the days following her TV appearance, the proverbial floodgates opened, with many papers published outside Victoria naming her. [You'll notice we're not naming her. We don't see the point in further embarrassing a troubled teenager trying to rebuild her life.] Predictably, the Sydney papers, the *Daily Telegraph* and the *Herald* named her, but their sister publications in Melbourne, the *Herald Sun* and *The Age*, didn't. *The Australian* named her in editions circulated outside Victoria (Overington 2011a). It was suggested at the time that media in Melbourne were taking an ethical, rather than a legal approach to the question of naming the teenager – because of her age and the potential risk to her health (Overington 2011a).

Questions for discussion:

1. In the early stages of the story there were two distinct groups – those who attacked the girl for embarrassing some of the biggest stars in the AFL, and others who wanted to help the girl because of what she alleged she'd been through. Research the story and debate your stand.
2. Who do you feel most sorry for – the girl (after you've read the complete story) or Nick Riewoldt and his mates?
3. Would you have mentioned her name as soon as you were able?
4. Were the Melbourne-based papers right in withholding the name, or just being over-cautious?
5. Why name her at all? What purpose does it serve?
6. Why not name her? She admitted that most of what she had alleged was lies.
7. Who has the greater right to privacy here – the young woman or the football celebrities involved?
8. Does someone like the young woman in this scenario have the right to be forgotten? What about the footballers and the manager?

13 Ethical decision-making in the newsroom

Thinking yourself into circles

> Being ethical does not always mean following the law. And just because something is possible doesn't mean it is ethical.
>
> (Swinton 2007)

No matter whether you are on the front lines of journalism, or a backroom manager, there is no escaping the ethico-legal paradox. However, somewhere within the nested paradox, you will, eventually have to make a decision. How will you know it's the right one? After reading this chapter you should at least know how to go about ethical thinking. The role of the ethical journalist as investigator, informant, explainer, educator, and sometimes entertainer, has never been more important than in the digital era. The public is swamped with information through more traditional sources as well as via the Internet, and its social media 'children', the bloggers, Facebook updaters and tweeters. How is the public to make sense of this tsunami of information swamping them every day? It is our contention that the 'new' role of the mass media is to sift through all that information (as they have always done, hence the inverted commas around 'new') and decide what the public really needs to know about, and interpret its relative importance. The gate-keeping role of journalists has not ended, but the number of non-journalistic gates is increasing and editors are competing against more sources, more outlets and more voices. For the news media to continue fulfilling its critical role of watchdog for the public interest, we, the public, need to be able to trust and believe what we read, see and hear in the mainstream media. So we have come full circle – we're back where we started in the Preface, highlighting the relatively low standing of journalists among the general community and asking 'who is a journalist nowadays'? The only way that trust will be regained by the MSM is by having journalists adhere to ethical principles in their reporting, investigating and writing. So far we have shown how ethical dilemmas are created by the movement of social forces within and around the news process; in this chapter we hope to give you some pointers that will help you navigate ethical fault lines and make sound decisions when confronted with ethical dilemmas.

There is no set of ten commandments for journalists; codes of ethics can never be more than a guide to action because circumstances will always be variable. The best approach is to adopt a reasoning and decision-making process that can help under most circumstances. As you have been reading this book and considering our arguments and cases, you will have soon realised that there are no simple solutions to ethical dilemmas in journalism. Editors, reporters, sub-editors and producers need to be aware at all times of both the practical and philosophical issues. We believe a familiarity with both approaches is necessary in preparing for the privilege and responsibility that comes with ethical editorial decision-making.

We also believe it is important for tertiary journalism students to consider the ethical dilemmas they may face in the future while still at university, where they can weigh up the merits of each case and arrive at a logical conclusion. In our view, you should have developed an ethical framework for how you will conduct yourself as a journalist before you do too many journalism assignments as part of your degree, and before you enter the media workforce. You certainly will have developed what we referred to in the early chapters as your 'world view' (of how you see things) long before you even reach university. Of course, once you are at university your views may change under the influence of new knowledge, new friends, independence from family and greater maturity. Once you are in the media you will need to make ethical decisions quickly. You won't be able to debate with your colleagues the various competing aspects as you will have done during your journalism ethics tutorials. In the classroom no one gets hurt by your decisions – except for the occasional bruised ego. In the media workforce, the results of your actions could have major effects on the people you are writing about. It will be rare that you will have the time to reflect too long on the various competing aspects of an ethical dilemma. Realise, though, that you are not what we call an 'ethical orphan'. There are other reporters in the newsroom you can consult. The senior staff at your media organisation should be made aware as early as possible of any ethical dilemma you are facing. They may take the decision out of your hands. By their very nature, many of the examples and case studies in this book have shown some reporters in anything but the best light, and we need to balance that by repeating what we have said in various contexts throughout the text: that the vast majority of journalists make simple, and sometimes complex, ethical decisions on a daily basis that go unnoticed because they don't create a ripple of attention.

In the classroom you will have been expected to take an ethical position on one of the arguments, or on the actions outlined in one of the case studies, and be prepared to defend it. And as you have seen, time and time again, there are never black and white answers to ethical dilemmas. If there were, they wouldn't be dilemmas. There are only varying shades of grey. In each instance you needed to weigh up the pros and cons (using the methods we're about to discuss) and reach a decision on the information before you – much as you will have to do once you join the media workforce.

The big questions – the who, what, where, when, why and how of ethical decision-making

We've spent many chapters discussing the ethical dilemmas, big and small, faced by journalists in the digital age. Now we're left with the all-important question, given all you've read earlier about various views of ethical behaviour and how journalists the world over have had problems reaching an ethical decision:

How do you go about making an ethical decision, given there are often so many conflicting ideas, information or positions?

If you're discussing an ethical dilemma in a university assignment or tutorial there are a number of aspects to consider. Among them are:

- What factors will have the most bearing on the decision – personal, social, economic, legal, or political? What effects are they likely to have on your decision – major or minor? Which is the most important if several are involved? How do you balance conflicting factors?

- Who are the various parties involved? Do you have any obligation to any of them (for example, respecting their confidence, or loyalty to a source)? What about the other obligations – to telling the truth to the public, your employer, your workmates or your colleagues in the profession?
- What are the relative merits of the various people involved?
- Will justice be served for all by your action?
- Will you be helping someone who deserves assistance by your action?
- Is the action prompted by a wrong you have committed and need to make amends for?
- What outcome would satisfy each of the parties involved? How will your chosen course of action affect each of them? (And that includes your boss.)
- What are the 'power dynamics' of the situation? Who might have power over you, or others involved in the issue, and what's your relationship with them? This could be colleagues, your employer, the sources you're using, or even someone close to you, like a partner, spouse, or close friend.
- What courses of action are open to you? What are the best and worst possible outcomes for the various scenarios?
- Will anyone be harmed by your preferred choice of action? By how much? Is the 'good' brought about by your action outweighed by the potential harm?
- How can you minimise unnecessary harm to all concerned?
- Are you just using a person as a means to an end without considering the effect your action will have on them?
- Would honouring any ideal or value you hold invalidate your chosen course of action?
- Are there any rules or principles – like Codes of Ethics or Charters of Editorial Independence – that would automatically invalidate your proposed course of action?
- Which of the alternative courses of action would generate the greatest benefit or the least harm for the greatest number?
- Are any of the alternative courses of action based on your or your organisation's best interests?
- And after reviewing all that, what would you do?

We believe this guide for ethical decision-making was first developed by the journalism staff at the University of Oregon in the United States and has been adapted by others over time, including by the authors in ethics units they have taught over many years. Circumstances may vary, but the fundamentals remain the same.

It might seem like an almost endless list of things to consider, and yes, the list is long, and it's long for a very good reason – any ethical decision is not to be taken lightly, without considering the ramifications of your actions. You could be about to ruin someone's career, expose them as a cheat, a liar, or a criminal.

The reality is that 'high end' ethical decisions will rarely be made by you in isolation. The more important the story, the more likely senior staff will become involved in any decision on content. But you will make ethical decisions every day – sometimes without realising it. We have mentioned earlier the decisions on who you will interview, what you will ask them, what of their replies you will use in your final story. They're all ethical decisions.

As we said above, you are not an 'ethical orphan' – seek advice on any dilemma you have with those colleagues in the office whose work ethics you admire. It might be a senior journalist who took you 'under their wing' when you first started. It might be the chief of staff, or editor. It might even be your university ethics lecturer. You don't need to make such decisions on your own – especially where there are seriously-conflicting positions you could take.

The decision-making process – stepping stones through the fault lines

There are often lots of issues to consider in making an ethical decision, which is why we say you need to have some strong ideas about your own ethical boundaries before you enter the media workforce. Have you sorted out your emotional attitudes and settled on a world view that is comfortable and represents who you are? This is not fixed and if you don't alter some of your opinions as you have more life experiences, then you are not really living; however, by young adulthood you should be critically self-aware enough to know if you are a 'theist', 'agnostic' or 'atheist'. Are you libertarian, conservative, liberal or leftwing in your political views? What makes you angry, sad or happy? Understand these issues and you will have a pretty good idea of your ethical values, too. Once you join the workforce as a reporter – or in any capacity really – you will need to distil your emotional attitudes into a manageable form to guide you in ethical decision-making in the future. As we said, once you are working in the mass media, there'll be precious little time for mulling over the ramifications of your actions. You'll need to make your decisions relatively quickly, and be prepared to justify them, if necessary. Over the years we have found that structuring your decision-making processes in a logical, step-by-step way can help overcome ethical doubts, fears, or dilemmas.

We call this method 'stepping stones' because, like using a series of rocks to step between and cross a river, you need to follow the logic of each step. The illustration overleaf shows an overview of this process and the steps you need to take in order to avoid the fault lines and ethical slips that will land you in hot water.

We start with the facts because, like any good journalist, you will want to know what the basic story is first, the news angle that you might take or have been asked to take on the issue, and the sources that you have or that you might need to complete the reporting assignment.

Step1: Finding the facts

The stepping stones are a series of prompts and the first one applies to every single reporting assignment you will ever do: do you know what the story is about? If you cannot confidently answer 'yes' to this question then you need to do more homework and research. Our strong belief is that 90 per cent of journalism – including making ethical decisions – occurs before you sit down to write up your story. Here are some prompts to help you determine what the story facts are:

- Do you have adequate information to determine that the story is worth pursuing? What have you got so far and what do you still need to make the story stand up? These are fundamental to all journalism and you will need to make sure that you are prepared to argue for the story at a news conference or with your chief of staff.

- What are the proposed or suggested angles on the story? Your angle frames the story – is it strong enough to generate interest?

- What are the news requirements of your organisation?
  Do you have a reasonable deadline? Do you know how much space or time you have to complete the story (word count, column centimetres or broadcast time)?

- What do you already know? What facts have you already gathered?
  Ninety per cent of journalism involves research and interviews. Can you fill in the holes in your story?

- What else do you need to know? Where are the gaps that might sink the story?
  Do you think there are 'unknown unknowns'? That is, could there be things that you don't even know you don't know about yet?

- What additional sources do you need?
  Do your proposed sources have credibility? Do they have any self-interest or prejudice that would colour their account of events or issues?

- How do you propose to reconcile differences in accounts that you are given?
  Are there different significant accounts of events or issues? If so, how do you intend to 'triangulate' and cross-reference between sources? This is important because you may not want to tip off a source that you are also talking to someone else. What would you do if you were asked this question directly and a source refuses to cooperate if you also speak to person 'X'?

- In a story with strong and divided opinions, do you have a sense of which side you might favour?
  Does your answer reflect a personal bias or is this position justified and supported by the facts as you have them to hand? Overcoming bias is one of the hardest things to do in journalism and it is also misunderstood. See below for our tips on dealing with bias.

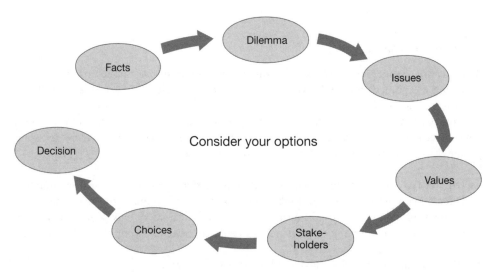

Figure 13.1　Steps to ethical decision-making

- Are you (and your editor) willing to change your minds about angles, sources and story outcomes on the basis of new information that comes to hand?

  You know already that you have to be flexible to work well in a busy news environment. Being willing to admit that you have been wrong and need to reconsider a story is a vital part of flexibility.

Step 2: Time out

When you have checked yourself against these opening questions, stop and think for a few moments about the potential ethical problems you might encounter.

- Is one of your sources likely to be lying to you? How do you respond?
- Is a source compromised if you use the information?
- Has the information given to you been obtained illegally by the source?
- Does the public interest outweigh your concerns about the problematic source?
- Is a source likely to be a child under 18? Do you need a guardian's or parent's permission to speak to them?
- Is the young person up to being interviewed?
- How would you approach the interview to ensure that no harm might come to the child?

If you don't take this step, and you react under pressure, you are more likely to make a bad decision. Remember, here, that we are using examples that would trigger alarm bells and are 'high stakes' for the organisation, the individual reporter, the source, the subjects of the story and are probably of high public interest value. However, under most circumstances, no matter how benign, it is always better to consider the potential issues so that you can prepare to manage them and the consequences.

Step 3: Actions have consequences

What are the potential repercussions from the story you are covering? Obviously simple stories or good news stories are likely to be very straightforward: there is a clear angle and the consequences are not going to be harmful to anyone. In fact, a good news story can actually make people feel good, or cheer them up. Sometimes the ethical issues around some 'feel good' stories are that they come with commercial strings. We're not talking about schools fetes, but sponsored events with high-profile, commercial stakes are often marketing focused. Coverage of these events has the look and feel of advertorial if it is not done with some critical distance.

However, any story involving the news values of conflict, drama, public interest, consequence or impact is also likely to upset someone. Journalists frequently have to make decisions about stories they're working on that do have real consequences for the subjects or sources involved. Nearly every decent story about an issue will paint someone in a potentially bad light; it may even go so far as to defame them – to lower their reputation in the eyes of their peers, or those who know them. Any story of substance involving organised conflict – from commercial and family legal disputes, to criminal allegations, government inquiries, political news, and so on – is bound to impinge on someone's good character at some point. Defamation is a soft ethico-legal paradox in that everyone accepts the rules of the game, to some degree; criticism, even personal criticism, is OK within certain boundaries. Legal precedents in the superior courts of most jurisdictions also set the limits to tolerated daily defamation in public life.

But consequences can do more than just damage egos or reputations. They can lead to commercial loss, personal harm to sources or subjects, or even a miscarriage of justice. So if you are working on a story with consequences, be sure you know what they are – rehearse them in your head, discuss them with a colleague or an editor beforehand if you're not sure.

It's one thing to know what the consequences are, it's another entirely to know if they are justified by the story outcome that you might be pursuing. This is the point in time where the public interest test must be applied. If the consequences are no more than tolerable defamation of one or more subjects, then the harm to reputation is likely to be relatively low. If, however, there are severe consequences, then the likely harm could be significant to someone involved. In that case, serious consideration must be given to just how high the public interest in the story is.

What are the issues that create the dilemma?

Step 4: What are the values you bring to the story?

By now you should be confident in your own values and in your emotional attitudes to why you are a journalist and to life in general. So, the step 4 questions involve an interrogation of these values in relation to the issues and potential ethical fault lines in your approach to the story. Three key questions might well be enough:

- Which values – either in a code of ethics, or social/moral values – are important to me? You will of course need to consider accuracy, bias, balance, the public interest, your attitudes to objectivity, truthfulness, fairness and requirements such as being able to honour a commitment to maintaining the confidentiality of a source. For example, have you considered using a different source who is willing to go on the record?

- Does doing this story violate any personal, corporate or social values that you are bound to? If so, is there another way to do the story that maintains your integrity? Which journalism values are important to the integrity of the story? Is the public interest sufficiently strong to warrant using confidential sources in the story? For instance, are you prepared for the consequences if you are compelled to reveal the identity of your secret source?

  It is useful to adapt some thoughts from virtue theory at this point and consider which virtues of journalism – honesty, truth-telling, public interest, do no harm, etc. – are upheld or violated (potentially) in the approach you're taking to the story.

- What values are important to the stakeholders – the subjects, sources and audience for your story?

  If you can triangulate evidence to support an anonymous source through other means of verification, then you will be able to protect your important anonymous source. If the issue has a high public interest stake, then taking steps to secure source anonymity is important. But other stakeholders may then also feel it is more important for them to pursue the identity of the source to plug a 'leak' in their operation.

  When considering the interests of stakeholders, you can also check them off against a simple list of questions. You can see that there is a method here: to reflectively ask and answer our simple questions in a logical sequence, step from stone to stone and cross the ravine in safety.

- Who is affected by the means used to gather the story together?
  Are you likely to damage someone's reputation inadvertently in the course of reporting and writing your story? If so, you should consider whether the impact on third parties is better avoided, or is there a way to ameliorate it – perhaps by fore-warning them of publication. In all cases, you should make sure the subject had been offered the right to comment. But this can be tricky, too. At what time prior to publication do you notify the subject? If the story is high-stakes they may well take action to get a 'stop writ', or use other methods to prevent publication.

- Who is affected by the ends?
  If you run the story with the angle you are considering, what will be the outcome? Could someone go to jail, or is someone's spouse or child likely to be emotionally hurt by the revelations in your story? Family members are often innocent bystanders, particularly when stories involve 'trial by media'. Can you live with that?

- Who is affected by the consequences?
  The subject is likely to be affected if the story casts them in a poor light, or exposes some wrongdoing. But what about collateral damage? Journalists are not often encour-aged to think about this, but Rawls' veil of ignorance thesis directs us to imagine how we might feel if it was us being exposed to ridicule, anger or public humiliation.

- How are third parties affected?
  Family members may be vulnerable for many reasons – you will remember in the Craig Thomson case that his wife was placed under a great deal of stress by an intrusive media while she was heavily pregnant.

- Where does the greatest good lie?
  The damage to reputation, or to family and friends, may be unavoidable, but is it justified because of the public interest? If the story has consequences and impact – it affects a whole town or school community, for example – collateral damage may well occur, but if the outcome of the story is that the town or school community benefits then J. S. Mill's utility principle is well served. While we would argue that in most cases the public interest takes precedence over potential consequential harm, it must be considered on a case-by-case basis.

- Are any of the consequences 'fatal'?
  By 'fatal' we don't just mean deadly or resulting in an otherwise unavoidable death – it could be fatal in that it kills the story, or it prevents any chance of a better story being told if you don't write what you know now, but hold off until a better time to tell it. It could also be 'fatal' in the sense that the damaging consequences are so great that there is no public benefit to the exposé and therefore you might decide not to do the story at all. Perhaps you really don't have that killer bit of the puzzle that completes the story. In which case, if what you have is strong, but not strong enough, do you wait and keep digging, or do you go and hope to flush out more material as the story develops?

It is important to know that you can make the decision not to proceed with a story at any time. Not every scoop is worth the downside consequences. That is why we are keen for you to internalise this method of self-questioning. There is no shame in deciding to ditch a story because the consequences are greater than you can handle personally, or are so nearly 'fatal' that you feel it better to abandon the yarn rather than cause further damage to yourself or stakeholders. Ethics must be about fearlessness in the face of some danger, but like Aristotle's 'Golden Mean', there is reason in moderation, too.

Who is most affected?

Step 5: From effects to choices

As you can see, every stepping stone is guiding us towards making a decision. On the basis of considering values and consequences, we may have already decided not to pursue a story that creates more harm than good. In our view, this decision is not made often enough, or early enough in the news cycle; far too often we see or read stories of little consequence in terms of public interest, but which cause grief for some or all of the stakeholders. There's enough important 'stuff' to report about without having to resort to half-thought-through stories that wreck the lives of otherwise innocent people.

We start to move from how our actions in writing a particular story might affect people to considering the options we have, with another series of simple questions:

- What choices do you have to make to bring about the best result for the most affected stakeholders?
  You clearly have a choice to do, or not do, the story that you're working on. You have a choice of angle, of who to speak to and of which sources to give prominence to. Having considered values, consequences and who the affected stakeholders are likely to be, you can consider your own options in terms of your approach to the story, the subject(s), the source(s) and your audience.

- Are you limited in the means you can apply?
  If you don't have a great deal of choice, for example around the sources you can use, is there a particular approach you should take that guarantees an outcome? If you need to approach a source in a delicate way that will not frighten them off, how would you do it? These choices are strategic as they inform the subsequent development of your story and that is why ethical thinking is valuable. Choices should always be informed and not made on the basis of a lottery. Every choice is a gamble, but you can, with some thoughtful self-reflection, manage the balance of probabilities a little better.

- Is the end you seek justified?
- The story may have an impact on some stakeholders that causes them harm or discomfort. Is the story worth it?
- Are the consequences manageable?
  If you answer 'yes', how do you intend to manage them? Is there support available for you, the subjects or the sources if things go pear-shaped after the story is published?

- Are you asking the right questions?
  This is an opportunity to return to the things you are certain about, elements that are evidence-based, and to the bits and pieces that you might not be so sure of about the story. This is as much about story structure as it is about ethics. Have you prepared your questions and research in such a way that it fills in the gaps? Have you asked yourself 'What's missing from this picture?'

  Like a detective (at least fictional ones) revisiting the scene of the crime and making deductions (informed guesswork) about motive and suspects and weapons of choice, sometimes a reporter must revisit their approach to a major news story. Unfortunately time constraints, the pressures of the continuous present and the tendency to pack mentality among reporters covering the same story means that too often this vital step is not taken. A key message of this book is that we must give ourselves more time to think, not less.

How are your choices constrained?

Step 6: What are my options?

We are now getting closer to crunch time, but before committing to a course of action, have you considered the alternatives that might be available? We have already mentioned finding new sources or means of verifying information about which you are unsure. If the story 'stands-up', which options for pursuing and writing the story will have the least adverse impact on stakeholders? What else might you do? Here's some advice:

Find more than two ways to approach the story.

If what you are considering doing makes you feel uncomfortable and your ethical dilemma is not solved to your satisfaction, then it is probably not the right thing to do. However, the story may be so important – to the public or to your editor – that you have to do it. When you can't ignore the story, but the means are bothering you, then think outside the square.

- Can you approach the story differently?
  You will have heard the expression 'there's more than one way to skin a cat'. We like cats so don't recommend skinning them in any way, but the idea is important in a newsroom context. If the story is necessary, or has a high public interest, but the consequences could be 'fatal' or near enough to one or more of the stakeholders, can you tackle it in such a way that minimizes the harm to those whom it would be good to protect? This might mean back-tracking and returning to your research phase in order to execute the story more effectively. That's OK; rushing a story because of the excitement of the moment or in anticipation of a career-boosting scoop will not always produce the best results. Take your time – 'measure twice, cut once.'

- Don't be afraid to seek advice.
  It is OK to be out of your depth; newsrooms are a daily learning experience and it is only through experience that you will know what to do. Getting to know your colleagues is really important. For both of us, throughout our careers, finding

co-workers who we could trust and who were willing to discuss job-related issues in context was important in ethical editorial decision-making. Talk the story over with an editor, a colleague or even a friend who is outside the newsroom. You will gain a fresh perspective by doing this. It is not a sign of weakness to ask for help or to admit that you are conflicted. The worst thing you can do is plough on regardless; it can only lead to harm for yourself (all that worry and angst is not good for anyone) and potentially fatal consequences for other stakeholders.

Consider the equal, lesser, greater, similar or conflicting consequences of your alternative story plan.

All options will have consequences and many of the main concerns you might have may not disappear just because you change course. That's OK, too. If, at the end of the deliberation process you decide to go ahead and to manage the consequences then you have made the right decision.

Choices you made

Step 7: From choice to decision

No matter how long it took you to get here, it was worth it. At some point you have to bring the deliberative process to an end. If the decision is to do the story then at this point double-check to expel any remaining doubts.

Choose the methods that deliver the best outcome

Approach the story with a suite of tools that gets the job done with the minimum of fuss for the maximum impact and ensuring the least amount of collateral damage. If possible, have a Plan B ready to put into action if there are unintended consequences that threaten to derail the story, or if unexpected obstacles are put in your way. Never undertake a high-stakes, risky reporting assignment without letting at least one or two trusted colleagues and friends know enough about it to get you out of serious trouble.

- Does your decision meet your own values paradigm?
  We would hope so. It can be very demoralising, particularly for young reporters, if they are forced to do a story that does not align with their own emotional attitudes, world view or journalistic values. Some codes of ethics contain a conscience clause that gives reporters an 'out' if something they are tasked with conflicts with their values. It used to be the case, and perhaps still is in some newsrooms, that older hands would claim young graduate recruits were too 'idealistic' for their own good. Lecturers like us would be blamed for introducing 'too much theory' into journalism degrees. In the end, it is something that we're quite proud of. We observe the work of our graduates from recent and distant past cohorts and, thankfully, not too many of them have made the 'walk of shame' on *Media Watch*. They are successful and, we continue to believe, act ethically and in the public interest on most working days.

  You will find camaraderie and lots of advice in most good newsrooms. In some, taking pride in the Code is part and parcel of joining a union or professional association. Some organisations are founded on high principles of public interest and disclosure. They have high standards in order to claim a right to hold others to account.

However, if there is not a good atmosphere in the newsroom it can be hard to say 'no' to your boss. We have seen first-hand and recounted throughout the book, the consequences of a management and leadership failure to hold to good standards. Even as we type these final words, there are recent echoes of the *News of the World* scandal with arrests now over 100 and the BBC's *Panorama* programme is caught up in another public relations disaster. A *Panorama* crew secretly accompanied a group of university students to Pyongyang at the height of diplomatic and military tension on the Korean peninsula. The London School of Economics denounced *Panorama* for putting the students at risk, embroiling the BBC in yet another major scandal.

Even the best-laid plans can go wrong. In hindsight it's always easy to shrug and say, 'What were they thinking?'. We think that was possibly another one of those moments for *Panorama*.

If things are difficult in the newsroom, our advice is to always seek advice and support – from the union or association if you can – before refusing an order to do a story in a particular way. If your chief of staff or editor is a bully, or the workplace is toxic, you should be able to take remedial action. Doing so with the support of colleagues is better than trying to tackle the office psychopath on your own.

- Does your approach satisfy the requirements of the story?
  The best answer is a simple 'yes', but a qualified 'yes' is OK if you are aware of the consequences – particularly any blowback that could land on your head, the newsroom or the heads of various stakeholders.

- Does your approach satisfy the requirements of the newsroom?
  We hope 'yes' again here. If it does then you should not have any problems and any consequences can be dealt with in a way that does not cause any harm to you, subjects or sources. If your answer to these last two questions is 'no', then you probably have a bit more work to do.

Crunch Time

Step 8: Monitor and modify

This process is self-reflective, which means that, when done consciously, it should provide you with a feedback loop that helps embed the 'lessons' into your memory for next time; it should also alert you to potential problems once the story is under way.

It is not enough to make the decision and then forget about ethical thinking while you get on with being a reporter. As you gather material, interview sources or check allegations with your triangulation methods, you should also be referencing your stepping stone responses. It may be a perfect plan and nothing can go wrong, but in our experience even the best-laid plans can be mucked up by unforeseen events, mishaps or mistakes. The simple rule is that we are only human and cannot think of everything, or plan for every contingency. As the Boy Scouts say: 'Be prepared.' Monitor and modify means keeping an eye on these final points:

- Always make your best effort working on any story – it always means more to someone else than it will ever mean to you.

- Take your responsibilities seriously; uphold the public interest and always act with the utmost honesty. But be prepared for mistakes and unintended consequences. Do the best job you can from start to finish.
- Always evaluate outcomes against predicted consequences.

Not every story will be a gem, some will be better than others. If you follow our stepping stones you will be in a position to learn from success and from failure.

- Did the story satisfy your public interest test?
- Were the consequences and outcomes what you expected?
- How did you handle the problems that came up?
- Were there any surprises?
- What would you do differently next time?

Eventually, and after some time in a newsroom or working freelance, you will have built up a store of experience that makes the decision-making process simpler and faster. The first few times you need to employ our methods it may seem cumbersome, slow and irksome. All we can say is, 'Stick to it.' If you are reflective you will soon understand the methods that work under certain circumstances and there is no doubt that you will need to employ them again on another story sooner or later. If you take a few moments at the completion of each reporting assignment to assess what worked and what didn't work you will know what to repeat and what to avoid when confronting ethical dilemmas in the future.

Simple questions about bias in reporting

Bias is perhaps the worst accusation that can be levelled against a journalist, but it is ironic, because everyone is biased. To avoid bias in your reporting, the stepping stone method works as a good process. Here are several questions that can be applied to news gathering in order to detect any bias in the reporter. You can apply them to yourself, too. They are not foolproof, but they will help in most cases:

- What is the author's/reporter's personal position? Does s/he belong to any professional association, church, community, social or political organisation that might influence how s/he reports a story?
- Does the reporter have any personal stake in the story, or the issues being covered?
- Does the story provide evidence beyond a simple re-telling of available information; has the reporter moved beyond the 'bias of convenience'?
- How credible are the sources or statistics that the journalist has used?
- Are there any obvious omissions from the data as presented?
- Is there another interpretation of the data that conflicts with the reporter's interpretation?
- Has this alternative viewpoint been fairly and accurately represented?
- Has the story covered enough background to overcome the 'perpetual present'?
- What arguments does the reporter use or choose to ignore in building their case?
- If alternative views are presented, is the reporter's summary accurate and fair?
- Is the language used to describe the various viewpoints balanced, or is one side presented in a negative fashion and the other in a positive tone?

- Does the reporter have the background knowledge, the insight, self-confidence, and emotional maturity to understand the story and the consequences of reporting it in a particular way?

Dealing with social media

We have talked extensively about the importance and pitfalls of using social media as a newsroom tool. Here's a short list of tips that will help you stay out of trouble on Facebook and Twitter.

- Be aware that what you say is public and affects your reputation and that it could also impact on the reputation of your employer.
- Things you say or write on Twitter or in a blog could affect your credibility as a reporter.
- Always be courteous and civil to your friends and even more so to your enemies; avoid personal attacks and offensive remarks.
- When in doubt, ask yourself if a given action might damage the company's or your reputation – if so, it's probably a bad idea.

What does the future look like for journalism and ethics?

Without access to a fortune teller's crystal ball, it is hazardous guesswork to try to predict future developments in journalism ethics, but the *News of the World* scandal, the Leveson inquiry in Britain, the Finkelstein review in Australia and worldwide concerns about media intrusions into privacy are having an impact on how journalists and journalism are seen by the public. Rebuilding trust in the news media will take some time. For ten years or more, the general public has grown more wary of journalists' pronouncements; the 'weapons of mass destruction' lie that led to war in Iraq in 2003, the use of spin and 'astro-turfing' to skew public debates and policy and the intrusion of advertising into information programming are all reasons that we love to hate journalists and news organisations.

Leveson, Finkelstein and the countless inquiries and legislative recommendations to deal with data and personal privacy are all responses to public unhappiness about news and journalism. But greater State regulation is not the answer. Further legal shackles on the freedom of journalists to investigate can only benefit the already powerful and those wealthy enough to afford 'super injunctions' against media organisations. In the long run, government regulation can have a 'chilling effect', eventually stifling reporting on things that the powerful want to keep secret, rather than things that should remain private.

Secrecy is the enemy of public interest. Secrecy is about hiding the truth from the public. It is citizens who have the right to know and also to act on information. State 'secrets' are often revealed to be cover-ups for spying, illegal detentions, torture and even State-sponsored mass killings. It is also about corporate corruption and generally disguising greed as 'progress'.

On the other hand, privacy is about keeping from the public that which merely titillates and has no public consequence. If new 'strict' privacy laws are only in place to prevent scrutiny of the rich and famous – those who can afford legal protection – then they will not benefit freedom of the press. The lives of ordinary people will still be subject to detailed scrutiny; physical and electronic surveillance will continue and expand behind the veil of 'information privacy'. 'Big Data' is already here, gathering millions of bits of information about who we are. Privacy laws will not stop that from happening.

A positive for the future of journalism?

We agree with critics who argue that greater policing of the news media by State agencies – no matter how well intentioned – will eventually erode freedom of the press for everyone. The idea that reporters should somehow be licensed by a government agency, in no matter how mild a form first proposed, is archaic and anathema to freedom of expression. Lessons from stage 2 of the Arab Spring revolutions – Morsi's attempts to silence his media critics, including left-wing journalists and academics – were a grave warning that it is only active revolutions that keep freedoms alive. As we have argued throughout this book, despite its revolutionary origins as a champion of individual rights, the ruling class today has little interest in real media freedom. If the role of the news media is to expose the hidden dealings of the rich and powerful and hold them to public account, then any government that helps to maintain the rule of the elite will not willingly assist in the exposure of their crimes. We have given a number of positive examples as cases for consideration throughout the book. Certainly the work of Berstein and Woodward since Watergate has continued to be impressive; others from the same generation are also still active. Seymour Hersh is still breaking stories. A new generation is also emerging, led by fearless reporters like Glenn Greenwald of *The Guardian*; inspired in part by WikiLeaks, foundations and collaborative projects are developing and independent new voices are emerging. It is early days for crowd-sourcing and other social media applications – and we are certainly not determinist – but the next few years represent a critical moment in which the news industry and traditional journalism are changing – either adapting, or dying out (Hirst 2011). Outside the gates of the old media castles it is a whole new landscape – vital and experimental. However, it is not just media for media's sake; the medium is not the message in this case. The real story is that information that challenges the status quo is emerging – and WikiLeaks is the model here, too – and this is coupled with crises both economic and social in scope. There is potential for widespread information anarchy.

News organisations have always exchanged stories within their particular stable of publications or accessed them through news agencies or by other financial arrangements. In Australia, the national broadcaster, the ABC and the Melbourne daily, *The Age*, have worked together on investigative journalism projects. Literally in the final days of writing this text, a new form of international media co-operation began to emerge giving hope for investigative journalists the world over. All the problems facing mainstream media have combined to limit costly investigative journalism in recent times, but an international consortium of investigative journalists announced in early April, 2013, they were about to start releasing stories about the murky workings of offshore tax havens. Apparently, the stories being compiled by a consortium of journalists involve analysing more than 2.5 million digital files about the finances of individuals in more than 170 countries (O'Donovan 2013). The WikiLeaks-size 'treasure trove' of files has yielded information on 120,000 offshore companies and nearly 13,000 individuals. The 15-month investigation involving 86 investigative journalists in 46 countries has been undertaken by the Washington-based International Consortium of Investigative Journalists (ICIJ) and headed by former Fairfax investigative journalist Gerard Ryle (*Mysterious mail to Australian journalist triggers global tax haven exposé* 2013). It seems to us to be a positive move forward for journalists everywhere, and a positive note on which to close our final chapter.

Figure 13.2 'Thank You and Goodbye', *News of the World*, 10 July 2011. Copyright News Syndication

Bibliography

2 jurors say they regret Jackson's acquittal. (2005, September 8). *Today* (US). Retrieved January 25, 2013, from www.today.com/id/8880663/site/todayshow/ns/today-entertainment/t/jurors-say-they-regret-jacksons-acquittal/

3 shots. Screams. Silence. 3 more shots. Blade Runner Pistorius 'murders lover'. (2013, February 15). *The Sun,* p. 1.

9/11: The image of The Falling Man that still haunts 10 years on. (2011, September 11). *The Mirror* (UK). Retrieved January 17, 2013, from www.mirror.co.uk/news/uk-news/911-the-image-of-the-falling-man-that-still-152974

11m views in two days: a social media super power. (2012, March 8). *The Sydney Morning Herald.* Retrieved March 8, 2012, from www.smh.com.au/technology/technology-news/11m-views-in-two-days-a-social-media-super-power-20120308-1ummi.html

87 not out. Nine Network. (1996).

2011: Journalists killed. (2012, November 10). *Reporters Without Borders.* Retrieved November 10, 2012, from http://en.rsf.org/press-freedom-barometer-journalists-killed.html?annee=2011

2012: Journalists killed. (2013, n.d.). *Reporters Without Borders.* Retrieved January 31, 2013, from http://en.rsf.org/press-freedom-barometer-journalists-killed.html?annee=2012

ABC Editorial Policies. (2007). Sydney: Australian Broadcasting Commission.

ABC Editorial policies: Principles and Standards. (2011). Sydney: Australian Broadcasting Corporation.

Ackland, R. (2011). Not so super: Attorney-General must stay alert to mighty gag orders. *National Times.* Retrieved from www.smh.com.au/opinion/politics/not-so-super-attorneygeneral-must-stay-alert-to-mighty-gag-orders-20111027-1mm4f.html

Ackland, R. (2012, May 4). Grotesque cases show failure of regulation. *The Sydney Morning Herald.* Retrieved May 4, 2012, from www.smh.com.au/opinion/society-and-culture/grotesque-cases-show-failure-of-regulation-20120503-1y1nt.html

Ackland, R. (2013, February 22). Say whatever you like, but it's a sorry day for freedom of the press. *The Sydney Morning Herald.* Retrieved February 22, 2013, from www.smh.com.au/opinion/politics/say-whatever-you-like-its-a-sorry-day-for-freedom-of-the-press-20130221-2euab.html

ACMA considers privacy of material sourced from Facebook. (2011). *Media Release.* Sydney.

Adams, R. and Vascellaro, J. (2010, November 30). To publish or not to publish? *The Wall Street Journal republished by The Australian.* Retrieved November 30, 2010, from   www.theaustralian.com.au/business/news/to-publish-on-not-to-publish/story-e6frg90x-1225963302392

Addley, E. (2011, April 6). Phone hacking: Hugh Grant taped former *NoW* journalist. *The Guardian*. Retrieved September 15, 2012, from www.guardian.co.uk/media/2011/apr/06/phone-hacking-hugh-grant-taped

Adjudication No. 1556: Debra Creevy and others/*Herald Sun* (November 2012). (2012) *Australian Press Council*.

Adrian Bayley to serve at least 35 years in jail for rape and murder of Jill Meagher. (2013, June 19). *ABC News*. Retrieved June 19, 2013, from www.abc.net.au/news/2013-06-19/adrian-bayley-sentenced-for-rape-and-murder-of-jill-meagher/4764318

Afghans protest after burning of Koran. (2012, March 27). *ABC News*. Retrieved November 10, 2012, from www.abc.net.au/news/2012-02-21/afghans-protest-after-korans-accidentally-burned/3843176

The Age code of conduct. (2002, n.d.). *The Age*. Retrieved September 19, 2011, from www.theage.com.au/ethicsconduct.html

Age found in contempt. (2006, December 9). *The Age*, p. 27.

Ahmed, T. (2012, October 15). Rueful confessions of an outed plagiarist. *The Australian*, p. 24.

Aide apologises for 'attacks memo' (2001, October 10). *BBC News*. Retrieved February 2, 2013, from http://news.bbc.co.uk/2/hi/uk_news/politics/1588323.stm

Akerman, P. (2013, July 16). Hinch contempt trial over Jill Meagher killer a 'test for social media'. *The Australian*. Retrieved July 20, 2013, from www.theaustralian.com.au/news/nation/hinch-contempt-trial-over-jill-meagher-killer-a-test-for-social-media/story-e6frg6nf-1226680027676

Alberici, E. (2011, October 4). American woman acquitted of sex murder in Italy. *ABC–AM*. Retrieved April 3, 2012, from www.abc.net.au/am/content/2011/s3331405.htm

Albrechtsen, J. (2010, March 31). Hey tabloid voyeurs! You are a threat to justice. *The Australian*. Retrieved March 31, 2010, from www.theaustralian.com.au/news/opinion/hey-tabloid-voyeurs-you-are-a-threat-to-justice/story-e6frg6zo-1225847686028

Alexander, L. and Moore, M. (2012). Deontological Ethics. *The Stanford Encyclopedia of Philosophy*. Retrieved from http://plato.stanford.edu/archives/win2012/entries/ethics-deontological/

Alfonso, F. (2012, April 11). Reporter's courtroom tweet leads to mistrial. *Daily Dot*. Retrieved April 12, 2012, from www.dailydot.com/news-ann-marie-bush-twitter-mistrial-jury-photo-topeka/

Allard, T. (2011, November 12). Rumours of TV deal rock Bali boy's case. *The Sydney Morning Herald*. Retrieved November 12, 2011, from www.smh.com.au/world/rumours-of-tv-deal-rock-bali-boys-case-20111111-1nbsc.html

Alldis, T. (2012, June 21). How PRs will need to adapt to the Fairfax and News Limited upheavals. *Mumbrella*. Retrieved June 22, 2012, from http://mumbrella.com.au/how-prs-will-need-to-adapt-to-the-fairfax-and-news-limited-upheavals-98657

Allen-Mills, T. (2012, December 10). Photo of doomed subway man raises ugly questions. *The Australian*, p. 9.

Altman, A. (2012). Civil Rights. *The Stanford Encyclopedia of Philosophy*. Retrieved from http://plato.stanford.edu/archives/fall2012/entries/civil-rights/

Altschull, J. H. (1990). *From Milton to McLuhan: The ideas behind American journalism*. White Plains, NY: Longman.

Alysen, B., Oakham, M., Patching, R. and Sedorkin, G. (2011). *Reporting in a Multimedia World*. (2nd edn). Sydney: Allen & Unwin.

Amanda Knox signs '$US4 million' book deal. (2012, February 17). *The Sydney Morning Herald*. Retrieved February 17, 2012, from www.smh.com.au/entertainment/books/amanda-know-signs-us4-million-book-deal-20120217-1tcnj.html

Amanda Knox: 'satanic whore' or saint? (2011, October 14). *The Week*, p. 16.

Amanda Lindhout talks candidly about abuse while in captivity. (2013). *CBC News Calgary*. Retrieved from www.cbc.ca/news/canada/calgary/story/2013/02/15/calgary-amanda-lindhout-speaks.html

Amiel, B. (2011, 8 August). The Sun King's alternate universe. *McLean's, 124*, 12–13.

Anderson, B. (2011, September 11). The Most Famous 9/11 Photograph No One Has Seen. *motherboard*. Retrieved January 17, 2013, from http://motherboard.vice.com/blog/the-most-famous-9-11-photograph-no-one-has-seen

Another 30m watch Kony film … in a day. (2012, March 9). *The Sydney Morning Herald*. Retrieved March 9, 2012, from www.smh.com.au/technology/technology-news/another-30m-watch-kony-film-in-a-day-20120309-1uoss.html

Anti-Islam film protests erupt in Sydney. (2012, September 15). *SBS World News*. Retrieved November 17, 2012, from www.sbs.com.au/news/article/1692867/Anti-Islam-film-protests-erupt-in-Sydney

AOL agrees to acquire the *Huffington Post*. (2011, February 7). Retrieved 9 April, 2013, from www.huffingtonpost.com/2011/02/07/aol-huffington-post_n_819375.html

Arnold, D. (2012). Syria: A war reported by citizen-journalists, social media. *Radio Free Europe*. Retrieved from www.rferl.org/content/syria-war-reported-by-citizen-journalists-social-media/24630841.html

Arnold, Z. (2012, August). I'm Craig Thomson's wife: This is my story. *The Australian Women's Weekly*, pp. 31–6.

Atherton, B. (2012, March 8). Who is Joseph Kony? *ABC News*. Retrieved March 8, 2012, from www.abc.net.au/news/2012-03-08/who-is-joseph-jony/3877490

Atton, C. and Hamilton, J. (2008). *Alternative Journalism*. London: Sage.

Atwood, R. A. (2011). Acta Diurna (IT, 59 BC–c. 222 AD). *The handwritten newspapers project*. Retrieved from http://handwrittennews.com/2011/06/20/acta-diurna-it-59-b-c/

Australians views on privacy in broadcast news and current affairs. (2011). *Australian Communications and Media Authority*. Melbourne.

Avery, D. (1995). Battle without a rule book. In L. Chiasson Jr (Ed.). *The press in times of crisis* (pp. 23–40). Westport, Conn: Praeger.

Avieson, J. (1992). Chequebook journalism: a question of ethics. *Australian Journalism Review*, 14(1), 44–50.

Ayres, C. (2005). *War Reporting for Cowards: Between Iraq and a hard place*. London: John Murray.

Azzopardi, S. (2013, January 18). Explainer: Showing some tact, journalists reporting on grief and Molly's Law. *upstart.net.au* Retrieved April 13, 2013, from www.upstart.net.au/2013/01/18/explainer-reporting-on-grief-right-to-privacy-and-mollys-law/

Babington, D. (2011, September 26). Amanda Knox is a 'she-devil', Italian court told. *Reuters*. Retrieved September 26, 2011, from www.reuters.com/article/2011/09/26/us-italy-knox-idUSTRE78P27Y20110926

Bacon, W. and Pavey, S. (2010, March 15). Who's really controlling the media message? *Crikey/Australian Centre for Independent Journalism*. Retrieved March 15, 2010, from www.crikey.com.au/2010/03/15/whos-really-controlling-the-media-message/

Badel, P. (2011, November 14). Sex assault claims emerge in Peter Roebuck death inquest. *The Daily Telegraph*. Retrieved November 14, 2011, from www. dailytelegraph.com.au/sport/sex-assault-claims-emerge-in-peter-roebuck-death-inquest/story-e6frexni-1226194021508

Bainbridge, J. (2009). Going down the hole: Beaconsfield, Celebrities and the Changing News Culture in Australia. *Cultural Studies Review*, 15(1), 43–64.

Baldasty, G. J. (1992). *The commercialization of news in the nineteenth century* (1st edn). Madison: The University of Wisconsin Press.

Ballard, D. (2011, November 29). Sound reporting or a sex-crazed media circus? *UPIU. com* Retrieved April 3, 2012, from www.upiu.com/culture-society/2011/11/29/Sound-reporting-or-a-sex-scrazed-media-circus/UPIU-6961322613835

The Bang Bang Club. Steven Silver (Director), Paramount Pictures (2010).

Banks, D. (2013, February 15). Oscar Pistorius: media unlikely to be in contempt, but could be libellous. *The Guardian*. Retrieved February 16, 2013, from www.guardian.co.uk/media/2013/feb/15/oscar-pistorius-media-contempt-libel/

Barns, G. (2009, March 9). How the media menaced Dennis Ferguson. *Crikey*. Retrieved March 9, 2009, from www.crikey.com.au/2009/03/09/how-the-media-menaced-dennis-ferguson

Barns, G. (2010, March 26). A very public campaign of vilification. *ABC–The Drum*. Retrieved March 29, 2010, from www.abc.net.au/unleashed/stories/s2856611.htm

Bates, D. and Moran, L. (2012, January 12). 'Disgusting' video is 'recruitment tool for the Taliban': Outrage across the world after footage emerged showing US troops 'urinating on dead Afghan bodies'. *The Daily Mail* (UK). Retrieved November 10, 2012, from www.dailymail.co.uk/news/article-2085378/US-troops-urinating-dead-Afghan-bodies-video-used-Taliban-recruitment-tool.html

Bates, S. (2011, May 11). William and the Middletons: the battle for privacy. *The Guardian*. Retrieved May 12, 2011, from www.guardian.co.uk/media/2011/may/11/william-middletons-battle-privacy

Batty, D. (2013, April 24). Two face charges over Duchess of Cambridge topless photos. *The Guardian*. Retrieved April 28, 2013, from www.guardian.co.uk/uk/2013/apr/24/duchess-cambridge-topless-photographs

Baum, G. (2011, November 14). Peter, we hardly knew you, but you told the game like no other. *The Sydney Morning Herald*. Retrieved November 14, 2011, from www.smh.com.au/sport/cricket/peter-we-hardly-knew-you-but-you-told-the-game-like-no-other-20111113-1ndvn.html

Bavas, J. (2013, January 23). Courier-Mail in hot water over custody case coverage. *ABC News*. Retrieved January 24, 2013, from www.abc.net.au/news/2013-01-23/dpp-examines-newspaper-over-custody-case/4480706

BBC defends Gaddafi death images. (2011, October 21). *Press Gazette*. Retrieved January 19, 2013, from www.pressgazette.co.uk/node/48102

Beaujon, A. (2012, September 7). *Columbia Spectator* fires editor who plagiarized from *New York Times* article. *Poynter Institute*. Retrieved September 19, 2012, from www.poynter.org/latest-news/mediawire/187744/columbia-university-editor-plagiarizes-from-new-york-times-article/

Beck, M. (2012, December 21). Fairfax bid to overturn subpoenas. *The Age*, p. 9.

Beck, M. (2013, January 25). Fairfax pair must take stand in bribery case, court rules. *The Age*. Retrieved February 2, 2013, from www.theage.com.au/victoria/fairfax-pair-must-take-stand-in-bribery-case-court-rules-20130125-2daz0.html

Beck, M. and Khokhar, A. (2011, March 7). St Kilda teen lied she was pregnant. *The Age*. Retrieved February 13, 2013, from www.theage.com.au/afl/afl-news/st-kilda-teen-lied-she-was-pregnant-20110306-1bjly.html

Beckham 'lover' nets $A1.9 million from claims: publicist. (2004, April 20). *ABC Online*. Retrieved April 20, 2004, from www.abc.net.au/news/2004-04-20/beckham-lover-nets-a19-million-from-claims/173152

Belsey, A. (1992). Privacy, publicity and politics. In A. Belsey and R. Chadwick (Eds), *Ethical dilemmas in journalism and the media* (pp. 77–92). London: Routledge.

Belsey, A. and R. Chadwick (Eds). (1992). *Ethical dilemmas in journalism and the media*. London: Routledge.

Bensinger, K. and Chang, A. (2013, April 20). Boston bombings: Social media spirals out of control. *Los Angeles Times*. Retrieved 28 April, 2013, from www.latimes.com/news/nationworld/nation/la-fi-boston-bombings-media-20130420,0,19541.story

Berg, C. (2012). *In defence of freedom of speech: From ancient Rome to Andrew Bolt*. Melbourne: Institute of Public Affairs/Mannkal Economic Education Foundation.

Berkovic, N. (2012, August 13). PM's $150m spin doctor brigade. *The Australian*. Retrieved January 15, 2013, from www.theaustralian.com.au/media/pms-150m-spin-doctor-brigade/story-e6frg996-1226448739077

Bernstein, C. (2011, July 9). Murdoch's Watergate? *Newsweek*. Retrieved July 13, 2011, from www.thedailybeast.com/newsweek/2011/07/10/murdoch-s-watergate.print.html

Bernstein, R. (2012) The Normative Core of the Public Sphere. *Political Theory*, 40(6), 767–78.

Berry, J. (2007, February 13). Reporters acted above law: judge. *The Sydney Morning Herald*. Retrieved January 8, 2013, from www.smh.com.au/news/national/reporters-acted-above-law-judge/2007/02/12/1171128899936.html

Bertram, C. (2012). Jean Jacques Rousseau. *Stanford Encyclopedia of Philosophy*. Retrieved from http://plato.stanford.edu/cgi-bin/encyclopedia/archinfo.cgi?entry=rousseau

The Bill of Rights: A brief history. (2002, March 4). ACLU. Retrieved 28 January, 2013, from www.aclu.org/racial-justice_prisoners-rights_drug-law-reform_immigrants-rights/bill-rights-brief-history

Bin Laden raid was revealed on Twitter. (2011, May 2). *BBC News*. Retrieved January 19, 2013, from www.bbc.co.uk/news/technology-13257940

Biography: Alan Johnston. (2007, September). *BBC*. Retrieved November 16, 2012, from www.bbc.co.uk/print/pressoffice/biographies/biogs/news/alan_johnston.shtml

Black, J. and Roberts, C. (2011). *Doing Ethics in Media: Theories and Practical Applications*. New York: Routledge.

Black, J., Steele, B. and Barney, R. (2005). *Doing Ethics in Journalism* (3rd edn). Boston: Allyn & Bacon.

Blair attacks 'feral' media. (2007, June 13). *ABC News*. Retrieved August 25, 2012, from www.abc.net.au/news/2007-06-13/blair-attacks-feral-media/66722

Blake, M. (2012, April 17). The picture that won the Pulitzer: Screaming girl stands amid the carnage of an Afghan suicide attack. *The Daily Mail* (UK). Retrieved January 16, 2013, from www.dailymail.co.uk/news/article-2131084/Pulitzer-Prize-winners-2012-Picture-screaming-girl-standing-amid-Afghan-suicide-attack-carnage.html

Blogger to defend suppression breach charges. (2009, December 26). *The New Zealand Herald*. Retrieved January 27, 2013, from www.nzherald.co.nz/nz/news/article.cfm?c_id=1&objectid=10617454

Blogger on trial for breaching suppressions. (2010, August 25). *The New Zealand Herald*. Retrieved January 27, 2013, from www.nzherald.co.nz/nz/news/article.cfm?c_id=1& objectid= 10668751

Bodey, M. and Ong, T. (2007, January 25). Shark survivor caught in media feeding frenzy. *The Australian*, p. 7.

Bolt, A. (2007, August 15). Costello shows Howard's finished–and so, perhaps is he. *Herald Sun*. Retrieved January 12, 2013, from http://blogs.news.com.au/heraldsun/ andrewbolt/index.php/heraldsun/comments/ costello_shows_howards_finished_and_so_perhaps_is_he

Bolt, A. (2010, October 8). Radio host went too far. *Herald Sun*, pp. 38–9.

Bolt, A. (2011, November 16). Roebuck eulogies mask harsh truth. *Herald Sun*. Retrieved November 16, 2011, from www.heraldsun.com.au/opinion/roebuck-eulogies-mask-harsh-truth/story-e6frfifx-1226196061091

Boreham, G. (2012). Convergence Review: Commonwealth of Australia.

Borger, J. (2005, October 10). Miller's twisted tale. *The Guardian*. Retrieved January 12, 2013, from www.guardian.co.uk/media/2005/oct/10/mondaymediasection

Bourdieu, P. (1998). *On television and journalism* (P. Parkhurst, Trans.). London: Pluto Press.

Bourke, E. and Binnie, K. (2010, February 25). Trinity's murder inflames Facebook debate. *ABC News*. Retrieved February 26, 2010, from www.abc.net.au/news/2010-02-25/trinitys-murder-inflames-facebook-debate/342764

Boynton, R. (2008). Checkbook journalism revisited. *Columbia Journalism Review*. January–February. Retrieved February 25, 2008, from www.cjr.org/essay/checkbook_journalism_revisited.php

Brennan, N., Bonney, N. and Brennan, K. (2011). *The Price of Life: A true story of kidnap and ransom*. Melbourne: Penguin Books.

Brent, P. (2012, February 23). Not so fast journalists. *Mumble blog, The Australian*. Retrieved February 25, 2012, from http://blogs.theaustralian.com.au/mumble/index.php/theaustralian/comments/media_hype/

Brislin, T. (2004). Empowerment as a universal ethic in global journalism. *Journal of Mass Media Ethics: Exploring Questions of Media Morality*, 19(2), 130–7.

Bristow, W. (2011). Enlightenment. *The Stanford Encyclopedia of Philosophy*. Retrieved from http://plato.stanford.edu/cgi-bin/encyclopedia/archinfo.cgi?entry=enlightenment

British Library. (n.d.). Magna Carta. Retrieved 12 February, 2013, from www.bl.uk/ treasures/magnacarta/index.html

Bronstein, S. and McIntyre, J. (2006, May 28). Investigation reveals new Tillman questions. *CNN.com*. Retrieved November 18, 2012, from http://edition.cnn.com/ 2006/US/05/27/pat.tillman/index.html

Brook, S. (2012, September 4). One in seven journalist jobs lost, says union. *The Australian*. Retrieved September 5, 2012, from www.theaustralian.com.au/media/one-in-seven-journalist-jobs-lost-says-union/story-e6frg996-1226464999203

Brown, A. (2012, August 31). Whistle-blower laws good for governance. *The Australian* p. 29.

Brown, M. (2012, June 9–10). Three decades to reach justice. *The Sydney Morning Herald*, p. 6 (News Review).

Brown, T. (2007). *The Diana Chronicles*. New York: Broadway Books.

Brown, T. (2011, July 4–11). Diana at 50: If She Were Here Now. *Newsweek*. Retrieved January 19, 2013, from www.thedailybeast.com/newsweek/2011/06/26/what-princess-diana-s-life-might-look-like-now.html

Brunton, R. (2002, 19 January). Bias depends on point of view. *Courier-Mail*, p. 28.

Bryant, C. (2013, February 15). A Political Life: Reeva Steenkamp, The Sun, and when the profit motive turns ugly. *The Independent* (UK). Retrieved February 17, 2013, from www.independent.co.uk/voices/comment/a-political-life-reeva-steenkamp-the-sun-and-when-the-profit-motive-turns-ugly-8497320.html

Bryant settles rape damaged claim. (2005, March 3). *The Sydney Morning Herald*. Retrieved January 25, 2013, from www.smh.com.au/news/Sport/Bryant-settles-rape-damages-claim/2005/03/03/1109700587313.html

Bullock, A. and Trombley, S. (Eds). (2000). *The new Fontana dictionary of modern thought* (3rd edn). London: HarperCollins.

Burnet, D. (1992). Freedom of Speech, the media and the law. In A. Besley and R. Chadwick (Eds), *Ethical dilemmas in journalism and the media* (pp. 49–61). London: Routledge.

Burns, E. (2006). *Infamous Scribblers: The founding fathers and the rowdy beginnings of American journalism*. New York: Public Affairs.

Burrell, I. (2012, August 21). Fake Sheikh's editor fails to find evidence for his grand claim to Leveson. *The Independent*. Retrieved September 12, 2012, from www.independent.co.uk/news/media/press/fake-sheikhs-editor-fails-to-find-evidence-for-his-grand-claim-to-leveson-8063485.html

Button, J. (2007, September 24). Madeleine and the media: a news frenzy fed by too few facts. *The Age*. Retrieved September 245, 2007, from www.theage.com.au/news/opinion/a-news-frenzy-fed-by-too-few-facts/2007/09/23/1190486129801.html

Buttry, S. (2012). Gatekeepers need to find new value when the fences have blown away. Retrieved from http://stevebuttry.wordpress.com/2012/04/30/gatekeepers-need-to-find-new-value-when-the-fences-have-blown-away/

Byrne, E. (2012, November 7). Court releases reasons for international custody case ruling. *ABC News*. Retrieved January 24, 2013, from www.abc.net.au/news/2012-11-07/court-releases-reasons-for-international-custody-case-ruling/4358228

Byrne, F. (2008, March 16). Carey sells story for $180,000. *The Daily Telegraph*. Retrieved March 16, 2008, from www.news.com.au/dailytelegraph/story/0,22049,23382073-5001021,00.html

Calame, B. (2007, April 22). Revisiting The Times's Coverage of the Duke Rape Case. *The New York Times*. Retrieved January 2, 2013, from www.nytimes.com/2007/04/22/opinion/22pubed.html

Caldwell, A. (2012, November 19). *The Age* sued by traumatised photographer. *ABC PM*. Retrieved December 19, 2012, from www.abc.net.au/pm/content/2012/s3636143.htm

Caldwell, A. (2013, April 3). Call for journalist protection amid legal threats. *ABC Current Affairs* (PM). Retrieved April 3, 2013, from www.abc.net.au/news/2013-04-02/journalist-protection-call-amid-legal-threats/4606302

Callick, R. (2012, June 30). The shrinking world of news. *The Australian*. Retrieved July 9, 2012, from www.theaustralian.com.au/news/world/the-shrinking-world-of-news/story-e6frg6ux-1226412666694

Calligeros, M. (2013). The *Courier-Mail* pleads guilty to family law breach in the Italian sisters' custody case. *Brisbane Times*. Retrieved from www.brisbanetimes.com.au/queensland/the-couriermail-pleads-guilty-to-family-law-breach-in-the-italian-sisters-custody-case-20130823-2sfii.html

Callinicos, A. (1987). *The revolutionary ideas of Marx*. London: Bookmarks.

Callinicos, A. (1995). *Theories and Narratives: Reflections on the philosophy of history.* Cambridge: Polity Press.

Campbell, K. (2011). Legal Rights. *The Stanford Encyclopedia of Philosophy.* Retrieved from http://plato.stanford.edu/archives/spr2011/entries/legal-rights

Cape Cod Times reporter fabricated sources. (2012, December 6). *The Australian.* Retrieved December 20, 2012, from www.theaustralian.com.au/media/cape-cod-times-reporter-fabricated-sources/story-e6frg996-1226530966574

Carr, D. (2012, December 5). Train Wreck: The New York Post's Subway Cover. *Media Decoder (The New York Times.)* Retrieved January 16, 2013, from http://mediadecoder.blogs.nytimes.com/2012/12/05/train-wreck-the-new-york-posts-subway-cover/

Cash for Comment. (2010, April 26). *The Australian*, p. 28.

Cebrian, M. (2013, February 6). False tweets a weapon with no defence. *The Australian.* Retrieved February 4, 2013, from www.theaustralian.com.au/media/opinion/false-tweets-a-weapon-with-no-defence/story-e6frg99o-1226567745653

Chadwick, P. and Mullaly, J. (1997). Privacy and the Media: Communications Law Centre.

Chambers, M. and Moran, S. (2013, January 8). Hoaxer snares coalmining investors and gullible media. *The Australian.* Retrieved January 8, 2013, from www.theaustralian.com.au/business/mining-energy/hoaxer-snares-coalmining-investors-and-gullible-media/story-e6frg9df-1226549202727

Channel Nine denies deal with Bali boy. (2011, November 7). *ABC News.* Retrieved November 7, 2011, from www.abc.net.au/news/2011-11-07/concern-over-bali-boy-tv-deal/3639124

Charges against journalists 'an attack on press freedom'. (2013). *The Age.* Retrieved from www.theage.com.au/victoria/charges-against-journalists-an-attack-on-press-freedom-20130405-2hcos.html

Cheney's aide was spy source. (2005, October 1–2). *The Weekend Australian*, p. 14.

Cherry, G. (2007, April 13). Rape racism: Case dropped. *The Daily Telegraph*, p. 19.

Cheshire, D. M. (1997). *Between facts and norms: Contributions to a discourse theory of law and democracy.* Paper presented at the Alta Conference on Argumentation.

Chiasson Jr, L. (Ed.). (1995). *The press in times of crisis.* Westport, Conn: Praeger.

Christensen, N. (2011, August 27). Pulver case reignites privacy debate. *The Australian*, p. 7.

Christensen, N. (2012, June 18). Queensland Police fall foul of Facebook followers. *The Australian.* Retrieved June 18, 2012, from www.theaustralian.com.au/media/monday-section/queensland-police-fall-foul-of-facebook-followers/story-fna1k39o-12263980 18259

Christensen, N. and Akerman, P. (2011, November 5–6). No-tweeting edict 'a timely reminder'. *The Weekend Australian*, p. 9.

Christensen, N. and Meade, A. (2012, February 27). Twitter: never wrong for long? *The Australian.* Retrieved February 27, 2012, from http://blogs.theaustralian.news.com.au/themediamachine/index.php/theaustralian/comments/twitter_never_wrong_for_long/

Chulov, M. (2007, July 5). Nightmare is over for BBC hostage. *The Australian*, p. 11.

Churcher, S. (2007, April 24). The most savage attack on Diana EVER. *The Daily Mail (UK).* Retrieved January 20, 2013, from www.dailymail.co.uk/femail/article-449912/The-savage-attack-Diana-EVER.html

Clayfield, M. (2012). Tweet the Press. *Metro*, pp. 92–7.

Code of Ethics. (1996, n.d.). *Society of Professional Journalists*. Retrieved February 20, 2013, from www.spj.org/ethicscode.asp

Cohen, M. (2011). The super injunction: what is it and does it matter? *The Drum*. Retrieved from www.abc.net.au/unleashed/2730684.html

Coleman, R. (2011). Journalists' moral judgment about children: Do as I say, not as I do? *Journalism Practice*, 5(3), 257–71.

Coleman, S. and Ross, K. (2010). *The public and the media: "Them" and "Us" in media discourse*. Chichester, UK: Wiley-Blackwell.

Colley, A. (2013, February 28). Union warns court rules could hurt new media. *The Australian*. Retrieved March 19, 2013, from www.theaustralian.com.au/media/recognised-journalists-exempt-from-court-security-rules/story-e6frg996-1226587743009

Collins, L., Bates, D., Boyle, L., Miller, D. and Stebner, B. (2012, December 5). 'There is no way I could have saved him': Photographer claims he was too far away to pull 'doomed' subway rider off train tracks. *The Daily Mail* (UK). Retrieved January 3, 2013, from www.dailymail.co.uk/news/article-2243344/Subway-death-New-York-Post-photographer-claims-help-doomed-Ki-Suk-Han.html

Collins, S-J. (2007, October 10). Snapshot of a soldier, a fisherman, a dad. *The Sydney Morning Herald*, p. 1.

Colossus of Canberra. (2003, June 4). *The Gold Coast Bulletin*, p. 1.

Columnist sacked over Logies Twitter 'jokes'. (2010, May 5). *ABC News*. Retrieved May 5, 2010, from www.abc.net.au/news/2010-05-05/columnist-sacked-over-logies-twitter-jokes/422704

Colvin, M. (2010, November 10). Truth at All Costs. *mariecolvin.org* Retrieved November 7, 2012, from mariecolvin.org/in-her-own-words

Connolly, K. (2013, April 4). Right to erasure protects people's freedom to forget the past, says expert. *The Guardian*. Retrieved from www.guardian.co.uk/technology/2013/apr/04/right-erasure-protects-freedom-forget-past

Conroy, P. and Ryle, G. (1996, May 1). Tasmanian DPP Warns Media On Use Of Photo. *The Age*, p. 2.

Conroy, S. (2013). Government response to Convergence Review and Finkelstein Inquiry. Media Release.

Constant, B. (2002). The Spirit of Conquest and Usurpation and their Relation to European Civilization. In B. Fontana (Ed.). *Constant: Political Writings*. Cambridge: Cambridge University Press.

Cook, J. (2011, May/June). Pay Up. *Columbia Journalism Review*. Retrieved June 27, 2011, from www.cjr.org/essay/pay_up.php

Cooper, M. and Raftery, I. (2011, October 4). A Court Fight and a Tireless Battle over an Image. Retrieved October 7, 2011, from www.nytimes.com/2011/10/05/us/court-fight-and-tireless-battle-over-an-image.html

Correcting the record: *Times* reporter who resigned leaves long trail of deception. (2003, May 11). *The New York Times*, p. 1.

Coultan, M. (2007, April 13). Soul-searching as lacrosse sex case exposes flawed American justice. *The Age*, p. 8.

Couric, K. (2009, February 11). What Really Happened To Pat Tillman? *60 Minutes*. Retrieved November 18, 2012, from www.cbsnews.com/8301-18560_162-4061656.html

Coward, R. (2007). What the butler started: Relations between British tabloids and the monarchy in the fall-out from the Paul Burrell trial. *Journalism Practice*, 1(2), 245–60.

Cowie, T. (2012, June 22). Hacks v flacks: the 'grave-dancing' publicist who created a storm. *Crikey.* Retrieved June 22, 2012, from www.crikey.com.au/2012/06/22/hacks-v-flacks-the-grave-dancing-publicist-who-created-a-storm/

Cozens, C. (2006, January 20). Eriksson to sue News of the World. *The Guardian.* Retrieved September 12, 2012, from www.guardian.co.uk/media/2006/jan/20/newsoftheworld.pressand publishing

Crawford, C. (2009, December 6). How a sly Tiger changed stripes to become king of the bungle. *The Sunday Mail* (Queensland), pp. 10–11.

Crikey 'gossip' dismissed in shield debate. (2011, October 26). *The Sydney Morning Herald.* Retrieved January 10, 2013, from news.smh.com.au/breaking-news-national/crikey-gossip-dismissed-in-shield-debate-20111026-1mjxk.html

Crook, A. (2010, October 6). The Pies' accused: why, this time, hasn't the media named them? *Crikey.* Retrieved January 3, 2013, from www.crikey.com.au/2010/10/06/the-pies-accused-why-this-time-hasnt-the-media-named-them/

Crook, A. (2011, August 15). *The Oz* runs different (sic) two different Morcombe stories. *Crikey.* Retrieved August 15, 2011, from www.crikey.com.au/2011/08/15/media-briefs-fairfax-paywall-review-rethinking-internet-freedom/

Cudd, A. (2012). Contractarianism. *The Stanford Encyclopedia of Philosophy.* Retrieved from http://plato.stanford.edu/archives/fall2012/entries/contractarianism/

Cuillier, D. (2009). Mortality Morality: Effects of death thoughts on journalism students' attitudes towards relativism, idealism and ethics. *Journal of Mass Media Ethics: Exploring Questions of Media Morality, 24*(1), 40–58.

Cullen, S. (2013, January 31). Police arrest MP Craig Thomson on 150 fraud charges. *ABC News.* Retrieved January 31, 2013, from www.abc.net.au/news/2013-01-31/craig-thomson-arrested/4493722

Cuneo, C. (2011, November 26). Bali teen gets a slap on the wrist. *Herald Sun,* p. 5.

Cuneo, C. (2012, February 8). Death on Facebook first–teen twins find out online brother killed in triple-fatal crash. *The Daily Telegraph.* Retrieved February 8, 2010, from www.dailytelegraph.com.au/news/death-on-facebook-first-teen-twins-online-find-their-brother-killed-in-triple-fatal-crash/story-e6freuy9-1225827634834

Cunningham, B. (2003). Re-thinking objectivity. *Columbia Journalism Review, 42*(2), 24–32.

Cunningham, S. B. (1999). Getting it right: Aristotle's 'Golden Mean' as theory deterioration. *Journal of Mass Media Ethics: Exploring Questions of Media Morality, 14*(1), 5–15.

Curran, J. (1991). Re-thinking the media as public sphere. In P. Dahlgren and C. Sparks (Eds), *Communication and citizenship: journalism and the public sphere in the new media age* (pp. 27–56). London & New York: Routledge.

Dadisman, S. (2007, June/July). Naming Names. *American Journalism Review.* Retrieved January 3, 2013, from www.ajr.org/article.asp?id=4380

Dale, A. (2012, November 21). Facing her demon. *The Daily Telegraph,* pp. 1 and 4.

Dale, H. (2008, January 4). Azaria again. *Online Opinion.* Retrieved January 4, 2008, from www.onlineopinion.com.au/print.asp?article=6833

Dalton, R. (2003, May 15). NY Times comes clean on reporter who made up the news. *The Australian,* p. 10.

Daniel, M. (2009). *Scandal and Civility: Journalism and the birth of American democracy.* New York: OUP.

Davidson, N. (2012). *How revolutionary were the Bourgeois Revolutions.* Chicago: Haymarket Books.

Davies, L. (2010, March 18). Ita Buttrose' nephew jailed for up to 16 years over cocaine haul. *The Daily Telegraph.* Retrieved August 27, 2012, from www.dailytelegraph. com.au/news/ita-buttroses-nephew-jailed-for-up-to-16-years-over-cocaine-haul/story-e6freuy9-1225842262288

Davies, N. (2008). *Flat Earth News.* London: Chatto & Windus.

Davis, G. (2011, November 8). Chequebook journalism in Bali drug boy case, irresponsible, stupid. *Pacific Media Centre.* Retrieved November 25, 2011, from www.pmc.aut.ac.nz/articles/chequebook-journalism-bali-boy-case-irresponsible-stupid

Davis, M. (2002, 12–13 January). Great white noise. *The Sydney Morning Herald,* pp. 4–5.

Dawtrey, Z. (2013, January 11). We're alive, we're a family ... not one hair on a child's head has been lost. *Hobart Mercury,* pp. 4–5.

Day, M. (2004, July 8). Truth will out, dirt will be dug, but slathering frenzy's not on. *The Australian,* p. 22.

Day, M. (2010, June 7). Sting on Fergie beyond the bounds. *The Australian (media section),* p. 27.

Day the reptiles rallied to the dopey duchess. (2010, May 25). *The Sydney Morning Herald.* Retrieved May 25, 2010, from www.smh.com.au/lifestyle/people/day-the-reptiles-rallied-to-the-dopey-duchess-20100525-w919.html

de Bruin, M. (2000). Gender, organizational and professional identities in journalism. *Journalism, 1*(2), 217–38.

Deans, J. (2011, June 2). Julian Assange wins Martha Gellhorn journalism prize. *The Guardian.* Retrieved June 22, 2012, from www.guardian.co.uk/media/2011/jun/02/julian-assange-martha-gellhorn-prize

Deards, H. (2009, January 19). Twitter first off the mark with Hudson plane crash coverage. *Editors Weblog.* Retrieved January 18, 2013, from www.editorsweblog.org/2009/01/19/twitter-first-off-the-mark-with-hudson-plane-crash-coverage

Death of a gangster. (2010, May 3). *Who magazine,* 1 and 21–6.

Deery, S. (2013). *The Age* journalists Royce Millar, Nick McKenzie and Ben Schneiders admit to illegally accessing ALP electoral database. *Herald Sun.* Retrieved from www.heraldsun.com.au/news/law-order/the-age-journalists-royce-millar-nick-mckenzie-and-ben-schneiders-admit-to-illegally-accessing-alp-electoral-database/story-fni0fee2-1226689435551

Defiant Derryn Hinch vows to continue campaign to name sex offenders. (2011, December 21). *news.com.au.* Retrieved January 27, 2013, from www.news.com.au/national-old/no-more-silent-nights-for-derryn-hinch/story-e6frfkvr-1226227172499

Defoe, D. (1704). An Essay on the Regulation of the Press. Retrieved from www.luminarium.org/renascence-editions/defoe2.html

The depressing tale of Johann Hari. (2011, September 15). *Bagehot's notebook (The Economist).* Retrieved September 21, 2012, from www.economist.com/blogs/bagehot/2011/09/unethical-journalism

Devine, M. (2012, April 24). Fair game for husband-stealers Retrieved May 2, 2012, from http://blogs.news.com.au/dailytelegraph/mirandadevine/index.php/dailytelegraph/comments/fair_game_ for_husband_stealers/

Dick, T. (2011, October 11). Naming the Bali boy. *The Sydney Morning Herald.* Retrieved September 8, 2012, from www.smh.com.au/opinion/blogs/media-matters/naming-the-bali-boy-20111010-1lge7.html

Dickinson, A. (2011, August 16). Experts warn of Facebook, Twitter contempt of court in Daniel Morcombe case. *The Courier Mail.* Retrieved August 16, 2011, from www.couriermail.com.au/news/technlogy/experts-warn-of-facebook-twitter-contempt-of-court-in-daniel-morcombe-case/story-e6frep1o-1226115509286

Digital Australians–Expectations about media content in a converging media environment. (2011, October 7). *Australian Communications and Media Authority.* Retrieved January 19, 2013, from www.acma.gov.au/webwr/_assets/main/lib410130/digital_australians-complete.pdf

Dillon Kinkead, L. (2003). Tabloid targets *Trib. Desert News.* Retrieved from: http://web.archive.org/web/20031212135711/http://deseretnews.com/dn/view/0,1249,485033665,00.html

Dodd, A. (2011a, February 15). Baffling logic in ACMA clearing Seven over Campbell outing. *Crikey.* Retrieved February 15, 2011, from www.crikey.com.au/2011/02/14/baffling-logic-in-acma-clearing-seven-over-campbell-outing/

Dodd, A. (2011b, July 13). Suppression-happy SA leaves naming of charged MP to social media. *Crikey.* Retrieved July 13, 2011, from www.crikey.com.au/2011/07/13/south-australia-mp-child-pornographycharges/

Don't shoot (cartoon). (2004, November 18). *The Australian,* p. 22.

Doomed. (2012, December 4). *New York Post,* p. 1.

Dorsett, J. and Seinor, B. (2013, February 18). British backpacker sells outback survival story. *ABC News.* Retrieved February 18, 2013, from www.abc.net.au/news/2013-02-17/british-backpacker-sells-outback-survival-story/4523858

Dowdell, A. (2012, September 24). Bernard Finnigan's name was all over the internet despite suppression order. *Adelaide Now.* Retrieved September 28, 2012, from www.adelaidenow.com.au/news/south-australia/bernard-finnigans-name-was-all-over-the-internet-despite-suppression-order/story-e6frea83-1226480605607

Dowsley, A. (2011, January 28). Collingwood stars cleared of sex assault. *Herald Sun.* Retrieved January 4, 2013, from www.perthnow.com.au/news/magpies-stars-in-the-clear/story-e6frg12c-1225996599077

Dowsley, A. and Harris, A. (2010, October 5). Pies Sex Quiz. *Herald Sun,* p. 1.

Dr David Kelly: Controversial death examined. (2011, December 17). *BBC News.* Retrieved January 9, 2013, from www.bbc.co.uk/news/uk-13716127

Dreyfus, S. (2013, April 2). Keeping us honest: protecting whistle-blowers. *The Conversation.* Retrieved April 2, 2013, from http://theconversation.com/keeping-us-honest-protecting-whistleblowers-13131

Duffy, M. (2003, October 13). Leaking with a Vengeance. *Time,* 28–36.

Duke, K. (2005). Journalists admit failing to check accuracy of leaked stories. *MediaGuardian.* Retrieved from www.guardian.co.uk/media/2005/sep/19/pressand publishing1

Dunlop, T. (2012, October 10). The gatekeepers of news have lost their keys. *ABC–The Drum.* Retrieved October 10, 2012, from www.abc.net.au/unleashed/4305220.html

Dunt, I. (2013, February 15). Outrage over *Sun's* Reeva Steenkamp front page. *Yahoo.com.* Retrieved February 17, 2013, from news.yahoo.com/outrage-over-suns-reeva-steenkamp-front-page-090616313.html

Dutton, W. H. (2009). The fifth estate emerging through the network of networks. *Prometheus: Critical studies in innovation, 27*(1), 1–15.

Edgar, A. (1992). Objectivity, bias and truth. In A. Belsey and R. Chadwick (Eds), *Ethical dilemmas in journalism and the media* (pp. 112–29). London: Routledge.

Editor sacked over 'hoax' photos. (2004, May 14). *BBC News*. Retrieved January 30, 2013, from news.bbc.co.uk/2/hi/uk_news/politics/3716151.stm

Editor said policeman's death would boost sales. (2010, September 10). *ABC News*. Retrieved September 10, 2010, from www.abc.net.au/news/2010-09-10/editor-said-policemans-death-would-boost-sales/2256212

Editorial–The Bulletin. (2008, September 2). *The Gold Coast Bulletin*, p. 4.

Editorial–We must be allowed to report freely. (2008, September 2). *The Gold Coast Bulletin*, p. 14.

Editorial Code of Conduct. (2011) *Herald and Weekly Times*.

Editorial Code of Conduct: Social Media Policy. (2011, September 12). *Herald and Weekly Times*. Retrieved February 8, 2013, from http://resources.news.com.au/files/2011/09/12/1226134/518211-hwt-social-media-policy.pdf

Edwards, M. (2010, May 21). Outing of David Campbell raises ethical questions. *ABC–PM*. Retrieved December 11, 2010, from www.abc.net.au/pm/content/2010/s2906275.htm

Eggerking, K. (1998). Review of Schultz. (1998). Reviving the fourth estate. *Australian Journalism Review, 20*(2), 164–8.

El-Hennawy, N. (2010). Leftwing journalists resurrect independent daily on the web. *Egypt Independent*. Retrieved www.egyptindependent.com/news/leftwing-journalists-resurrect-independent-daily-web

Elks, S. (2013, April 5). *Courier Mail* newspaper in court over custody battle photos. *The Australian*. Retrieved April 5, 2013, from www.theaustralian.com.au/media/courier-mail-newspaper-in-court-over-custody-battle-photos/story-e6frg996-1226613146431?sv=e611581da 972de3b46c0d0d8011312a8

Elliott, F. (2012, October 10). Teen icon targeted by Taliban. *The Australian*. Retrieved November 17, 2012, from www.theaustralian.com.au/news/world/taliban-shoots-teen-activist-in-head/story-fnb64oi6-1226492525865

Elliott, T. (2011, June 25). Hostage for 462 days … tale of survival out of Africa. *The Sydney Morning Herald*. Retrieved November 16, 2012, from www.smh.com.au/national/hostage-for-462-days–tale-of-survival-out-of-africa-20110624-1gjmb.html

English, B. (2004, April 12). Second woman tells of two-year Beckham affair. *The Courier Mail*, p. 3.

Este, J. (2003, June 12–18). Shabby sheik's chequebook heist fails to add up for *NoW*. *The Australian (media section)*, p. 10.

EU judges to hear Google 'right to be forgotten' case. (2013). *The Telegraph*. Retrieved from www.telegraph.co.uk/technology/google/9895279/EU-judges-to-hear-Google-right-to-be-forgotten- case.html

Evans, M. (2011, December 19). Hero or traitor? Private Manning fronts court over Wikileaks 'betrayal'. *The Australian*, p. 7.

Facebook bows to police demands over hate pages related to the killing of Jill Meagher. (2012, October 3). *The Australian*. Retrieved October 4, 2012, from www.theaustralian.com.au/news/nation/facebook-bows-to-police-demands-over-hate-pages-related-to-the-killing-of-jill-meagher/story-e6frg6nf-1226487331653

Fair Game (2010). Doug Liman (Director), Summit Entertainment.

Fairfax Media Group Social Media Policy. (2011, July 1). *Fairfax Media*. Retrieved February 8, 2013, from http://resources.news.com.au/files/2011/09/12/1226134/518423-fairfax-social-media-policy.pdf

Farhi, P. (2012, December 21). How race to report overtook the facts. *The Washington Post*, reproduced by *The Sydney Morning Herald*. Retrieved December 21, 2012, from www.smh.com.au/world/how-the-race-to-report-overtook-the-facts-20121220-2bpc6.html

Faris, P. (2010, May 22–23). Silenced by 'risk of unfair trial'. *The Weekend Australian*, p. 2.

Farnsworth, S. (2012, November 19). Former *Age* photographer sues over Bali trauma. *ABC News*. Retrieved November 19, 2012, from www.abc.net.au/news/2012-11-19/former-age-photographer-sues-over-job-trauma/4380042

Fearing incitement of violence Obama vetoes pix release. (2011, May 5). *APN News*. Retrieved January 19, 2013, from http://apnnews.com/2011/05/05/fearing-incitement-of-violence-obama-vetoes-pix-release/

Feighery, G. (2009). Two visions of responsibility: How national commissions contributed to journalism ethics, 1963–75. *Journalism and Communication Monographs, 11*(2), 167–210.

Feldman, C. (2012). No time to think: Journalism, news and speed in the US presidential race 2012. Paper presented at the *Critical Times? Changing journalism in a changing world*, JEAA Conference, Melbourne.

Ferguson, J. and Le Grand, C. (2012, October 19). *Age* trio faces DPP scrutiny on ALP files. *The Australian*. Retrieved October 19, 2012, from www.theaustralian.com.au/national-affairs/state-politics/age-trio-faces-dpp-scrutiny-on-alp-files/story-e6frgczx-1226498896792

Ferguson, S. (2009a, May 11). Code of Silence. *Four Corners*. Retrieved July 12, 2012, from www.abc.net.au/4corners/content/2009/s2567972.htm

Ferguson, S. (2009b). *Sport, sex and journalism–what's the story?* Paper presented at the George Munster Forum, Sydney.

Fiasson, J. (2010, May 21). David Campbell: Media Shame. *The Daily Bludge*. Retrieved December 11, 2010, from http://dailybludge.com.au/2010/05/david-campbell-media-shame

Fife-Yeomans, J. (2012, April 24). Caroline Byrne's dad slams 60 Minutes after they paid Gordon Wood $200,000. *The Daily Telegraph*. Retrieved April 24, 2012, from www.news.com.au/national/caroline-byrnes-dad-slams-60-minutes-after-they-paid-gordon-wood-200000-for-an-interview/story-e6frfkvr-1226336629024

Filleting Facebook. (2007, October 29). *Media Watch*. Retrieved October 30, 2007, from www.abc.net.au/mediawatch/transcripts/s2074079.htm

Finkelstein, R. and Ricketson, M. (2012). *Report of the Independent Inquiry into the Media and Media Regulation*.

Fish, S. (1994). *There's no such thing as free speech: and it's a good thing, too*. New York: OUP.

Flash Harry: Prince's 'strip billiards' photos spark a right royal row. (2012, August 23). *The Sydney Morning Herald*. Retrieved August 23, 2012, from www.smh.com.au/lifestyle/celebrity/flash-harry-princes-strip-billiards-photos-spark-a-right-royal-row-20120823-24ngq.html

Flitton, D. (2012, September 27). No-ransom policy to stay. *The Sydney Morning Herald*. Retrieved November 18, 2012, from www.smh.com.au/opinion/political-news/noransom-policy-to-stay-29120926-26lii.html

Fonseca, P. (2013). Snowden journalist to publish UK secrets after Britain detains partner. Reuters. Retrieved from www.reuters.com/article/2013/08/19/us-usa-security-snowden-brazil-idUSBRE97I0LZ20130819

Forbes, M. (2004, June 26). Axis of Deceit. *The Age*. Retrieved January 11, 2013, from www.theage.com.au/articles/2004/06/24/1088046216900.html

Force, P. (2009). Voltaire and the necessity of modern history. *Modern Intellectual History, 6*(3), 457–84.

Foreman, J. (2011, n.d.). Dirty Hari. *Commentary magazine*. Retrieved September 21, 2012, from www.commentarymagazine.com/article/dirty-hari/

Forgive me sponsors for I have sinned: Tiger slammed over 'staged' apology. (2010, February 21). *The Sunday Mail* (Queensland), p. 14.

Former PM John Howard says he didn't send troops to Iraq based on WMD 'lie'. (2012). AAP/AP. *news.com.au*. Retrieved from www.news.com.au/national-news/former-pm-john-howard-says-he-didnt-send-troops-to-iraq-based-on-wmd-lie/story-fncynjr2-1226616928637

Former staff photographer sues Age over 2002 Bali trauma. (2012, November 19). *The Australian*. Retrieved November 19, 2012, from www.theaustralian.com.au/media/former-staff-photographer-sues-age-over-2002-bali-trauma/story-e6frg996-1226519822099

Fountein, L. (2013, January 31). MP's child porn trial to be reconsidered. *ABC News*. Retrieved January 31, 2013, from www.abc.net.au/news/2013-01-30/state-mp-on-child-pornography-charges/4491340

Franklin, B. (1722, July 2). *The New-England Courant*. Retrieved from www.ushistory.org/franklin/courant/issue49.htm

Franklin, B. and Carlson, M. (Eds). (2011). *Journalists, sources and credibility: New perspectives*. New York, London: Routledge.

Franklin, M. (2007, August 15). Costello 'lies' on challenge. *The Australian*. Retrieved January 12, 2013, from www.theaustralian.com.au/news/costello-lies-on-challenge/story-e6frg6no-1111114186282

Frater, J. (2008, 9 June). Top 10 reasons the Dark Ages were not dark. *listverse* Retrieved 12 February, 2013, from http://listverse.com/2008/06/09/top-10-reasons-the-dark-ages-were-not-dark/

Freed Australian describes hostage ordeal. (2009, November 26). *ABC News*. Retrieved November 26, 2009, from www.abc.net.au/news/2009-11-26/freed-australian-describes-hostage-ordeal/1157210

Freed female sailor feared death. (2007, April 9). *ABC News*. Retrieved April 9, 2007, from www.abc.net.au/news/newsitems/200704/s1892634.htm

Freeman, S. (2012). Original Position. *Stanford Encyclopedia of Philosophy*. Retrieved from http://plato.stanford.edu/archives/spr2012/entries/original-position/

Freund, C. P. (1999, June 1). The Atrocity Exhibition: A War Fuelled by Imagery. *Reason Magazine*. Retrieved January 17, 2013, from http://reason.com/archives/1999/06/01/the-atrocity-exhibition

Friend, C. and Singer, J. B. (2007). *Online journalism ethics: Traditions and transitions*. New York: M.E. Sharpe.

Frost, C., Hutchings, S., Miazhavich, G. and Nickels, H. (2011). Between impartiality and ideology: the BBC's paradoxical remit and the case of Islam-related television news. *Journalism Studies, 12*(2), 221–38.

Gallup. (2011, December 1). *Honesty/Ethics in Professions*. Retrieved June 24, 2012, from www.gallup.com/poll/1654/honesty-ethics-professions.aspx

Gandy, O. (1982). *Beyond Agenda Setting: Information Subsidies and Public Policy*. Norwood, New Jersey: Ablex Publishing.

Gayle, D. (2011, Octover 21). Milly Dowler's family receive 2m pounds settlement from Rupert Murdoch over *News of the World* phone hacking. *The Daily Mail* (UK). Retrieved August 20, 2012, from www.dailymail.co.uk/news/article-2051974/Milly-Dowlers-family-receive-2m-settlement-Rupert-Murdoch-News-World-phone-hacking.html

Glionna, J. (2013, May 15). Simpson seeks new trial in robbery case. *Los Angeles Times*, republished by *The Sydney Morning Herald*. Retrieved May 15, 2013, from www.smh.com.au/world/simpson-seeks-new-trial-in-robbery-case-20130514-2jkf0.html

Glover, D. (2004). *Orwell's Australia: From Cold War to Culture Wars*. Melbourne: Scribe.

Godfrey, A. (2012, June 12). As it happened: Coroner rules Azaria Chamberlain died as a result of a dingo attack. *The Daily Telegraph*. Retrieved March 6, 2013, from www.dailytelegraph.com.au/archive/national-old/the-azaria-chamberlain-inquest-live/story-e6freuzr-1226392517376

Gomes, P. (2013, May 2). It's a good policy to have rules in writing. *The New York Times*. Retrieved from www.nytimes.com/roomfordebate/2013/04/02/should-social-media-activity-cost-you-your-job/its-a-good-policy-to-have-social-media-rules-in-writing

Goodman, J. D. and Ruderman, W. (2013). Police Dept. sets rules for officers' use of social media. *The New York Times*. Retrieved from www.nytimes.com/2013/03/29/nyregion/new-york-police-dept-issues-guidelines-for-social-media.html?_r=0

Gordon, D. A., Kittross, J. M., Merrill, J. C., Babcock, W. and Dorsher, M. (2011). *Controversies in Media Ethics* (3rd edn). New York: Routledge.

Gossman, L. (2004). *Between Passion and Irony: Benjamin Constant's Liberal Balancing Act*. The George R. Havens Memorial Lecture. Speech. Ohio State University. Retrieved from www.princeton.edu/~lgossman/constant.pdf

Gough, A. (2011, June 19). Police social media site a disgracebook. *The Sunday Mail* (Queensland). Retrieved January 26, 2013, from www.couriermail.com.au/news/queensland/police-social-media-site-a-disgracebook/story-e6freoof-1226077672110

Gowans, C. (2012). Moral Relativism. *The Stanford Encyclopedia of Philosophy*. Retrieved from http://plato.stanford.edu/archives/spr2012/entries/moral-relativism/

Graham, D. W. (2011). Heraclitus. *The Stanford Encyclopedia of Philosophy*. Retrieved from http://plato.stanford.edu/archives/sum2011/entries/heraclitus/

Graphic designer—the most popular cultural occupation. (2012, December 20). *Australian Bureau of Statistics*. Retrieved January 7, 2013, from www.abs.gov.au/AUSSTATS/abs@.nsf/mediareleasesbyReleaseDate/836D4B1D297F1DC7CA2573FB000E2A19

Grattan, M. (1991). Ideological spectacles: Reporting the 'Ratpack'. *Media Information Australia* (60), 7–10.

Grattan, M. (2011, May 23). Pushed to the limit, Bob goes in guns blazing. *The Sydney Morning Herald*. Retrieved August 27, 2012, from http://smh.com.au/opinion/politics/pushed-to-the-limit-bob-goes-in-guns-blazing-201105221-1exil.html

Green, E. and O'Leary, J. (2012). Ensuring a Fair Trial for an Accused in a Digital Era: Lessons for Australia. In P. Keyzer, J. Johnston and M. Pearson (Eds), *The Courts and the Media*. Braddon, ACT: Halstead

Green, J. (2013, January 31). Why wait for mainstream media to catch up? *The Drum (ABC News)*. Retrieved February 6, 2013, from www.abc.net.au/news/2013-01-31/green-why-wait-for-the-mainstream-media-to-catch-up/4491818

Greene, G. (1955). *The Quiet American*. London: William Heinemann.

Greenhouse, S. (2013). Even if it enrages your boss, social net speech is protected. *The New York Times*. Retrieved from nytimes.com website: www.nytimes.com/2013/01/22/technology/employers-social-media-policies-come-under-regulatory-scrutiny.html?pagewanted=all

Greenslade, R. (2008, March 19). McCanns take on the *Express* at last. Retrieved March 13, 2008, from www.guardian.co.uk/media/greenslade/2008/mar/13/mccannstakeontheexpressat?INTCMP= SRCH

Greenslade, R. (2009, December 9). Tiger Woods cannot plead privacy now to escape media storm. *London Evening Standard*. Retrieved December 10, 2009, from www.standard.co.uk/business/markets/tiger-woods-cannot-plead-privacy-now-to-escape-media-storm-6767145.html

Greenslade, R. (2010, May 24). Why the *News of the World* was right to expose the Duchess of York. *The Guardian*. Retrieved June 2, 2010, from www.guardian.co.uk/media/greenslade/2010/may/24/newsoftheworld-prince-andrew

Greenslade, R. (2012a, May 24). Public wants stricter press regulation and tighter limits on ownership. *The Guardian*. Retrieved May 25, 2012, from www.guardian.co.uk/media/greenslade/2012/may/24/pcc-polls

Greenslade, R. (2012b, August 20). *Sunday Times* inquiry fails to support Fake Sheikh's claims. *The Guardian*. Retrieved September 12, 2012, from www.guardian.co.uk/media/greenslade/2012/aug/20/mazher-mahmood-sundaytimes

Greenslade, R. (2012c, October 18). Taliban target media critical of Malala's shooting. *The Guardian*. Retrieved October 19, 2012, from www.guardian.co.uk/media/greenslade/2012/oct/18/malala-yousafzai-taliban/

Greenslade, R. (2012d, August 1). TV documentary to expose the Fake Sheikh's sting operations. *The Guardian*. Retrieved September 12, 2012, from www.guardian.co.uk/media/greenslade/2012/aug/01/mazher-mahmood-newsoftheworld

Greenslade, R. (2013, February 15). *The Sun*'s Oscar Pistorius front page: 'lechery over a corpse'. *The Guardian*. Retrieved February 16, 2013, from www.guardian.co.uk/media/greenslade/2013/feb/15/sun-oscar-pistorius/

Greenwood, C. (2011, November 4). We will never be able to trust cricket again: Judge's damning verdict as three shamed Pakistani stars are jailed for corruption. *The Daily Mail*. Retrieved September 6, 2012, from www.dailymail.co.uk/news/article-2056982/Pakistan-spot-fixing-players-corrupt-agent-jailed-cricket-betting-scandal.html

Grieving mum's anger prompts 7 *News* backlash. (2012, July 23). *ABC News*. Retrieved August 1, 2012, from www.abc.net.au/news/2012-07-23/grieving-mum27s-anger-prompts-seven-news-backlash/4148250

Gunter, J. (2011, August 11). Cameron: media has a responsibility to hand over riot footage. *journalism.co.uk* Retrieved September 15, 2012, from www.journalism.co.uk/news/cameron-media-has-a-responsibility-to-hand-over-riot-footage/s2/a545570/

Gunter, J. (2012, January 10). *Telegraph* paid middleman 150,000 pounds for expenses data. *The Daily Telegraph*. Retrieved January 12, 2012, from www.journalism.co.uk/news/relegraph-paid-middleman–150-000-for-expenses-data/s2/a547418/

Habermas, J. (1984). *The theory of communicative action, vol. 1: Reason and the rationalization of society* (T. McCarthy, trans.). Boston, MA: Beacon Press (original work published in German, 1981).

Habermas, J. (1987). *The theory of communicative action, vol. 2: Lifeworld and system: A critique of functionalist reason* (T. McCarthy, trans.). Boston, MA: Beacon Press (original work published in German, 1981).

Habermas, J. (1989). *The structural transformation of the public sphere* (T. Burger with F. Lawrence, trans.). Cambridge, MA: MIT Press (original work published in German, 1962).

Habermas, J. (1990) *Moral consciousness and communicative action* (C. Lenhardt and S. W. Nicholson, trans.). Cambridge: Polity Press (original work published in German 1983).

Habermas, J. (1992). Further reflections on the public sphere. In C. Calhoun (Ed.), *Habermas and the public sphere*. Cambridge, MA: MIT Press, pp. 421–461.

Haddow, D. (2010, April 7). Grim truths of WikiLeaks Iraq video. *The Guardian*. Retrieved November 11, 2012, from www.guardian.co.uk/commentisfree/libertycentral/2010/apr/07/wikileaks-collateral-murder-iraq-video/

Hall, L. (2012a, February 2). Judge orders journalists to name sources. *The Age*. Retrieved February 2, 2012, from www.theage.com.au/national/judge-orders-journalists-to-name-sources-20120201-1qtdz.html

Hall, L. (2012b, September 21). Lawyer's comments to journalist should be allowed in Liu case: Fairfax says. *Newcastle Herald*. Retrieved January 9, 2013, from www.theherald.com.au/story/350275/lawyers-comments-to-journalist-should-be-allowed-in-liu-case-fairfax/

Hallas, D. (1988). The Bourgeois Revolution. *Socialist Review* (105), 17–20.

Halliday, J. (2011, December 5). Gaddafi death footage not too graphic for TV, rules Ofcom. *The Guardian*. Retrieved January 19, 2013, from www.guardian.co.uk/media/2011/dec/05/gaddafi-death-footage

Halliday, J. (2012a, May 28). *Independent on Sunday* editor defends using images of dead Syrian children. *The Independent on Sunday* (UK). Retrieved January 17, 2013, from www.guardian.co.uk/media/2012/may/28/independent-sunday-dead-syrian-children

Halliday, J. (2012b, February 16). Journalists' employers must protect sources, says Lords committee chair. *The Guardian*. Retrieved from guardian.co.uk website: www.guardian.co.uk/media/2012/feb/16/journalists-sources-lords-committee

Hallin, D. C. (1989). *The "uncensored war": The media and Vietnam*. Berkeley: University of California Press.

Hallin, D. C. (1994). *We keep America on top of the world*. London; New York: Routledge.

Hanitzsch, T. (2007). *Deconstructing Journalism Culture: Towards a Universal Theory*. Paper presented at the International Communication Association.

Hanitzsch, T. and Hanusch, F. (2012). Does gender determine journalists' professional views? A reassessment based on cross-national evidence. *European Journal of Communication*, 27(3), 257–77.

Hansen, J. (2012, December 9). Don't blame prank callers for suicide. *The Sunday Mail* (Queensland), p. 46.

Hanson, P. (n.d.). Pauline Hanson. Retrieved August 25, 2012, from http://paulinehanson.com.au/

Hanusch, F. (2013a). Whose views skew the news? Media chiefs ready to vote out Labor, while reporters lean left. *The Conversation*. Retrieved from theconversation.com/whose-views-skew-the-news-media-chiefs-ready-to-vote-out-labor-while-reporters-lean-left-13995

Hanusch, F. (2013b). Women overtake men in the media, but not in pay or power. *The Conversation.* Retrieved from theconversation.com/women-overtake-men-in-the-media-but-not-in-pay-or-power-14479

Harcup, T. (2007). *The ethical journalist.* London: Sage.

Harding, L. and Stephen, C. (2012, September 12). Chris Stevens, US Ambassador to Libya, killed in Benghazi attack. *The Guardian.* Retrieved February 25, 2013, from www.guardian.co.uk/world/2012/sep/12/chris-stevens-us-ambassador-libya-killed

Harding, T. (2007, March 31). Blair's disgust as Iran TV parades captives. *The Age.* Retrieved March 31, 2007, from www.theage.com.au/news/world/blairs-disgust-as-iran-tv-parades-captives/2007/03/30/1174761752080.html

Hargreaves, I. (2003). *Journalism: Truth or Dare?* Oxford: Oxford University Press.

Hari, J. (2011, September 15). Johann Hari: A personal apology. *The Independent.* Retrieved September 21, 2012, from www.independent.co.uk/voices/commentators/johann-hari/johann-hari-a-personal-apology-2354679.html

Harris, B. (1996). *Politics and the rise of the press: Britain and France, 1620–1800.* London & New York: Routledge.

Harrison, D. (2011, March 10). Hinch loses High Court challenge. *The Age.* Retrieved January 27, 2013, from www.theage.com.au/national/hinch-loses-high-court-challenge-20110310-1bp2u.html

Harry grabs the family jewels. (2012, August 23). *The Sun,* p. 1.

Hart, H. L. A. (1955). Are there any natural rights? *The Philosophical Review, 64*(2), 175–91.

Hartigan, J. (2012). The Courts and the Media in the Digital Era: A Media Perspective. In P. Keyser, J. Johnston and M. Pearson (Eds), *The Courts and the Media* (pp. 16–23). Braddon, ACT: Halstead Press.

Hartley, J. (1996). *Popular Reality: Journalism, Modernity, Popular Culture.* London: Arnold.

Hassan, G. (2011, July 15). Can celebrities expect privacy? *BBC News.* Retrieved March 7, 2013, from www.bbc.co.uk/news/entertainment-arts-14151678

Haughney, C. (2012, August 10). CNN and Time Suspend Journalist After Admission of Plagiarism. *The New York Times blog: Media Decoder.* Retrieved August 11, 2012, from http://mediadecoder.blogs.nytimes.com/2012/08/10/time-magazine-to-examine-plagiarism-accusation-against-zakaria/

Hausman, C. (2011, March 14). Hidden-Camera Sting Sparks Ethics Debate. *Ethics Newsline.* Retrieved March 15, 2011, from www.globalethics.org/newsline/2011/03/14/hidden-camera-stings/

Haywood, B. (2004, August 23). The Price of a Good Story. *The Age,* p. 12.

Headless Body in Topless Bar. (2008). *New York Post.*

Heilpern, J. (2012, August 1). Onward, Christiane. *Vanity Fair.* Retrieved August 1, 2012, from www.vanityfair.com/culture/2012/08/christiane-amanpour-on-marie-colvin

Heir it is! Pic of naked Harry you've already seen on the internet. (2012, August 24). *The Sun,* p. 1.

Helicopter horror crash. (2013, January 16). *London Evening Standard,* p. 1.

Hermida, A. (2012). Tweets and truth. *Journalism Practice, 6*(5/6), 659–68.

Hermida, A., Fletcher, F., Korell, D. and Logan, D. (2012). Share, Like, Recommend. *Journalism Studies, 13*(5/6), 815–24.

Hey Dad! scandal: child star to launch civil action. (2011, March 8). *The Sydney Morning Herald.* Retrieved March 8, 2011, from www.smh.com.au/entertainment/tv-and-radio/hey-dad-scandal-child-star-to-launch-civil-action-20110308-1blgs.html

Higgins, E. and Packham, B. (2013, February 1). NSW authorities deny strip-search of Craig Thomson was intended intimidation. *The Australian*. Retrieved February 1, 2013, from www.theaustralian.com.au/national-affairs/nsw-authorities-deny-strip-search-of-craig-thomson-was-intended-intimidation/story-fn59niix-1226566731327

Hildebrand, J. (2011, November 30). Rat calls not all nasty for Speaker Peter Slipper. *The Daily Telegraph*. Retrieved February 2, 2012, from www.dailytelegraph.com.au/news/sydney-news/rat-calls-not-all-nasty-for-speaker-peter-slipper/story-e6freuzi-1226209653020

Hillsborough Independent Panel. (2012). The report of the Hillsborough Independent Panel. London: House of Commons.

Hinch, D. (2010). *Human Headlines*. Melbourne: Cocoon Lodge.

Hirst, M. (1997). MEAA Code of Ethics for journalists: an historical and theoretical overview. *Media International Australia*(83), 63–77.

Hirst, M. (2001). Journalism in Australia: hard yakka? In S. Tapsall and C. Varley (Eds), *Journalism: Theory in practice* (pp. 55–70). Melbourne: Oxford University Press.

Hirst, M. (2003). *Grey collar journalism: The social relations of news production*. Charles Sturt University, Bathurst, NSW.

Hirst, M. (2009). The witches of Facebook–lynch mobs dribblejaws' style. *Ethical Martini* (17 February). Retrieved from http://ethicalmartini.wordpress.com/2009/02/17/the-witches-of-facebook-lynch-mobs-dribblejaws-style/

Hirst, M. (2011). *News 2.0: Can journalism survive the Internet?* Sydney: Allen & Unwin.

Hirst, M. (2012a). The cultural politics of journalism: Quotidian intellectuals and the power of media capital. In M. Hirst, S. Phelan and V. Rupar (Eds), *Scooped: The politics and power of journalism in Aotearoa, New Zealand* (1st edn). Auckland, NZ: AUT University Media.

Hirst, M. (2012b). *One tweet does not a revolution make: Technological determinism, media and social change*. Paper presented at The Arab Spring: A Symposium on Social Media and the Politics of Reportage Swinburne University, Melbourne.

Hirst, M. (2013). *Rebuildng a 'failed' State: Does the terror frame still dominate media coverage of Iraq in 2012?* Paper presented at the symposium Iraq 10 years on: Intervention, Occupation, Withdrawal and Beyond, Melbourne. www.deakin.edu.au/arts-ed/ccg/events/symposiums/2013/13-australia-iraq/

Hirst, M. and Harrison, J. (2007). *Communication and New Media: Broadcast to Narrowcast*. Melbourne: Oxford University Press.

Hirst, M. and Patching, R. (2005). *Journalism Ethics: Arguments and Cases*. Melbourne: Oxford University Press.

Hirst, M. and Patching, R. (2007). *Journalism Ethics: Arguments and Cases* (2nd edn). Melbourne: Oxford University Press.

Hobbes, T. (1651). Leviathan or The Matter, Forme and Power of a Common Wealth Ecclesiasticall and Civil. Retrieved from http://ebooks.adelaide.edu.au/h/hobbes/thomas/h68l/

Hofschneider, A. (2013, February 8). Hawaii Celebrity Privacy Bill Pushed By Steven Tyler, Mich Fleetwood. *The Huffington Post*. Retrieved February 15, 2013, from www.huffingtonpost.com/2013/02/09/hawaii-celebrity-bill-steven-tyler_n_2652524.html

Hohmann, J. (2011, May). 10 Best Practices for Social Media. *American Society of News Editors*. Retrieved February 9, 2013, from http://asne.org/Files/pdf/10_Best_Practices_for_Social_Media.pdf

Holmes, J. (2010, May 24). Seven Goes Public on the Private. *Media Watch*. Retrieved February 14, 2011, from www.abc.net.au/mediawatch/transcripts/s2907661.htm

Holmes, J. (2012a, June 29). Independence is the cornerstone of good journalism. *ABC News–The Drum*. Retrieved July 2, 2012, from www.abc.net.au/news/2012-06-29/holmes-independence-is-the-cornerstone-of-good-journalism/4100222

Holmes, J. (2012b, November 26). Longing for a new idea. *Media Watch*. Retrieved December 19, 2012, from www.abc.net.au/mediawatch/transcripts/s3641249.htm

Holmes, J. (2012c, December 21). Trivial pursuit: When *The Australian* gets personal. *The Drum*. Retrieved from www.abc.net.au/news/2012-12-21/holmes-trivial-pursuits-when-the-australian-gets-personal/4438872

Holmes, J. (2013, February 18). You wouldn't Tweet about it. *Media Watch*. Retrieved from www.abc.net.au/mediawatch/transcripts/s3693024.htm

Hookway, C. (2010). Pragmatism. *The Stanford Encyclopedia of Philosophy*. Retrieved from http://plato.stanford.edu/archives/spr2010/entries/pragmatism/

Hopkins, N. (2013, January 21). How the MoD gambled to keep Prince Harry safe–from reporters. *The Guardian*. Retrieved January 22, 2013, from www.guardian.co.uk/uk/2013/jan/21/mod-gamble-prince-harry-afghanistan/

Horne, D. (1994). A marketplace of ideas? In J. Schultz (Ed.). *Not just another business* (pp. 7–10). Sydney: Pluto Press.

Hornery, A. (2013a, February 7). Chrissie Swan: 'I was protecting my children'. *The Sydney Morning Herald*. Retrieved February 7, 2013, from www.smh.com.au/lifestyle/private-sydney/chrissie-swan-i-was-protecting-my-children-20130207-2dzzo.html

Hornery, A. (2013b, February 13). Woman's Day spend up to $150,000 on pregnant Kate. *The Age*. Retrieved February 14, 2013, from www.theage.com.au/lifestyle/private-sydney/womens-day-spends-up-to-150000-on-pregnant-kate-photos-20130213-2eczg.html

Hornery, A. and Jacobsen, G. (2010, March 27). *Hey Dad!* star to see police over sex claims. *The Sydney Morning Herald*. Retrieved March 27, 2010, from www.smh.com.au/lifestyle/people/hey-dad-star-to-see-police-over-sex-claims-20100326-r31o.html

Hough, A. (2013, April 23). Revealed: the best jobs to pursue as a career. *The Telegraph*. Retrieved from www.telegraph.co.uk/finance/jobs/10012272/Revealed-the-best-jobs-to-pursue-as-a-career.html

Howe, P. (2011, March 3). Richard Drew. *Digital Journalist*. Retrieved January 17, 2013, from http://digitaljournalist.org/issue0110/drew.htm

Hoyt, C. (2009, July 5). Journalistic Ideals, Human Values. *The New York Times*. Retrieved July 7, 2008, from www.nytimes.com/2009/07/05/opinion/05pubed.html?_r=0

Huff, R. (2012, January 23). Lara Logan: Life is not about dwelling on the bad. *New York Daily News*. Retrieved January 24, 2012, from http://articles.nydailynews.com/2012-01-22/news/30651720_1_sexual-assault-lara-logan-jeff-fager

Hughes, M. and Sanches, R. (2012, June 7). Barbara Walters email furore: Assad's aide says TV host is a family friend. *The Sydney Morning Herald*. Retrieved June 7, 2012, from www.smh.com.au/lifestyle/celebrity/barbara-walters-email-furore-assads-aide-says-tv-host-is-a-family-friend-20120607-1zxjs.html

Hull, C. (2006, May 13). Forum for 13 May 2006: Miners and Media. Retrieved November 25, 2011, from www.crispinhull.com.au/2006/05/13/forum-for-13-may-2006-miners-and-media/

Hull, L. (2011, October 7). Wayne Rooney's father and uncle arrested over 'football betting scam'. *The Daily Mail* (UK). Retrieved August 27, 2012, from www.dailymail.co.uk/news/article-2045989/Wayne-Rooneys-father-uncle-Richie-arrested-football-betting-scam.html–ixzz24iDzU3zR

Humphrey, C. S. (1995). Selling the American Revolution. In L. J. Chiasson (Ed.). *The Press in Times of Crisis* (pp. 1–22). Westport, CT: Praeger.

Hunt, I. (1993). *Analytical and Dialectical Marxism*. Aldershot, UK: Avebury.

Hurst, J. and White, S. (1994). *Ethics in Australian News Media*. Melbourne: Macmillan Education.

Hypocrisy Unlimited. (2009, March 16). *Media Watch*. Retrieved March 18, 2009, from www.abc.net.au/mediawatch/transcripts/s2517612.htm

I loved Clive James, Leanne Edelsten tells *A Current Affair*. (2012, April 24). *The Daily Telegraph*. Retrieved May 2, 2012, from www.news.com.au/entertainment/celebrity/i-loved-clive-james-leanne-edelsten/story-e6frfmgi-1226336608308

The influence game: How news is sourced and managed today. (2012) *Global digital journalism study 2012*, Oriella PR Network.

Ingram, D. (2013, May 21). Court rules Bin Laden death photos can stay secret. Retrieved August 3, 2013, from www.reuters.com/article/2013/05/21/us-usa-courts-binladen-idUSBRE94K0MZ20130521

Innes, P. (2012). Suppression Orders: The More Things Change, the More They Stay the Same. In P. Keyser, J. Johnston and M. Pearson (Eds), *The Courts and the Media* (pp. 82–5). Braddon, ACT: Halstead Press.

International Affairs: #1 "Kony 2012". (2013, n.d.). *yahoo.com*. Retrieved February 11, 2013, from http://news.yahoo.com/year-in-review-2012-international-affairs-kony-2012-011843817.html

Internet Encyclopedia of Philosophy. John Rawls (1921–2002). *Internet Encyclopedia of Philosophy*. Retrieved from www.iep.utm.edu/rawls/–SH2c

Internet Encyclopedia of Philosophy. John Stuart Mill (1806–73). *Internet Encyclopedia of Philosophy*. Retrieved from www.iep.utm.edu/milljs/–SSH2d.i

Irby, K. (2011, March 2 (originally posted April 2, 2003)). *L. A. Times* Photographer Fired Over Altered Image. *Poynter Online*. Retrieved January 21, 2013, from www.poynter.org/how-tos/newsgathering-storytelling/9289/l-a-times-photographer-fired-over-altered-image/

Irfan, A. (2010). Is there an ethics of terrorism? Islam, globalisation, militancy, South Asia. *Journal of South Asian Studies, 33*(3), 487–98.

Is this woman pregnant? Decide for yourself. (2012, September 15). *The Gold Coast Bulletin*, p. 38.

Italy's court order retrial for Amanda Knox in murder case. (2013, March 27). *The Sydney Morning Herald*. Retrieved March 27, 2013, from www.smh.com.au/world/italys-court-orders-retrial-for-amanda-knox-in-murder-case-20130326-2gskj.html

Jabour, B. (2013a, January 23). *Courier-Mail* 'highly likely' to be charged over custody dispute coverage. *Brisbane Times*. Retrieved January 24, 2013, from www.smh.com.au/queensland/couriermail-highly-likely-to-be-charged-over-custody-dispute-coverage-20130123-2d6kz.html

Jabour, B. (2013b, August 6). Gina Rinehart fails to force journalist to reveal sources. *The Guardian*. Retrieved from www.theguardian.com/business/2013/aug/06/gina-rinehart-fails-journalist-sources

Jackson, J. (1992). Honesty in investigative journalism. In A. Belsey and R. Chadwick (Eds), *Ethical dilemmas in journalism and the media* (pp. 93–111). London: Routledge.

Jackson, S. (2003, April 17–23). Journalists the first casualties in reporting the truth of war. *The Australian (media section)*, p. 7.

Jackson, S. (2008, June 5). Fearing the rise of 'churnalism'. *The Australian*, p. 33.

Jackson, S. (2010a, May 10). Devine's 'gay slur' on Twitter. *The Australian*, p. 3.

Jackson, S. (2010b, April 26). Editors pour cold water on price rumours. *The Australian (media section)*, pp. 28 (part 1) and 26 (part 2).

Jackson, S. (2010, March 22). I was abused on set of *Hey Dad! Woman's Day*, 16–17.

Jackson, S. (2010c, May 3). Williams death a reporting dilemma. *The Australian*, p. 40.

Jackson, S. (2011, May 5). Women's mags report record wedding sales. *The Australian*. Retrieved May 5, 2011, from www.theaustralian.com.au/business/media/womens-mags-report-record-wedding-sales/story-e6frg996-1226050454998

Jackson, S. (2012, December 7). New privacy laws needed: Leveson. *The Australian*. Retrieved December 20, 2012, from www.theaustralian.com.au/media/new-privacy-laws-needed-leveson/story-e6frg996-1226531931189

Jackson, S. and Bodey, M. (2012, August 27). Moral outrage over mortal matters sparks press action. *The Australian*, p. 29.

Jameson, F. (2009). *Valences of the Dialectic*. London: Verso.

Jennings-Enquist, G. and Kodila, S. (2011, March 7). Did 60 Minutes break the law in revealing girl? *Crikey*. Retrieved March 7, 2011, from www.crikey.com.au/2011/03/07/did-60-minutes-break-the-law-in-revealing-girl/

Jericho, G. (2012). *The rise of the fifth estate: Social media and blogging in Australian politics*. Brunswick, Vic: Scribe.

Jesser, P. R. and Young, P. (1997). *The media and the military: From the Crimea to Desert Strike*. London: Macmillan.

Jimmy Savile a suspect in 199 crimes, 31 rapes. (2012, December 13). *The Australian*. Retrieved December 20, 2012, from www.theaustralian.com.au/news/world/jimmy-savile-a-suspect-in-199-crimes-31-rapes/story-e6frg6so-1226535918129

Johnson, G. (2012). *Hack: Sex, drugs and scandal from inside the tabloid jungle*. London: Simon & Schuster.

Johnson, R. (2012). Kant's Moral Philosophy. *The Stanford Encyclopedia of Philosophy*. Retrieved from http://plato.stanford.edu/archives/sum2012/entries/kant-moral/

Johnston, A. (2007, October 25). Alan Johnston: My kidnap ordeal. *BBC*. Retrieved November 16, 2012, from http://news.bbc.co.uk/2/hi/programmes/from_our_own_correspondent/7048652.stm

Johnston, A. (2011). *Kidnapped: And Other Dispatches*. London: Profile Books.

Johnston, M. (2012, November 29). There'll be no rats in the house, media told. *The Australian*. Retrieved February 2, 2013, from www.theaustralian.com.au/news/therell-be-no-rats-in-the-house-media-told/story-e6frg6n6-1226526126341

Jones says PM's father 'died of shame'. (2012, September 30). *ABC News*. Retrieved September 30, 2012, from www.abc.net.au/news/2012-09-30/jones-says-pms-dad-27died-of-shame27/4287770

Jones, G. and Kamper, A. (2010, May 21). Minister quits in sex club scandal. *The Daily Telegraph*, p. 1.

Jones, J. (2011, December 12). Record 64% Rate Honesty, Ethics of Members of Congress Low. *Gallup*. Retrieved June 24, 2012, from www.gallup.com/poll/151460/Record-Rate-Honesty-Ethics-Members-Congress-Low.aspx

Jones, S. (2005, January 13). Royal family caught up in Nazi row. *The Guardian*. Retrieved August 23, 2012, from www.guardian.co.uk/media/2005/jan/13/royalsandthemedia.pressandpublishing/

Jonsson, P. (2009, December 3). Tiger Woods scandal: the impact of his larger-than-life persona. *The Christian Science Monitor*. Retrieved December 12, 2009, from www.csmonitor.com/2009/1203/p02s15-ussc.htm

Jordan, B. (2012, May 21). Front page no place for kids caught in family disputes. *The Australian*, p. 26.

Joseph Kony top bodyguard killed. (2013, January 21). *The Telegraph* (UK). Retrieved February 11, 2013, from www.telegraph.co.uk/news/worldnews/joseph-kony/9815000/Joseph-Kony-top-bodyguard-killed.html

Journalistic sources and the law: blowing the whistle on truth-tellers. (2013). *The Guardian*. Retrieved from www.guardian.co.uk/commentisfree/2013/feb/17/journalistic-sources-law-editorial

Journalists avoid jail over contempt. (2007, June 25). *The Sydney Morning Herald*. Retrieved January 8, 2013, from www.smh.com.au/news/national/journalists-avoid-jail-over-contempt/2007/06/25/1182623785133.html

Judge orders mistrial. (2008, March 12). *The Gold Coast Bulletin*, p. 11.

Judge upholds charge against Bradley Manning in the WikiLeaks case. (2012, April 27). *The Australian*. Retrieved April 27, 2012, from www.theaustralian.com.au/in-depth/wikileaks/judge-upholds-charge-against-bradley-manning-in-the-wikileaks-case/story-fn775xjg-1226340511094

Judges ban story of unrelated murder. (2010, May 22–23). *The Weekend Australian*, p. 2.

Junod, T. (2003, September). The Falling Man. *Esquire Magazine*. Retrieved January 17, 2013, from www.esquire.com/features/ESQ0903-SEP_FALLINGMAN

Just Bloody mindedness. (2004, June 16). *Press Gazette*. Retrieved February 23, 2006, from www.pressgazette.co.uk/node/26062

Justice for Chantelle as jealous killer jailed for 35 years. (2012, April 17). *The Sydney Morning Herald*. Retrieved April 17, 2012, from www.smh.com.au/national/justice-for-chantelle-as-jealous-killer-jailed-for-35-years-20120417-1x4ko.html

Justin Bieber calls for crackdown after paparazzo death. (2013, January 3). *The Guardian*. Retrieved January 4, 2013, from www.guardian.co.uk/music/2013/jan/03/justin-bieber-crackdown-paparazzo-death

Kamber, M. (2011). Photographing conflict for the first time. *Lens, 2011* (23 November).

Kampfner, J. (2003, May 24–25). American lynches truth. *The Weekend Australian*, p. 5.

Kant, I. (1996). *The metaphysics of morals*. Cambridge: Cambridge University Press.

Kaplan, R. L. (2006). The news about New Institutionalism: Journalism's ethic of objectivity and its political origins. *Political Communication, 23*, 173–85.

Kapunda murder trial prompts Facebook alarm. (2010, November 19). *ABC News*. Retrieved January 26, 2013, from www.abc.net.au/news/2010-11-18/kapunda-murder-trial-prompts-facebook-alarm/2341746

Keane, B. (2010). Peter Garrett and the perpetual present of politics. *Crikey*. Retrieved from www.crikey.com.au/2010/02/19/peter-garrett-and-the-perpetual-present-of-politics/

Keane, B. (2011, July 25). Essential: trust in media slumps following phone hacking. *Crikey*. Retrieved from www.crikey.com.au/2011/07/25/essential-trust-in-media-slumps-following-phone-hacking/

Keane, B. (2012a, February 28). Bagging the gallery isn't the whole story on the leadership 'beat up'. *Crikey*. Retrieved February 28, 2012, from www.crikey.com.au/2012/02/28/bagging-the-gallery-isnt-the-whole-story-on-the-leadership-beat-up/

Keane, B. (2012b, July 2). Essential: the 'meh' about newspapers edition. *Crikey*. Retrieved from www.crikey.com.au/2012/07/02/essential-the-meh-about-newspapers-edition/

Keane, B. (2012c, June 26). Our trust in the media begins to recover, but only for some. *Crikey*. Retrieved from www.crikey.com.au/2012/06/26/our-trust-in-media-begins-to-recover-but-only-for-some/

Keane, B. (2012d, September 4). Which social media do Australians use most? *Crikey*. Retrieved September 4, 2012, from www.crikey.com.au/2012/09/04/which-social-media-do-australians-use-most/

Keane, B. (2012e, October 30). Wilkie tires of waiting on whistle-blower laws. *Crikey*. Retrieved October 30, 2012, from www.crikey.com.au/2012/10/30/wilkie-tires-of-waiting-on-whistleblower-laws/

Keller, B. (2011, May 5). The Inner Lives of Wartime Photographers. *The New York Times Magazine*. Retrieved January 18, 2013, from www.nytimes.com/2011/05/08/magazine/mag-08lede-t.html

Kennedy, S. (2012, March 30). Teen shooting forces US to look at itself in the mirror. *ABC News*. Retrieved April 3, 2012, from www.abc.net.au/news/2012-03-29/kennedy-teen-shooting-forces-america-to-look-at-itself/3919502

Ker, P. (2013, January 12). Whitehaven hoax sparks call to slow news flow. *The Sydney Morning Herald*. Retrieved January 12, 2013, from www.smh.com.au/national/whitehaven-hoax-sparks-call-to-slow-news-flow-20120111-2clav.html

Kessing, A. (2009, September 14). Allan Kessing: my side of the story. *Crikey*. Retrieved September 17, 2009, from www.crikey.com.au/2009/09/14/allan-kessing-my-side-of-the-story/

Khouri, R. G. (2006). The courage of journalists in the Middle East. *Nieman Reports, 60*(2), 42.

Kicking the Cornerstone of Democracy: The state of press freedom in Australia. (2012). Media, Entertainment and Arts Alliance, Sydney.

Kidder, R. (2008, November 17). A Journalist's Kidnapping, an Editors' Dilemma. *Global Ethics Newsline*. Retrieved November 18, 2008, from www.globalethics.org/newsline/2008/11/17/editors-dilemma/

Kidder, R. (2010, December 13). The Ethics of WikiLeaks. *Institute of Global Ethics*. Retrieved January 11, 2011, from www.globalethics.org/newsline/2010/12/13/the-ethics-of-wikileaks

Kidnap of Beckham Trial Axed. (2003, June 4). *The Gold Coast Bulletin*, p. 2.

Kieran, M., Morrison, D. E. and Svennevig, M. (2000). Privacy, the public and journalism: Towards an analytic framework. *Journalism, 1*(2), 145–69.

Kissane, K. (2011, October 5). Tears of freedom, now the bidding war begins. *The Sydney Morning Herald*, p. 9.

Kissane, K. (2012, November 13). Cameron joins growing fury at BBC payout. *The Age*. Retrieved November 14, 2012, from www.theage.com.au/world/cameron-joins-growing-fury-at-bbc-payout-20121113-29918.html

Knight, A. (2011, August 14). Queensland police unleash a social media lynch mob. *Online Journalism*. Retrieved August 15, 2011, from http://alanknight.wordpress.com/2011/08/14/queensland-police-unleash-a-social-media-lynch-mob

Knight, E. (2012, July 30). Degrees of detachment: The Journalist's role in a tragedy. Retrieved July 31, 2012, from www.editorsweblog.org/print/2012/07/30/degrees-of-detachment-the-journalists-role-in-a-tragedy

Knightley, P. (2003). *The First Casualty*. London: André Deutsch.

Knott, M. (2012a, December 10). Press Council breaches: *Herald Sun* worst culprit in '12. *Crikey*. Retrieved January 4, 2013, from www.crikey.com.au/2012/12/10/press-council-breaches-herald-sun-worst-culprit-in-12/

Knott, M. (2012b, December 19). Where are they now: losses at News, Fairfax are PR's gain. *Crikey*. Retrieved December 19, 2012, from www.crikey.com.au/2012/12/19/where-are-they-now-losses-at-news-fairfax-are-prs-gain/

Knott, M. (2013, March 26). Labor's whistle-blower bill just window dressing without change. *Crikey*. Retrieved March 26, 2013, from www.crikey.com.au/2013/03/26/labors-whistleblower-bill-just-window-dressing-without-an-overhaul/

Kravets, D. (2013). Osama Bin Laden photo flap heading to Supreme Court. *Wired*. Retrieved from www.wired.com/threatlevel/2013/08/bin-laden-death-pics/

Kyriacou, K. and Murray, D. (2013, March 21). Gerard Baden-Clay committed to stand trial for murder of wife Alison, tells court 'I am not guilty'. *The Courier Mail*. Retrieved April 5, 2013, from www.couriermail.com.au/news/queensland/gerard-baden-clay-committed-to-stand-trial-for-murder-of-wife-alison-tells-court-i-am-not-guilty/story-e6freoof-1226602014708

Lacrosse rape case collapses. (2007, April 13). *The Australian*, p. 9.

Lappeman, S. (2008, July 5–6). Rapist release becomes right to know row. *The (Gold Coast) Weekend Bulletin*, p. 7.

Law denies what readers want (and can get). (2012, August 24). *The Courier Mail*, p. 9.

Le Blanc, P. (2006). Uneven and combined development and the sweep of history: Focus on Europe. *International Viewpoint*. Retrieved from http://internationalviewpoint.org/spip.php?article1125

Le Grand, C. (2011, December 2). It's now or never for action on a privacy tort: Kirby. *The Australian*. Retrieved August 8, 2012, from www.theaustralian.com.au/business/legal-affairs/its-now-or-never-for-action-on-a-privacy-tort-kirby/story-e6frg97x-1226211757368

Lee, A. (2011). Moving the Overton Window. Retrieved from http://bigthink.com/daylight-atheism/moving-the-overton-window

Lee, J. and Oakes, D. (2012, October 6). States to tackle social media laws after alarm over fair trial for accused. *The Sydney Morning Herald*. Retrieved October 6, 2012, from www.smh.com.au/technology/technology-news/states-to-tackle-social-media-laws-after-alarm-over-fair-trial-for-accused-20121005-274py.html

Lee, K. (2012, September 17). Royal legal threats fail to stop publication of photos. *The Australian*, p. 28.

Lehman, J. (Ed.) (2008). West's Encyclopedia of American Law. Retrieved from http://law-journals-books.vlex.com/source/wests-encyclopedia-american-law-2707#

Leigh, D. (2011, December 13). Milly Dowler and the tabloid: trail that led to phone-hacking story. *The Guardian*. Retrieved August 20, 2012, from www.guardian.co.uk/media/2011/dec/13/milly-dowler-phone-hacking-story

Lette, K. (2012, September 10). Republicans beware: a royal baby will help the monarchy. *The Sydney Morning Herald*. Retrieved September 10, 2012, from www.smh.com.au/opinion/society-and-culture/republicans-beware-a-royal-baby-will-help-the-monarchy-20120909-25m5a.html

Leveson, B. (2012). *Privacy and the Internet: Privacy in the Twenty-first Century*. Sydney: Communications Law Centre.

Levs, J. and Cratty, C. (2013, January 10). Court considers demand that US release photos of bin Laden's body. *CNN*. Retrieved January 19, 2013, from http://edition.cnn.com/2013/01/10/world/bin-laden-photos/index.html

Levy, M. (2012a, September 17). British press slams 'perverts, peeping Toms' over topless Kate pics. *The Age*. Retrieved September 17, 2012, from www.theage.com.au/lifestyle/celebrity/british-press-slams-perverts-peeping-toms-over-topless-kate-pics-20120917-2612r.html

Levy, M. (2012b, December 21). Customs security warnings ignored 10 years ago: Xenophon. *The Sydney Morning Herald*. Retrieved December 21, 2012, from www.smh.com.au/national/customs-security-warnings-ignored-10-years-ago-xenophon-20121221-2bqc7.html

Levy, M. (2012c, December 17). 'IT WASN'T ME': brother's plea shows up online failings as police consider charging impersonators. *The Sydney Morning Herald*. Retrieved December 17, 2012, from www.smh.com.au/technology/technology-news/it-wasnt-me-brothers-plea-shows-up-online-failings-as-police-consider-charging-impersonators-20121217-2biw2.html

Lewis, J. Williams, A. and Franklin, B. (2008). A compromised fourth estate? *Journalism Studies, 9*(1), 1–20.

Leys, N. (2012a, May 22). News outlets reject Thomson's reporting claims. *The Australian*. Retrieved May 22, 2012, from www.theaustralian.com.au/national-affairs/news-outlets-reject-thomsons-reporting-claims/story-fndsip4d-1226362835761

Leys, N. (2012b, March 1). Uhlmann: let it all hang out on Twitter. *The Australian*. Retrieved March 1, 2012, from www.theaustralian.com.au/media/uhlmann-lets-it-all-hang-out-on-twitter/story-e6frg996-1226285846673

Leys, N. and Kelly, J. (2012, October 4). Alan Jones row: Lib event 'was not private'. *The Australian*. Retrieved October 4, 2012, from www.theaustralian.com.au/media/alan-jones-row-lib-event-was-not-private/story-e6frg996-1226487739991

Lidberg, J. (2012, October 3). Victoria and WA pass shield laws for journalists. *Arts On Line: Monash University*. Retrieved January 9, 2013, from http://artsonline.monash.edu.au/news-events/victoria-and-wa-pass-shield-laws-for-journalists/

Linder, D. (2002). The Trial of Socrates. Retrieved from http://law2.umkc.edu/faculty/projects/ftrials/socrates/socratesaccount.html

Littlely, B., Jean, D. and Noonan, A. (2010, November 19). It's Facebook justice for alleged killer. *Adelaide Now*. Retrieved November 19, 2010, from www.adelaidenow.com.au/news/south-australia/kapunda-youth-appears-in-elizabeth-magistrates-court-charged-with-triple-murder/story-e6frea83-1225954934820

Lloyd, P. (2010). *Inside Story*. Crows Nest, Sydney: Allen & Unwin.

Loong, P. (2008, November 8). Blackout on Canadian reporter's kidnapping posed dilemma for media. *The Globe and Mail* (Canada). Retrieved November 18, 2008, from http://v1.theglobeandmail.com/servlet/story/RTGAM.20081108.wmedia1108/business/Business/Business/

Lord, P. (2012, June 20). 'Molly's Law' needed to stop vile intrusion into grief. *The Australian*. Retrieved April 13, 2013, from www.theaustralian.com.au/media/from-the-paper/mollys-law-needed-to-stop-vile-intrusion-into-grief/story-fna1k39o-1226438036605

Lowe, A. (2012, September 28). 'Trial by social media' worry in Meagher case. *The Age*. Retrieved January 26, 2013, from www.theage.com.au/technology/technology-news/trial-by-social-media-worry-in-meagher-case-20120928-26pe4.html

Lucy, N. and Mickler, S. (2006). *The war on democracy: Conservative opinion in the Australian press*. Perth: UWA Press.

Lydall, R., Allen, P. and Murphy, J. (2012, September 14). Wills and Kate furious at topless pictures. *The Evening Standard* (London), p. 1.

Lyons, J. (2012, March 19). Assad rewrites rules of war reporting. *The Australian*, p. 28.

MacBean, N. (2009, March 20). Hanson nude pics: editor admits not checking facts. *ABC News*. Retrieved March 20, 2009, from www.abc.net.au/news/stories/2009/03/20/2521575.htm

Macleod, S. (1994, September 12). The Life and Death of Kevin Carter. *Time Magazine*.

Maddie's parents cleared as suspects. (2008, July 22). *The Sydney Morning Herald*. Retrieved July 22, 2008, from www.smh.com.au/articles/2008/07/22/1216492393632.html

Magazine 'proud' to publish Kate photos. (2012, September 20). *ABC News*. Retrieved September 20, 2012, from www.abc.net.au/news/2012-09-19/danish-mag-to-publish-topless-kate-photos/4270890

Magna Carta (Great Charter). (c. 1215, 8 December 2012) Retrieved 12 February, 2013, from www.constitution.org/eng/magnacar.htm

Maguire, T. (2012, April 26). Should only people we like be paid for their stories? *The Punch*. Retrieved September 6, 2012, from www.thepunch.com.au/articles/should-only-people-we-like-be-paid-for-their-stories/asc/

Mahmood, M. (2013, February 24). Boxing champ Herbie Hide peddles cocaine and offers to throw title fight. *Sun on Sunday*. Retrieved February 25, 2013, from www.thesun.co.uk/sol/homepage/news/4809904/Herbie-Hide-peddles-cocaine-and-offers-to-throw-title-fight.html

Malone, N. (2012, June 6). Barbara Walters Tried to Help Ex-Assad Aide Get a Job in the States. *New York Magazine*. Retrieved June 7, 2012, from http://nymag.com/daily/intel/2012/06/walters-tried-to-help-ex-assad-aide-get-job.html

Manker, R. (2012, December 6). Would you choose to come to the rescue or capture the moment? *The Daily Telegraph*, p. 30.

Maras, S. (2013). *Objectivity in journalism*. Cambridge: Polity Press.

Marcus, C. (2012, September 25). MP on child porn charges now named. *ABC News*. Retrieved January 29, 2013, from www.abc.net.au/news/2012-09-24/bernard-finnigan-facing-child-porn-charges/4277868

Marcus, C. and Domjen, B. (2012, March 11). World hunts warlord: Obscurity to instant infamy. *The Sunday Mail* (Queensland), p. 17.

Marinovich, G. and Silva, J. (2000). *The Bang-Bang Club: Snapshots from a Hidden War*. London: William Heinemann.

Marks, V. (2011, November 15). An expansive man who could not share the demons within. *The Guardian* republished in *The Age*. Retrieved November 15, 2011, from www.theage.com.au/sport/cricket/an-expansive-man-who-could-not-share-the-demons-within-20111114-1nfjq.html

Marshall, J. (2012, June 10). FAKE-arazzi: celebrity set-ups. *The Sunday Telegraph*. Retrieved June 17, 2012, from www.dailytelegraph.com.au/fake-arazzi-celebrity-phono-set-ups-exposed/story-fn6b3v4f-1226390073261

Marshall, S. (2012, July 9). Report: More people share news by email than Twitter. *journalism.co.uk* Retrieved July 9, 2012, from www.journalism.co.uk/news/report-email-is-second-most-important-way-of-sharing-news-after-facebook/s2/a549803/

Martin, J. (2006, May). Arab journalism comes of age. *Middle East*, 50–54.

Martin, R. (1981). Tacitus. Retrieved from http://penelope.uchicago.edu/Thayer/E/ Roman/Texts/secondary/SMIGRA*/Acta.html

Massola, J. (2010). Controversial political blogger unmasked as a federal public servant. *The Australian*. Retrieved from theaustralian.com.au website: www.theaustralian. com.au/media/controversial-political-blogger-unmasked-as-a-federal-public-servant/ story-e6frg996-1225929679443

Masters, C. (1987). The Moonlight State. *Four Corners*, ABC Television, broadcast May 11.

McArthur, G. (2012, September 12). Bid to broaden protection for journalists has been rejected. *Herald Sun*. Retrieved September 12, 2012, from www.heraldsun.com.au/ news/victoria/bid-to-broaden-protection-for-journalists-has-been-rejected/story-e6frf7kx- 1226472200253

McAthy, R. (2011, September 22). Broadcasters ordered to hand riot footage to police. *journalism.co.uk* Retrieved September 24, 2011, from www.journalism.co.uk/news/ broadcasters-ordered-to-hand-riot-footage-to-police/s2/a546109/

McAthy, R. (2012, June 21). Study: 75% of UK journalists source news from known social media contacts. *journalism.co.uk* Retrieved June 22, 2012, from http:www. journalism.co.uk/news/study-75-percent-journalists-source-news-from-sontacts-on- social-media/s2/a549652/

McBride, K. (2007, April 11). Winners and Losers in the Duke Lacrosse Story. *Poynter Online*. Retrieved April 13, 2007, from www.poynter.org/latest-news/everyday-ethics/ 81712/winners-and-losers-in-the-duke-lacrosse-story/

McBride, K. (2009, June 24). Journalists Can't Uphold Standard Set by News Blackout of Rhode Kidnapping. *Poynter Online*. Retrieved June 30, 2009, from www.poynter. org/column.asp?id=67&aid=165629

McBride, K. (2011, March 2 (originally published October 31, 2003)). Tabloid Publishes Prom Picture of Kobe's Accuser. *Poynter Institute*. Retrieved January 25, 2013, from www.poynter.org/latest-news/everyday-ethics/poynter-ethics-journal/17889/tabloid- publishes-prom-picture-of-kobes-accuser/

McBride, K. (2012a, September 18). 'Patchwriting' is more common than plagiarism, just as dishonest. *Poynter Institute*. Retrieved September 19, 2012, from www.poynter. org/latest-news/everyday-ethics/188789/patchwriting-is-more-common-than-plagiarism- just-as-dishonest/

McBride, K. (2012b, March 23). Trayvon Martin story reveals new tools of media power, justice. *Poynter Institute*. Retrieved March 26, 2012, from www.poynter.org/ latest-news/making-sense-of-news/167660/trayvon-martin-story-a-study-in-the-new- tools-of-media-power-justice/

McChesney, R. W. (2000a). The political economy of communication and the future of the field. *Media, Culture & Society*, 22(1), 109–116.

McChesney, R. W. (2000b). *Rich Media, Poor Democracy: Communication politics in dubious times*. New York: The New Press.

McChesney, R. W. (2001). Global media, neoliberalism and imperialism. *Monthly Review*, 52(10).

McChesney, R. W. (2007). *Communication Revolution: Critical junctures and the future of media*. New York and London: The New Press.

McChesney, R. W. (2008). The problem of journalism, in *The political economy of media: Enduring issues, emerging dilemmas* (pp. 25–66). New York: Monthly Review Press.

McClellan, A. (2005, October 27). *NY Times* hangs 'woman of mass destruction' out to dry. *The Australian,* p. 16.

McDonald, T. (2010, May 21). Campbell sex scandal sparks privacy debate. *ABC News.* Retrieved December 11, 2010, from www.abc.net.au/news/2010-05-21/campbell-sex-scandal-sparks-privacy-debate/836580

McElroy, D. (2013, March 28). North Koreans send Photoshop army into battle. *The Age.* Retrieved March 28, 2013, from www.theage.com.au/digital-life/digital-life-news/north-koreans-send-photoshop-army-into-battle-20130328-2gvmp.html

McGeough, P. (2013a). Afghanistan: when the West pulls out, wild west rides in. *The Sydney Morning Herald.* Retrieved from smh.com.au website: www.smh.com.au/comment/afghanistan-when-west-pulls-out-wild-west-rides-in-20130321-2git0.html

McGeough, P. (2013b, July 31). Bradley Manning cleared of aiding enemy but still facing up to 136 years in jail. *The Age.* Retrieved August 1, 2013, from www.theage.com.au/world/bradley-manning-cleared-of-aiding-enemy-but-still-faceing-up-to-136-years-in-jail-20130731-2qxr8.html

McGuire, E. (2010, October 8). Edited Transcript, Triple M, *Herald Sun,* p. 5.

McKenna, M. (2004, May 1). Legal carnival as Jackson faces first court hearing. *The Courier Mail,* p. 17.

McKnight, D. (2012). *Rupert Murdoch: An investigation of political power.* Sydney: Allen & Unwin.

McLuhan, M. (1967). *Understanding media: The extension of man.* London: Sphere Books.

McManus, M. M. (2013, March 6). Hawaii's Senate passes Steven Tyler Act celebrity privacy Bill. *Reuters.* Retrieved March 12, 2013, from www.reuters.com/article/2013/03/07/entertainment-us-usa-paparazzi-hawaii-idUSBRE92603D20130307

McQueen, H. (1977). *Australia's Media Monopolies.* Melbourne: Widescope.

MEAA. (1997). *Ethics in journalism/report of the Ethics Review Committee, Media Entertainment and Arts Alliance, Australian Journalists' Association Section.* Carlton VIC: Melbourne University Press.

MEAA Code of Ethics. (1999, n.d.). *Media Entertainment and Arts Alliance.* Retrieved August 27, 2012, from www.alliance.org.au/documents/codeofethics.pdf

Meade, A. (2012a, April 24). *A Current Affair*'s dirty new low. *The Australian.* Retrieved May 2, 2012, from http://blogs.theaustralian.com.au/themediamachine/index.php/theaustralian/comments/a_current_affairs_dirty_new_low/

Meade, A. (2012b, August 27). Family urges Conroy to curb press intrusion. *The Australian,* p. 30.

Meade, A. (2012c, August 14). Paper sorry for family's anguish. *The Australian.* Retrieved August 14, 2012, from www.theaustralian.com.au/media/paper-sorry-for-familys-anguish/story-e6frg996-1226450069543

Meade, A. (2012d, September 11). SMH columnist Tanveer Ahmed on ice amid plagiarism claims. *The Australian.* Retrieved September 11, 2012, from www.theaustralian.com.au/media/smh-columnist-on-ice-amid-plagiarism-claims/story-e6frg996-1226471388456

Media and contempt (2006, February 27). *Media Watch.* Retrieved March 15, 2006, from www.abc.net.au/mediawatch/transcripts/s1579630.htm

Media coverage may hurt Robert Hughes' chances of a fair trial: lawyer. (2013, July 26). *The Australian.* Retrieved July 26, 2013, from www.theaustralian.com.au/news/nation/media-coverage-may-hurt-robert-hughes-chances-of-a-fair-trial-lawyer/story-e6frg6nf-1226686180816

Media Monitors. (2010a, March 15). *The Australian*, p. 27.

Media Monitors. (2010b, March 22). *The Australian*, p. 34.

Media standards: a Tawdry TV tale. (2012, June 15–21). *The Week*, p. 16.

Media to blame. (2013, January 10). *ABC News*. Retrieved January 10, 2013, from www.abc.net.au/news/2013-01-10/hoaxer-defiant-despite-facing-up-to-10-years-jail/4459208

Mendte, L. (2011, October 3). Punk'd: How TV News Skirts Ethics. *Philadephia Post*. Retrieved September 21, 2012, from http://blogs.phillymag.com/the_philly_post/2011/03/10/punkd-how-tv-news-networks-skirt-ethics/

Merrill, J. C. (1989). *The dialectic in journalism: toward a responsible use of press freedom*. Baton Rouge: Lousiana State University Press.

Merritt, C. (2009a, October 30). Allan Kessing's conviction 'tainted'. *The Australian*. Retrieved October 30, 2009, from http://theaustralian.com.au/story/0,25197,26279289-7582,00.html

Merritt, C. (2009b, September 7). Half-baked laws need recooking. *The Australian*. Retrieved September 7, 2009, from www.theaustralian.com.au/business/story/0,28124,26036333-17044,00.html

Merritt, C. (2012a, August 31). Media leaks must be protected: Wilkie. *The Australian*, p. 29.

Merritt, C. (2012b, August 31). Time arrives for Labor to show it's not all talk on whistle-blowers. *The Australian*. Retrieved August 31, 2012, from www.theaustralian.com.au/business/opinion/time-arrives-for-labor-to-show-its-not-all-talk-on-whistleblowers/story-e6frg98f-1226461991298

Merritt, C. (2013, March 22). Wilkie was right: whistle-blower bill comes up short. *The Australian*. Retrieved March 22, 2013, from www.theaustralian.com.au/business/opinion/wilkie-was-right-whistleblower-bill-comes-up-short/story-e6frg9uf-1226602921014

Middletons shop the paparazzi over 'press intrusion'. (2011, April 8). *The Age*. Retrieved April 8, 2011, from www.theage.com.au/lifestyle/people/middletons-shop-the-paparazzi-over-press-intrusion-20110408-1d77e.html

Mill, J. S. (1859). On Liberty, Harvard Classics Volume 25 (1909). Retrieved from http://ebooks.adelaide.edu.au/m/mill/john_stuart/m645o/

Millar, L. (2013, July 15). Zimmerman verdict divides a nation. *ABC News*. Retrieved July 30, 2013, from www.abc.net.au/news/2013-07-15/millar-zimmerman-martin-verdict/4819812

Miller, N. (2013, April 2). Media struck dumb over nameless entertainer. *The Sydney Morning Herald*. Retrieved April 3, 2013, from www.smh.com.au/world/media-struck-dumb-over-nameless-entertainer-20130402-2h3y1.html

Milligan, L. (2003, 28–29 June). Gay artist error ties Fairfax up in court. *The Weekend Australian*, p. 3.

Milly hack gave Dowler parents false hope. (2011, November 21). *Channel 4 News* (UK). Retrieved August 20, 2012, from www.channel4.com/news/hacking-inquiry-hears-from-milly-dowlers-parents

Milton, J. (1644). *Areopagitica: A speech for the liberty of unlicensed printing to the Parliament of England* (J. Boss and D. Widger, Eds). Retrieved from www.gutenberg.org/files/608/608-h/608-h.htm

Miranda, C. (2012a, December 5). Baby joy is great news for royals. *Herald Sun*, pp. 4–5.

Miranda, C. (2012b, August 24). Brits turn the other cheek for Harry. *The Advertiser*, p. 11.

Miranda, C. (2012c, September 22). Hunted royals hit back. *The Gold Coast Bulletin*, p. 40.

Miranda, C. (2013, July 6). Maddie may still be alive, say police. *The Gold Coast Bulletin*, p. 33.

Mirkinson, J. (2011, June 8). Sexual Assault Of Journalists: Committee To Protect Journalists' New Report. *The Huffington Post*. Retrieved June 27, 2011, from www.huffingtonpost.com/2011/06/08/sexual-assault-of-journalists-committee-to-protect-n-873391.html

Mirkinson, J. (2013, February 15). *The Sun*'s Oscar Pistorius Front Page Called 'Disgusting,' 'Despicable' For Picture Of Reeva Steenkamp. *The Huffington Post*. Retrieved February 17, 2013, from www.huffingtonpost.com/2013/02/15/the-sun-pistorious-steenkamp-front-page-disgusting_n_2693803.html

Mitchell, N. (2010, October 8). Edited Transcript, 3AW. *Herald Sun*, p. 4.

Monaghan, E. (2003, July 24). US fetes its mythical heroine. *The Australian*, p. 8.

Moore, B. (1997). The Australian Concise Oxford Dictionary. Melbourne: OUP.

Moore, M. (2010, May 24). Politicians' private lives in the media's sights. *The Sydney Morning Herald*. Retrieved March 7, 2013, from www.smh.com.au/nsw/politicians-private-lives-in-the-medias-sights-20100523-w430.html

Moos, J. (2011a, June 13). 5 reasons broadcasters pay licensing fees for stories and why it corrupts journalism. *Poynter Institute*. Retrieved September 7, 2012, from www.poynter.org/latest-news/top-stories/135226/5-reasons-broadcasters-pay-licensing-fees-for-stories-and-why-it-corrupts-journalism/

Moos, J. (2011b, July 26). ABC ends checkbook journalism, will no longer pay for interviews. *Poynter Institute*. Retrieved September 6, 2012, from www.poynter.org/latest-news/mediawire/140596/abc-ends-checkbook-journalism-will-no-longer-pay-for-interviews/

Moos, J. (2011c). Few US front pages feature dead Gadhafi, many international papers show body. *Poynter Institute*. Retrieved January 18, 2013, from www.poynter.org/latest-news/top-stories/150386/few-us-front-pages-feature-dead-gadhafi-many-international-papers-show-body/

Moos, J. (2012, December 5). *NY Post* photos: 'Every time I close my eyes, I see the image of death'. *Poynter Institute*. Retrieved January 16, 2013, from www.poynter.org/latest-news/mediawire/197176/ny-post-subway-photog-every-time-i-close-my-eyes-i-see-the-image-of-death/

Mosco, V. (1996). *The Political Economy of Communication: Rethinking and Renewal*. London: Sage.

Mosco, V. (1999). New York.Com: A Political Economy of the 'Informational' City. *The Journal of Media Economics, 12*(2), 103–116.

Moses, A. (2013, February 18). Privacy fears as drones move into mainstream. *The Age*. Retrieved February 18, 2013, from www.theage.com.au/technology/technology-news/privacy-fears-as-drones-move-into-mainstream-20130217-2elcj.html

Moss, H. (2011, August 28, originally posted July 27). Princess Diana and Kate Cover *Newsweek*. *Huffington Post*. Retrieved January 18, 2013, from www.huffingtonpost.com/2011/06/27/diana-kate-middleton-newsweek_n_885594.html

MPs voice concern for Thomson's wellbeing. (2012, May 25). *ABC News*. Retrieved May 25, 2012, from www.abc.net.au/news/2012-05-24/mps-voice-concern-for-thomsons-wellbeing/4031960

Muammar Gaddafi photos: did media go too far? (2011, October 22). *The Australian*. Retrieved January 18, 2013, from www.theaustralian.com.au/media/muammar-gaddafi-photos-did-media-go-too-far/story-e6frg996-1226173747203

Muller, D. (2007, August 17). Ethics and the Peter Costello dinner: a last word. *Crikey*. Retrieved January 12, 2013, from www.crikey.com.au/2007/08/17/ethics-and-the-peter-costello-dinner-a-last-word/

Muller, D. (2010, December 21). Muller: what WikiLeaks means for media ethics. *Crikey*. Retrieved December 21, 2010, from www.crikey.com.au/2010/12/21/muller-what-wikileaks-means-for-media-ethics/

Murphy, D. (2011, November 26–27). Celebrities spill the beans on tabloids. *The Sydney Morning Herald*, p. 8 (News Review)

Murphy, K. (2012, June 7). Channel Nine aired ex-prostitute's claim on Thomson, even when she said it wasn't true. *The Age*. Retrieved June 7, 2012, from www.theage.com.au/opinion/political-news/channel-nine-aired-exprostitutes-claim-on-thomson-even-when-she-said-it-wasnt-true-20120606-1zwre.html

Murray, D. (2009, December 13). Nicole Kidman slams Australia. *Herald Sun*. Retrieved August 25, 2012, from www.heraldsun.com.au/entertainment/nicole-kidman-slams-australia/story-e6frf96o-1225809750069

Myers, S. (2012, July 10). NPR unpublishes intern's execution story after discovering parts were plagiarised. *National Public Radio*. Retrieved July 11, 2012, from www.poynter.org/latest-news/mediawire/180462/npr-removes-first-person-account-after-discovering-parts-were-plagiarised

Mysterious mail to Australian journalist triggers global tax haven exposé. (2013). *The Age*. Retrieved from www.theage.com.au/business/world-business/mysterious-mail-to-australian-journalist-triggers-global-tax-haven-expose-20130405-2hak3.html

The 'napalm girl' image that haunted the world turns 40. (2012, June 1). *Herald Sun*. Retrieved June 1, 2012, from www.heraldsun.com.au/news/more-news/the-napalm-girl-image-that-haunted-the-world-turns-40/story-e6frf7lf-1226379741233

Narain, H. (1973). *Evolution of the dialectic in Western thought*. Delhi: Motilal Banarsiass.

Neate, R. (2013, February 6). News corporation's quarterly profits double. *The Guardian*. Retrieved February 7, 2013, from www.guardian.co.uk/media/2013/feb/06/news-coporation-quarterly-profits

Nettle, S. (2010, February 11). Meeja chokes hard on another shark story. *Crikey*. Retrieved from: www.crikey.com.au/2010/02/12/meeja-chokes-hard-on-another-shark-story/

New Idea slammed for Harry story. (2008, February 29). *The Australian*. Retrieved February 29, 2008, from www.theaustralian.news.com.au/story/0,25197,23295795-7582,00.html

New Idea: regrets 'lapse of judgment' over Prince Harry story. (2008, March 10). *The Daily Telegraph*. Retrieved March 10, 2008, from www.news.com.au/dailytelegraph/story/0,22049,23348304-5001021,00.html

The New York Times Company Policy on Ethics in Journalism. (2005, October). *The New York Times*. Retrieved September 7, 2012, from www.nytco.com/press/ethics.html

New York Times reporter accused of plagiarism resigns. (2010, February 18). *The Age*. Retrieved February 18, 2010, from www.theage.com.au/world/new-york-times-reporter-accused-of-plagiarism-resigns-20100218-oeau.html

Newman, M. (2013, 21 February). All animals are equal, but some want to tell us what we can say, *The Australian*, p. 10.

News again targeted by Chinese hackers: Murdoch. (2013, February 6). *The Australian*. Retrieved February 7, 2013, from www.theaustralian.com.au/media-news-again-targeted-by-chinese-hackers-murdoch/story-e6frg996-1226571778439

Newspaper Review: Syrian children massacre image shown. (2012, May 27). *BBC News*. Retrieved January 17, 2013, from www.bbc.co.uk/news/uk-18224720

Nickel, J. (2013). Human Rights. *The Stanford Encyclopedia of Philosophy*, (Spring). Retrieved from http://plato.stanford.edu/archives/spr2013/entries/rights-human/

'No Hero' but Harry wants to go back. (2008, March 3). *The Gold Coast Bulletin*, p. 10.

No Rest For The Wicked: Disguises of a monster. (2008, July 5–6). *The Gold Coast Weekend Bulletin*, p. 7.

No tears for death of child sex fiend. (2013, January 1). *The Gold Coast Bulletin*, p. 11.

Nohrstedt, S. A., Kaitatzi-Whitlock, S., Ottosen, R and Riegert, K. (2000). From the Persian Gulf to Kosovo–War Journalism and Propaganda. *European Journal of Communication, 15*(3), 383–404.

Nothing but the Truth. (2008). R. Lurie (Producer), Yari Film Group.

Novack, G. (1968). Understanding History. Retrieved from www.marxists.org/archive/novack/works/history/index.htm

Nude photos 'a help for Hanson'. (2009, March 16). *The Australian*, p. 5.

NUJ Code of Conduct. (2011, September 16). *National Union of Journalists*. Retrieved February 20, 2013, from http://media.gn.apc.org/nujcode.html

Nyst, C. (2009, March 14–15). Innocent 'til proven guilty. *The Gold Coast Weekend Bulletin*, p. 46.

O'Brien, N. (2008, July 19–20). ABC correspondent in Singapore drug arrest. *The Weekend Australian*, p. 9.

O'Brien, N. (2011, January 16). Seven cleared over Campbell's outing. *The Sydney Morning Herald*. Retrieved January 22, 2011, from www.smh.com.au/nsw/seven-cleared-over-campbells-outing-20110115-19rvm.html

O'Brien, S. (2012, May 15). Politicians must accept scrutiny of private life. *Herald Sun*. Retrieved March 7, 2013, from www.heraldsun.com.au/opinion/politicians-must-accept-scrutiny/story-fn56aaiq-1226355181715

O'Carroll, L. (2013, January 16). Twitter pictures put in spotlight following London helicopter crash. *The Guardian*. Retrieved September 17, 2013, from www.guardian.co.uk/technology/2013/jan/16/twitter-pictures-london-helicopter-crash-copyright

O'Donovan, C. (2013). Intercontinental collaboration: How 86 journalists in 46 countries can work on a single investigation. *Nieman Journalism Lab*. Retrieved from www.niemanlab.org/2013/04/intercontinental-collaboration-how-86-journalists-in-46-countries-can-work-on-a-single-investigation/

O'Driscoll, P. (2005, March 3). Kobe Bryant, accuser settle her civil lawsuit. *USA Today*. Retrieved January 25, 2013, from http://usatoday30.usatoday.com/sports/basketball/nba/2005-03-02-bryant-settles_x.htm

O'Neill, J. (1992). Journalism in the marketplace. In A. Belsey and R. Chadwick (Eds), *Ethical dilemmas in journalism and the media*. London: Routledge.

O'Shea, K. (2011, September 9). Social Media and our courts. *Law Institute of Victoria*. Retrieved February 14, 2013, from www.aija.org.au/Criminal Justice 2011/Papers/O'Shea.pdf

Oberei, S. (2012, August 22). The Vulture and the Starving Child: The Most Iconic Photograph of the Century. *thincQuisitive* Retrieved January 17, 2013, from http://thincquisitive.com/2012/08/22/the-vulture-and-the-starving-child-the-most-iconic-photograph-of-the-century/

Oberhardt, M. and Odgers, R. (2008, August 13). Ferguson free on bail. *The Courier Mail*, p. 5.

Odone, C. (2011, December 2). US magazine argues that Johann Hari is getting away with it because he is anti-Israel and anti-USA. *The Telegraph* (UK). Retrieved September 21, 2012, from http://blogs.telegraph.co.uk/news/cristinaodone/100121232/us-magazine-argues-johann-hari-is-getting-away-with-it-because-he-is-anti-israel-and-anti-usa/

Officials: Bush upset by Hussein hanging video. (2007, January 10). *CNN*. Retrieved January 19, 2013, from http://edition.cnn.com/2007/POLITICS/01/10/bush.hussein/index.html

Oliver, A. (2011, June 29). *Newsweek* imagines Diana aged 50 with her admiring daughter-in-law ... in article that claims the Botoxed Princess would be Facebook friends with Camilla. *The Daily Mail* (UK). Retrieved January 18, 2013, from www.dailymail.co.uk/femail/article-2008914/Newsweek-Princess-Diana-aged-50-Kate-Middleton-cover.html

Omari, S. (2013). 1,000 deaths: Journalists who gave their lives. CPJ Blog. Retrieved from cpj.org/blog/2013/08/1000-deaths-journalists-who-gave-their-lives.php

Orden, E. and Steel, E. (2012, March 12). Video on Kony sets web record. *The Australian*, p. 10.

Orwell, G. (1946). Why I write. In S. Orwell and I. Angus (Eds), *The Penguin Essays of George Orwell* (pp. 7–13). London: Penguin.

Orwell, G. (1988). *Nineteen Eighty-four*. London: Penguin.

Over half your news is spin. (2010, March 15). *UTS–Crikey*. Retrieved March 15, 2010, from www.crikey.com.au/2010/03/15/over-half-your-news-is-spin/

Overington, C. (2010a, March 27–28). More at stake in molester affair than a reputation. *The Weekend Australian*, p. 10.

Overington, C. (2010b, May 22–23). Title withheld for legal reasons. *The Weekend Australian Magazine*, pp. 14–19.

Overington, C. (2011a, March 12). Dilemma behind naming AFL girl. *The Weekend Australian*. Retrieved February 13, 2013, from http://blogs.theaustralian.news.com.au/mediadiary/index.php/theaustralian/comments/dilemma_behind_naming_afl_girl/

Overington, C. (2011b, May 16). A family's never-ending ordeal. *The Australian*, p. 15.

Owen, J. (2012, May 24). Police probe complaint against newspaper. *The Australian*. Retrieved May 24, 2012, from www.theaustralian.com.au/media/police-probe-complaint-against-newspaper/story-e6frg996-1226365010210

Owen, M. (2012, November 21). State defers shield reforms. *The Australian*. Retrieved November 21, 2012, from www.theaustralian.com.au/nationa-affairs/state-politics/state-defers-shield-reforms/story-e6frgczx-1226520715781

Oxford Dictionary. (n.d.) Oxford Dictionary Online, oxforddictionaries.com

Packham, B. and Vasek, L. (2012, May 24). Leave me alone: Craig Thomson's plea. *The Australian*. Retrieved May 24, 2012, from www.theaustralian.com.au/national-affairs/in-depth/leave-me-alone-craig-thomsons-plea/story-fndsip4d-1226365480273

Paedophile saga to end badly. (2009, September 25). *The Gold Coast Bulletin*, p. 26.

Pandaram, J. and Levy, M. (2007, January 24). From the jaws of a shark comes a ripping yarn. *The Sydney Morning Herald*. Retrieved September 5, 2012, from

www.smh.com.au/news/national/diver-saved-from-jaws-of-a-shark/2007/01/23/1169518
709539.html

Papal Encyclicals. (1515). Fifth Lateran Council 1512–17 AD *Papal Encyclicals*.
Retrieved from www.papalencyclicals.net/Councils/ecum18.htm

The parents of missing British girl Madeleine McCann have appeared before the Leveson
media inquiry. (2011, November 24). *The Australian*. Retrieved November 24, 2011, from
www.theaustralian.com.au/business/in-depth/the-parents-of-missing-girl-madeleine-mccann-
have-appeared-before-the-leveson-media-inquiry/story-fn9eci82-1226204263748

Patching, R. (2011). *The Private lives of Australian cricket stars: a study of newspaper
coverage 1945–2010*. Unpublished PhD thesis. Bond University.

Paterno, S. (1998). The intervention dilemma. *American Journalism Review*. Retrieved
from www.ajr.org/article.asp?rel=ajrpaterno1.html

Patterson, P. and Wilkins, L. (1994). *Media Ethics: Issues and cases* (2nd edn). Dubuque,
Iowa: Brown & Benchmark.

Pearson, Mark (2005). *The Privacy Mandela: Towards a newsroom checklist for ethical
decisions*. Paper presented at the Journalism Education Association, Gold Coast.

Pearson, Mark (2011, June 20). Police Facebook wall raises fair trial questions. *journlaw*
Retrieved January 26, 2013, from http://journlaw.com/2011/06/20/police-facebook-
wall-raises-fair-trial-questions/

Pearson, Mark (2012, June 14). Queensland's biggest publisher–the police–try to calm
the FB lynch mob. *journlaw* Retrieved June 16, 2012, from http://journlaw.com/2012/
06/14/queenslands-biggest-publisher-the-police-try-to-calm-the-fb-lynch-mob/

Pearson, Michael (2012, December 6). Newspaper takes heat over haunting subway
photo. *CNN*. Retrieved January 3, 3013, from http://edition.cnn.com/2012/12/04/us/
new-york-subway-death/index.html

Pearson, M. and Polden, M. (2011). *The Journalist's Guide to Media Law*. (4th edn),
Crows Nest, Sydney: Allen & Unwin.

Pelton, R. Y. (2013). Syria: Wish you were here. *Dangerous Magazine*. Retrieved from
Dangerous website: http://dangerousmagazine.com/2013/03/29/syria-wish-you-were-
here/

Penberthy, D. (2010, May 21). Why David Campbell has a lesser right to privacy. *The
Punch*. Retrieved August 1, 2013, from www.thepunch.com.au/articles/why-david-
campbell-has-a-lesser-right-to-privacy

Penberthy, D. (2012, March 11). Hashtag battle with a warlord. *The Sunday Mail*
(Queensland), p. 49.

Perez-Pena, R. (2009, June 29). Keeping News of Kidnapping Off Wikipedia. *The New
York Times*. Retrieved July 7, 2009, from www.nytimes.com/2009/06/29/technology/
internet/29wiki.html

Petraeus mistress feels devastated. (2012, November 20). *The Gold Coast Bulletin*, p. 13,

Petraeus Resignation Highlights Moral No-Man's Land at Intersection of Private Lives and
Public Responsibility. (2012, November 12). *Institute of Global Ethics*. Retrieved
November 14, 2012, from www.globalethics.org/newsline/2012/11/12/petraeus-resignation/

Petrecca, L. and Eversley, M. (2012, December 4). Should *NJ Post* have printed photo of
man about to die? *USA Today*. Retrieved January 3, 2013, from www.usatoday.com/
story/news/nation/2012/12/04/nyc-subway-death-push/1744875/

Petrie, A. (2010, April 29). Williams story has magazine in strife. *The Sydney Morning
Herald*. Retrieved April 29, 2010, from www.smh.com.au/victoria/williams-story-has-
magazine-in-strife-20100428-tsht.html

Pexton, P. (2011, March 18). The damage done by *Post* reporter Sari Horwitz's plagiarism. *The Washington Post*. Retrieved April 1, 2011, from www.washingtonpost.com/wp-dyn/content/article/2011/03/18/AR2011031805543.html

Pilger, J. (1998). *Hidden Agendas*. London: Vantage.

Pilkington, E. (2013a, February 28). Manning plea document: Americans had a right to know 'true cost of war'. *The Guardian*. Retrieved March 1, 2013, from www.guardian.co.uk/world/2013/feb/28/bradley-manning-trial-plea-statement/

Pilkington, E. (2013b, February 28). Manning says he first tried to leak to *Washington Post* and *New York Times*. *The Guardian*. Retrieved March 1, 2013, from www.guardian.co.uk/world/2013/feb/28/manning-washington-post-new-york-times

Pilling, M. (2006, April 18). Prince Swills' shame. *The Gold Coast Bulletin*, p. 9.

Plaisance, P. L. (2002). The journalist as moral witness: Michael Ignatieff's pluralistic philosophy for a global media culture. *Journalism*, 3(2), 205–22.

Plunkett, J. (2012, February 8). Don't break stories on Twitter, BBC journalists told. *The Guardian*. Retrieved February 9, 2012, from www.guardian.co.uk/media/2012/feb/08/twitter-bbc-journalists

Police set up *Hey Dad!* strike force. (2010, March 29). *ABC News*. Retrieved March 29, 2010, from www.abc.net.au/news/stories/2010/03/29/2858843.htm

Police warn of more arrests after Sydney protests. (2012, September 17). *ABC News*. Retrieved September 17, 2012, from www.abc.net.au/news/2012-09-19/police-warn-of-more-arrests-after-sydney-protests/4264512

Policinski, G. (2012, December 20). First Amendment predictions for 2013 include disputes over leaks. *First Amendment Center*. Retrieved January 10, 2013, from www.firstamendmentcenter.org/first-amendment-predictions-for-2013-include-disputes-over-leaks

Porter, C. (2013, February 13). Conspiracies grow over LAPD's call for #Dorner blackout. *news.com.au* Retrieved February 14, 2013, from www.news.com.au/technology/lapd-calls-for-dorner-twitter-blackout/story-e6frfro0-1226577048844

Porwancher, A. (2011). Objectivity's Prophet: Adolph S Ochs and the *New York Times*, 1896–1935. *Journalism History*, 36(4), 186–95.

Posetti, J. (2009, June 21). Top 20 Take Away Tips for Tweeting Journos. *j-scribe.com* Retrieved June 23, 2009, from www.j-scribe.com/2009/06/top-20-tips-for-journo-twits.html

Posetti, J. (2012, September 28). Avoiding 'trial by social media' in the #JillMeagher case. *storify.com* Retrieved September 29, 2012, from http://storify.com/julieposetti/avoiding-trial-by-social-media-in-the-jillmeagher

Poulantzas, N. (1978). *Classes in contemporary capitalism* (D. Fernbach, Trans.). London: Verso.

Power, J. and Hall, L. (2012, May 9). Pell's threat to sue Twitter highlights law's use-by date. *The Sydney Morning Herald*. Retrieved May 9, 2012, from www.smh.com.au/technology/technology-news/pells-threat-to-sue-twitter-highlights-laws-useby-date-20120508-1yb33.html

Prescott hits at *Sun*'s 'titillating' Reeva Steenkamp cover. (2013, February 15). *The Week*. Retrieved February 17, 2013, from www.theweek.co.uk/media/oscar-pistorius/51532/prescott-hits-sun%E2%80%99s-titillating-reeva-steenkamp-cover

Price, J. (2010, May 28). Journalists condemn Channel Seven. *Crikey*. Retrieved May 28, 2010, from www.crikey.com.au/2010/05/28/journalists-educators-tell-ch-7-what-you-did-to-david-campbell-is-deplorable

The price of truth. (2012, February 23). *The Times* (London), p. 1.

Prince and the paparazzi: William to adopt zero tolerance (2010, November 22). *Sunday Telegraph* (London), republished in *The Sydney Morning Herald*. Retrieved November 22, 2010, from www.smh.com.au/lifestyle/people/prince-and-the-paparazzi-william-to-adopt-zero-tolerance-policy-20101122-183dj.html

'Princess Diana' Walking with Kate on *Newsweek* Cover–Cool or Creepy? (2011, June 28). *Gossip Cop*. Retrieved January 19, 2013, from www.gossipcop.com/princess-di-photoshop-kate-middleton-diana-newsweek-cover-2011-picture-photo-twitter-facebook-iphone/

Privacy Guidelines for broadcasters. (2011): Australian Communications and Media Authority.

Profile: Glenn Mulcaire. (2012, July 24). *BBC News*. Retrieved August 24, 2012, from www.bbc.co.uk/news/uk-14080775

Prosser, W. (1960). Privacy. California Law Review, 48(3), 383–423.

Pulitzer, J. (1904). The College of Journalism. *The North American Review*, 178(570), 641–80.

Rainey, J. (2011, March 11). On the Media: NPR video stings ethics too. *Los Angeles Times*. Retrieved September 21, 2012, from http://articles.latimes.com/2011/mar/11/entertainment/la-et-onthemedia-20110312

Ralson, N. (2013, May 14). Paid interviews may risk trial. *The Age*. Retrieved May 14, 2013, from www.theage.com.au/entertainment/tv-and-radio/paid-interviews-may-risk-trial-20130513-2ji96.html

Ralston, N. (2012, December 14). *Hey Dad!* star granted bail on sex charges. *The Sydney Morning Herald*, p. 4.

Ramadge, P. (2011). Personal Interview with Roger Patching.

Ravens, T. (2012, September 15–16). French magazine's photos of topless Kate leave William distraught. *The Sydney Morning Herald* p. 20.

Ravi, N. (2005). Looking beyond flaws journalism: How National Interests, Patriotism and Cultural Values Shaped the Coverage of the Iraq War. *Harvard International Journal od Press/Politics*, 10(1), 45–62.

Rayner, G. (2011, June 24). Profile: Levi Bellfield, sexual predator who treated women with 'distain'. *The Telegraph* (London). Retrieved August 20, 2012, from www.telegraph.co.uk/news/uknews/crime/8597604/Profile-Levi-Bellfield-sexual-predator-who-treated-women-with-disdain.html

Rayner, G. and Evans, M. (2010, January 29). Judge lifts super injunction over John Terry affair with team-mate's girlfriend. *The Telegraph* (London). Retrieved August 24, 2012, from www.telegraph.co.uk/sport/7102733/Judge-lifts-super-injunction-over-John-Terry-affair-with-team-mates-girlfriend.html

Redmond, R. (2008, September 2). Coverage under fire. *The Gold Coast Bulletin*, p. 4.

Reeves, S. (2010, May 24). Britain's Duchess of York apologises after paper sting. *The Age*. Retrieved May 24, 2010, from http://news.theage.com.au/breaking-news-world/britains-duchess-of-york-apologises-after-paper-sting-20100524-w51h.html

Reich, Z. (2010). Measuring the impact of PR on published news in increasingly fragmented news environments. *Journalism Studies*, 11(6), 799–816.

Reidy, P. (2010, February 1). Could Trafigura and Terry signal the demise of the superinjunction? *The Guardian*. Retrieved November 11, 2010, from www.guardian.co.uk/media/2010/feb/01/john-terry-superinjunction-courts/

Reluctant Heroes. (2013, January 11). *Mercury* (Hobart), p. 1.

Remeikis, A. (2012, May 27). Fair trials face a web challenge. *Brisbane Times*. Retrieved Mat 31, 2012, from www.brisbanetimes.com.au/national/fair-trials-face-a-web-challenge-20120527-1zciy.html

Report Copied. (2011, March 19). *The Gold Coast Bulletin*, p. 19.

Reporter sexually assaulted by mob in Egypt. (2011, February 16). *ABC News*. Retrieved February 16, 2011, from www.abc.net.au/news/2011-02-16/reporter-sexually-assaulted-by-mob-in-egypt/1944662

Retief, J. (2002). *Media Ethics: An introduction to responsible journalism*. Cape Town: Oxford University Press.

Reynolds, D. (1995). Words for war. In L. Chiasson (Ed.). *The Press in Times of Crisis* (pp. 85–101). Wesport, CT: Praeger.

Ricchiardi, S. (2011). Out of the Shadows. *American Journalism Review*, June/July.

Richards, I. (2002). Adjusting the focus: Levels of influence and ethical decision-making in journalism. *Australian Journalism Review, 24*(2), 9–20.

Riley, R. (2009, March 15). Don't stand if you can't cop heat. *Sunday Herald Sun*, p. 23.

Roberts, C. (2012). Public relations and Rawls: An ill-fitting veil to wear. *Journal of Mass Media, Ethics: Exploring Questions of Media Morality, 27*(3), 163–76.

Robinson, J. (2011a, December 6). Leveson inquiry: subterfuge can be in public interest, says *Guardian* reporter. *The Guardian*. Retrieved December 8, 2011, from www.guardian.co.uk/media/2011/dec/06/leveson-inqury-david-leigh-evidence

Robinson, J. (2011b, November 14). Phone hacking: 58% of UK public say they have lost trust in papers. *The Guardian*. Retrieved November 15, 2011, from www.guardian.co.uk/media/2011/nov/14/phone-hacking-public-trust

Rolf Harris charged with indecent assault on girls. (2013). *BBC News*. Retrieved from www.bbc.co.uk/news/uk-23880768

Romano, C. (2009). We need 'philosphy of journalism'. *The Chronicle of Higher Education*. Retrieved from http://chronicle.com/article/We-Need-Philosophy-of/49119/

Rosen, J. (2003, June). All about the retrospect. *American Journalism Review*. Retrieved September 19, 2012, from www.ajr.org/Article.asp?id=3020

Rosen, J. (2010). The web means the end of forgetting. *The New York Times*. Retrieved from www.nytimes.com/2010/07/25/magazine/25privacy-t2.html?pagewanted=all

Rosen, J. (2012). A grave new threat to free speech from Europe. *New Republic*. Retrieved from www.newrepublic.com/article/politics/100664/freedom-forgotten-internet-privacy-facebook

Rosenberg, H. and Feldman, C. (2008). *No Time to Think: The Menace of Media Speed and the 24-hour News Cycle*. New York: Continuum Books.

Rouse, T. (2012, April 27). Press Freedom group launches Journalist Security Guide. *journalism.co.uk* Retrieved April 27, 2012, from www.journalism.co.uk/news/press-freedom-group-launches-journalist-security-guide/s2/a548986/

Roy Morgan image of professions survey 2012: Nurses still most highly regarded, politicians at 14 year lows. (2012, May 14). *Roy Morgan Research*. Retrieved May 25, 2012, from www.roymorgan.com/news/polls/2012/4777/index.cfm

Royals sue magazine over nude pictures of Kate Middleton. (2012, September 15). *The Daily Telegraph*. Retrieved September 15, 2012, from www.dailytelegraph.com.au/news/royal-fury-as-nude-pictures-of-kate-middleton-hit-newsstands-in-paris/story-e6freuy9-1226474490476

Rozenberg, J. (2013, November 28). Does the internet mean game over for contempt of court? *The Guardian*. Retrieved March 6, 2013, from www.guardian.co.uk/law/2012/nov/28/internet-contempt-of-court-law-commission

Rubinsztein-Dunlop, S. (2010, February 11). Investigation launched into Sydney shark attack claims. *ABC News*. Retrieved February 11, 2010, from www.abc.net.au/news/stories/2010/02/11/2816740.htm

Rudé, G. (1964). *Revolutionary Europe 1783–1815*. London: Fontana/Collins.

Rumours and Facts. (n.d.). *lindychamberlain.com* Retrieved March 5, 2013, from www.lindychamberlain.com/content/rumours_and_facts

Rupert Murdoch at Leveson: Hitler Diaries 'major mistake'. (2012, April 25). *BBC News*. Retrieved January 15, 2013, from www.bbc.co.uk/news/uk-17838201

Russell, M. (2012, September 29–30). Husband warns of social media's negative influence on trial. *The Sydney Morning Herald (weekend edition)*, p. 3.

Russell, M. (2013a, April 9). Hinch to face contempt charge on Meagher case. *The Age*. Retrieved from www.theage.com.au/victoria/hinch-to-face-contempt-charge-on-meagher-case-20130409-2hi31.html

Russell, M. (2013b, April 18). *Age* reporters won't have to give evidence. *The Age*. Retrieved April 30, 2013, from www.theage.com.au/victoria/age-reporters-wont-have-to-give-evidence-20130418-2i2df.html

Ryan, M. (2006, August 15). The death of Kevin Carter and one indelible image. *Chicago Tribune*. Retrieved December 12, 2012, from http://featuresblogs.chicagotribune.com/entertainment_tv/2006/08/the_death_of_ke.html

Saddam Hussein executed. (2006, December 30). *The Guardian*. Retrieved January 19, 2013, from www.guardian.co.uk/world/2006/dec/30/iraq.iraqtimeline/

Sanchez, R. (2012, June 5). Barbara Walters apologises over links to Syrian aide to Bashar al-Assad. *The Daily Telegraph* (London). Retrieved June 5, 2012, from www.telegraph.co.uk/news/worldnews/middleeast/syria/9312558/Barbara-Walters-apologises-over-links-to-Syrian-aide-of-Bashar-al-Assad.html

Sanders, K. (2003). *Ethics and Journalism*. London: Sage.

Santora, M., Glanz, J. and Tavernise, S. (2006, December 30). Dictator Who Ruled Iraq With Violence Is Hanged for Crimes Against Humanity. *The New York Times*. Retrieved January 18, 2013, from www.nytimes.com/2006/12/30/world/middleeast/30hussein.html

Savage, C. (2013, March 1). I did it to make the world a better place: Manning. *The Sydney Morning Herald*. Retrieved March 1, 2013, from www.smh.com.au/world/i-did-it-to-make-the-world-a-better-place-20130301-2f9y3.html

Sawyer, D. (2003). Jessica Lynch interview. *60 Minutes* (November 16).

Scathing Harry reveals 'anger' at press intrusion. (2013, January 21). *ITV News*. Retrieved January 22, 2013, from www.itv.com/news/2013-01-21/prince-harry-media-press-intrusion-anger/

Schlein, L. (2012, July 9). UN says journalists Need Greater Protection. *Voice of America News*. Retrieved July 10, 2012, from www.voanews.com/content/un-says-journalists-need-greater-protection/1365383.html

Schlesinger, D. (2010, November 10). Our need to be in the midst of danger. *blogs.reuters.com* Retrieved November 10, 2012, from http://blogs.reuters.com/reuters-editors/2010/11/10/our-need-to-be-in-the-midst-of-danger/

Schlesinger, F. and Malvern, J. (2012, August 23). Naked Prince Harry 'letting off steam' but photos prompt security questions. *The Australian*. Retrieved August 23, 2012, from www.theaustralian.com.au/news/world/clarence-house-confirms-nude-photos-of=prince-harry-are-genuine/story-e6frg6so-1226456274337

Schmidt, S. and VanderHei, J. (2005, September 30). *N.Y. Times* Reporter Released From Jail. *The Washington Post*. Retrieved October 1, 2005, from www.washingtonpost.com/wp-dyn/content/article/2005/10/19/AR2005101900795.html

Schoenberg, T. (2013, January 11). Calls to release Bin Laden burial photos. *The Sydney Morning Herald*. Retrieved January 11, 2013, from www.smh.com.au/world/calls-to-release-bin-laden-burial-photos-20130111-2cjps.html

Schorn, D. (2009, February 11). Duke Rape Suspects Speak Out. *Sixty Minutes*. Retrieved January 2, 2013, from www.cbsnews.com/8301-18560_162-2082140.html

Schultz, J. (1994). The paradox of professionalism. In J. Schultz (Ed.). *Not just another business: Journalists, citizens and the media*. Sydney: Pluto Press in association with Ideas for Australia, National Centre for Australian Studies, Monash University.

Schultz, J. (1998). *Reviving the Fourth Estate: Democracy, Accountability and the Media*. Melbourne: Cambridge University Press.

Self Care Tips for News Media Personnel Exposed to Traumatic Events. (2007) *Dart Centre Australasia, Melbourne*.

Serwer, A. (2012, December 14). How the Press Got It Wrong on the Newtown Shooter. *Mother Jones*. Retrieved December 19, 2012, from www.motherjones.com/mojo/2012/12/ryan-lanza-newtown-shooting-media-fail

The shameless airing of an un-current affair. (2012, April 30). *Media Watch*. Retrieved May 2, 2012, from www.abc.net.au/mediawatch/transcripts/s3492282.htm

Shanahan, L. (2012, February 2). *The Age* told by court to reveal sources. *The Australian*. Retrieved February 2, 2012, from www.theaustralian.com.au/media/the-age-told-by-court-to-reveal-sources/story-e6frg996-1226260078237

Shank, J. B. (2010). Voltaire. *The Stanford Encyclopedia of Philosophy*. Retrieved from http://plato.stanford.edu/archives/sum2010/entries/voltaire/

Shaver, N. (2011, April 23–24). Clear, open justice denied by suppression order secrecy. *The Weekend Australian*, p. 15.

Sheehan, P. (2003). *The electronic whorehouse*. Sydney: Pan MacMillan.

Sherwin, A. (2007, July 14–15). BBC says sorry to palace over faked walkout. *The Weekend Australian*, p. 17.

Shooter charged over death of US teen. (2012, April 12). *ABC News*. Retrieved April 12, 2012, from www.abc.net.au/news/2012-04-12/shooter-charged-in-death-of-us-teen/3944864

Shovelan, J. (2005, June 14). Jackson goes free after trial victory. *ABC News*. Retrieved January 25, 2013, from www.abc.net.au/news/2005-06-14/jackson-goes-free-after-trial-victory/1592488

Shovelan, J. (2009, December 10). Sponsors give Woods the cold shoulder. *ABC News*. Retrieved December 10, 2009, from www.abc.net.au/news/stories/2009/12/10/2767122.htm

Silvester, J. (2012, September 29). 'Meet me at the pub'. *The Age*. Retrieved September 29, 2012, from www.theage.com.au/victoria/meet-me-at-the-pub-20120928-26r4d.html

Simkin, J. (1997). Alfred Harmsworth, Lord Northcliffe. *Spartacus Educational*. Retrieved 14 November, 2012, from www.spartacus.schoolnet.co.uk/index.html

Simmons, L. (Ed.) (2007). *Speaking truth to power*. Auckland: Auckland University Press.

Simons, M. (2010, October 8). The boredom of Mitchell on naming rights and wrongs. *Crikey*. Retrieved January 4, 2013, from www.crikey.com.au/2010/10/08/the-boredom-of-mitchell-on-naming-rights-and-wrongs/

Simons, M. (2011a, August 19). Contempt laws ... news media means a national approach needed. *Crikey*. Retrieved January 24, 2013, from www.crikey.com.au/2011/08/19/contempt-laws-new-media-means-a-national-approach-needed/

Simons, M. (2011b). Simons: to tweet or not to tweet from court ... *Crikey*. Retrieved from www.crikey.com.au/2011/11/04/simons-to-tweet-or-not-to-tweet-from-court/?wpmp_switcher=mobile

Singer H. (2006). *The Falling Man* (documentary). New York.

Sjovaag, H. (2010). The reciprocity of journalism's social contract: The political-philosophical foundations of journalistic ideology. *Journalism Studies, 11*(6), 874–88.

Skorpen, E. (1989). Are journalistic ethics self-generated? *Journal of Mass Media Ethics: Exploring Questions of Media Morality, 4*(2), 157–73.

Smile hid newsreader's 10-year depression battle (2010, March 12). *The Gold Coast Bulletin*, p. 25.

Smith, E. G. (2013, January 15). News outlets improperly used photos posted to Twitter: judge. *Reuters*. Retrieved January 17, 2013, from www.reuters.com/article/2013/01/15/us-socialmedia-copyright-ruling-idUSBRE90E11P20130115

Smith, G. (2013). Media Release: Status Quo for technology in court.

Smith, W. (Ed.) (1875). A Dictionary of Greek and Roman Antiquities. London: John Murray.

Smyth, F. (2013, February 28). Do news blackouts help journalists held captive? *Committee to Protect Journalists*. Retrieved March 1, 2013, from http://cpj.org/security/2013/02/do-news-blackouts-help-journalists-held-captive.php

Snow, J. (2012, January 23). Poised for journalism's golden age. *Hugh Cudlipp lecture*. Retrieved from http://blogs.channel4.com/snowblog/hugh-cudlipp-lecture-poised-journalisms-golden-age/17044

Social Media Guidelines for AP employees, January 2012. (2012). *Associated Press*

Social Media Guidelines for AP Employees, July 2012. (2012). *Associated Press*

Social Networking, Microblogs and other Third Party Websites: BBC Use. (n.d.). *BBC*. Retrieved February 8, 2013, from www.bbc.co.uk/editorialguidelines/page/guidance-blogs-bbc-full

Soldier David Pearce killed after just 15 months in army. (2007, October 9). *The Daily Telegraph*. Retrieved January 19, 2013, from www.dailytelegraph.com.au/archive/national-old/digger-leaves-wife-2-children/story-e6freuzr-1111114603137

Sottek, T. (2013, February 12). Sheriff's department asks media to stop tweeting as Christopher Dorner manhunt reaches bloody climax (update). *The Verge*. Retrieved February 13, 2013, from www.theverge.com/2013/2/12/3982256/sheriff-asks-media-to-stop-tweeting-christopher-dorner

Sparks, C. (2006). Contradictions in capitalist media practices. In L. Artz, S. Macek and D. Cloud (Eds), *Marxism and Communication Studies: The point is to change it* (pp. 111–32). New York: Peter Lang.

Sparrow, A. (2001, October 10). Sept 11: 'a good day to bury bad news'. *The Telegraph* (UK). Retrieved February 2, 2013, from www.telegraph.co.uk/news/uknews/1358985/Sept-11-a-good-day-to-bury-bad-news.html

The spin cycle: how your newspaper fared. (2010, March 15). *Crikey/Australian Centre for Independent Journalism*. Retrieved March 15, 2010, from www.crikey.com.au/2010/03/15/the-spin-cycle-how-your-newspaper-fared/

Spratling, S. (2010). Tiger's Transgressions: A Look at How Sports Coverage Has Changed. *USC Annenberg*. Retrieved March 4, 2010, from http://blogs.uscannenberg.org/neontommy/2010/01/tigers-transgressions-werent-a.html

Stableford, D. (2010, December 16). For the *New York Post*, Tiger Woods More Important Than 9/11. *The Wrap*. Retrieved March 4, 2009, from www.thewrap.com/ind-column/new-york-post-tiger-woods-more-important-911-11987

Staines, P. (2004). About Guido's Blog. Retrieved from http://order-order.com/2004/01/09/about-guidos-blog/

Standard: Suicide Reporting. (2011, August 2). *Australian Press Council*. Retrieved May 18, 2012, from www.presscouncil.org.au/document-search/standard-suicide-reporting/

Stassen, W. (2010). Your news in 140 characters: Exploring the role of social media in journalism. *Global Media Journal–African Edition, 4*(1).

Statement of Privacy Principles. (2011, August). *Australian Press Council*. Retrieved August 27, 2012, from www.presscouncil.org.au/uploads/52321/ufiles/APC_Statement_of_Privacy_Principles.pdf

Statements in full: McCann case. (2008, March 20). *BBC News*. Retrieved March 20, 2008, from http://news.bbc.co.uk/go/pr/fr/-/1/hi/uk/7304747.stm

Staveley, D. (n.d.). Dragons and Serpents in Sussex. *Sussex Archeology and Folklore*. Retrieved 17 October, 2012, from www.sussexarch.org.uk/saaf/dragon.html

Steele, J. (2002). *War junkie: One man's addiction to the worst places on earth*. Sydney: Bantam Press.

Steel, J. (2012). *Journalism and free speech*. London & New York: Routledge.

Stein, G. (2011, November 15). Roebuck in despair over sex assault claim: Maxwell. *ABC News*. Retrieved November 15, 2011, from www.abc.net.au/news/2011-11-15/maxwell-details-roebucks-final-moments/3666356

Stelter, B. (2011, April 30). Reporter breaks code of silence on sexual assault. *The Sydney Morning Herald*. Retrieved April 30, 2011, from www.smh.com.au/world/reporter-breaks-code-of-silence-on-sexual-assault-20110429-1e0je.html

Stelter, B. and Carter, B. (2011, June 12). For Instant Ratings, Interviews With a Checkbook. *The New York Times*. Retrieved June 24, 2011, from www.nytimes.com/2011/06/13/business/media/13payments.html

Stephens, M. (2007). *A history of news* (3rd edn). New York and Oxford: Oxford Univeristy Press.

Stilgherrian. (2010, November 5). Timeline of misinformation: Twitter's plane crash down to human error. *Crikey*. Retrieved February 9, 2013, from www.crikey.com.au/2010/11/05/timeline-of-misinformation-twitters-plane-crash-down-to-human-error/

Stilgherrian. (2011, March 4). Journo shield law covers bloggers, independent media. *Crikey*. Retrieved January 10, 2013, from www.crikey.com.au/2011/03/04/journo-shield-law-covers-bloggers-independent-media/

Stockwell, S. (1999). Beyond the fourth estate: Democracy, deliberation and journalism theory. *Australian Journalism Review, 21*(1), 37–49.

Stone, I. F. (1979). The Trial of Socrates. *The New York Times Magazine*. Retrieved from http://law2.umkc.edu/faculty/projects/ftrials/socrates/ifstoneinterview.html

Strupp, J. (2010, March 24). SPJ Issues Major Statement Condemning 'Checkbook Journalism'. *Media Matters for America*. Retrieved June 23, 2011, from http://mediamatters.org/print/blog/201003240053

Suich, M. (2003). The electronic whorehouse. *The Sydney Morning Herald*. Retrieved from www.smh.com.au/articles/2003/11/07/1068013375925.html

The Sun defies royals to publish naked Prince Harry photos. (2012, August 24). *The Australian*. Retrieved August 24, 2012, from www.theaustralian.com.au/media/the-sun-defies-royals-to-publish-naked-prince-harry-photos-story-e6frg9976-1226457161784

The Sun explains decision to print naked Prince Harry pictures. (2012, August 23). *The Sun*. Retrieved August 23, 2012, from www.thesun.co.uk/sol/homepage/news/4501937/Why-The-Sun-is-printing-naked-prince-harry-photos.html

Suppression Orders. (2012, September 10). *Guidelines and Directions Manual*. Retrieved January 27, 2013, from www.cdpp.gov.au/Publications/Guidelines-and-Directions/CDPP-GDM-Suppression-Orders.pdf

The Suspected Killer–Young, Rich And Wild. (1996, April 30). *The Age*, p. 1.

Swan, J., Ireland, J. and Bright, D. (2013, January 9). Milne endorses Whitehaven hoax. *The Sydney Morning Herald*. Retrieved January 9, 2013, from www.smh.com.au/opinion/political-news/milne-endorses-whitehaven-hoax-20130108-2cerk.html

Swan, R. (2012). The 'Dark Ages' were a lot brighter than we give them credit for. *The Independent*. Retrieved from www.independent.co.uk/voices/our-voices/battle-of-ideas/the-dark-ages-were-a-lot-brighter-than-we-give-them-credit-for-8215395.html

Sweeney, M. and Conlan, T. (2013). BBC *Panorama* producer resigns after developer's 'bribery' allegation. *The Guardian*. Retrieved from www.guardian.co.uk/media/2013/apr/05/bbc-panorama-harlequin

Sweiringa, M. (2013). Howard ignored official advice on Iraq's weapons and chose war. *The Canberra Times*. Retrieved from www.canberratimes.com.au/comment/howard-ignored-official-advice-on-iraqs-weapons-and-chose-war-20130411-2hogn.html

Swinton, L. (2007). Ethical decision making: How to make ethical decisions in 5 steps. *mftrou.com*. Retrieved from www.mftrou.com/ethical-decision-making.html

The *Sydney Morning Herald* code of ethics. (n.d. 2006). *The Sydney Morning Herald*. Retrieved September 6, 2012, from www.smh.com.au/ethicscode/

Sykes, T. (2012, July 10). William and Kate Honeymoon Photos Published. *The Daily Beast*. Retrieved July 12, 2012, from www.thedailybeast.com/articles/2012/07/10/william-and-kate-honeymoon-photos-published.html

Szabo, C. and Nunn, T. (2011). Media Ethics Survey 2011. *Center for International Media Ethics*

Tanner, S. J. (2005). *Journalism ethics at work*. Frenchs Forest, N.S.W.: Pearson Education.

Taylor, L. (2012, May 21). Mud, splat and tears on judgment day. *The Age*. Retrieved May 21, 2012, from www.theage.com.au/opinion/politics/mud-splat-and-tears-on-judgment-day-201210521-1z0jm.html

Taylor, P. (2010, October 16–17). Presenter's suicide preventable: inquest. *The Weekend Australian*, p. 3.

Tenore, M. J. (2011a, June 20). Have newsrooms relaxed standards, sanctions for fabrication and plagiarism? *The Poynter Institute*. Retrieved June 21, 2011, from www.poynter.org/how-tos/leadership-management/136198/have-newsrooms-relaxed-standards-sanctions-for-fabrication-and-plagiarism/

Tenore, M. J. (2011b, August 8). What journalists need to know about libellous tweets. *Poynter Institute*. Retrieved August 9, 2011, from www.poynter.org/latest-news/top-stories/141987/what-journalists-need-to-know-about-libelous-tweets/

'Terrified of their own shadow': Nude Harry photos give British tabloids a headache. (2012, August 24). *The Sydney Morning Herald*. Retrieved August 24, 2012, from www.smh.com.au/lifestyle/celebrity/terrified-of-their-own-shadow-nude-harry-photos-give-british-tabloids-a-headache-20120824-24pii.html

The Free Dictionary. (n.d.) The Free Dictionary. Retrieved from www.thefree dictionary.com

'This man is about to die': anger over photographer's role in subway death. (2012, December 5). *The Age*. Retrieved December 19, 2012, from www.theage.com.au/world/this-man-is-about-to-die-anger-over-photographers-role-in-subway-death-20121205-2atw9.html

Thompson, E. P. (1963). *The Making of the English Working Class* (1st edn). London: Victor Gollancz.

Thompson, H. S. (1994, June 16). He was a crook. *Rolling Stone*.

Thomson lawyer threatens to sue O'Farrell. (2013, February 1). *ABC News*. Retrieved February 1, 2013, from www.abc.net.au/news/2013-02-01/thomson-lawyer-threatens-to-sue-over-ofarrell-remarks/4496618

Thomson strip-searched by 'goons': lawyer. (2013, February 1). *ABC News*. Retrieved February 1, 2013, from www.abc.net.au/news/2013-02-01/thomson-strip-searched-by-corrective-service-lawyer-says/4494808

Thomson's loophole closes. (2012, December 22–23). *The Weekend Australian*, p. 4.

Tierney, B. (2001). *The idea of natural rights: Studies on natural rights, natural law, and church law, 1150–1625*. Grand Rapids, MI: Wm. B Eerdmans Publishing Company

Tiger Woods apology biggest media event since Bill Clinton's Monica confession. (2010, February 20). *The Australian*. Retrieved February 20, 2010, from www.theaustralian.com.au/business/media/tiger-woods-apology-biggest-media-event-since-bill-clintons-monica-confession/story-e6frg996-1225832456324

Tiger Woods' 120 affairs. (2010, April 29). *The Daily Mail* (UK), republished by *The Daily Telegraph*. Retrieved April 29, 2010, from www.dailytelegraph.com.au/news/tiger-woods-120-affairs/story-e6freuy9-1225860115803

Timms, D. (2006, January 24). Sven admits role of *NoW* sting in exit. *The Guardian*. Retrieved September 12, 2012, from www.guardian.co.uk/media/2006/jan/24/newsoftheworld.privacy

Tippet, G., Schneiders, B., Kennedy, L. and Smith, K. (2006, February 20). Party night turns to horror as five young lives are gone. *The Age*, p. 1.

Tomaselli, S. (2012). Mary Wollstonecraft. *The Stanford Encyclopedia of Philosophy*. Retrieved from http://plato.stanford.edu/archives/win2012/entries/wollstonecraft/

Tovey, J. (2010, March 29). *Hey Dad!* cast gather to back Monahan. *The Sydney Morning Herald*. Retrieved 2010, March 29, from www.smh.com.au/lifestyle/people/hey-dad-cast-gather-to-back-monahan-20100328-r59d.html

Townsend, M. (2012, August 24). Breivik verdict: Norwegian extremist declared sane and sentenced to 21 years. *The Guardian*. Retrieved January 21, 2013, from www.guardian.co.uk/world/2012/aug/24/breivik-verdict-sane-21-years

Tran, M. (2008, December 5). OJ Simpson jailed for 15 years. *The Guardian*. Retrieved January 24, 2013, from www.guardian.co.uk/world/2008/dec/05/oj-simpson-jailed

Travis, C. (2010). John Rawls, Philosophy, Ethics, and Justice. *Yahoo! Voices*. Retrieved from http://voices.yahoo.com/philosophy-summary-explanation-john-rawls-theory-5594246.html

Trenwith, C. (2012, September 28). Whistle-blowers, journalists protected under new law. *WA Today*. Retrieved September 19, 2012, from www.watoday.com.au/wa-news/whistleblowers-protected-under-new-law-20120918-264qv.html

Turnbull, N. (2012, July 27). Come in Spinner: will retrenched journos take PR jobs? *Crikey*. Retrieved July 27, 2012, from www.crikey.com.au/2012/07/27/come-in-spinner-will-retrenched-journos-take-pr-jobs/

Tweet like you mean it. (2012, June 13). *The Australian*. Retrieved June 13, 2012, from www.theaustralian.com.au/media/media-diary/tweet-like-you-mean-it/story-fnab9kgj-1226393400329

Twitter outings undermine 'super injunctions'. (2011, May 10). *The Sydney Morning Herald*. Retrieved May 10, 2011, from www.smh.com.au/technology/technology-news/twitter-outings-undermine-super-injunctions-20110510-1eg7r.html

Twitter Reaction to Events Often at Odds with Overall Public Opinion. (2013, March 4). *Pew Research Centre*. Retrieved March 6, 2013, from www.pewresearch.org/2013/03/04/twitter-reaction-to-events-often-at-odds-with-overall-public-opinion/

UK threat to storm embassy to take Assange. (2012, August 16). *The Sydney Morning Herald*. Retrieved August 16, 2012, from www.smh.com.au/world/uk-threat-to-storm-embassy-to-take-assange-20120816-249pe.html

Uncovered. (2009, March 15). *Sunday Herald Sun*, p. 1.

The Universal Declaration of Human Rights. United Nations. Retrieved September 27, 2013, from www.un.org/en/documents/udhr/

Urquhart, C. (2012, January 20). Johann Hari leaves the *Independent* after plagiarism storm. *The Guardian*. Retrieved January 23, 2012, from www.guardian.co.uk/media/2012/jan/20/johann-hari-quits-the-independent

US launches air strikes on Libya. (1986, April 15). *BBC News*. Retrieved November 10, 2012, from http://news.bbc.co.uk/onthisday/hi/dates/stories/april/15/newsid_3975000/3975455.stm

US Marine filmed shooting prisoner. (2004, November 17). *The Gold Coast Bulletin*, p. 11.

US reporter jailed in CIA trial. (2005, July 6). *BBC News*. Retrieved January 12, 2013, from http://news.bbc.co.uk/2/hi/americas/4654969.stm

US Soldier charged with murder of civilians. (2012, March 23). *Al Jazeera*. Retrieved November 10, 2012, from www.aljazeera.com/news/americas/2012/03/201232222412129838.html

Use of Social Media Policy. (2011, September 27). *ABC*. Retrieved February 8, 2013, from http://about.abc.net.au/wp-content/uploads/2012/06/UseOfSocialMediaPOL.pdf

van der Zijpp, N. (1953). Coornhert, Dirk Vokertsz (1522–90). *Global Anabaptist Mennonite Encyclopedia Online*. Retrieved from www.gameo.org/encyclopedia/contents/coornhert_dirk_volkertsz_1522_1590

'Victimised' whistle-blower loses appeal. (2008, December 19). *ABC News*. Retrieved December 19, 2008, from www.abc.net.au/news/2008-12-19/victimised-whistleblower-loses-appeal/245424

Victims' families 'betrayed' by verdict. (2008, March 11). *The Gold Coast Bulletin*, p. 5.

Vincent, M. and Bainbridge, A. (2012, June 7). Thomson tabloid TV war sparks privacy concerns. *ABC News*. Retrieved June 7, 2012, from www.abc.net.au/news/2012-06-07/tabloid-war-over-thomson-sparks-privacy-concerns/4056916

Violence erupts as protesters burn cars and throw rocks at US military base in Afghan capital over anti-Islam video. (2012, September 17). *The Daily Mail* (UK). Retrieved November 17, 2012, from www.dailymail.co.uk/news/article-2204400/Innocence-Muslims-protests-Rioters-burn-cars-throw-rocks-U-S-military-base-Afghan-capital-anti-Islam0video.html

Voorhees, J. (2013, February 15). Today's Front Pages, Global Edition: 'Blade Slays Blonde'. *slate.com* Retrieved February 17, 2013, from www.slate.com/blogs/the_slatest/2013/02/15/reeva_steenkamp_oscar_pistorius_front_pages_south_african_murder_case_dominates.html

Vultee, F. (2009). Jump back Jack, Mohammed's here. *Journalism Studies, 10*(5), 623–38.

Wacko wobbles. (2005, March 23). *Northern Territory News*, pp. 1 and 16.

Walford, C. and Ramdani, N. (2012, February 23). 'She wanted one more story': Mother of veteran war reporter Marie Colvin said her daughter was due to leave Syria on SAME DAY she was killed in rocket attack. *The Daily Mail* (UK). Retrieved November 7, 2012, from www.dailymail.co.uk/news/article-2104711/Marie-Colvin-Sunday-Times-reporter-leave-Syria-day-dies-says-mother.html

Walker, C. and Cubby, B. (2013, January 11). Moylan camp is feeling the heat in more ways than one. *The Sydney Morning Herald*. Retrieved January 11, 2013, from www.smh.com.au/business/moylan-camp-is-feeling-the-heat-in-more-ways-than-one-20130110-2cj49.html

Walker, P. (2010). Octavia Nasr fired by CNN over tweet praising late ayatollah. *The Guardian*. Retrieved from www.guardian.co.uk/media/2010/jul/08/octavia-nasr-cnn-tweet-fired

Wallace, R. (2012, September 17). Anti-journalist 'death squads must be investigated' *The Australian*. Retrieved September 17, 2012, from www.theaustralian.com.au/media/anti-journalist-death-squads-must-be-investigated/story-e6frg996-1226475199175

Ward, S. J. A. (2010). *Global journalism ethics*. Toronto: McGill-Queen's University Press.

Watch: Taliban thugs execute woman for 'adultery' near Kabul. (2012, July 8). *New York Post*. Retrieved November 17, 2012, from www.nypost.com/p/news/international/watch_taliban_thugs_execute_woman_esUphvrl3yQ0YrIruHOZ3O

Watson, T. and Hickman, M. (2012). *Dial M for Murdoch: News Corporation and the corruption of Britain*. London: Allen Lane.

Wayne Rooney's father faces no further action on betting scam claims. (2012, April 23). *The Guardian*. Retrieved August 27, 2012, from www.guardian.co.uk/football/2012/apr/23/wayne-rooney-father-no-action

We don't believe you. (2012, May 22). *Herald Sun*, p. 1.

We may never know how Milly Dowler's voicemails were deleted. (2012, May 9). *Channel 4 News* (UK). Retrieved August 20, 2012, from www.channel4.com/news/leveson-inquiry-milly-dowlers-voicemail-was-hacked

Wells, J. (2012). Rinehart loses suppression order bid. *ABC News*. Retrieved from ABC News website: www.abc.net.au/news/2012-02-02/gina-rinehart-loses-application-for-suspension-order/3808124

Wenar, L. (2011). Rights. *The Stanford Encyclopedia of Philosophy*. Retrieved from http://plato.stanford.edu/archives/fall2011/entries/rights/

West, B. and Smith, R. L. (2003). *The March Up: Taking Baghdad with the 1st Marine Division.* London: Pimlico.

Whale Oil may appeal convictions. (2010, September 14). *The New Zealand Herald.* Retrieved January 27, 2013, from www.nzherald.co.nz/nz/news/article.cfm?c_id=1& objectid = 10673417

Whittaker, J. (2011). 'Bali boy' in grubby TV rights deal: Nine's cameras ready to roll? *Crikey.* Retrieved from: www.crikey.com.au/2011/11/09/bali-boy-in-grubby-tv-rights-deal-are-nines-cameras-ready-to-roll/

Whittington, D. (1977). *Strive to be fair: An unfinished autobiography.* Canberra: Australian National University Press.

Who's Who in the UK Phone-hacking Scandal. (2011, July 29). *Time Magazine.* Retrieved August 24, 2012, from www.time.com/specials/packages/article/ 0,28804,2084083_2084082_2084120,00.html

Wien, C. (2005). Defining objectivity within journalism. *NORDICOM Review, 26*(2), 3–15.

Wiggins, G. (1995). Journey to Cuba: The yellow crisis. In L. Chiasson (Ed.). *The Press in Times of Crisis* (pp. 103–19). Westport, CT: Praeger.

WikiLeaks. (2010a, 10 July). Collateral Murder. Retrieved 21 April, 2013, from www. collateralmurder.com./

WikiLeaks. (2010b, 28 November). Secret US Embassy Cables. Retrieved 21 April, 2013, from http://wikileaks.org/cablegate.html

WikiLeaks takes top journalism award. (2011, November 28). *The Advertiser*, p. 14.

Wilkie, A. (2004). *Axis of Deceit.* Melbourne: Black Inc.

Williams, R. (1989). *Keywords: A vocabulary of culture and society* (3rd edn). London: Fontana Press.

Wills and Kate: Our Island Paradise. (2012, July 16). *Woman's Day*, 1; 22–25

Wilson, P. (2007, September 20). Reputations trashed in an echo chamber of unnamed sources. *The Australian (Media section)*, p. 34.

Wilson, P. (2011, October 10). How newspapers got Knox verdict wrong. *The Australian*, p. 29.

Wilson, P. (2012, September 29–30). *Hey Dad!*'s 'trial by media'. *The Weekend Australian*, p. 9.

Windschuttle, K. (1988). *The media: A new analysis of the press, television, radio and advertising in Australia.* Ringwood (Vic): Penguin.

Wolfe, L. (2011). The silencing crime: Sexual violence and journalists. *Committee to Protect Journalists.*

Wolff, M. (2008). *The man who owns the news: Inside the secret world of Rupert Murdoch.* New York: Random House.

Wolper, A. (2012, September 13). Ethics corner: The News Hole Is No Place For PR Copy. *Editor and Publisher.* Retrieved September 18, 2012, from www. editorandpublisher.com/Newsletter/Columns/Ethics-Corner–The-News-Hole-Is-No-Place-For-PR-Copy

A woman of extraordinary bravery who charmed tyrants. (2012, February 23). *The Telegraph* (London), republished by *The Sydney Morning Herald.* Retrieved February 23, 2012, from www.smh.com.au/national/obituaries/a-woman-of-extraordinary-bravery-who-charmed-tyrants-20120223-1tp5B.html

Woman's Day editor defends decision to publish Catherine baby bump pictures. (2013, February 14). *The Australian.* Retrieved February 14, 2013, from www.theaustralian.

com.au/media-editors-defend-decsion-to-publish-kate-baby-bump-pics/story-e6frg996-1226577639564

Wood, A. (2011, October 5). Riveting, yet wrong, in race for first report. *The Sydney Morning Herald*, p. 9.

Wright, J. (2012, May 21). Opposition, media unleashed a lynch mob–Thomson. *The Sydney Morning Herald*. Retrieved May 21, 2012, from www.smh.com.au/opinion/political-news/opposition-media-unleashed-a-lynch-mob-thomson-20120521-1z025.html

Wright, J. and Ireland, J. (2012, May 24). 'Enough is enough': Thomson. *The Sydney Morning Herald*. Retrieved May 24, 2012, from www.smh.com.au/opinion/political-news/enough-is-enough-thomson-20120524-1z63o.html

Wuth, R. (2012, November 22). Crime Expert Abuse Claims. *The Gold Coast Bulletin*, p. 1.

Younge, G. (2005, October 24). Colleagues call for removal of *New York Times* journalist in CIA leak case. *The Guardian*. Retrieved January 12, 2013, from www.guardian.co.uk/media/2005/oct/24/pressandpublishing.usnews

Zhang, M. (2012, December 4). Photograph of Doomed Man on Subway Tracks Sparks Outrage, Debate. *petapixel* Retrieved January 3, 2013, from www.petapixel.com/2012/12/04/photogra%5Bph-of-doomed-man-on-subway-tracks-sparks-outrage/

Zimmerman faces court. (2012, April 14–15). *The Weekend Australian*, p. 10.

Index